PERU

Alain Legault

ULYSSES
TRAVEL PUBLICATIONS
Travel better... enjoy more

Author
Alain Legault

Collaboration
Suzanne Murray
Jean Roger
Daniel Desjardins
Marc Rigole

Translation
Tracy Kendrick
Sarah Kresh
Danielle Gauthier
Christina Poole
Suzanne Murray

Project Supervisor
Pascale Couture

Editing
Tara Salman
Stephanie Heidenreich

Layout
Stephanie Heidenreich
Tara Salman

Cartography
André Duchesne
Assistants
Patrick Thivièrge
Isabelle Lalonde
Marc Rigole

Series Director
Claude Morneau

Cover Photograph
Agence Visa

Interior Photographs
Tibor Bognar
Patrick Escudero
Alain Legault;

Design
Patrick Farei
(Atoll Direction)

Illustrations
Marie-Annick Viatour.

Thanks to Roxana and Karmen (Promperú), Enrique Velasco, Juan Stuessell, Enrique Pollack, Ugo Ugoletti, Ruth Guzmán, José Luis, Christian, Carlos Canales, Francisco, Pancho, Ray, Lupe, Fioreen, Agnés, Sophia, and the Peruvian Consul in Montréal.

DISTRIBUTORS

AUSTRALIA: Little Hills Press, 11/37-43 Alexander St., Crows Nest NSW 2065, ☎ (612) 437-6995, Fax: (612) 438-5762

BELGIUM AND LUXEMBOURG: Vander, Vrijwilligerlaan 321, B-1150 Brussel, ☎ (02) 762 98 04, Fax: (02) 762 06 62

CANADA: Ulysses Books & Maps, 4176 Saint-Denis, Montréal, Québec, H2W 2M5, ☎ (514) 843-9882, ext.2232, 800-748-9171, Fax: 514-843-9448, www.ulysses.ca

GERMANY AND AUSTRIA: Brettschneider, Fernreisebedarf, Feldfirchner Strasse 2, D-85551 Heimstetten, München, ☎ 89-99 02 03 30, Fax: 89-99 02 03 31, Brettschneider_Fernreisebedarf@t-online.de

GREAT BRITAIN AND IRELAND: World Leisure Marketing, Unit 11, Newmarket Court, Newmartket Drive, Derby DE24 8NW, ☎ 1 332 57 37 37, Fax: 1 332 57 33 99

ITALY: Centro Cartografico del Riccio, Via di Soffiano 164/A, 50143 Firenze, ☎ (055) 71 33 33, Fax: (055) 71 63 50

NETHERLANDS: Nilsson & Lamm, Pampuslaan 212-214, 1380 AD Weesp (NL), ☎ 0294-494949, Fax: 0294-494455, E-mail: nilam@euronet.nl

PORTUGAL: Dinapress, Lg. Dr. Antonio de Sousa de Macedo, 2, Lisboa 1200, ☎ (1) 395 52 70, Fax: (1) 395 03 90

SCANDINAVIA: Scanvik, Esplanaden 8B, 1263 Copenhagen K, DK, ☎ (45) 33.12.77.66, Fax: (45) 33.91.28.82

SPAIN: Altaïr, Balmes 69, E-08007 Barcelona, ☎ 454 29 66, Fax: 451 25 59, altair@globalcom.es

SWITZERLAND: OLF, P.O. Box 1061, CH-1701 Fribourg, ☎ (026) 467.51.11, Fax: (026) 467.54.66

U.S.A.: The Globe Pequot Press, 6 Business Park Road, P.O. Box 833, Old Saybrook, CT 06475, ☎ 1-800-243-0495, Fax: 800-820-2329, sales@globe-pequot.com

Other countries, contact Ulysses Books & Maps (Montréal), Fax: (514) 843-9448

Canadian Cataloguing in Publication Data, see p 6.

© January 1999, Ulysses Travel Publications.
All rights reserved
Printed in Canada
ISBN 2-89464-122-2

While supper was preparing, orders were given to show them the city, where they saw public structures that reared their lofty heads to the clouds; the marketplaces decorated with a thousand columns; fountains of spring water, besides others of rose water, and of liquors drawn from the sugarcane, incessantly flowing in the great squares, which were paved with a kind of precious stone that emitted an odor like that of cloves and cinnamon.

– Voltaire in *Candide*

TABLE OF CONTENTS

WRITE TO US

The information contained in this guide was correct at press time. However, mistakes can slip in, omissions are always possible, places can disappear, etc. The authors and publisher hereby disclaim any liability for loss or damage resulting from omissions or errors.

We value your comments, corrections and suggestions, as they allow us to keep each guide up to date. The best contributions will be rewarded with a free book from Ulysses Travel Publications. All you have to do is write us at the following address and indicate which title you would be interested in receiving (see the list at the end of guide).

Ulysses Travel Publications
4176 Rue Saint-Denis
Montréal, Québec
Canada H2W 2M5
www.ulysses.ca
E-mail: guiduly@ulysses.ca

CATALOGUING

Canadian Cataloguing in Publication Data:

Legault Alain, 1967 June 12-
    Peru

      (Ulysses Travel Guide)
      Translation of: Pérou.
      Includes index.

      ISBN 2-89464-122-2

      1. Peru - Guidebooks.   I. Title II. Series.

F3409.5.L4313 1999   918.504'633   C98-941545-7

"We acknowledge the financial support of the Government of Canada through the Book Publishing Industry Development Program (BPIDP) for our publishing activities." We would also like to thank SODEC for their financial support.

Canadä

LIST OF MAPS

MAP SYMBOLS

Map symboles

Bus Station	Tourist Information	Museum
Train Station	Hospital	Camping
Airport	Post Office	Ruins
Police	Bank	Mountains, Volcano
Passenger Ferry	Telephone	Church
Car Ferry		

SYMBOLS

🚢	Ulysses' favourite
☎	Telephone number
≈	Fax number
≡	Air conditioning
⊗	Ceiling fan
♯	Fireplace
≈	Pool
ℜ	Restaurant
ℝ	Refrigerator
K	Kitchenette
△	Sauna
⊖	Exercise room
tv	Colour television
ctv	Cable television
pb	Private bathroom
sb	Shared bathroom
ps	Private shower
hw	Hot water
bkfst	Breakfast

ATTRACTION CLASSIFICATION

★	Interesting
★★	Worth a visit
★★★	Not to be missed

HOTEL CLASSIFICATION

The prices in the guide are for one room, double occupancy in high season, not including taxes and service charges.

RESTAURANT CLASSIFICATION

$	US$6 or less
$$	US$7 to $12
$$$	more than US$20

The prices in the guide are for a meal for one person, not including taxes, drinks and tip.

All prices in this guide are in American dollars.

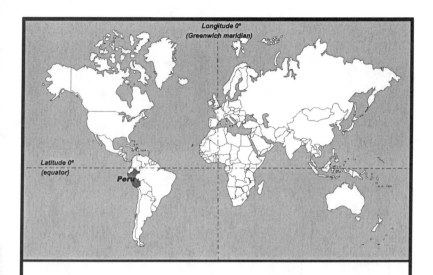

Where is Peru ?

Peru	
Capital :	Lima
Area :	1 285 216 km²
Population :	23 944 000 inhab.
Languages :	Spanish and Quechua (official)
	Aymara (dialect)
Currency :	*nuevo sol*

Longitude 0°
(Greenwich meridian)

Latitude 0°
(equator)

Peru

Caribbean Sea

Venezuela

Guyana

Suriname

French Guyana

Colombia

Latitude 0°
(equator)

Ecuador

Pacific
Ocean

PERU

Brazil

Atlantic
Ocean

Bolivia

Paraguay

Chile

Argentina

Uruguay

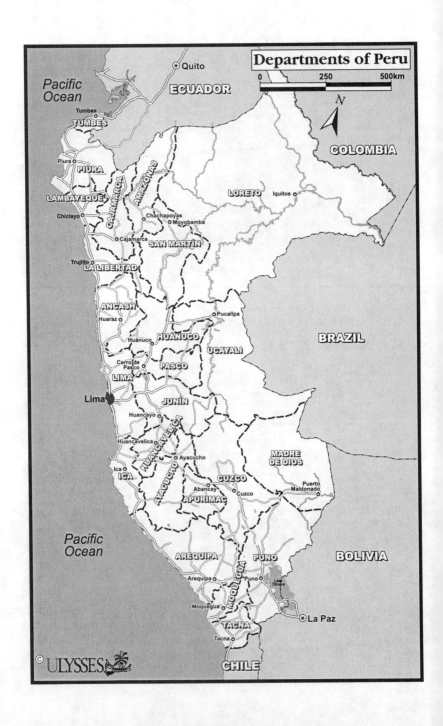

PORTRAIT

A trip to Peru, that faraway and mysterious land pounded by the sun in some parts and shrouded in mist in the mountains and in the lush tropical forest, is a disorienting yet fascinating foray into the history of a medley of peoples who joined together to create one of the most intriguing countries in Latin America.

Once home to the magnificent Inca civilization, Peru continues to hold an almost mythical fascination for anyone interested in this part of the world. Though its image has been tarnished by a recent wave of terrorism, Peru still extends a gracious welcome to visitors who are captivated by its enigmatic history, imbued with poetry yet punctuated by bloody conflicts, and by the remarkable contrasts that characterize its territory which is strewn with ageless treasures and has been inhabited since time immemorial.

Everyone knows about Peru's magnificent Inca ruins, of which Machu Picchu is the most notable, and about the famous Lake Titicaca, but few have heard of the incredible fortress of Chán-Chán, on the north coast, or the strange, remote religious site of Chavín de Huantar, perched at an altitude of 3,190 metres between the Cordillera Blanca and the Cordillera Negra. And then there are Cajamarca and Arequipa, which boast some of the finest colonial architecture in the country, and the enigmatic Nazca Lines, which remain one of the biggest unsolved mysteries on the planet, perplexing scientists and tourists alike. People still inhabit the coastal desert, the luxuriant Selva and the magnificent, windswept Andes, whose jagged peaks stand out against the sky. These regions are scattered with little villages, whose residents look like the last survivors of a forgotten era. Finally, the countless creatures great and small that inhabit the immense Amazon forest and a whole slew

Birou

According to oral tradition, a Spanish navigator who had sailed southward across the Equator in search of El Dorado happened to cross paths with a Native American in a small boat. The navigator asked the Native American where he had set out from, and the Native American responded, "*Birou*". Over the years, *birou* became "Peru". *Birou* is actually an Amerindian word for "river", but no one knows which river the man was referring to.

of unusual sights, both manmade and natural, make this an altogether unique destination.

GEOGRAPHY

Bounded by the Pacific Ocean to the west, Ecuador and Colombia to the north, Brazil and Bolivia to the east and Chile to the south, Peru covers an area of 1,285,216 square kilometres, making it the third largest country in South America after Brazil and Argentina. It is divided into three very distinct geographical regions: the Costa, the Sierra and the Selva.

The Costa

The Costa is a narrow strip of sandy, rocky, desert-like land that is continually scorched by the sun and accounts for barely 10% of the country's area. Bounded by the Pacific Ocean to the west and the Andes to the east, this region varies in width from fewer than a hundred to several hundred kilometres, and stretches from Chile to Ecuador, a distance of nearly 3,000 kilometres. The cold Humboldt Current, which flows northward from southern Chile, prevents rain from reaching this coastal area. The only vegetation found here grows in valleys watered by rivers that flow down from the Cordillera Occidental, forming a series of oases along the coast.

The Sierra

Peru is the quintessential Andean country. Its central region, known as the Sierra, is studded with towering mountains, which form the backbone of the country, culminating with Huascarán, an extinct volcano, at an altitude of 6,768 metres. This is a segment of the world's longest chain of mountains which stretches over 10,000 km, from Alaska in the north to Tierra del Fuego at the southern tip of South America. The Sierra covers about a third of the country's total area and actually consists of several ranges, some of which include active volcanoes. Between these cordilleras are valleys and lofty plateaux known as *altiplanos* (the Lake Titicaca area). To the east, the towering mountains contrast sharply with the dense tropical forests at their feet, known collectively as the Selva.

The Selva

Probably because of its stifling humidity, jungle of greenery and formidable rivers, the Selva was one of the few regions that the Incas did not settle. Located east of the Sierra, the Selva is a huge, somewhat swampy peneplain that extends all the way to the Atlantic and is crossed by the Amazon River and its numerous affluents. This region covers 760,000 square kilometres in Peru alone, just over 60% of the country's area, but is home to less than 5% of the population. The people who do live here are clustered in rustic villages that are largely self-sufficient and by a network of navigable rivers. The only way to travel from Lima to Iquitos, the largest town in the Selva, is by plane.

Geology

Peru's present geological features are the result of the various movements that affected the earth's crust in this part of the world in the past, as well as a number of events that have gradually shaped its geography. The most important events in shaping Peru's landscape and, consequently, its climate, are those that contributed to the emergence of the Andes mountain range, since the country straddles this famous chain of mountains. The entire history of the formation (orogenesis) of the Andes can be deduced from the country's present geographical relief.

The emergence of the Andes began with the westward drift of the South American continent, which resulted in a collision between the continental shelf, still known as the Guyano-Brazilian Shield, to the east, and the ocean crust or Pacific plate to the west. Gradual as it was, this collision was marked by countless earth tremors and volcanic eruptions. The slow drift and impact of the two tectonic plates ended up fracturing and displacing both the continental shelf and the Pacific plate, causing the latter to gradually lodge itself under the former. During the Cretaceous period (a geological period 144 to 65 million years ago), the fractures and the subduction of the Pacific plate (occurring at a speed of up to 10 centimetres per year) caused magma from the depths of the lithosphere to rise up, creating intense volcanic activity on the surface. The abundant flow of lava

eventually created a solid mass of rock, which now forms the backbone of the mountain range. The "pillow lava" found here indicates that these eruptions occurred underwater – that is, before the emergence of the Andes. During this period, the pressure caused by the continental shelf's westward shift transformed the fractured blocks of crystalline rock of which it was composed, and gradually forced them upward.

It was then that the two major geological zones that now characterize Peru took their identity: the coastal regions and northern parts of the Cordillera Occidental have a substratum of volcanic rock, while the entire Amazon region and the Cordillera Oriental have a substratum of crystalline metamorphic rock. The widespread upward thrust of the Andes occurred during the Eocene epoch, just over 50 million years ago, and continues to this day.

This lifting has been accompanied by severe erosion throughout the Andes; a phenomenon that has led to a significant amount of sediment accumulating at the foot of the mountains, mainly on the Amazon shield, to the east. This sediment and the organic debris it contains provide a favourable environment for the formation and accumulation of hydrocarbons, a resource Peru is beginning to capitalize on.

FLORA AND FAUNA

Thanks to its topography and varied climate, Peru is home to a remarkable variety of plants and animals. Each of the regions described above has its own distinctive vegetation. Just as an example: there are over 1,300 species of orchids alone!

Flora

The desert-like Costa does not provide a favourable environment for plant life. However, the thick fog (*garúa*) that blankets the region for about half the year does make it possible for some sparse vegetation to grow. In addition to various kinds of cactus, there are a few fig trees and acacias. Furthermore, some 40 rivers flow down the slopes of the Cordillera Occidental into the desert, creating fertile valleys and forming a string of oases all along the coast. Luxuriant tropical vegetation, particularly sugarcane and lemon, palm and fig trees, often grows in these areas and is cultivated intensively.

The Selva is home to giant trees up to 60 metres high which rise up majestically in the tropical rain forest. Their branches are very high, while their broad, flattened tops are made up of dark green leaves, which often end in a narrow point to drain off rainwater. These trees are entwined by lianas, which hang from the leafy canopies. Only slivers of light make their way through the dense, luxuriant foliage. Surprisingly, the Selva's giant trees have very shallow roots, and even the tallest ones are often felled by the wind, the rain or the countless insects that gnaw upon them mercilessly.

The rain forest is home to an astonishing array of medicinal plants, which are used to treat countless illnesses. The most recently discovered of these is the **uña del gato**, or cat's claw, a member of the *Rubiaceae* family that is indigenous to the Peruvian rain forest and has remarkable healing qualities. Though the tribes who live in the Selva have long been aware of this plant's existence, the modern world only learned about its curative properties for diabetes and arthritis a few years ago. Cat's claw is even being used in experimental cancer therapy.

For a century now, the **eucalyptus**, a precious plant imported from Australia, has been thriving in Peru, quickly adapting to the country's widely varied climate. Unfortunately, the eucalyptus absorbs a lot of the substances it feeds on, thus drying out and impoverishing the soil. Furthermore, its dead leaves, which contain toxins that affect the soil when they fall, preventing other plant species from growing.

The *Páramo* is typical of the Andes. One of the first definitions of this term was provided by the Spanish, for whom it meant a very high and inhospitable stretch of land that was cold, windy and rainy. Today *Páramos* can be found at altitudes ranging from 3,000 to 3,500 metres. They are home to fascinating plants known as **fralejones**, which have lots of little thorns, spread out gracefully and can protect themselves from wind, sun and ice.

At even higher altitudes than *páramos*, *punas* are inhospitable areas at elevations of 3,500 to 4,000 metres on the *altiplano*. Only a few stunted shrubs manage to grow in these wind-whipped areas. One of these is the *ichu*, used as roofing material by local native people. The **puya raimondi**, meanwhile, is a strange, beautiful and rare plant that can grow to up to 10 metres tall and live to 100, but only blooms once – right before it dies.

High in the Andes, the Amerindians chew **coca leaves** to help fight off the cold and stave off hunger. Coca leaves should not be confused with cocaine, even though they are indeed the source of that highly-addictive drug. It is far more dangerous to consume cocaine than coca leaves. It was in 1859 that scientists first isolated the alkaloid

Mangrove tree

known as cocaine and used it as a local anesthetic.

In towns and villages high in the mountains, such as Cuzco or Puno, you might be offered tea made with coca leaves, which is reputed to help your metabolism adapt to the altitude. Don't worry: this brew is non-addictive and entirely legal.

The Mangrove Swamp

The mangrove swamp is home to several species of mangrove trees, distinguished by their large roots. These trees can grow as high as 30 metres and are able to withstand submersion and salt. The red mangrove is one of the varieties found in the salty waters along the shore of the Costa. A great many sea birds and all sorts of insects inhabit this strange forest.

Fauna

The lush Amazon forest is home to all sorts of animals. Some waterways are infested with voracious **piranhas**. These carnivorous fish are attracted by blood and can devour a man or an animal within a few minutes. There are some 30 species of piranha in Peru, though not all of them are carnivorous.

Much more appealing than piranhas in many people's opinion, is the **giant sea otter**, a curious creature that haunts the rivers of Amazonia. Overhunted for its skin, it is now an endangered species. It weighs between 24 and 35 kilograms, rarely swims alone and is difficult to observe. These animals have a small head and powerful flippers that enable them to move swiftly through the water. Sea otters are usually seen in groups of five to eight. When alarmed, they all surface at the same time, stick their necks out of the water and make loud snorting noises.

At first glance, it is hard to tell the difference between a **crocodile** and an **alligator**. Both of these amphibious reptiles have a menacing gaze and a formidable set of teeth. However, a crocodile's upper and lower teeth can be seen when its jaws are closed, while only the upper set is visible on an alligator.

Caimans and alligators (with the exception of the Chinese alligator) are native

Rupicola

to the Americas, while crocodiles can also be found in Australia, Africa and Asia.

The **black caiman** is another endangered species, overhunted for its flesh. This crocodilian has sharp teeth and a powerful jaw and can measure up to seven metres in length. If you keep your eyes peeled, you might spot one on the riverbanks.

The **red caiman**, better known as the **dwarf caiman** because it is smaller than other caimans, has dark brown skin, weighs between 15 and 20 kilograms and can grow up to two metres long.

The Selva is also inhabited by a large number of snakes, the most notorious being the **anaconda**. To get an idea of what this creature looks like, watch the movie *Anaconda*, which was filmed in Peru. Thanks to the magic of 3-D software, the anaconda in the movie is much larger than its real counterpart, which is still pretty big – almost 10 metres long! An aquatic snake belonging to the boa family, it originally lived in the sea and is now found in the Orinoco basin. Though the anaconda is not poisonous, it is still dangerous, because it wraps around its prey and crushes it before swallowing it.

The **condor** is an endangered bird of prey with black plumage, except for some white feathers on the wings, and can be seen flying over the lofty Andean peaks. It has a wingspan of up to three metres and weighs up to 12 kilograms. A vulture, it feeds exclusively on carrion.

The **Puma** and the **jaguar** are two of the carnivorous mammals that live in the Selva. However, chances are relatively slim that you will see either, since both flee at the slightest sign of danger – which is just as well!

Hummingbird

The **morpho** is the most eye-catching butterfly in the Selva with its bright, metallic blue colour, and has a wing-span of up to 20 centimetres.

The **manatee** is a sea mammal that looks like a prehistoric creature. It has a short muzzle, a round head and a racket-shaped tail. There are three kinds of manatee: the first is found in the Amazon (*Trichechus inunquis*), the second in Africa and the third in Florida, the Gulf of Mexico and the Caribbean. This endearing herbivore presents no danger to human beings and is quite defenseless, making it easy prey for its predators.

The **sloth** has a short snout and a round head. Aptly named, it moves extremely slowly. It has three large-clawed toes on each foot (some have only two), with which it easily hangs on to tree branches. Sloths have about 20 teeth with no enamel on them and feed on seaweed, which they often use as camouflage, as well.

In addition to dazzling visitors with their vibrant plumage, **parrots** never cease to amaze people with their unique ability to imitate human sounds, though they don't understand what they're saying.

The **rupicola** got its name for its red crest, which looks like a rounded rooster comb, and is another of the tropical forest's fascinating winged inhabitants.

Hummingbirds are tiny, brilliantly col-oured birds that can beat their wings an amazing 75 times per second.

The largest monkey in the Selva is the **spider monkey**, which gets its name from its long limbs. This herbivorous primate lives in the treetops.

Members of the Camel Family

Llamas, which adapt well to changes in temperature, can be found high in the mountains of Peru, Ecuador, Bolivia as well as certain parts of Colombia, Chile and Argentina. Llamas are ruminants belonging to the camel family. There are two wild breeds, the guanaco and the vicuña, and two domesticated breeds, the alpaca and the llama, raised for their meat and their wool. The best-known by far is the llama, which can weigh up to 140 kilograms. Used as a pack animal, it is very strong and can carry sizeable loads over long distances.

The **alpaca** is smaller than the llama, weighing up to 80 kilograms. It is bred for its wool, which is longer and finer than the llama's. Unlike its cousin, however, it is not used as a beast of burden. Alpacas are found near swampy areas where there are lots of lush pastures suitable for their dietary needs.

The **vicuña** weighs barely 55 kilograms and is distinguished by its gracefulness and its thin neck and frail-looking legs, which give it a dainty appearance. Its wool is extremely soft and warm, and is considered the finest animal fibre after silk. In fact, for years the vicuña was so aggressively hunted for its high-quality wool that the species was on the brink of extinction. Fortunately, a concerted effort was made to protect vicuñas all over the continent, and their numbers are once again on the rise.

Finally, the **guanaco** weighs an average of 90 kilograms. A good swimmer, it can also run very fast – up to 55 kilometres per hour. Like the vicuña, it has reddish-brown wool, is difficult to domesticate, lives in small herds and is rarely spotted.

Besides being valued for their wool, used by Amerindians to make clothing, the various members of the camel family still serve as pack animals and a source of meat for inhabitants of the Andes. Residents of the Costa don't care for this kind of meat, so you are unlikely to find it on the menu in that part of the country. You might be able to sample an alpaca steak in the mountains, though.

HISTORY

Historians generally agree that the first inhabitants of the American continent were Asian nomads who crossed the Bering Strait some 20,000 years ago; it is believed that human habitation of present-day Peru dates all the way back to that period. Over time, these groups were followed by Polynesians, who apparently crossed the Pacific Ocean by canoe and ended up on this continent, fishing and hunting to survive. Then, around 5,000 BC, sudden changes in the temperature made the animals they fed on more scarce, forcing them to find a new means of subsistence. They thus took up farming and became sedentary.

Around 3,000 BC, these Native Americans discovered maize (corn), began making pottery and erected a few monuments, most notably those at Kotosh in the central Peruvian Andes. Their architecture and pottery became increasingly sophisticated up until about 500 BC. The Sechín ruins, north of Lima, right near Casma, are typical of the architecture of this period.

Pre-Inca Civilizations

A large number of civilizations rose and fell before the rise of the Inca empire and the arrival of the Spanish. A few

Moche vase

ruins remain – silent but evocative witnesses to a rich but oft-forgotten past.

Chavín Culture (1,000 - 250 BC)

The Chavín cult was the first group of people in Peru to worship a divine power. Their civilization emerged around 1,000 BC in the central Andes, at 3,190 metres above sea level in the Callejón de Huaylas, in what is now the department of Ancash. They are named after the little village of Chavín de Huantar, which is located right near the ruins of a huge stone temple known as El Castillo.

It was the Peruvian archaeologist Julio C. Tello who first discovered the Chavín culture, which some historians consider the precursor of the region's later civilizations. Its sphere of influence extended to Cuzco and into Bolivia. Because the stone sculptures of the Chavín civilization are similar to those at certain Olmec sites in Mexico, experts believe that kingdom might have been founded by migrants from Central America. The Chavín people worshipped a feline god with a terrifying set of teeth. The decorative vestments woven for the temple priests show that they were skilled artisans. There is also evidence that they were accomplished goldsmiths, silversmiths and potters. The civilization mysteriously vanished around 250 BC.

Paracas Culture (800 BC - AD 200)

In 1920, Julio C. Tello, the archeologist who discovered the Chavín culture, excavated two sites on the Península de Paracas, south of Lima: the Paracas Cavernas and the Paracas Necrópolis. The Paracas civilization is believed to have appeared around 800 BC and vanished around AD 200.

The Paracas Cavernas are essentially a group of subterranean burial vaults. A narrow passage about 10 metres long leads down to a large cave where about 30 mummified bodies were laid out, surrounded by objects that were supposed to accompany their souls on their journey to the afterlife. The Paracas Necropolis is a group of over 400 *fardos* – tombs containing mummies wrapped in sumptuous, colourful fabric. Because of the desert's arid climate, the fabric is beautifully preserved; 190 different patterns have been indentified.

Mochica or Moche Culture (200 BC - AD 600)

The first of the great civilizations to develop along the ocean shore, the Mochica culture appeared around 200 BC and occupied almost the entire north coast over the next six centuries. These skilled farmers turned the desert into arable land by using guano as fertilizer and developing irrigation systems that were highly advanced for the time. They also built magnificent, stepped, adobe pyramids, whose ancient walls are still adorned with colourful frescoes. The Temples of the Sun and Moon, near the modern-day town of Trujillo, are the finest examples of these. Mochica leaders claimed to be direct descendants of the gods they worshipped and believed that human sacrifices would appease their gods' anger. The Mochica's brightly coloured and wonderfully detailed pottery was mass-produced and depicts their daily life, as well as religious, erotic and war themes. This civilization also mysteriously disappeared, around AD 600 Some historians link its decline to the effects of the powerful ocean current El Niño (see p 60).

Nazca Culture (200 BC - AD 600)

Nazca culture, which emerged on the coast south of Lima, was probably an offshoot of the declining Paracas civilization. It is notable for its priests, who made astounding advances in astrology, mathematics and geometry. Like the Mochicas, the Nazcas developed irrigation systems to survive in the arid climate of the Costa. Some of their pottery is decorated with a type of zodiac, which might be related to the enigmatic Nazca Lines – huge geometric designs carved into the coastal desert that continue to baffle historians. The Nazca civilization died out around AD 700.

Wari or Huari (AD 600 - 1000) and Tiahuanaco Culture(100 BC - AD 1000)

Although the Tiahuanaco appeared on the scene several centuries before the Wari, historians often refer to these two cultures together. Wari civilization flourished in the Andes, near the city of Ayacucho, halfway between Lima and Cuzco. Little is known about the Tiahuanaco culture, which reached its peak just as the Nazca and Mochica civilizations began to decline. According to historians, this civilization emerged on the shores of Lake Titicaca, in the Andean highlands of present-day Bolivia, and eventually extended all the way to northern Chile and southern Peru. The Incas believed that Viracocha created the universe at Tiahuanaco, a site on the shores of Lake Titicaca, and that the monoliths found there were men that he had created then turned to stone. The Tiahuanaco culture disappeared inexplicably around 1000 BC, right before the Inca civilization emerged in the same region.

PORTRAIT

Chimú Culture (AD 900 - 1470)

The Chimús, who appeared around the 10th century, settled on former Mochica territory, reactivating the irrigation networks already in place to redirect the waters of the Río Moche. With somewhere between 80,000 and 250,000 inhabitants, Chán-Chán, the capital of their empire, located near present-day Trujillo, was the largest city in the Andes. Masterful artisans of precious metals, they depicted their daily lives, sex and all, in remarkable detail. They buried their dead in family groups, including wives, children and servants. The Chimús also managed to assimilate the neighbouring Sicán tribe into their culture. In short, they took over where the Mochica had left off. Ultimately, the Chimús surrendered to the expanding Inca empire. When the Incas laid siege to Chán-Chán and cut off the water supply, the Chimús chose to assimilate rather than enter into a bloody conflict. Following their victory, the Incas sent the finest Chimú silver- and goldsmiths to Cuzco, the capital of their empire.

The Inca Civilization
(AD 1200 to 1532)

Starting in the 13th century, this people formed a vast empire known as *Tahuantinsuyu*, a Quechuan word meaning "the four directions of the world". The Inca empire stretched along the Andes mountain range from Chile to modern-day Colombia, making it difficult to unify. It was ruled by an emperor believed to be a direct descendant of Inti, the Sun God; this connection entitled him to the powers of an uncontested monarch. His people approached him with great veneration, fear and humility, and he only communicated with others through an intermediary, never looking at the person before him. Always surrounded by an escort, he was carried about on a richly decorated litter drawn by men. Inca society was based on a rigid social structure that included privileged classes: at the top of the pyramid was the nobility, made up of the Inca's male descendants and war chiefs, and the priesthood, essentially the sacrificers and dignitaries of the solar cult, and the people were at the bottom. The *allyu*, the basic unit of Inca society, formed an extended family grouped into a village. War booty plundered from the neighbouring peoples was distributed among the various classes of Inca society. The conquered peoples were uprooted from their land, and sent to other parts of the empire to prevent any attempt at rebellion. Here, they were enslaved and finally assimilated.

Historians believe the first emperor was Manco Cápac, who was succeeded by 12 other Incas. The last two, Atahualpa and Huáscar, were engaged in a bitter feud for control of the empire, which had become too big and difficult to govern. It is believed that the empire was founded in Cuzco around AD 1300, but didn't really develop until the reign of Pachacutec, the ninth Inca.

Inca Emperors

Manco Cápac
Sinchi Roca
Lloque Yupanquí
Maya Cápac
Cápac Yupanquí
Inca Roca
Yahuar Huacac
Viracocha
Pachacutec
Tupac Yupanquí
Huayna Cápac
Huáscar/Atahualpa

Pachacutec was the most influential of the Incas. A military genius, he is considered the mastermind and architect of the empire. No one before him had ever undertaken projects of such a large scale. He centralized the government in Cuzco and established a pyramidal structure for the empire, which he divided into four administrative districts known as *suyos*, each governed by a lord, or *curaca*. These *curacas* ranked below the aristocracy and were not pure-blooded Incas. The empire was highly centralized, since each of the *curacas* reported directly to the nobility, who relayed the information to the Inca, the empire's supreme ruler.

Under Pachacutec, the empire expanded considerably. The conquered peoples were forced to adopt the Quechua language, and those who opposed the Inca's authority were uprooted and relocated in some remote place to prevent them from organizing a rebellion.

The empire branched out in four directions. Pachacutec began his reign at the dawn of the 15th century with a victory over the Chanca, a fierce neighbouring tribe. He subsequently took over present-day Bolivia and northern Chile, and headed north, along the Peruvian coast, to conquer Pachacamac before defeating the Chimú near Trujillo. Not content to rest on his laurels, he pushed even farther north, to southern Ecuador, before handing the reins over to his son, Tupac Yupanquí.

When Pachacutec died, Tupac proved himself to be his father's son. Determined to build an ever larger and more powerful empire, he pushed inexorably northward, conquering the Cañaris and the Quitus, among other peoples. In 1528, Tupac Yupanquí passed the torch to his son, Huayna Cápac. Around that time, word reached the emperor that a group of mysterious, bearded white men had arrived in the land; this turned out to be none other than Francisco Pizarro and his gang of adventurers. Shortly after this rumour had circulated and before the Incas had even laid eyes on these mysterious strangers, an insidious illness, most probably smallpox, spread through the empire, killing large numbers of people including Huayna Cápac himself.

Before he died, Huayna Cápac married a Quitu princess who had bore him a son named Atahualpa. Upon Huayna Cápac's death, a war of succession broke out between Atahualpa, his illegitimate son, from Quito, and Huáscar, his full-blooded Inca son, from Cuzco. This fratricidal war drastically influenced the course of history and had dire consequences for the Incas. Hungry for wealth and conquests, the conquistadors took advantage of the empire's weakened state and started colonizing the territory on Spain's behalf. After several years of war, Atahualpa's forces managed to invade Peru from Quito, and crushed Huáscar's troops near the city of Ambato, in the Ecuadoran Andes, in 1532. Atahualpa thus became king of a crippled and more or less divided empire.

Chasquis

Though the Incas worshipped Inti, the Sun God, the round, shining star, the Incas did not use wheels for transportation, since this invention was unknown to them. To convey information from one part of the empire to another, they relied on messengers known as *chasquis*. These young, vigorous and extremely fit runners were groomed from an early age to tear along the roads of the empire, and lived in small groups of about six in roadside shelters known as *tampus*. A new runner would take over every four or five kilometres. If the *chasqui* were alive today, they would be Olympic gold-medalists. According to oral tradition, they were so efficient that the Inca, who lived in the

Atahualpa

A man of imposing stature, with chiselled features and a penetrating gaze, Atahualpa was the son of Huayna Cápac and a Shyri princess. He was crowned king of the Incas after defeating and killing his half-brother Huáscar in a war of succession, becoming the last emperor to rule over his people. His reign ended with the arrival of the Spanish conquistadors, led by Francisco Pizarro, who captured him and held him for a huge ransom. Once this was paid, Pizarro betrayed Atahualpa, killing him in 1533, but christening him beforehand.

mountains in Cuzco, could eat fresh fish from the coast for dinner each day.

The *Quipu*

Though the Incas did not know how to write, they kept records with the *quipu*, a thick piece of rope that extended horizontally, with a series of smaller ropes hanging from it. The smaller ropes, which were also of different colours, were tied in single, double or triple knots. These knots were used to record harvests, profits, tributes paid to the Inca and the size of the population. Other *quipus* were used to record the history of the empire.

Mita

People were required to donate their labour to projects such as road maintenance, coca production, harvesting crops, etc. for the good of the empire. These tasks were referred to as *mita*. When the Spanish took power, they appropriated this Inca institution for their own ends, forcing the Incas to exploit the country's natural resources under appalling conditions for the sole benefit of the mother country.

Quechua

Quechua was the official vernacular of the Inca empire *Tahuantinsuyu*. With the arrival of the conquistadors, Spanish soon became the country's major language. Although the use of Quechua diminished considerably, it did not disappear altogether. Today, it is spoken by Amerindian communities living on the plateaus of the Andes in Ecuador, Peru, Bolivia and Northern Chile. Still, in those places where it is commonly spoken, Quechua is enjoying something of a revival. Some Quechua words, such as condor, poncho and puma, have even been incorporated into the English language.

Inca Women

An Inca woman's life was no picnic, and there was absolutely nothing romantic about it. The most beautiful girls in the realm were taken from their families and locked up inside a house when they were about 12 years old. Here, they spent their time weaving clothing and preparing food for the Inca. These young women had either to remain chaste or become one of the Inca ruler's numerous concubines. If such a girl lost her virginity to a commoner, she faced one of the cruelest punishments imaginable: to be buried alive. Her lover didn't fare much better: he would be hanged, along with his entire family – including parents, children and servants. Their houses were burned and the ground was covered with salt so that nothing could grow there. The Inca's lawful wife was his own sister, known as the *Colla*, but the emperor, like the rest of the aristocracy, practiced polygamy. Common people, on the other hand, had to be monogamous or risk suffering the grim fate described above.

The Arrival of the Spanish in the New World

After Columbus's "discovery" of America in 1492, Vasco Núñez de Balboa's "discovery" of the Pacific Ocean in 1513 and Cortez's conquest of Mexico in 1519, all sorts of adventurers started dreaming about colonizing the New World, where they hoped to find wealth and glory.

Early in the 16th century, a rumour spread all the way to Panamá, that aroused a great deal of interest. Supposedly, an empire overflowing with riches existed to the south of the isthmus. Several Spanish adventurers tried in vain to find it.

In 1524 Francisco Pizarro, an illiterate Spanish captain of illegitimate birth, joined forces with Diego de Almagro, and the two set off to seek their fortune, having convinced Father Hernando de Luque to finance their long, costly and perilous expedition. Pizarro and his men made three voyages before meeting with any success. The first took place in 1524; the Spaniards discovered nothing but hostile Native Americans and swamp-strewn forests during their brief stay on the Colombian coast.

A second expedition set out at the end of 1526. Guided by Pizarro, the Spanish sailed along the Pacific shoreline and dropped anchor at the mouth of the Río San Juan, in Colombia. Pizarro sent his captain, Bartolomé Ruiz de Andrade, ahead as a scout. Ruiz and his men continued down the Pacific coastline, landing at Esmeraldas on September 21, 1526. Ruiz thus became the first European to set foot on Ecuadoran soil. He named the area Bahía de San Mateo, as September 21 is St. Matthew's Day. He was greeted by the natives, who presented him with gifts as a sign of welcome and token of friendship. Ruiz then continued southward, and was no doubt the first European to cross the Pacific equator. Farther south, he met men decked out in gold and sumptuous fabrics sailing boats made of balsa wood.

Satisfied with his discoveries, Ruiz backtracked and rejoined Pizarro in Colombia. Unfortunately, Pizarro was ordered to return to Panamá with his troops. At that point, he took out his sword, drew a line in the sand, and told his men that anyone who didn't want to continue the expedition was free to go back to Panamá. He warned them, however, that those who did would be derided, tried and perhaps even thrown in prison, while those who crossed the line to follow him would become rich and famous. Thirteen soldiers accepted the challenge. This tale has survived the centuries and is now known as "Los trece del Isla de Gallo".

Pizarro and his 13 men sailed southeast along the coast and landed at Tumbes, a Peruvian town located south of the present-day border of Ecuador. The Europeans were given a warm reception by the natives who presented them with jewels, gold and fabrics. They found the coveted Inca empire in the midst of a crisis, and realized that the various various peoples colonized by the Incas had only recently been subjugated. Delighted with this knowledge, Pizarro returned to Spain toward the

Francisco Pizarro (1475-1541)

Born out of wedlock in Spain's rugged Extremadura region, Francisco Pizarro grew up poor and illiterate. Who could have known that he would one day bring about the collapse of the Inca empire. Though, he was born into unfortunate circumstances, Pizarro was highly intelligent, which enabled him to take part in numerous South Seas expeditions, thereby launching his career as a conquistador. He was serving under Vasco Nuñez de Balboa when the latter crossed the Isthmus of Darién (Panamá) and discovered the Pacific Ocean in 1513. Later, he became fascinated by Hernando Cortez's fabulous exploits in Mexico. In 1520, although he was already 45 years old at the time, he was determined to make new discoveries and to attain the same fame as Cortez and Balboa. With the help of Diego de Almagro, he decided to try to conquer Peru for King Charles V of Spain. After several failed attempts, Pizarro succeeded in vanquishing the Inca empire and betraying, and ultimately killing the Inca Atahualpa. In 1541, shortly after putting his ex-partner, Almagro, to death, Pizarro himself was killed by Almagro's son, Diego el Mondo.

end of 1528 with a great deal of information on this enigmatic land. He also brought back several natives, whom he would later use as interpreters, and the gifts he had received, which he hoped would convince the King of Spain that he might have found El Dorado. No such luck: instead, he was locked up for disobeying orders and unpaid debts. Then he was summoned to appear before King Charles V, who freed him from prison and granted him permission to conquer and govern the kingdom of El Dorado in the name of the Spanish Crown.

The Spanish Conquest

After planning his expedition carefully, Pizarro set sail with the firm intention of colonizing the territory and carrying off the possessions of the so-called kingdom. In 1531 he landed at Tumbes, accompanied by just 300 men: about 60 cavalrymen and nearly 200 foot soldiers.

In the meantime, Atahualpa had emerged victorious in his duel with Huáscar in central Ecuador and was slowly making his way back to Cuzco. News quickly spread of the mysterious strangers' arrival on the coast, and soon everyone was talking about the Spaniards. Lured by the promise of riches, Pizarro and his faithful companions-in-arms travelled across a windswept desert beneath the scorching sun before tackling the cold and hostile steppes, surrounded by mountains that rise three to four thousand metres toward the sky.

Pushing ever onwards, they made their way north up a mountainside to the village of Cajamarca. Along the way, they passed through war-ravaged villages and met local inhabitants who had suffered disgraceful treatment under the Inca Atahualpa's rule and were eager for revenge. Atahualpa unleashed the full force of his wrath on anyone who defied him. Through their interpreters, the Spanish learned that Atahualpa was in Cajamarca, a populous town whose inhabitants were seasoned warriors, intelligent and extremely well-organized, as was evident by the network of paved mountainside roads they had built to make it easier to get around.

Though they refused to admit it to themselves, the situation didn't look promising for the Spanish. Only greed and a kind of madness drove them ahead. Even the men began to question the wisdom of their enterprise, but Pizarro coaxed them onward. They did, however, start to exercise some caution.

The Fall of the Inca Empire

Exhausted, nervous and wary, the conquistadors finally arrived in Cajamarca on November 15, 1532. Atahualpa greeted them amicably, but Pizarro realized that he and his men were vastly outnumbered, and that it would require both force and cunning to conquer the Inca empire. He decided to lay a trap for Atahualpa by setting up a meeting with him. Pizarro and his men ambushed the Inca and his men when they arrived. Taking full advantage of the Inca's surprise, the Spanish went into a bloodthirsty frenzy in which countless Incas were slaughtered within a short time. Atahualpa was taken prisoner, but treated in a manner befitting his royal status. He was even permitted to keep his clothing and his concubines.

In the hope of saving his own life, Atahualpa made a deal with Pizarro: in exchange for his freedom, he would fill a room in his house with several dozen tons of gold. Before this could be done, however, a rumour reached Pizarro's ears: the Incas were secretly plotting a counter-attack to liberate the emperor. Furious, Pizarro reneged on his promise and instead of setting Atahualpa free, set up a puppet court to try him for treachery: he was condemned to be burnt at the stake. Atahualpa was terrified of being cremated, because his body would be completely destroyed. He therefore converted to Catholicism

and was strangled instead. He died on August 29, 1533.

Pizarro and his soldiers left for Cuzco early in September of that same year. Before their departure, the Spaniards melted all the gold they could lay their hands on to decorate the churches, palaces and monasteries they were planning to build.

After Atahualpa's execution, a climate of uncertainty descended on the empire. Who was going to succeed him? To avoid another war of succession, the quick-thinking Pizarro put Manco, Huáscar's young, naive and easily manipulated half-brother, on the throne. Manco was in fact so naive that he viewed the Spanish as liberators who were going to restore the power and prestige of the emperor. He was to learn the hard way what the Spaniards' intentions really were. They had absolutely no respect for the and eventually locked him up in a cage where his guards urinated on him and raped his wives before his very eyes. After finally realizing that the Spaniards were motivated only by greed for the people's gold and other riches, Manco Cápac managed to escape to the depths of the Amazon forest, where he began to organize a rebellion.

In the meantime, Francisco Pizarro and his men had already left for the coast, where they founded the city of Lima in 1535, declaring it the capital of the viceroyalty of Peru. In order to rule his foreign colonies more effectively, the King of Spain established viceroyalties, which were directly under his jurisdiction. The *Tahuantinsuyo* (Inca) empire was gradually supplanted by the viceroyalty of Peru.

Bartolomé de Las Casas

Born in Seville in 1474, Bartolomé de Las Casas arrived in the New World in 1502, after having trained for the priesthood. He took his vows in 1513 and was granted an *encomienda*. He renounced his land the following year, horrified by the ill-treatment inflicted on the Amerindians, and spent the rest of his life fighting for the rights of Native Americans. It was thanks to his efforts that slavery was gradually abolished. He died in Madrid in 1566, at the age of 92. His testimony at a historic trial held before the papal legate ensured that his name would be remembered. The trial was significant because it acknowledged that Amerindians were men and women created by God, and thus deserved the same respect as to all members of the human race

In 1536, the Inca Manco and his men besieged the city of Cuzco for nearly a year. The troops sent by Pizarro to assist his fellow-Spaniards trapped in Cuzco were mercilessly slaughtered by the Incas. In 1537, Diego de Almagro returned from Chile, where he had tried in vain to find gold and other riches. He helped the Spanish liberate Cuzco, plotting to usurp Pizarro's power all the while. The following year, he was assassinated by Pizarro's men while trying to take control of the city. Pizarro himself was killed in Lima by Almagro's son in 1540.

It took just over 200 years for the Incas to build their formidable empire and only around 15 for the conquistadors to completely destroy it. The Spaniards' decadence made Peru the battleground of two rival factions, the Almagrists and the Pizarrists, plunging it into an abyss of violence and bloodshed.

The Spaniards set up the *encomienda* system to meet the labour needs of the new empire. However, this system forced native people to work in atrocious conditions.

The *Encomienda* System

The *encomienda* system was intended to reward Spanish soldiers and encourage them to settle on Spanish lands in the New World. It was a form of feudalism, under which each soldier was granted a parcel of land and control over all indigenous people living on it. Unfortunately, this "control" was often abused and took on the form of punishment, spawning all sorts of injustice. In addition to working the land, the Amerindians were exploited by the Spanish in other areas of activity, as well, including household work and mining. This deplorable practice has survived into the 20th century; today, it is better known as the *hacienda* system. The *encomienda* system angered the king of Spain, because it made it harder for him to collect taxes owed him. He thus decided to send over some representatives to try to abolish the practice.

Not satisfied with the riches they had accumulated, the Spaniards decided to conquer even more territory. In March 1541, Gonzalo Pizarro (Francisco's half-brother) and Francisco de Orellana led an expedition into Amazonia in search of El Dorado. The men descended from the high plateaus in the Andes and slowly made their way into the depths of the dense tropical forest, where it rained continually, and they had to clear a path with their swords as they went. Many of them succumbed to exhaustion and mysterious illnesses. Realizing that the mission wasn't progressing and that supplies were running low, Orellana offered to scout ahead along the waterways. Bitter, tired of waiting and believing that Orellana had deceived him, Pizarro decided to return to Quito. Meanwhile, Orellana and his men, failing to find sufficient food or gold, followed the Río Napo and the Amazon to the Brazilian coast, thus becoming the first Europeans to cross the South American continent.

The following year, in 1542, the New Laws (*Nuevos Leyes*) came into effect, thanks in part to the testimony of Bartolomé de Las Casas, who denounced the atrocities suffered by the Amerindians at the hands of the Spanish. As a result, both slavery and the *encomienda* system were eventually abolished. The situation didn't improve overnight, however. In 1545, after pillaging Cuzco and other towns that virtually glittered with gold, the Spaniards continued searching in the Andean highlands. Here they discovered the Cerro de Potosí and its huge silver deposits at nearly 4,000 metres above sea level. Located in Bolivia, this *cerro rico* is famous for its astounding number of silver lodes and massive mines in which countless Amerindians lost their lives under the Spaniards' rule.

Meanwhile the Inca Manco, unable to create a united front among his people, was assassinated by the Almagrists. His sons, Sayri Tupac and Titu Cusi tried to pick up where he had left off, but their efforts proved to be in vain and they, too, met their death.

Numerous Amerindian uprisings have taken place since the beginnings of the Spanish conquest, leading to much bloodshed. One of these was led by Tupac Amarú, who considered himself to be the last Inca. The rebellion was violently put down in 1572, and Tupac Amarú himself was taken prisoner and brought to Cuzco, where he was savagely murdered and decapitated in front of his distraught followers.

Much later, in 1780, about 60,000 Amerindians revolted against the Spanish. They were led by the Peruvian patriot José Gabriel Condorcanquí, who adopted the name of one of his ancestors, Tupac Amarú, the Inca who had been executed some 200 years earlier in Cuzco. Outraged by the ill-treatment Amerindians continued to endure, he kidnapped and executed a *corregidor*. (In the 18th-century, *corregidores* were representatives of the Spanish Crown and as such governed entire regions and paid tribute to the King.)

Though initially successful, the insurrection came to a bloody halt on January 18, 1781, when Condorcanquí, who had been captured, was tortured and then drawn and quartered in Cuzco while thousands of his loyal companions looked on, terror-stricken.

Another revolt was crushed in 1814. Later, however, opposition to the Spanish began to spread throughout Latin America. The revolts were led mainly by mestizos, who had Spanish blood but were born in Latin America and had long harboured deep resentment towards the ruling minorities, whose status was superior to their own.

Around the same time, the German naturalist and geographer Alexander von Humboldt arrived in Peru, where he carried out numerous climatological, geographical and botanical studies.

Alexander von Humboldt (1769-1859)

Born in Berlin in 1769, Alexander von Humboldt sailed to the Americas with the French doctor and naturalist Aimé Goujau Bonpland. From June 1799 to August 1804 he travelled over 10,000 kilometres in North, Central and South America, including some particularly dangerous regions, to conducted extensive geographical, botanical and climatological research. He introduced the public to numerous discoveries theretofore unknown to Europeans. Humboldt arrived in South America at the beginning of the 19th century. He described the ruins of the Inca empire and succeeded in measuring and identifying the cold ocean current of the Pacific that flows along the coast of South America and now bears his name. He also proved that the American continent was older than was commonly believed, counted over 400 terrestrial volcanoes, inventoried an incredible number of plant and animal species and frankly denounced the atrocities committed during the colonization of South America.

Independence: From Revolt to Revolution

In the early 19th century, news of the victories of the French and American revolutions and Napoleon's invasion of Spain spread to South America as far as Peru. By 1809, independence movements were taking shape all over the continent.

The idea of getting out from under the Spanish yoke did not originate in Peru, however. In September 1820, nearly 11 years after the first independence movements, the Argentine soldier and patriot José de San Martín, who had defeated Spanish forces in Chile, arrived at the port of Pisco, south of Lima, with an invading army. On July 12, 1821, he and his men marched straight into Lima, which had been abandoned by the Spanish troops. Peru was officially declared independent on July 28, 1821. The battle against the Spanish was continued by the Venezuelan revolutionary hero Simón Bolívar, who arrived in Peru with his troops in 1822 and defeated the Spanish at the Battles of Junín (August 6, 1824) and Ayacucho (December 9, 1824).

The *Caudillo* Era (1826-1862)

The *claudillo* era was extremely chaotic. Bolívar, who left for Gran Colombia in 1826, was succeeded by a whole string of marshals, or *caudillos*, who had distinguished themselves at the Battle of Ayacucho. Thus, no sooner had Peru become independent than it entered a new era of upheaval.

The *caudillos* were former lieutenants who had served under Bolívar and Sucre. Each built up a small army with the intention of taking over the presidency and eliminating anyone who stood in their way. One *caudillo* after another ruled the republic until the early 1860s. It was a seemingly endless cycle: one *caudillo* would take power and remain in control until the people, led by another *caudillo*, overthrew him. The entire notion of a national presidency conflicted with Bolívar's dream of creating a federation of Spanish-speaking South American states.

Andrés Santa Cruz ruled Peru until 1827, when he was replaced by José Lamar, who was in turn ousted by Agustín Gamarra in 1829. Gamarra

Simón Bolívar

Born in Caracas, Venezuela in 1783, this illustrious general will always be remembered as the first person to try to consolidate the countries of Latin America into one nation. After waging a long battle against Spanish domination, he succeeded in liberating Venezuela, Colombia (which at the time included present-day Panamá) and Ecuador. With these victories under his belt, he founded the Republic of Gran Colombia which encompassed all the aforementioned countries, and became president of the fledgling nation. The first Panamerican Congress was held in Panamá, but Bolívar, in spite of his military success, could not manage to keep the country unified. Driven to despair, he died in Santa Marta, Colombia, in 1830. Bolívar is considered a true hero, and places all over Latin America bear his name.

ruled the country until 1833. Meanwhile, Santa Cruz had become president of Bolivia. In 1836, he invaded Peru and formed a Bolivian-Peruvian confederation, which lasted barely three years. Gamarra then returned to power.

The country did not see a lasting peace until 1845, when Ramón Castilla, another marshal who had fought at Ayacucho, seized power. He proved to be a fairly wise ruler and launched a whole series of major reforms during his two terms in office (1845 to 1851 and 1855 to 1862), including the abolition of slavery, the construction of railroads and telegraph facilities and the adoption of a liberal constitution in 1860. Castilla also began exploiting the country's rich nitrate and guano deposits. Guano is composed mainly of the accumulated dung of sea birds nesting along the shore and is used as fertilizer. The dry coastal climate allows the dung, which would otherwise be dissolved by the rain, to build up. By the end of the 19th century guano, which was very valuable in those days, had become one of the country's principal resources.

Despite his achievements, Castilla was first and foremost a *caudillo* so his record is not entirely admirable. Though

he abolished slavery, he replaced the black and Amerindian labour force with Asian immigrants. Some people also hold him responsible for plunging the country into serious debt.

The War Against Spain

In 1864, Peru went to war against Spain, which was trying to appropriate the guano-rich Chincha Islands. Ecuador, Bolivia and Chile backed Peru, forcing the Spanish troops to retreat in 1866. The resulting treaty, signed in 1878, was Spain's first formal recognition of Peruvian sovereignty.

The Pacific War (1879-1883)

In 1879, Chile declared war on Bolivia in order to seize the nitrate fields of the Atacama Desert, now part of Chile. Thus began a four-year conflict known as the Pacific War. Peru tried to help Bolivia, while Chile received support from a large detachment of British troops. In 1882, Peru suffered a crushing defeat. The conflict had severely depleted its financial resources, and relations between Chile and Peru remained strained for a long time. Bolivia lost its access to the sea, and Peru had to give up Tacna (which it recovered in 1929), Tarapacá and Arica.

APRA

In 1924, Victor Rául Haya de la Torre founded the American Popular Revolutionary Alliance, or APRA, before going into exile in Mexico for fear of reprisals. His concerns were well-founded: in 1927, the military assassinated nearly 1000 members of the movement at the ruins of Chán-Chán.

For the next 25 years, Peru was governed by a series of dictators, each of whom seized power only to be ousted by the next.

The War Against Ecuador

In 1941, an armed conflict broke out between Peru and Ecuador over a border dispute dating back to about 1880. At the end of the war, the borders of the two countries were permanently defined under the Protocol of Rio de Janeiro. Four other countries (Argentina, Brazil, Chile and the United States) participated in the negotiations and cosigned the treaty. Since then, a number of prominent Ecuadorans have raised questions about the validity of this treaty. In fact, the boundaries indicated on maps published in Ecuador are not the same as those recognized by the United Nations and the international community. In 1998, however, Ecuador signed a treaty with Peru in which Ecuador officially recognized the territory as being part of Peru.

After the War

During World War II, Peru provided limited assistance to the Allied cause. It broke off relations with the Axis powers (Berlin, Rome) and recalled its ambassador from Austria, which had been invaded by German troops. The country only entered the war officially in February 1945, just three months before Germany capitulated, so that it could become a signatory of the United Nations charter. That same year, José Luis Rivero, backed by a coalition of leftist and liberal political parties, including APRA, was elected president.

A great many liberal reforms relating to civil rights and freedom of the press were introduced during Rivero's presidency, and certain powers more befitting a dictator than a democratically elected president were abolished by constitutional amendment. In October 1948, however, right-wing insurgents ousted Rivero, seized control of the government and outlawed APRA.

On July 2, 1950, Manuel A. Odría, the leader of the 1948 coup d'état, was elected president. The name of his leading opponent did not appear on the ballot. The Odría administration strengthened the Peruvian armed forces, launched an extensive public-works program and concluded a series of economic and cultural accords with Brazil, thus strengthening ties between the two countries. In 1952, Ecuador, Chile and Peru signed the Declaration of Santiago, which extended their territorial waters to 300 kilometres off the mainland, thereby reinforcing the unilateral declarations they had made in 1948. The declaration was greeted with a volley of protests from the United States, since a large number of American fishing vessels regularly sailed the fish-stocked coastal waters of South America.

Former president Manuel Prado y Ugarteche won the elections of 1956 and immediately began launching major liberal reforms. However, his efforts were soon hindered by strikes and

The *Sendero Luminoso* (Shining Path)

The Shining Path is a terrorist movement that originated in the Andes, more specifically in the town of Ayacucho. It was founded by Abimaël Guzmán Reynoso, a professor of philosophy at Ayacucho's San Cristóbal de Huamanga University. Guzmán's revolutionary ideas started to gel during a 1965 trip to China, and he was quite fanatical by the time he returned to Peru. Over the following years, he devoted his time to recruiting followers, implementing his plans and spreading his extremist philosophy. He didn't really take action, however, until 15 years later, when he set fire to some ballot boxes during the 1980 elections. These modest and relatively harmless early efforts gave little forewarning of the wave of violence that was to follow, which included car bombs, assassinations and kidnappings. At the time, the movement had an estimated 3,000 members. In 1981, President Alan García launched a major counter-attack. In response, the Shining Path liberated 300 of its members from the Ayacucho prison. Two years later, some journalists from Lima went to Huanta to find out what was happening and were savagely murdered by inhabitants of the Andean village of Uchuracay. In 1986, 250 members of the Shining Path serving time in a Lima jail were killed during a prison revolt. However, it was the next president, Alberto Fujimori, who succeeded in dealing the group its most serious blow. In September 1992, during his first term, he captured its leader, Abimaël Guzmán himself. Shortly thereafter, Guzmán was given an expeditious trial. The judge wore a mask so that he could not be recognized, while Guzmán, locked in a huge iron cage, was garbed in a standard, striped prisoner's uniform. Sentenced to life in prison, Guzmán spends most of his time in his cell and is only permitted to leave it for half an hour each day, just long enough to catch a glimpse of sunlight. The horrific rash of terrorism that swept through Peru claimed the lives of some 25,000 people.

uprisings related to political instability and soaring inflation. In 1959, the government introduced measures to curb the incoming flood of US businesses, encourage domestic industry and attract foreign investors. Within one year, the economy had improved dramatically and foreign capital was pouring into the country in the form of loans and development contracts. In October of that same year, the government received permission from the National Congress to nationalize most of the country's oil-production facilities over a period of time. In the presidential elections of 1962, none of the candidates received the minimum number of votes required (one third of the total), and a military junta took power.

General Ricardo Pérez Godoy took over the presidency in July, only to be ousted by the junta in March 1963. Three months later, Fernando Belaúnde Terry came to power. During the second half of his term in office, increased political opposition and rising inflation resulted in the devaluation of the national currency in 1967.

A lengthy dispute involving the claims of the International Petroleum Company (IPC), a subsidiary of the New Jersey-based Standard Oil Company, which was drilling in the rich La Brea y Parinas oilfields, was finally resolved by the Belaúnde government in August 1986. However, public opposition to the settlement forced the cabinet to resign in

The Tupac Amarú

The Tupac Amarú Revolutionary Movement (MRTA) was founded in 1984 by Victor Polay and Nestor Serpa. Tupac Amarú was the Inca Manco's son, whose name Gabriel Condorcanquí adopted a century later when he led a futile revolt against the Spanish. Both men met the same grim fate of being drawn and quartered on Cuzco's Plaza de Armas as their grief-stricken people looked on. Though the MRTA's methods are not as violent or expeditious as the Shining Path's, they still qualify as acts of terrorism. When terrorist activity in Peru was at its peak, the MRTA kidnapped and killed more than its share of victims. In February 1989, the group leader, Victor Polay, was captured by the police and immediately incarcerated. Nearly a year and a half later, in July 1990, Polay and 46 of his companions managed to escape through a 315-metre-long tunnel they had dug. On June 10, 1992, he was recaptured and sent back to prison, where he remains to this day. Once he was locked up, everyone thought the movement was dead and buried, not realizing that they were in for the rudest of awakenings: On December 17, 1996, MRTA commandoes took over the Japanese embassy in the middle of a reception. More than 400 people were taken hostage, but were gradually released. Negotiations went on for months. Then, on April 22, 1997, the Peruvian army launched a surprise attack on the embassy, during which all the terrorists, including the group leader, Nestor Serpa, were killed.

October 1968. Two days later, Belaúnde was driven out of office. Once again, the constitution was suspended and a military junta, this time led by General Juan Velasco, head of the joint chiefs of staff, took power. His government expropriated the IPC's assets, thereby antagonizing the United States. Relations between the two countries deteriorated even further in February 1969, when a Peruvian frigate inspected two American fishing vessels off the Peruvian coast, claiming that the ships were fishing illegally in Peruvian waters.

The next year, in 1970, a major earthquake in the Callejón de Huaylas claimed the lives of some 50,000 people and left 600,000 others homeless. Despite the political situation, the United States sent aid to the stricken area.

In the early 1970s, the Velasco government tried to overhaul the economic and social system, seizing foreign-owned estates, putting a ceiling on prices for basic goods and services and instituting bold agrarian reforms.

The anchovy fishing industry suffered a serious blow in 1972, due to a considerable change in the Humboldt Current.

In 1975, the government was continuing to carry out its nationalization program. However, President Velasco's health had become precarious, and a series of strikes and public demonstrations paved the way for a bloodless coup d'état led by the leaders of the armed forces. The next day, General Francisco Morales Bermúdez, who had been prime minister and minister of war under Velasco, was sworn in as president.

After about a decade of military dictatorship, presidential elections were finally held in 1980, returning former president Fernando Belaúnde Terry to office in July just as a new constitution was coming into effect. Over the next five years, the per capita income declined, foreign debt climbed and violence increased as the Shining Path stepped up its activities and the government's counter-revolutionary forces responded in kind. In the presidential elections of 1985, voters chose APRA candidate Alan García Pérez, who proved unable to halt the country's rapid economic decline. At the same time, the Shining Path was planting more and more bombs and increasing its killings of innocent people. Plagued by inflation, corruption and violence, the country was sinking into a state of utter chaos.

The presidential elections of 1990 marked a surprising turnaround in the political situation when agricultural economist Alberto Fujimori defeated the famous Peruvian author Mario Vargas Llosa, who had been considered the people's favourite. Fujimori, who had entered the running with left-wing support, imposed a program of economic austerity. In the early 1990s, these draconian measures prompted the Shining Path to increase its terrorist activities. Claiming that Congress and the judiciary had thwarted his efforts to curb the drug trade and wipe out the Shining Path, Fujimori suspended the constitution, dissolved the legislature and succeeded in putting the leader of the Shining Path behind bars i n April 1992. Three years later, Fujimori was elected to a second term in office, defeating another popular candidate, Javier Pérez de Cuéllar, the former secretary general of the United Nations.

The beginning of 1995 saw the mobilization of Ecuadoran and Peruvian troops in the Amazon, in a disputed border zone located some 500 kilometres south of Quito, in the northernmost part of Peru. Ecuador lost this area under the Protocol of Rio de Janeiro, signed on January 29, 1942, and has been disgruntled ever since, causing an ongoing controversy over the demarcation of the border in this remote mountainous region in the heart of the Amazon jungle.

The border conflict elicited strong reactions on the international community, and peace negotiations initiated by the co-signatories of the Protocol of 1942 (the United States, Argentina, Brazil and Chile) seem to have temporarily resolved the dispute. In fact, in 1998, Ecuador officially recognized this area as part of Peru.

Terrorist activity appeared to have come to a halt in 1996, and Fujimori was taking credit for putting an end to the violence. Then, shortly after Christmas, the Japanese embassy in Lima became the scene of a spectacular hostage crisis. The Tupac Amarú terrorist group, slightly less well-known than the Shining Path, managed to take over the embassy and holed up there for several months while the entire world held its breath. The crisis ended in a bloodbath when the Peruvian army launched a surprise attack on the building. One police officer and all the terrorists were killed during the operation. All the hostages but one were liberated unharmed.

Important Dates in the History of Peru

Late 15th century: The Inca Pachacutec hands over power to his son Tupac Yupanquí, who extends the Inca empire as far as Ecuadoran territory.

1493: Death of Tupac Yupanquí. His son, Huayna Cápac, succeeds him and extends the Inca empire to the Colombian border.

1527: Death of the Inca Huayna Cápac.

1530-1532: War breaks out between Huayna Cápac's two sons, Huáscar and Atahualpa, over the succession. The latter crushes his half-brother's troops.

1531: Conquistador Francisco Pizarro lands at Tumbes, in northern Peru.

1532: Pizarro and his men lay a trap for Atahualpa and take him prisoner in Cajamarca, Peru.

1533: Atahualpa is assassinated.

1535: Pizarro founds the city of Lima.

1536: The Inca Manco lays siege to the city of Cuzco.

1541: Francisco de Orellana sets out in search of El Dorado. He does not find gold, but becomes the first European to navigate the full length of the Amazon, all the way to the Atlantic Ocean.

1551: The University of San Marcos, the first university in South America, is founded in Lima.

1563: The Audiencia Real de Lima, a political body with territorial and judicial powers, but responsible to the Spanish Crown, is created.

1570: The Inquisition reaches Lima.

1572: The Inca Manco's son, Tupac Amarú, is executed in Cuzco.

1579: The English privateer Sir Francis Drake destroys the port of Callao.

1767: The Jesuits are expelled from the continent.

1780: Gabriel Condorcanquí adopts the name Tupac Amarú and leads a revolt against the Spanish regime.

1821: Peru declares independence.

1824: The Spanish are defeated at Junín and Ayacucho.

1826: Simón Bolívar leaves Peru.

1854: Slavery is abolished.

1864: Spain tries to seize the Chincha Islands.

1879: The Pacific War (involving Peru, Bolivia and Chile) begins.

1883: The Pacific War ends. Bolivia loses its access to the sea and Peru cedes Tarapacá.

1941: The Peruvian army invades southern Ecuador.

1942: Ecuador loses a large portion of its territory to Peru through the Rio de Janeiro treaty.

1979: Peru joins the Andean Pact, which promotes free trade among member countries. The other members are Colombia, Chile and Ecuador.

1980: The Shining Path (*Sendero Luminoso*) terrorist group becomes active.

1984: The Tupac Amarú Revolutionary Movement (MRTA) becomes active.

1985: Alan García is elected president.

1986: Some 200 incarcerated Shining Path members are killed during a prison revolt.

1989: Victor Polay, the leader of the MRTA, is captured.

1990: Victor Polay and 46 of his comrades escape from prison.

PORTRAIT

Alberto Fujimori

Everyone has a different opinion about Alberto Fujimori, who burst onto the chaotic political scene during the presidential elections of 1990, defeating the famous author Mario Vargas Llosa. Nicknamed *El Chino* because of his Japanese origins, Fujimori took the country firmly in hand in April 1992. Realizing that his opponents were intent on putting obstacles in his way and that he was surrounded by corruption, he carried out an *autogolpe* (self-directed coup), during which he suspended the constitution, dissolved the legislature and put the leaders of both the Shining Path and the MRTA behind bars. These exploits put him on the cover of *Time* magazine as the South American Man of the Year in 1993. A decline in terrorist activity and an economic upswing in which Peru had of the highest growth rates in the world (13% in 1994), won Fujimori 62% of the vote in the 1995 elections, and another five years in office. A year later, just before Christmas, the Japanese embassy in Lima was stormed by the MRTA, marking the beginning of a hostage crisis that would last several months. Fujimori categorically refused to collaborate with the terrorists and ordered the Peruvian army to launch a surprise attack on the embassy, during which one hostage, one police officer and all the terrorists were killed. The other hostages were released unharmed. Once again, Fujimori's expeditious actions roused the ire of humanitarian organizations. Then, in 1997, questions were raised about Fujimori's place of birth and thus the legitimacy of his presidency (the Peruvian constitution requires the president to have been born in the country). The controversy made headline news and was blown out of proportion by Fujimori's opponents.

1990: Against all odds, Alberto Fujimori wins the presidential elections.

1991: A cholera epidemic sweeps through the country.

1992: Victor Polay is recaptured and sent back to prison.

1994: Fujimori is elected to a second term in office.

1995: Fighting on the Ecuadoran border in early January.

1996: The MRTA takes a group of people hostage at the Japanese embassy.

1997: Peru withdraws from the Andean Pact on April 11.

1997: On April 22, the Peruvian army launches Operation Chavín de Huantar, a surprise attack on the terrorists occupying the Japanese embassy. One hostage, one soldier and all the terrorists are killed. The other hostages are liberated unharmed.

1997: Peru rejoins the Andean Pact on June 25.

1998: Ecuador officially recognizes the territory it ceded in the Rio de Janeiro treaty of 1942 as Peru's.

CULTURE AND TRADITION

Language

Spanish and Quechua (a vernacular spoken by Andean peoples since Inca times) are the two official languages of Peru. Aymara and a few other dialects are also spoken in remote areas around Lake Titicaca. English is understood in major tourist cities like Lima, Cuzco, Arequipa and Trujillo.

Religion

The majority of Peruvians are Roman Catholic. However, since the constitution recognizes freedom of religious expression, other Christian religions are also represented, albeit on a small scale, throughout the country.

POLITICS

Peru is a social democratic republic with a government elected by universal suffrage. In order to become president, a candidate must win at least 50% of the vote. The president is elected to a five-year term. The current president of Peru is Alberto Fujimori.

ECONOMY

Peru produces and exports raw materials. Gas, petroleum and copper are three of its major natural resources. The fish-stocked waters of the Pacific Ocean make fishing another important part of the economy. In fact, Peru is the world's leading exporter of fish meal. Agricultural products include cotton, sugar and coffee. Now that the terrorist epidemic is over, tourism has also become important to the economy. Though Peru only ranks twelfth on the list of gold-producing nations, its precious mineral resources have been coveted since the Spanish first arrived. Peru is the world's second largest producer of silver, third of tin, fourth of lead and zinc, sixth of copper and twelfth of gold.

THE ARTS

Like other colonial powers, the Spanish brought their religion to the lands they conquered and imposed it on the native peoples. It is not surprising, therefore, that religious themes are prevalent in colonial painting and sculpture.

After defeat the Incas, the Spanish wasted no time in building their palaces and churches. It was through the decoration of their interiors that a specifically Peruvian form of sacred art was born. Under the guidance of Spanish and Flemish monks, several schools of painting emerged; first in Lima, then elsewhere in the country. The painting of the Lima schools was strongly influenced by the Italian Renaissance artist Bernado Bitti.

Shortly thereafter, around the 18th century, the Cuzco School emerged, distinguished by the use of gold dust and the representation of saints venerated throughout Europe; here, however, the figures were given typically Amerindian features. The best-known painters of this movement were Pedro Loaiza, Basilio Santa Cruz and Marcos Zapata.

The *Escuela Cuzqueña* (The Cuzco School)

The Spanish had definite plans for Peru when they arrived: to conquer the native peoples and impose their dogmas on them. After succeeding, against all odds, in toppling the Inca empire, they wanted to reshape everything, from the art and architecture to people's beliefs. In order to promote a new surge of artistic activity, they brought Italian masters over to teach the natives how to paint and express themselves through various artistic media.

Using the Bible as a major source of inspiration, these Italian artists focussed mainly on painting baroque religious figures. One man in particular influenced this new school of painting: Bernado Bitti, who painted long, stylized figures characteristic of the Mannerist style. Bitti arrived in Lima around 1574 and opened schools in Cuzco, Puno and La Paz.

Thus was born the *Escuela Cuzceña*, whose evolution can be divided into three periods, which correspond to the different centuries (16th-18th).

In the 16th century, there were two distinct groups: the Italian masters, who knew how to paint and sculpt, and the natives, who were there to learn from them. The themes were exclusively European and religious, and the canvases were unsigned, because the Europeans considered Amerindian paintings to be mere copies of the masters' works, and forbade them the natives to sign their works.

In the 17th century, Amerindian painters became more confident and began to include plants, animals and landscapes in their compositions. Student paintings of this era are generally characterized by a lack of perspective and an exaggerated representation of human anatomy.

Among all the native students of this era, one stands out from the rest: **Diego Quispe Tito**, whose remarkable talent earned him the opportunity to complete his artistic training in Europe.

He studied in Flanders, Holland and, of course, Spain. Upon his return, he put everything he had learned into practice and also took a few subtle liberties, such as signing his paintings – not with his own name or initials, but with symbols such as hummingbirds.

Scenes of richly clothed, red-cheeked nuns whose bodies are shaped like mountains are also typical of 17th-century painting. Forbidden to worship their gods, including those of mountains, the natives skillfully integrated the shape of a mountain into the nun's appearance. The red cheeks are a reference to the Spaniards, whose skin would burn in the blazing Peruvian sun.

Seventeenth-century sculpture is typified by graphic representations of Christ, which vividly evoke the terrible suffering and torture inflicted on the natives by the Spanish. Unlike European representations of Christ, which show him looking up at the sky, these depict him with his eyes closed and his head bent downward in the submissive pose to which the natives had become accustomed.

In the 18th century, Peruvian painting was very baroque, and increasingly mixed native elements and traditional European religious images.

In the 19th century, Peruvian painting was republican, with artists depicting everyday scenes and socially prominent individuals.

Literature

Peru has a substantial number of nationally renowned novelists and poets. However, very few Peruvian authors have been translated into other languages; novelists Mario Vargas Llosa and Alfredo Bryce-Echenigue and poet

César Vallejo are three exceptions. An accurate reflection of the times, the literature of the past and present gives valuable insights into this perpetually changing society.

Mario Vargas Llosa

One of the giants of Latin American literature, Mario Vargas Llosa is among Peru's most prolific and most controversial writers. A harsh critic of the status quo, he has published numerous novels dealing with social and political issues, with the occasional foray into humour. His body of work also includes a large number of articles, essays and plays.

Vargas Llosa was born in Arequipa in 1936. A journalist and professor turned novelist, he won tremendous acclaim for his novel *La ciudad y los perros*. Vargas Llosa draws his inspiration from his tumultuous childhood and his experiences at the Leoncio Prado military academy, an authoritarian and intolerant institution where he was sent by his father to make him a man. Instead, the institution brought out the rebel in him and made him determined to expose the hypocrisy and corruption not only of the school, but of his country's leaders as well. At the age of 27, he won the prestigious *Biblioteca Breve* prize, thereby making a name for himself in the literary circles of the Spanish-speaking world. A wave of protest swept through Lima, and a thousand copies of his novel were burned at the gates of the military college. Vargas Llosa, an intellectual and man of letters, thus became a controversial figure both loved and hated by the Peruvian public. He left Lima, which he detested, and headed off to Europe.

Vargas Llosa's many novels are the work of a remarkably supple mind. *La*

Tía Julia y el escribador (*Aunt Julia and the Scriptwriter*, 1977, translated 1982), a humourous account of the marriage of a 19-year-old young scriptwriter and his 32-year-old aunt, won France's award for the best foreign book in 1980. Some people feel that *La casa verde* (*The Green House*, 1965) is the quintessential Spanish-American novel because of its descriptions of the landscape, its historical authenticity and its characters, whose stories blend together into a single narrative. The more political *Conversación en la catedral* (*Conversation in the Cathedral*, 1969) is a favourite among Peruvians. It deals with social divisions and recalls the despotic regime of General Odría. Finally, Vargas Llosa captures the violence of a bloody 19th-century rebellion in Brazil in *La guerra del fin del mundo* (*The War of the End of the World*, 1981), and draws a parallel with the tumultuous history of Latin America.

While he was living in Europe, Vargas Llosa decided to give up writing. In 1990 he returned to Peru to run for presidency as the Democratic Front candidate. He lost to Alberto Fujimori, the son of Japanese immigrants. It was a bitter failure for him, one which he explored in his autobiography published in 1993. He has since become a Spanish citizen and only returns to Peru for vacations.

Alfredo Bryce-Echenigue

Alfredo Bryce-Echenigue was born in 1939, just a few years after Mario Vargas Llosa. In Peruvian literary circles, he is considered Vargas Llosa's heir. He published a collection of stories entitled *Huerto Cerrado* in 1967, but is best known for *Un mundo para Julius* (*A World for Julius: A Novel*, 1970, translated 1992).

Ramón Ribeyro

Novelist Julio Ramón Ribeyro vividly depicts the poverty and misery of Lima's shantytowns in the 1950s. *Gallizanos sin plumas* tells the disturbing story of Efraín and Enrique, two young brothers whose tyrannical grandfather forces them to sift through garbage. This heartrending tale, which is as relevant today as when it was written, inspired Peruvian director Francisco Lombardi's 1989 film *Caídos del cielo*. Ribeyro has made a tremendous contribution to Spanish-American literature by capturing the realities of urban life in his writing, and is now recognized as one of Peru's leading contemporary writers.

José María Arguedas

The Peruvian literary scene also includes an important contingent of anthropological writers, who focus on the values and traditions of the country's indigenous peoples. Novelist and anthropologist José María Arguedas (1911-1969) developed a fascination with Quechua culture and language very early in life. He learned Quechua from his family's servants before mastering Spanish, his parents' first language. Later, he learned about Quechua customs at an native community near Andahuaylas. He was one of the greatest defenders of the Quechua language before he committed suicide in 1969. His work deals with Amerindian traditions: *El sueño del Pongo*, for example, is an adaptation of a legend from the Cuzco area. He examines the Amerindian spirit more closely in *Yawar Fiesta* (translated 1985) which describes a violent clash between Amerindian and Spanish traditions. In addition to his novels, poems and translations of Quechua works, Arguedas wrote about the Amerindian migration to the city and the challenges involved in national unification and modernization. Arguedas's style is a reflection of his own character: an imaginative blend of Quechua and Spanish influences.

Ciro Alegría

Born in the province of Huamachuco in the northern Andes, Ciro Alegría (1909-1966) began his career as a journalist before venturing into politics. Because of his involvement with APRA, he spent 22 years in exile in Chile, where he published *La serpiente de oro* (1935), the first volume of a trilogy that would place him among the most famous authors in South America. Alegría built on this success with *Los perros hambrientos* and *El mundo es ancho y ajeno* (*Broad and Alien Is the World*, 1941, translated 1983), a gripping and highly acclaimed portrayal of the Amerindian struggle against exploitation.

Poetry

Peruvian poetry, like that of other Latin American nations, has a critical stance towards the status quo and the crises that rock the country. Poetry and activism are closely allied, and dissenting voices are often poetic. Poets, like novelists, reflect on the national conscience, which is one of the most common themes in Spanish-American verse. Two of South America's most famous poets, César Vallejo and José Santos Chocano, were born in Peru.

César Vallejo

Born at the turn of the century in a northern Andean town, César Vallejo is one of the most critically acclaimed poets of the 20th century. He studied literature in Lima, then, tired of his bohemian lifestyle, set out to explore his country. He developed a strong interest in social causes and political issues, which aggravated those in power. He then took off for Europe to fight in the Spanish Civil War. Inspired by the French symbolists and various socio-political works, his poems have a modern view of traditional values and his country's tribulations. His angry verse denounces violence and challenges authority. Vallejo died in Paris in 1938, at the age of 46. His vast body of work includes *Los heraldos negros* (*The Black Heralds*, translated 1990), *España aparta de mi este caliz* (*Spain, Take This Cup from Me*, translated 1997) and *Poemas humanos*.

José Santos Chocano

José Santos Chocano was born in Lima in 1875, just before the war between Chile and Peru, which affected him deeply. He became interested in literature and political movements at a very young age, and his poetry would always have a political slant. His poems, such as *Los Conquistadores*, are heavily influenced by Spanish poetry and deal with history and culture. A man of strong convictions, he joined various ideological movements and protested against the military government. In 1895, at the tender age of 20, he published *Iras Santas*, followed by *En la Aldea* in 1896. An adventurous soul, he then set out to explore Central and South America. His travels introduced him to all sorts of people who shared his interest in politics and with whom he could discuss his political and social opinions. His idealism earned him fame but also aroused the ire of those in power, forcing him to move around. During this period, he published a number of works; poetry and prose alike. Upon his return to Peru he entered a dark period in his life, during which he was incarcerated after a fatal confrontation with one of his opponents. In

1928, eager to leave his tarnished reputation behind, he went to Chile, where he wrote *Primicias de Oro de Indias*. In 1934, in an dramatic incident straight out of a movie script, he was assassinated by a madman.

Women Writers

Women authors have finally started to break into the literary world, a world that had for a long time been dominated by men. Among the new generation of feminist poets, three writers have distinguished themselves by their passionate and intimate prose and their perception of day to day life in Peru.

María Emilio Cornejo

The young poet María Emilio Cornejo, who committed suicide in 1972, left an indelible mark on Peruvian poetry. Highly introspective, her work is notable for its trenchant style. Steeped in eroticism, her verse throws human values and is a mixture of the good and the bad, the personal and the political. Her family published a posthumous collection of her works entitled *En la mitad del camino recorrido* in 1989.

Carmen Ollé

With the publication of *Noches de adrenalina* in the early 1980s, Carmen Ollé proudly thumbed her nose at the male-dominated literary world. Brushing aside inhibitions and prejudice, she presented the female body not as an object but as the source of a distinct point of view, thereby ushering in a new, unapologetically feminist and highly erotic trend in poetry.

Giovanna Pollarola

Tacna poet and screenwriter Giovanna Pollarolo's work is in tune with contemporary Peruvian society. Her poem *Entre Mujeres Solas*, published in 1991, focusses on middle-class women and their changing relationships with one another. Pollarola has also written the scripts for numerous Peruvian films, including *La boca del lobo* and *Caídos del cielo*.

Music

Peruvian music reflects both Amerindian and European influences. Pre-Columbian instruments included flutes and percussion instruments made with shells and bones. Later, string instruments like the guitar, the harp and the violin were introduced by the Spanish. All these contributions helped shape Peruvian music as we know it today. It is most often heard in *peñas*, where both young and old come to dance to the sounds of Peruvian folk music.

The Colonial Flute

The flute is one of the oldest wind instruments. There are four different kinds: the recorder, the transverse flute, the straight flute and the double flute.

Transverse flutes are made with several materials, such as reeds and metal, have six holes and are painted differently according to the tribe to which they belong. The fife and the *rondador*, the equivalent of the panpipe (shepherd's pipe or syrinx), also fall into the flute category.

Panpipes

The first panpipe was made with reeds of various lengths and circumferences tied together with plant fibres. Over time, the instrument became associated with the Greek god Pan, who supposedly created it out of his passionate love for the nymph Siringa; it is thus referred to in certain places as the *siringa* (syrinx).

The **panpipe** is a wind instrument with an extremely soft sound. It comes in all different sizes, from tiny ones with only eight pipes, to big ones with 20, 30 or more.

The tiny **pentaphone panpipe**, which has five sounds, is used in certain places in Peru only once a year, as it is considered a ritual instrument. It is used in the festivities held during the autumnal equinox (September), when locals pay homage to the sun.

The **large panpipe** has six sounds and is used by some Amerindians to practice their scales.

Reed panpipes are traditional flutes made of bone, wood, feather shafts or reeds and strips of leather.

The **condor-feather panpipe** is made up of feather shafts of various lengths, attached side by side with a delicate wire.

Andean horns are bull's horns with a thin reed attached at the tip, from which the sound is emitted.

The **marimba** has keys of various sizes, made with the wood of palm trees. The resonance chamber is made up of pieces of bamboo positioned like a panpipe under each key; the sound is created by hitting them with two or more sticks, also made of palm-tree wood and covered with several layers of rubber at the tips. The instrument sits on two supports known as *burros*. The marimba is tuned by binding the laths tightly together with linen strings. When they play the marimba, the mestizos often form a traditional orchestral ensemble that typically includes a bass drum, four *guasás* and two *cununos*.

Ranulfo Fuentes

Ranulfo Fuentes is a guitarist from Ayacucho who writes and sings in Quechua, so that families from poor areas, who usually can't afford to buy books in Quechua, can hear their language in his music.

Yma Súmac

Singer Yma Súmac was born about 70 years ago, but no one knows exactly when or where. In musical circles, she is known as "the bird" because she can reach such incredibly high notes. In fact, when her first records came out, critics thought that the sound had been doctored. Her first North American shows, in the 1940s, enthralled audiences and critics alike. Súmac's life remains shrouded in mystery. She claims that she is of Inca descent and was born in the Peruvian Andes, but a number of music writers say that she is an American, and that "Yma Súmac" is a pseudonym.

PRACTICAL INFORMATION

Whether you are travelling on your own or in a group, getting around in Peru is an easy matter. Planning ahead will help you get the most out of your visit. This section is intended to help you organize your trip to Peru by providing general information and practical advice. **Please note that all prices in this guide are in U.S. dollars.**

ENTRANCE FORMALITIES

Before leaving home, make sure you have the official documents that will allow you to enter and leave Peru. Though the requirements may seem lax, without the proper documents you will not be able to travel within the country. Safeguard these documents and always have them on your person.

Passport

To enter Peru, travellers from Canada, the United States, Great Britain, Australia and New Zealand must have a passport that is valid for the length of their stay. This document is the official proof of identity.

Travellers are advised to keep a photocopy of the most important pages of their passport, as well as to write down its number and date of issue. If ever this document is lost or stolen, this will facilitate the replacement process (do the same with your birth certificate, and other important pieces of identification). In case of such an event, contact your country's embassy or consulate (see addresses in Lima chapter) in order to be reissued an equivalent document as soon as possible.

Tourist Card

Besides your passport, you must have a tourist card (*tarjeta de turismo*) to enter the country. In most cases, this card is issued on the plane or at the airport when you arrive. The card allows all visitors (Canadians, Americans, British, Australians, New Zealanders) to stay in the country for 90 days. The airfare or package price usually includes the cost of the card, which is $10 per person. The card must be returned upon departure, so don't lose it.

For stays of 90 days or more in Peru, you must visit the Ministerio del Interior *(Paseo de la República 585, ☎427-6927)* to obtain a 30-day extension for approximately $25. Another option is to visit a neighbouring country for a couple of days. Upon re-entering Peru, your stay will automatically be extended by 30 days, without having wasted a single day of your trip dealing with bureaucracy. For information on crossing the border into other countries, see the corresponding chapter.

Visa

Canadian, American, British, Australian, and New Zealand travellers do not need a visa to enter Peru. Other travellers should check with the Peruvian embassy or consulate in their country to see if they need a visa.

Departure Tax

Everyone leaving Peru must pay a departure tax of $25 at the airport upon checking in. Be sure to have this amount in cash ($ or *soles*), since credit cards are not accepted. A $4 departure tax is applied to all domestic flights.

Customs

Those entering the country may have in their possession up to one litre of alcohol, 200 cigarettes and $300 worth of goods (besides personal items). Drugs and firearms are of course forbidden. The export of archaeological artefacts from Peru is subject to stringent regulations, so think twice before taking something back to furnish your home.

EMBASSIES AND CONSULATES

Embassies and consulates representing your home country can provide valuable assistance in the event of health emergencies, legal problems or the death of a travel companion. Only urgent cases are dealt with, however. Visitors are responsible for any costs incurred as a result of services provided by these official bodies. You can also receive mail here.

See the "Practical Information" section in the Lima chapter (see p 104) for foreign consulates and embassies in Peru.

PERUVIAN EMBASSIES AND CONSULATES ABROAD

Consulates

Canada
550 Rue Sherbrooke Ouest, Suite 970, Montréal, Québec, H3A 1B9, ☎(514) 844-5123, ⬝(514) 843-8425, perou@globale.net.

10 St. Mary Street, Suite 301, Toronto, Ontario, M4Y 1P9, ☎(416) 963-9696, ⬝(416) 963-9074.

260-505 Burrard Street, Vancouver, British Columbia, V7X 1M6, ☎(614) 662-8880, ⇐(614) 662-3564.

Embassies

Australia
Qantas House, Suite 1, 9th Floor, 97 London Circuit, Canberra, ACT 2601, P.O. Box 971, Civic Square, ACT 2608, ☎(06) 257-953, ⇐257-5198.

Belgium
Avenue de Tervueren 179, 1150 Brussels, ☎(32-3) 735-9927, ⇐ (32-3) 733-4819, embassy.of.peru@unicall.be.

Bolivia
Fernando Guachalla, corner of 6 de Agosto, La Paz, ☎(591-2) 353.550 or 352.352, ⇐(591-2) 796.164, embbol@caoba.entelnet.bo.

Brazil
Avenida des Nacoes, Lote 43, 70428-900 Brasilia, ☎(55-61)242.9933 or 242.9835, ⇐(55-61) 244.9344, emb.peru@nutelnet.com.br.

Canada
130 Albert Street, Suite 1901, Ottawa, Ontario, K1P 5G4, ☎(613) 238-1777, ⇐ (613) 232-3062, emperuca@magi.com.

Chile
Avenida Andrés Bello 1751, Providencia, Santiago, ☎(562) 235.6451 or 235.2356, ⇐ (562) 235.8139, embstgo@entelchile.net.

Denmark
Rosenvaengets Alle 20, 2 TV, 2100 Copenhagen, ☎(45-3) 526-5848 or 526-2397, ⇐(45-3) 526-8406.

Ecuador
Avenida República de El Salvador 495, corner of Irlanda, Quito, ☎(593-2) 468.410 or 468.389, ⇐ (539-2) 468.411, embeecu@ui.satnet.net.

Germany
Godesberger Alle 125-127, 53175 Bonn, ☎(228) 37.30.45, ⇐(228) 37.94.75.

Great Britain
52 Sloane Street, London SW1X 9SP, ☎(171) 235-1917, ⇐(171) 235-4463.

Italy
Via Po 22, 00198 Rome, ☎(39-06) 841-6556 or 841-7265, ⇐ (39-06) 853-54447, amb.peru@agora.stm.it.

Netherlands
Nassauplein 4, 2585 EA, The Hague, ☎ (31-70) 365-3500, ⇐(31-70) 365-1929, embperu@bart.nl.

Portugal
Rua Castillho 50, 4th Floor, 1250 Lisbon, ☎(351-1) 386-1552 or 385-5569, ⇐ (351-1) 386-0005, embperu@mail.telepac.pt.

Spain
Príncipe de Vergara 36, 5D, 28001 Madrid, ☎(1) 431-4242, ⇐(1) 577-6861.

Switzerland
Thunstrasse 36, CH-3005 Berne, ☎ (41-31) 351.8555, ⇐ (41-31) 351.8570, peru02@embaperu.int.ch.

United States
1700 Massachusetts Avenue NW, Washington DC 20036, ☎(202) 833-9860, ⇐(202) 659-8124, lepruwash@aol.com.

GETTING TO PERU

By Plane

Most European airlines service Peru via the United States or other Latin American countries. Depending on your departure location, many combinations are possible. For instance, British Airways offers flights to Lima via New York. KLM flies from London and Amsterdam, and Lufthansa has a direct connection from Frankfurt to Lima.

There are no direct flights from Canada to Peru. Canadians must first fly to the United States or to a Latin American country before embarking on a flight to Lima.

Airports

Most visitors fly to one of Peru's two international airports. The **Jorge Chávez Airport** (*☎575-1712*) welcomes the greater number of incoming passengers and is located in the northern part of Lima. The **Cuzco Airport** welcomes flights mostly from La Paz, Bolivia.

By Bus

From Ecuador: Buses travel from Huaquillas (Ecuador) to two Peruvian cities: Aguas Verdes and Tumbes.

From Bolivia: Buses cross the border into Peru from small Bolivian towns such as Yunguyo or Desgraruadero.

Border crossings are generally open from 8am to either 5pm or 8pm. Offices are closed from noon to 1 or 2pm depending on which day of the week it is.

TRANSPORTATION

Though most highways are in good condition, distances can be considerable in Peru, especially since it is impossible to go any faster than 40 km/h on the smaller roads. It is therefore very important to plan your itinerary well, and above all, avoid driving at night.

Renting a Car

If you are over 25, have a valid driver's license and enough money, renting a car in Peru is easy. Most of the major car-rental agencies have offices in the country. Expect to pay on average $40 per day (plus about 20¢ per kilometre in certain cases) for a small car, not including insurance and taxes. A four-wheel-drive vehicle is more expensive, between $50 and $70 per day. This last option is worth serious consideration if you plan on taking the smaller roads. Choose a car in good condition and one that is relatively new. A few local companies charge less, but their vehicles are often in much worse shape. When renting, be sure to take sufficient insurance to cover the costs of an accident. A $1,000 down-payment is often required (in cash or by credit card). Before signing the rental contract, ensure that the method of payment is clearly indicated. Remember that when you sign, your credit card must cover not only the rental cost but also the insurance deductible. Certain credit cards (gold cards) automatically insure you against vehicle theft or collisions, but they often do not cover four-wheel-drives.

Driving and the Highway Code

Though it can be very practical to have your own set of wheels to take you off

Table of distances (km)
Via the shortest route

Example : The distance between Lima and Cuzco is 1102km.
1 mile = 1.62 kilometres
1 kilometre = 0.62 miles

© ULYSSES

	Arequipa	Ayacucho	Cajamarca	Cerro de Pasco	Cuzco	Chiclayo	Huancayo	Huanuco	Huaráz	Ica	Lima	Piura	Pucallpa	Puerto Maldonado	Puno	Tacna	Trujillo
Ayacucho	1135																
Cajamarca	1865	1439															
Cerro de Pasco	1314	573	1161														
Cuzco	518	582	1958	1155													
Chiclayo	1779	1353	260	1075	1872												
Huancayo	1307	318	1154	255	900	1068											
Huanuco	1419	678	1266	105	1260	1180	300										
Huaráz	1426	1002	631	724	1521	545	717	354									
Ica	706	429	856	608	799	1073	416	713	722								
Lima	1009	583	528	305	1102	770	298	410	419	303							
Piura	2047	1621	1641	1343	2140	268	1336	375	813	1341	1038						
Pucallpa	1794	1053	2487	480	1635	1555	735	1448	729	1088	785	1823					
Puerto Maldonado	948	1111	2188	1684	529	2401	1429	1789	2050	1328	1631	2661	2164				
Puno	323	971	2149	1544	389	2102	1289	1649	1751	1024	1332	2370	2024	819			
Tacna	368	1419		1598	768	2063	1477	1703	1712	990	1293	2331	2078	1198	379		
Trujillo	1570	1144	295	866	1663	209	859	971	336	864	561	477	1346	2192	1893	1854	
Tumbes	2329	1903	810	1625	2422	550	1678	1730	1095	1623	1320	282	2105	2951	2652	2613	759

PRACTICAL
INFORMATION

the beaten path, we do not recommend driving in Peru. With all due respect to Peruvians, they have a tendency to drive dangerously fast, and though the highways and main roads are generally in good condition, they are winding, sometimes slippery and accidents waiting to happen. The PanAmerican highway that runs north-south along the coast is probably the best maintained in the country. Driving in the Andes cordillera is a whole other story. Here, the most roads are in poor condition and are quite treacherous if you aren't used to curvy roads with sheer drops in some places. During the rainy season, roads often become blocked because of landslides and sections of the road collapsing.

And despite the fact that there is no shoulder, traffic still runs at a fair clip. The occasional pothole here and there is a problem. Then there is the rock 'n' roll passing style: if you're lucky the car behind you will give a few warning honks on the horn before he pulls out face to face with the oncoming traffic to pass you! The lack of lighting, the steep mountain terrain and the poor signage of Peruvian roads make driving at night something to be avoided. Not to mention that some cars don't have headlights, and it gets dark quickly this close to the equator.

Driving on the secondary roads is a whole other can of worms. These are often gravel roads; some are paved, and most are pockmarked with potholes of all sizes. Traffic moves slowly. Also, animals of all kinds, but mostly dogs, are continually crossing the road. For some reason, our canine friends feel the need to chase after all cars, all the while foaming at the mouth and barking wildly. If this happens, above all, don't stop or get out of your vehicle. The best course of action for travellers in this case is to stay calm, slow down so as not to hit the dog and continue on their merry way.

Small villages line these secondary roads, and drivers must be careful of the numerous pedestrians. Speed bumps have been placed in village streets to slow down drivers. Unfortunately, these are poorly indicated; they are usually located on the way into town. Roads signs are also few and far between (there are hardly any speed limit, stop or yield signs). Also, directions are poorly signed out, if they are indicated at all. Thus, to find your way around, the only alternative is to ask directions from the locals.

Driving in Lima

Traffic is heavy in Lima, where drivers weave dangerously in and out of traffic. The elementary rules of the road as travellers may know them are nonexistent, and use of the turn signal has been replaced by a constant and repetitive leaning on the horn. Few drivers check their blind spot before passing. Furthermore, pedestrians must be especially careful when crossing the street: just because the light is red does not mean the cars will stop.

Finally, never leave your car unattended. Try to pick a hotel with a private parking lot. What's more, many Peruvians will offer to watch your car during your absence. Accept on good faith, but only pay once you return and only pay one person. This service usually costs about two *soles*.

Car Service

In certain regions of the country, young Peruvians will offer to wash your car; sometimes they'll even do it without asking you. Of course, they expect a little something for their trouble. Even if you don't or didn't want your car washed, it is better to pay them (and avoid a scratched car or worse). Expect to pay about two *soles*.

Police

Police and military checks along the highway are routine to monitor drivers. Officers have the right to stop anyone who breaks one of the rules of the road, or simply to check their papers. Be sure to always have your passport or a photocopy of it certified by your embassy or consulate. Otherwise, you will have trouble proving your identity, which can cause trouble. Generally speaking, officers are obliging, and will help out if you have car trouble.

Police: ☎105.

Gas

Gas (petrol) stations are located throughout the country, but it is recommended that you keep a spare tank of gas in case of an emergency. Gas costs about 60¢ a litre. Gas stations are called *grifos*. Few stations accept credit cards.

By Taxi

Taxis are available in most larger towns and of course in the major cities. The cars are often quite old, but will get you where you are going. In most cases, the fare is not determined by a meter, but rather set in advance. If you set the price ahead of time, be clear on what it includes before accepting, and only pay at the end.

Negotiating the Price

The price of a taxi or motorcycle taxi ride can be bargained down slightly.

Shared Taxis

In shared taxis (*taxis ruta)* the fare is shared by all the passengers even if they have different destinations. These are found mostly in Guayaquil.

Motorcycle Taxis

These are three-wheel motorcycles equipped with a back seat that can accommodate two to three passengers. The fare is lower than that of a standard taxi and must be mutually agreed upon prior to departure.

By Bus

The whole country is well served numerous bus companies. Few cities have a *terminal terrestre* from which all buses arrive and depart. Rather, each company has its own terminal, but there is no direct service connecting these stations. To take the bus, simply go to the local company's depot or hail one from the side of the road. Buses stop frequently, and are often very crowded. Nevertheless, it is possible to buy your ticket in advance at the station. This is a good idea if you are taking a long trip; tall people can thus avoid getting stuck in the seat over the wheel. Remember that the back seats do not always recline and make for a much bumpier ride thanks to the less-than-perfect road conditions. Bus fares are fixed.

Bus drivers generally travel at breakneck speeds, which may cause first-time passengers to experience a few

PRACTICAL INFORMATION

heart palpitations or break out in a cold sweat. Many buses are equipped with VCRs that generally play low-budget, violent and insipid movies for passengers' enjoyment or displeasure. Also, bus drivers love to listen to the radio, sometimes at irritatingly loud volumes. Finally, most buses do not have toilets, so use the bathroom right before getting on – it's now or never!

Some companies like Ormeño, Cruz del Sur and Tepsa, have relatively comfortable, air-conditioned buses. Stops are less frequent and the trip is a lot faster. Fares are slightly higher, of course, but for long distances, the time saved and greater comfort more than outweigh the extra cost.

By Helicopter

Helicopter travel is rare and expensive, except between Cuzco and Aguas Calientes. However, it is a fast and spectacular way of getting to the ruins of Machu Picchu. One company to try is **HeliCusco** *(Lima, Paseo de la Repœblica 5663, Miraflores, ☎01-447-104 or 447-110, ≈467-197).*

By Boat

In the tropical forest, boats are often the only available means of transport. This is the only way of getting to the islands of Lake Titicaca.

By Plane

Flying is a practical, though not necessarily economical, way of getting around the whole country. A one-way flight from Lima to Cuzco takes close to an hour and costs around $75. Iquitosis is 90 minutes away from Lima and costs around $200 for the return

flight. Aeroperú is the biggest national airline and offers daily flights to the major cities. Aerocontinente flies to the same interior destinations as Aeroperú. Aerocondor flies to the smaller cities such as Chimbote and Cajamarca. The fares are roughly the same. Always confirm your flight a few days prior to departure.

N.B.: There is a departure tax of about $4 on all domestic flights.

A relatively economical option for travellers planning on taking several successive flights within a relatively short period of time is the *Tour Pass*. This excursion ticket entitles you to several domestic flights within a given period, at reduced rates. The concept is similar to that of rail passes in Europe. Most airlines offer this special at competitive rates.

By Train

Travelling by train is a wonderful way to admire Peru's picturesque landscapes, but it is also the slowest and least reliable means of transportation. Take the bus or plane instead. **ENAFER** *(Empresa Nacional de Ferrocarriles)* is the national railway company *(Lima, Jr. Ancash 207, ☎428-9440 or 427-6620, ≈428-0905, enafer@amauta.rcp.net.pe).*

Lima - La Oroya - Cerro de Pasco

This is the highest train route in the world and undoubtedly one of the most spectacular on the planet. A veritable technological masterpiece, this railway once treated passengers to fabulous landscapes, and runs through some sixty tunnels, spans numerous waterways, climbs dizzying mountainsides to a height of 4,781 metres before de

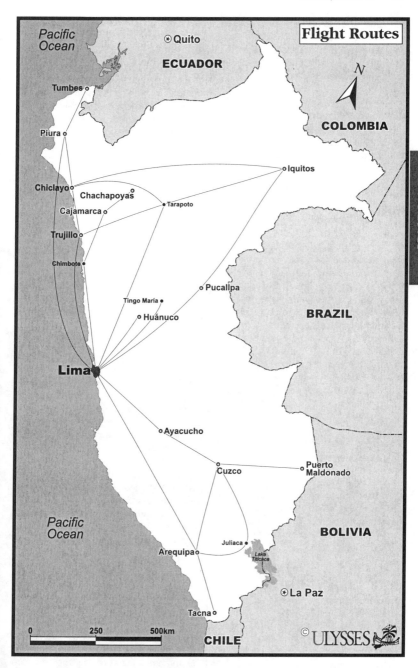

scending to its final destination. Unfortunately for tourists, this line is now only used to ship ore from the mines near La Oroya and Cerro de Pasco, in the Central Andes, to Lima.

Huancayo - Huancavelica

There is a passenger railway line linking Huancayo and Huancavelica in the Central Andes.

Cuzco - Quillabamba
(via Aguas Calientes)

Aside from going by helicopter or hiking, taking the train is one of the few ways of reaching Machu Picchu. Although most travellers disembark in the small village of Aguas Calientes and take the bus to the famous Machu Picchu ruins, locals continue by train to Quillabamba. This is probably the most reliable rail line in the country, and one of the busiest, because it goes to Machu Picchu, the archaeological site which draws most foreign travellers visiting Peru.

Cuzco - Juliaca - Puno

This rail line is not very reliable and service on it may be cut when the road that links Cuzco and Puno is completed around the end of 1998. The road is designed to follow roughly the same route as the train, so the scenery will be just as spectacular.

Cuzco - Juliaca - Arequipa and
Arequipa - Juliaca - Puno

Once again, the train is not always reliable. Delays and breakdowns are frequent due to mechanical problems.

Hitchhiking

If you have time, it is possible to hitchhike your way around. People are friendly and like talking to strangers, but usually expect a small payment. Of course, a certain amount of caution is advised. Women travelling alone should not hitchhike. Given the low cost of a bus ticket, hitchhiking should really be a last resort.

Other

In remote areas, trucks and other vehicles will often take along passengers for a few *soles*

INSURANCE

Cancellation Insurance

This type of insurance is usually offered by your travel agent when you purchase your plane tickets or tour package. It covers any non-refundable payments to travel suppliers such as airlines, and must be purchased at the same time as initial payment is made for air tickets or tour packages. Trip cancellation insurance comes into effect if a traveller has to call off a trip for valid medical reasons or because of a death in the family. This type of insurance can be useful, but weigh the likelihood of your using it against the price.

Theft Insurance

Most Canadian residential insurance policies cover a percentage of personal belongings against theft if the items are stolen outside the country. If you plan on travelling with valuable objects, check your policy or with an insurance agency to see if additional baggage insurance is necessary. It is recommended that travellers from Europe insure their luggage against theft so that they are prepared in case it occurs. To file an insurance claim for a theft incurred while on holiday, you will need a police report from the country you are visiting. Generally, 10% of your total coverage is applicable to theft occurring during your travels.

Life Insurance

By purchasing your tickets with certain credit cards you will get life insurance. However, many travellers already have another form of life insurance and do not need extra insurance.

Health Insurance

Health insurance is the most important type of insurance travellers can get. A comprehensive health insurance policy that provides a level of coverage sufficient to pay for hospitalization, nursing care and doctor's fees is recommended. Keep in mind that health care costs are rising quickly everywhere. The policy should also have a repatriation clause in case the required care is not available in Peru. As patients are sometimes asked to pay for medical services up front, find out what provisions your policy makes in this event. Always carry your health insurance policy with you when travelling to avoid problems if you are in an accident, and get receipts for any expenses incurred.

HEALTH

Peru is a wonderful country to explore; however, travellers should be aware of and protect themselves from a number of health risks associated with the region, such as malaria, typhoid, diphtheria, tetanus, polio and hepatitis A. Cases of these diseases are rare but there is a risk. **Travellers are therefore advised to consult a doctor (or travellers' clinic) for advice on what precautions to take.** Remember that it is much easier to prevent these illnesses than it is to cure them and that a vaccination is not a substitute for cautious travel.

Illnesses

Please note that this section is intended to provide general information. If you are travelling with prescription medication, bring the prescription as customs officials may ask to see it.

Malaria

The only place where you risk contacting malaria in Peru is in the Selva region. If you visit this area, take the necessary precautions and use the medication prescribed by a physician.

Malaria (paludism) is caused by a parasite in the blood called *Plasmodium sp.* This parasite is transmitted by anopheles mosquitoes, and cannot be passed from person to person. The symptoms of malaria include high fever, chills, extreme fatigue and headaches as well as stomach and muscle aches. There are several forms of malaria, including one serious type caused by *P. falciparum*. The disease can take hold while you are still on holiday or up to 12 weeks following your return; in some cases the symptoms can appear months later. While most people recover from malaria, it is important to take all possible precautions against the disease. A doctor can prescribe anti-malarial medication to be taken before and after your trip (various types exist, depending on the destination, length of trip, your physical condition, etc.). Since the parasite that causes malaria is constantly evolving, anti-malarial medication is not foolproof. Travellers should avoid getting bitten by mosquitoes as much as possible (see section on mosquitoes, p 58).

Hepatitis A

This disease is generally transmitted by ingesting food or water that has been contaminated by faecal matter. The symptoms include fever, yellowing of the skin, loss of appetite and fatigue, and can appear between 15 and 20 days after infection. An effective vaccination is available. Besides the recommended vaccine, good hygiene is important. Always wash your hands before every meal, and ensure that the food and preparation area are clean.

Typhoid

This illness is caused by ingesting food that has come in contact (direct or indirect) with an infected person's stool. Common symptoms include high fever, loss of appetite, headaches, constipation and occasionally diarrhea, as well as the appearance of red spots on the skin. These symptoms will appear one to three weeks after infection. Which vaccination you get (it exists in two forms, oral and by injection) will depend on your trip. Once again, it is always a good idea to visit a travellers' clinic a few weeks before your departure.

Diphtheria and Tetanus

These two illnesses, against which most people are vaccinated during their childhood, can have serious consequences. Thus, before leaving, check that your vaccinations are valid; you may need a booster shot. Diphtheria is a bacterial infection that is transmitted by mucous or by skin lesions on an infected person. Symptoms include sore throat, high fever, general aches and pains and occasionally skin infections. Tetanus is caused by a bacteria that enters your body through an open wound that comes in contact with contaminated dust or rusty metal.

Soroche (mountain sickness)

Dizziness, headaches, loss of appetite and vomiting are the major symptoms of *soroche*. The cause is simply a lack of oxygen; your system does not have a chance to produce the excess of red blood cells required to oxygenate the blood at higher altitudes. The best treatment is rest, but a medication called Diamox is also available. It comes in pill form and can be taken before climbing high summits. A physician will be able to give you more advice about this drug. In Arequipa, a temporary headache is probably the worst effect you will experience. Avoid heavy meals, cigarettes and alcohol, and drink lots of liquids. If the symptoms persist, however, it is a good idea to head downhill where you can breathe easier. If you plan to spend time at higher altitudes than Arequipa, spend a few days in the city first to allow your system to adjust. It may ease your system to have a *mate de coca* upon arriving in mountaintop villages at high altitudes. The coca leaf used in this tea is not cocaine, and therefore is not addictive.

Never take any sleep-inducing medication, which can slow down your breathing and thus your oxygen intake. Descending to a lower altitude is the only treatment available.

Soroche can affect anyone, young or old, even those in top physical shape. Anyone who heads to over 2,400 metres too quickly is at risk.

Rabies

The risk of rabies is very high in Peru. This illness is usually transmitted by dog bites. Despite numerous educational campaigns, many dogs roam unvaccinated. Bats, squirrels and wolves can also carry the disease.

The virus, which is transmitted by the saliva of the infected animal, attacks the nervous system and ultimately the brain. Symptoms include violent fits and localized paralysis. The illness can be fatal. Luckily, it only develops after a few weeks. If you are bitten, wash the wound with soap and water, then with alcohol, and consult a doctor as soon as possible.

The conventional treatment involves several painful injections in the stomach, which are administered over several days. Many clinics in Lima provide this treatment.

Cholera

Cholera is an intestinal infection caused by the bacteria *vibrio comma*. Symptoms include severe watery diarrhea (the stool is a colourless, odourless liquid without substance), and vomiting can occur in more serious cases. The incubation period is several hours, and the illness lasts two to three days. Though it is highly contagious, cholera is easy to avoid and cure. There is no need to panic like before modern medicine when cholera was a real cause for

concern. To avoid catching it, drink only bottled water or other drinks that come in sealed containers (soda, beer, etc.), or beverages made with boiled water (coffee or tea) in countries which do not have adequate sanitation systems or which have had cholera outbreaks within the last 10 years. Also, do not eat salad or uncooked vegetables, and peel fruits, even if you have washed them. It is recommended to eat only cooked foods that are still warm. People who are already malnourished are often the hardest hit by the disease. Westerners who are in good health have a very high resistance to the bacteria, and are at little risk of becoming ill, even if they come into contact with it. If, despite everything, you do become sick, make sure to drink lots of fluids and continue to eat, or you can become extremely dehydrated, which can be fatal. Also, consult the nearest clinic, pharmacy or hospital, especially if symptoms get worse. Bring along rehydrating salts, and drink as much of them as possible if you do come down with acute diarrhea. Although they don't taste great (they have a salty-sweet flavour), they are very effective. Aside from maintaining good hygiene and liquid intake, there is no effective medication or vaccine against cholera.

Other illnesses

Cases of illnesses like hepatitis B, **AIDS** and certain venereal diseases have been reported; it is therefore a good idea to be careful. Remember that condoms are the best protection against these illnesses.

Fresh water is often contaminated by an organism that causes **schistosomiasis**. This infection, which is caused by a parasite entering the body and attacking the liver and nervous system, is difficult to treat. It is therefore best to avoid swimming in fresh water.

PRACTICAL INFORMATION

Remember that consuming too much alcohol, particularly during prolonged exposure to the sun, can cause severe dehydration and lead to health problems.

Due to a lack of available funds, medical facilities in Peru are generally not as modern as those in industrialized countries. Consequently, should you require medical attention during your stay in Peru, don't expect the same service you would normally get at home. Furthermore, clinics in more remote areas are usually smaller and under-equipped. In tourist zones, it should be relatively easy to find an English-speaking doctor. Finally, in case of a blood transfusion, make sure that the blood has been properly tested and is safe. It is best to carry your own syringes and other emergency medication.

Insufficiently treated water, which can contain disease-causing bacteria, is the cause of most of the health problems travellers are likely to encounter, such as stomach upset, diarrhea or fever. Throughout the country, it is a good idea to drink bottled water (when buying bottled water, make sure the bottle is properly sealed), or to purify your own with iodine or a water purifier. Most major hotels treat their water, but always ask first. Ice cubes should be avoided, as they may be made of contaminated water. In addition, fresh fruits and vegetables that have been washed but not peeled can also pose a health risk. Make sure that the vegetables you eat are well-cooked and peel your own fruit. Do not eat lettuce, unless it has been hydroponically grown (some vegetarian restaurants serve this type of lettuce; ask). Remember: cook it, peel it or forget it.

If you do get diarrhea, soothe your stomach by avoiding solids; instead, drink carbonated beverages, bottled water, or weak tea (avoid milk) until you recover. As dehydration can be dangerous, drinking sufficient quantities of liquid is crucial. Pharmacies sell various preparations for the treatment of diarrhea, with different effects. Pepto Bismol and Imodium will stop the diarrhea, which slows the loss of fluids, but they should be avoided if you have a fever as they will prevent the necessary elimination of bacteria. Oral rehydration products, such as Gastrolyte, will replace the minerals and electrolytes which your body has lost as a result of the diarrhea. In a pinch, you can make your own rehydration solution by mixing one litre of pure water with one teaspoon of sugar and two or three teaspoons of salt. After, eat easily digested foods like rice to give your stomach time to adjust. If symptoms become more serious (high fever, persistent diarrhea), see a doctor as antibiotics may be necessary.

Nutrition and climate can also cause problems. Pay attention to food's freshness and the cleanliness of the preparation area. Good hygiene (wash your hands often) will help avoid undesirable situations.

Mosquitoes

A nuisance common to many countries, mosquitoes are no strangers to Peru. They are particularly numerous during the rainy season. Protect yourself with a good insect repellent. Repellents with DEET are the most effective. The concentration of DEET varies from one product to the next; the higher the concentration, the longer the protection. In rare cases, the use of repellents with high concentrations (35% or more) of DEET has been associated with convulsions in young children; it is therefore important to apply these products sparingly, on exposed skin, and to wash it off once back inside. A concentration of 35% DEET will protect for four to six hours, while 95% will last from 10 to 12 hours. New formulas with DEET in lesser concentrations are available and last just as long.

To further reduce the possibility of getting bitten, do not wear perfume or bright colours. Sundown is an especially active time for insects. When walking in wooded areas, cover your legs and ankles well. Insect coils can help provide a better night's sleep. Before bed, apply insect repellent to your skin and to the headboard and baseboard of your bed. If possible, get an air-conditioned room, or bring a mosquito net.

Lastly, since it is impossible to completely avoid contact with mosquitoes, bring along a cream like calomine lotion to soothe the bites you will invariably get.

Dangerous Animals

The list of all the wild animals found in Peru is long and might discourage even the most hardy travellers from exploring the countryside. Keep in mind, though, that wild animals do not roam all regions of the country and definitively steer clear of cities and populated areas. The chances of encountering a wild beast are next to nil.

If you intend to travel in riskier areas, such as the tropical forest, here are some basic rules to reduce the danger of potential attacks:

Before you turn in for the night, move the bed a few centimetres from the wall.

Cover your boots or shoes with a plastic bag and secure it tightly with an elastic band or scotch tape.

Make sure your backpack or luggage is closed properly.

Before getting dressed, vigorously shake out your clothes and footwear.

Never leave out food that might attract insects or animals.

Snakes

The fact is, snakes are as fearful as they are dangerous, and flee at the slightest sign of danger. Consequently, very few instances of deadly snake bites have been reported.

What to do if you are bitten by a snake?

If you are one of the unlucky few to be bitten by a snake, forget popular foolhardy advice, such as killing the snake, which is as ridiculous as it is dangerous. The best thing to do in this unlikely situation is to stay calm and try to identify its species. Wearing a tourniquet might help as long as you remove it every quarter of an hour for a minute or so to avoid cutting blood circulation. Finally, get to a doctor as quickly as you can.

The Sun

Its benefits are many, but so are its harms. Always wear sunscreen. Many creams on the market do not offer adequate protection; ask a pharmacist. Too much sun can cause sunstroke (dizziness, vomiting, fever, etc.). Be careful, especially the first few days, as it takes time to get used to the sun. Take sun in small doses and protect yourself with a hat and sunglasses.

First Aid Kit

A small first aid kit can prove very useful. Bring along sufficient amounts of any medications you take regularly; it can be difficult to find certain medications in small towns in Peru. Also, bring a valid prescription in case you lose your supply. Other medications such as anti-malaria pills and Imodium (or an equivalent), can be hard to find in Peru. Finally, don't forget self-adhesive bandages, disinfectant cream or ointment, analgesics (pain-killers), antihistamines (for allergies), an extra pair of sunglasses or contact lenses and medicine for upset stomach.

CLIMATE

In Peru, the word "climate" takes on a whole new meaning. Because of its position just below the equator and its steep terrain, the country has different climates, which change over short distances depending on the altitude and the region you're in.

On the coast, summer lasts from December to April. During this time, the temperature hovers between 26°C and 36°C on the coast. The Costa south of Lima is affected by the cold Humboldt Current, which leads to cooler summer temperatures and an intense heat from May to November.

East of the coast, the almost vertical heights of the Andes cause numerous temperature changes in the various geographic areas. The temperature in the Sierra drops to an average between 14°C and 18°C because of its higher altitude. Of course, the higher up you go, the colder it gets, and temperatures can even reach the freezing point. Bear in mind that even if the temperatures are lower than in the costal regions, the sun's rays are just as strong. The rainy season is from November to April.

The hot, humid and rainy climate of the Selva has average temperatures between 24°C and 29°C, but it can also rise to anywhere between 30°C and 40°C. The rainy season is from November to April.

El Niño

El Niño is a powerful and unusually warm water current that originates in the Pacific Ocean off the shores of Panama and flows south to the Peruvian coastline. It reaches its peak during the Christmas period, hence its name "El Niño" (Baby Jesus). El Niño causes heavy rains that can either benefit arid regions or develop into full-blown tropical storms. The complex phenomenon is becoming better understood thanks in part to satellite observation. For instance, the American satellite Seastar allows scientists to study photographs of this climatic anomaly and record its impact on the biosphere. Occasionally, as was the case in 1982 and in 1997, El Niño is particularly strong and its abnormally warm waters linger longer in certain areas and cause considerable damage to land and marine ecosystems. In 1997, El Niño was one of the strongest ever recorded and affected the entire planet: torrential rains and unusually high temperatures were reported in Peru, droughts and forest fires in Indonesia, downpours in California, flooding in the south-eastern part of the United States, and an ice storm in Quebec.

La Niña

Close on the heels of El Niño comes its chilly counterpart La Niña, coined "little girl" because of its opposite effects.

La Niña originates from cold-water masses that flow from South America to the middle of the Pacific Ocean. This climatic aberration lasts for approximately one year and can either cause dry spells or floods in South America and Africa, and monsoons in Australia and Asia. Like El Niño, la Niña is still not fully understood by scientists, and its frequency is difficult to predict.

Packing

Given that temperatures in Peru vary from one region to the next, what type of clothing you bring depends entirely on the time of year and which region you will be visiting. Generally speaking, however, loose-fitting cotton clothing is best. Wear shoes rather than sandals when exploring the Sierra, as they will protect you from cuts that could get infected. If you plan on doing any hiking in the mountains, be sure to bring along proper hiking boots and warmer clothes. For cooler evenings, a long-sleeved shirt or jacket will come in handy. A small umbrella or raincoat will protect you from showers. In fact, clouds regularly cover up clear blue skies causing surprise rainstorms.

Women in miniskirts are frowned upon, except on the beaches of the Costa. Bring a few fancier items for nights out as many places have dress codes.

The Amazon region is characterized by its hot, humid and rainy climate. Bring casual, comfortable clothes that dry quickly if you are heading to this part of the country.

For more information on packing for a trip in the Selva, see p 286. If you are planning to go hiking in the mountains, bring rain gear and good walking shoes that cover your ankles

A Packing Checklist

- insect repellent
- insect coils
- sunscreen
- condoms
- first-aid kit (see p 60)
- flashlight
- sunglasses
- hat
- walking shoes
- light wind-breaker
- plastic sandals for shower and beach
- "ziploc" plastic bags (for wet bathing suits, documents, sea shells, etc.)
- mosquito netting (if you plan on travelling outside large cities)
- water purification system (iodine tablets, water purifier, etc.)
- travel laundry line or bungee cord
- earplugs (for noisy hotel rooms or long bus and boat trips)
- extra pair of glasses or contact lenses

PRACTICAL INFORMATION

WHEN TO GO

The tourist high season in Peru runs from the end of May to the beginning of November. If you plan on visiting during these periods be sure to reserve well in advance, especially if you are heading to the ruins at Macchu Picchu, Arequipa or other popular tourist destinations. The beaches of the Costa are literally overrun by vacationing Peruvians in January and March. Also, numerous religious and commemorative holidays take place throughout the year. During important festivities like l'Inti Raimi in Cuzco, El Señor de los Milagros in Lima or independence day celebrations on July 28, hotel prices go up. Also, events like the Semana Santa à Huaráz tie up traffic on the region's thoroughfares which are congested by the pious. For a list of holidays, see p 77. If you are an avid walker, avoid the rainy season when the paths are muddy, the showers are frequent and outdoor conditions are generally unpleasant.

Making a Quick Stop in Peru

Spending less than a week in a country as vast and richly diverse as Peru does not give you enough time to see everything. One way to cover a lot of ground, provided you have the financial means and are not prone to altitude sickness, is through a tour agency that flies part of the way. A typical itinerary for a visit of this length is as follows: upon arriving in Lima, you head to the historic district of the city then spend an hour or so in a museum before rushing off to the Barranco neighbourhood for *ceviche* and a *pisco sour* as you take in the ocean view. Next, fly south to catch a view of the mysterious Nazca Lines, then make your way up the Andes to visit the pretty colonial city of Arequipa and its Monasterio de Santa Catalina, and climb even higher to Lake Titicaca or to the city of Cuzco, before finally reaching the country's star attraction, Machu Picchu, and heading home.

A Week in Peru

If your schedule limits you to a single week in Peru, it is best to concentrate on specific areas instead of getting caught up in a whirlwind tour of the country. Day one: spend some time touring the historic district of the nation's capital. Day two: fly directly to Cuzco, giving yourself a full day to become acclimatized to the city which sits at an altitude of 3300 metres. Enjoy a *mate de coca* and a quiet stroll through the city's streets and neighbouring Inca ruins before heading to the imposing Machu Picchu ruins. At this point, at least three days will have passed. For the time remaining, you have a number of options. For example, you can stay in Cuzco and explore its surroundings, climb higher to famous Lake Titicaca, or visit Arequipa. Alternately, you can return to Lima and from there set off to Nazca to enjoy an aerial view of its mysterious lines, or the picturesque northern city of Trujillo, or to the lush tropical forest. Of course, the longer you stay in Peru, the more you can see.

Tour Agencies

While you are planning your trip to Peru (or elsewhere for that matter), you should first decide what kind of trip you have in mind: is it an organized tour, a backpacking expedition, or something between the two?

If you long to soak up the sun and linger by the deep blue sea, you will probably prefer the ease and comfort of staying in the same hotel for your entire trip. Travel agencies and a few airlines offer reasonably priced all-inclusive tour packages that guarantee hassle-free holidays, but you'll have to put up with the same boring buffet food at your hotel.

On the other hand, if you prefer to explore the countryside, consider organized tour groups, backpacking, or a combination of both. Tour groups are great for older travellers, as well as travellers who want to take it easy and let others do most of the planning. Tour groups offer carefully thought-out itineraries, comfortable vehicles, reserved lodgings and safer trips. However, they do have their share of drawbacks: schedules are less flexible, and being in the same group all the time might feel confining and isolate you from the local population.

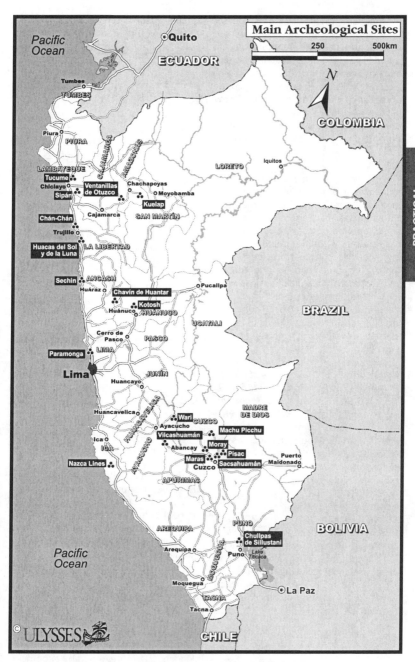

Main Archeological Sites

0   250   500km

Pacific Ocean

ECUADOR

Quito

COLOMBIA

Tumbes

TUMBES

Piura

PIURA

LORETO

Iquitos

LAMBAYEQUE

Tucume

Chiclaye

Sipán

Ventanillas de Otuzco

Chachapoyas

Moyobamba

Kuelap

Chán-Chán

Cajamarca

SAN MARTÍN

Trujillo

LA LIBERTAD

Huacas del Sol y de la Luna

Sechin

ANCASH

Huáraz

Chavín de Huantar

Kotosh

Pucalpa

BRAZIL

Huánuco

HUANUCO

UCAYALI

Cerro de Pasco

PASCO

Paramonga

LIMA

Lima

Huancayo

JUNÍN

Huancavelica

HUANCAVELICA

MADRE DE DIOS

Wari

CUZCO

Ayacucho

Machu Picchu

Vilcashuamán

Ica

IGA

AYACUCHO

Abancay

Moray

Písac

APURIMAC

Maras

Cuzco

Sacsahuamán

Puerto Maldonado

Nazca Lines

AREQUIPA

PUNO

Chullpas de Sillustani

BOLIVIA

Arequipa

Puno

Lake Titicaca

Pacific Ocean

MOQUEGUA

Moquegua

La Paz

TACNA

Tacna

CHILE

© ULYSSES

Independent travel allows you to draw up your own schedules and itineraries, and eat and sleep where you want. On the downside, some destinations are harder to reach for personal security or geographic reasons, unless you hire an authorized guide. It helps to know several languages and to be flexible in order to deal with unexpected situations and to overlook minor inconveniences.

Finally, even independent travellers should supplement their journey with one or more organized excursions through one of Peru's many tourist agencies who can take you to one of the country's prime destinations or embark on a week-long journey to remote regions such as the tropical forest. Smaller local agencies are listed in the "Practical Information" section of each chapter of this guide. The following agencies provide all kinds of quality excursions within the various regions of Peru.

Coltur *(Avenida Kennedy 456, Lima, Miraflores,* ☎241-5551, ≈446-9392 *or 446-8073, www.coltur.com.pe, postmaster@coltur.com.pe)* is a well-established agency offers a wide selection of popular excursions such as city tours, flights over the Nazca lines, and visits to Machu Picchu. Service is professional and courteous.

Kantu *(Avenida Ricardo Palma L-8, Cuzco,* ☎221-381 *or 232-021,* ≈233-155, *kantupe@mail.cosapidata. com.pe)* offers standard excursions (city tours, Inca Trail, Machu Picchu, etc.) and outdoor activities such as hiking in the mountains or the Amazon, whitewater rafting, or motorcycling through the country.

Condor Travel *(Mayor Armando Blondet 249, Lima, San Isidro,* ☎442-7305, ≈442-1000, *condortravel@mcimail.com.)* is a good

agency which organizes various popular excursions throughout the country.

Tourist Organizations

Promperú:
Calle Uno Oeste - Edificio Mitinci, Ministerio de Industria, Comercio, Turismo y Integración URB, CORPAC, San Isidro, 14th floor, ☎442-9280, www.rcp.net.pe/promperu.

Latin American Travel Consultant:
P.O. Box 17-17-908, Quito, ☎(02) 562-566, latc@pi.pro.ec, www.amerispan.com/latc or www.greenarrow.com.com/latc.htm. Three times a year, this organization publishes an interesting news bulletin on Latin American issues such as security, health, temperature, travel costs, economy, and politics.

South American Explorer's Club (see p 102).

SAFETY AND SECURITY

Is Peru a dangerous country to visit? A few years ago when Peru was in the grip of terrorism, going there was not the best idea. Today, calm has returned and one can travel to most regions. However, it is preferable to contact the specialized tourist agencies in Lima (see p 103) before venturing off the beaten path without a guide. While terrorism has declined drastically, drug trafficking is fast on the rise. Also, partisan political factions can be found in remote areas such as the Andes and the central Selva.

Let us set the record straight without turning a blind eye to the facts. In Peru, you are more likely to be robbed than kidnapped or threatened by extremists. Government anti-terrorist measures have inevitably widened the gap between the rich and the poor, and muggings are a direct result of this economic reality. Crime is on the rise in cities like Chimbote and Trujillo, as well as the poorer neighbourhoods of Lima, which is the country's most densely populated city. Be particularly cautious in crowds as this is where you're most likely to get pickpocketed. Other unsafe areas are open markets, bus depots, dark and deserted streets and isolated parks. If you stay alert and don't flaunt your wealth, you can avoid this and many other misfortunes.

Thieves usually work in pairs. One diverts your attention while the other discretely picks your pockets and takes off with your personal belongings. Be especially cautious if a stranger suddenly bombards you with questions or if a person collapses right in front of you. Also, think twice if someone points you to money lying on the ground. Why would they show this to you if they could take it for themselves? It only takes a fraction of a second for them to distract you and empty your pockets. Finally, if you are sitting on an outdoor terrace or even inside a restaurant, wrapping the shoulder strap of your bag around your chair's legs and keeping a close watch on your belongings is an extra precaution that can save you many troubles.

If you are carrying valuable objects, keep a watchful eye on them at all times or entrust them to someone you know well. Most of the better hotels provide safes in which you can store valuables, so you don't have to worry about them. Don't forget that, to most people, your luxury items items (camera, leather luggage, video camera, jewellery, etc.) represent a lot of money. A degree of caution can help avoid many problems. Leave valuable jewellery at home, store your electronic equipment in a non-descript shoulder bag, and avoid revealing the contents of your wallet when making your purchases. Remember: the less attention you attract, the less likely you are to be robbed. Wearing a money belt beneath your clothing can be useful for hiding your most valuable items (passport, travellers' checks and money). Make photocopies of your passport and write down your traveller's cheque numbers; store copies of these on you and in separate bags. Another tip is to always keep your passport in the same place so that putting it away becomes an automatic gesture.

Never accept food or drinks from strangers; not only can they make you sick, but you might wake up several days later in a strange place with your money and luggage stolen. If possible, avoid overnight bus rides, because bandits occasionally set up road blocks and hold up travellers. If you rent a car, avoid driving at night. In addition to the risks described above, most roads are not lit at night and many Peruvians drive dangerously fast. During the rainy season, some mountain roads are closed. In the Andes, roads are winding, and visibility often decreases as you reach higher altitudes.

Terrorism

The two major guerilla groups, the Shining Path and the Tupac Amaru (MRTA), no longer target foreign travellers. The heads of both organizations are presently behind bars, and the sound of bombs has been silenced. Although there are still partisan factions in remote areas, they rarely target tourists.

Women Travellers

A few years ago, a friend who was travelling abroad decided to draw less attention to herself by chopping off her lovely red hair and boldly wearing a T-shirt with a feminist slogan proclaiming: "A woman needs a man like a fish needs a bicycle." This might sound a little radical, despite the fact that blondes and redheads *do* attract more attention. But rest assured: women can travel alone in Peru without too much trouble. The most you are likely to encounter is catcalling and whistling from macho men. Remember; this is a Latin country and the cultural rules are not always the same as in North America or Europe. Just ignore them and they will go away. In any event, you can usually avoid attracting too much unwanted attention by dressing a little more conservatively and saving your skimpier clothes for the beach. Wearing a wedding ring is also a good idea, since most men are quite respectful of married women.

If you are lost, ask someone who looks trustworthy for help: do not wait for someone to come to your rescue. Be on your guard if strangers come up to you and are overly insistent. Do not disclose where you are staying to strangers, or you may receive unexpected (and unwanted) calls or visits. The best way to play it safe is to say that you are travelling with a group and that friends are expecting you back at the hotel. Always walk confidently with your head up and keep loose change in your pockets in case you suddenly need to call a taxi.

Finally, bring your own feminine hygienic products because your favourite brands might not be available in Peru. Some clinics provide gynaecological services.

Independent Travellers

The good thing about travelling alone is that you have no obligations to anyone. You can always change your plans and still be right on schedule. Travelling as a pair does have certain advantages, however, like being able to go to the bathroom without having to lug all your bags with you. During long bus rides, one person can sleep soundly, knowing that the other will keep an eye on the belongings. As well, unless you really like being alone, it is always nicer to share a meal or your thoughts with a companion. Furthermore, travelling as a pair splits the cost of accommodations.

Children

You can travel with your children in Peru without major difficulties, but remember that distances can be long and planes and buses are sometimes late. Carry small toys to entertain your kids in case they get cranky during the long waits and extended time on the road which are quite common when travelling.

Handicapped Travellers

Peru is not very well equipped for handicapped travellers. Only a handful of the best hotels and restaurants in Lima have wheelchair access, but call ahead to check what facilities are available at specific establishments.

Homosexuality

Being openly gay or lesbian in Peru is not the best idea. Homosexuality is formally forbidden by the State and can lead to imprisonment. There are a few

---

Exchange Rates

$1 CAN	=	$0.65 US	$1 US	=	$1.53 CAN
1 EURO	=	$1.10 US	$1 US	=	0.91 EURO
1 £	=	$1.65 US	$1 US	=	0.60 £
1 DM	=	$0.59 US	$1 US	=	1.68 DM
1 SF	=	$0.71 US	$1 US	=	0.87 SF
10 BF	=	$0.27 US	$1 US	=	37.03 BF
100 Pesetas	=	$0.54 US	$1 US	=	178.57 Pesetas
1000 Lire	=	$0.56 US	$1 US	=	1785.7 Lire
1 N. SOL	=	$0.34 US	$1 US	=	2,94 N. SOL

All prices in this guide are in US dollars

---

clandestine gay bars in Lima and Cuzco, though they are difficult to find.

MONEY AND BANKING

Currency

The currency in Peru is the *nuevo sol*, which everyone refers to as simply the *sol*. The bills come in denominations of 100, 50, 20 and 10 *soles*, and coins of 5, 2 and 1 *sol*, and 50, 20 and 10 centavos.

Banks

Apart from banks in Lima, which are open Monday to Friday from 9:30am to 5pm, and sometimes on Saturday morningsl, banks generally open at irregular hours in other Peruvian cities, generally from Monday to Friday from 9:30am to noon and 3pm to 5pm. They are found in all the major cities and towns. Most will exchange US dollars; fewer exchange traveller's cheques or other foreign currencies. Always carry some cash. Major hotels can also exchange your dollars or traveller's cheques, but the rates will not be as good as those at the banks.

Casas de Cambio or Exchange Offices

Casas de cambio are open from Monday to Friday, from 9am to 6pm and occasionally on Saturday from 9am to 1pm. They offer the same rates as the banks, but sometimes refuse to accept traveller's cheques. Service is considerably faster here.

To get the best rate it is always preferable to exchange your money in a big city like Lima, Cuzco, Arequipa or Trujilo.

American Money

American money should be the currency of choice for travellers to Peru. It is easier to exchange and enjoys a better rate than other currencies.

Cambistas

Changing money on the street is legal in Peru. In several cities, you will notice people with a calculator in one hand and a wad of bills in the other trying to attract your attention by shouting: *"Dolares! Dolares!"* Some are clad in a special uniform attesting to their profession, while others simply pretend to be *cambistas* – at your expense. These street dealers will offer you a slightly better rate than official banking institutions. Be careful, though, because there are many counterfeit bills in circulation and rip-offs are common. Never let money changers leave with your cash: they will tell you to wait while they go get some bills, and then never come back. Also, count your bills carefully before making a transaction to avoid getting swindled. Given these possibilities, it may be wiser to use a bank or a *casa de cambio* (exchange office).

Traveller's Cheques

Generally, the exchange rate for traveller's cheques is not as good as for US dollars. However, only traveller's cheques are refundable if they are lost or stolen. Thus, it is always a good idea to carry part of your money in the form of traveller's cheques. They are sometimes accepted in restaurants, hotels and certain shops, and are generally easy to cash in banks or exchange offices. Keep a list of your cheque numbers separate from your cheques so that they can be cancelled and replaced if they are lost or stolen. Always carry some cash.

MAIL

There is a post office in almost every city. Some hotels can also mail your letters and sell you stamps. Wherever you send your mail from, expect it to take quite a while to reach its destination. The postal service is a bit slow. If you have something urgent to send, use the fax service at Telefónica del Perú. Stamps are sold in post offices and in certain shops.

TELECOMMUNICATIONS

Telephones and Faxes

Peru's telephone system was one of the worst in Latin America until 1994 when the government decided to sell the network to foreign companies. A consortium led by Telefónica Internacional de España bought two of the state enterprises: Empresa Nacional de Telecomunicaciones del Perú and Compañía Peruana de Teléfonos. This means that by 1999, the Spanish telephone company will hold the monopoly on all local, national and international calls, as well as fax and Internet services.

International and local calls can be made from Telefónica del Perú offices, which are located in almost every city or in the major hotels. Calling overseas is easy from these offices. It also saves you the extra high fees that hotels usually charge. You don't need to collect your change either, since the length of your call is recorded by computer and you pay at the counter fater making your call. To make a call, simply go to the counter, give the person the telephone number you want to reach, including the country code, and wait to be directed to a booth. The connection will be established when you lift the receiver of the ringing telephone. Telefónica del Perú also offers fax service. You must pay cash, except in hotels. Public telephones are rare; a few can be found in major cities, airports or universities. A few Telefónica del Perú offices sell *fichas* (tokens) for local calls. A minimum of three minutes is charged for international calls.

Three minutes to North America or Europe costs about $12.

The Telefónica del Perú personnel will explain in Spanish, or maybe in broken English, how to call overseas from Peru.

Area Codes

The area code for Peru is 51.

Abancay:	084
Arequipa:	054
Ayacucho:	064
Cajamarca:	044
Cerro de Pasco:	064
Chiclayo:	074
Chimbote:	074
Chincha:	034
Cuzco:	084
Huancavelica:	064
Huancayo:	064
Huánuco:	064
Huaráz:	044
Ica:	034
Iquitos:	094
Jauja:	064
Juliaca:	054
La Merced:	064
La Oroya:	064
Lambayeque:	074
Lima:	01
Moyobamba:	094
Nazca:	034
Pisac:	084
Pisco:	034
Piura:	074
Purto Maldonado:	084
Pucallpa:	064
Puno:	054
Tacna:	054
Tarapoto:	094
Tarma:	064
Trujilo:	044
Tumbes:	074

Apart from Lima, where telephone numbers have seven-digits, all Peruvian cities have six-digit phone numbers.

International access numbers allow you to place calls through an operator in your country. Some of these operators will accept any calling card, while others only serve card-holders of that company. The major companies are:

Canada Direct: ☎0-800-502-90 toll free
Sprint: ☎176
MCI: ☎0-800-50010
AT&T: ☎0-800-50000
British Telecom: ☎0-800-50080

Police: ☎105

Fire: ☎116

International Phone Calls: ☎103

Cell Phones

Celular phones are becoming increasingly popular throughout the country. Many stores rent out these phones.

Internet

This means of communication is quickly gaining popularity in Peru. Internet access is available in most of the country's major cities, including some at the Telefónica del Perú offices. Most upscale hotels also offer this service to their clients. Free web-based E-mail addresses are available at www.hotmail.com; with these accounts, you only pay for the time spent at the computer terminal.

A Few Useful Internet Sites

MAGICPERU
www.magicperu.com
General information about Peru.

TRAFICO
www.traficoperu.com

PRACTICAL INFORMATION

Web page with information on transportation, visas and border customs in Peru.

AHORA
Asociación Peruana de Hoteles, Restaurantes y Afines, Avenida José Pardo 620, Of. 306, Lima 18, ☎/≈446-8773, ahora@correo.dnet.com.pe, www.ahoraperu.com.

 # ACCOMMODATIONS

Most major hotels accept credit cards; smaller hotels usually do not.

Hotels

Hotels rooms can be found in just about every town in Peru. The quality and comfort of these rooms varies from one town to the next, but it is generally easy to find a room that will suit you. If you are travelling on a limited budget, you can almost always find a room with a double bed for about $10 per night. There are many affordable hotels, but their cleanliness tends to be haphazard and their comforts spartan. If you are prepared to stretch your budget and spend an additional ten dollars on your hotel room, you will notice quite a difference. Obviously, the more you pay, the better the quality of the service. It is always advisable to ask to see the room before taking it. Check for cleanliness and ask whether breakfast is included. Also, depending on the region, check if the room has hot water, mosquito netting and a fan. Note that on market days and local holidays, the best hotels are usually full. To avoid an upset, reserve in advance or arrive the day before the market or festival.

Motels

Motels are dubious places where the rooms are often rented out by the hour and amount to little more than houses of ill-repute.

Apart-hotels

Apart-hotels are like hotels in that they offer all the services, but like apartments because rooms include kitchenettes equipped with dishes and utensils. This is a very economical option for longer stays.

Cabañas

Cabañas differ little from hotels, except that rooms are often located in small, individual pavilions or cabins. They are generally inexpensive and sometimes include a kitchenette.

Bed & Breakfasts

Very few people have adapted their homes to receive guests. The level of comfort varies greatly from one place to the next. These rooms usually do not have private bathrooms.

Youth Hostels

There are several youth hostels in Peru. They can be found in Lima, Cuzco and Huáraz, and some other places. Contact the **Asosiación Peruana de Albergues** *(in Lima, Avenida Casimiro Ulloa 328, Miraflores, ☎446-5488)*.

Camping

Camping is permitted in certain national parks and some beaches along the coast.

 RESTAURANTS

Many restaurants serving all sorts of fare, from local to international, can be found near the major tourist sites. Depending on which city you visit, it is almost always possible to find a restaurant within your budget range. Most places have *un menu del día*, a daily special at a good price, which includes an entrée (soup), *un segundo* (main dish: pasta, meat or fish) and a drink. A 20% tax is added to the price of the meal. Prices mentioned are for a meal for one person, not including drinks and tax.

$	$6 and less
$$	$7 to $12
$$$	more than $12

Tipping

A delicate subject indeed. Whether at a hotel or a restaurant, clients and staff alike do not agree on the amount of tip to be left. The situation in Peru is the same as elsewhere. Good service means a good tip. Guides, bus drivers and waiters and waitresses live off a ridiculously low salary and count on tips to survive. If you are in a position to pay for a meal in a good restaurant or an excursion with a quality tour company, you are also able to leave a tip, which should come to about 15% of the bill. More upscale restaurants include the tip in the price. Bellboys expect about $1 for their services. Unless you have received truly extraordinary service, taxi drivers do not expect a tip.

PERUVIAN CUISINE

Peruvian food is a delicious combination of international flavours and gastronomic traditions based on the earth, the sea and the beliefs of Peru's native peoples. The presentation of its unique national dishes with their Hispanic, African, Asian and Italian flavours, reflect Peru's cultural richness.

Since Pre-Columbian times, three foods have become cooking staples in Peru: chili peppers, potatoes and corn.

Chilies, or *ajís* (called *uchu* or *rocoto* in ancient times), spice up Peruvian cuisine with their various flavours. Chilies are a basic ingredient in all sauces, and the many different varieties bring a unique flavour to every dish they complement. Their aroma alone is enough to make any gourmand's mouth water. Chilies are used differently in the country's various regions to enhance the taste of dishes and rouse the taste buds. In the Andes, for example, copious amounts of spices are added to food. On the coast, fish and seafood are often served with a sauce delicately flavoured with chilies and onions. In the Amazon, however, chilies are used sparingly to prepare medium-spicy meals.

Peru has five major varieties of *ají*, different in colour, shape and flavour:

● Cultivated in the Andes, the red or yellow *rocoto* (the latter being milder) goes into every dish in the country, most particularly in the highlands. Thin strips of *rocoto* are often added to soups to perk them up.

PRACTICAL INFORMATION

• Despite its name, *ají verde* is yellow or orange. When dried, it is nicknamed *ají mirasol* and used to flavour such dishes as *ají de gallina*.

• Of a darker hue, *ají colorado* is better as a dried spice. Like *ají mirasol*, it has to be soaked in water before it is used.

• *Ají limo* packs a punch despite its small size. This chili, which comes in every colour of the rainbow (purple, blue, green, red and white), is added to *ceviche*, the Peruvian dish par excellence.

• Lastly, *ají pajarito* is certainly one of the hottest peppers commonly used in the Peruvian jungle.

If you are not accustomed to eating spicy food, you should avoid consuming too many chili peppers, because they can cause diarrhea in the uninitiated.

The Potato

Originally cultivated in the Andes, the *papa*, or potato, is the staple food of Peru. An estimated 600 varieties of potatoes are grown and exported, including the yellow *limeña* and the purple potato. Varieties peculiar to the Lake Titicaca plateau, *chuño* and *moraya* potatoes are dehydrated by continuous exposure to the sun and frost. Potato starch is made from them and is used to thicken and flavour soups.

In the Andes, many dishes are potato-based. *Ocopa* is a hearty dish of boiled potatoes covered with spicy peanut sauce, accompanied by rice, hard-boiled eggs and olives. *Papa a la huancaína* is a plate of potatoes smothered in a white-cheese and hot-pepper sauce. *Huancaína*, is also served as a

dipping sauce for fried *yucca*. *Papa rellena* is a potato stuffed with meat, onions, olives, hard-boiled eggs and raisins. *Lomo saltado*, a spicy specialty also enjoyed along the coast, is a delicious blend of fried potatoes, thin strips of sautéed beef, tomatoes and rice.

Corn

Corn served not only as a currency and a divine offering in Pre-Columbian times, but was also a staple food in Peruvian cuisine. An amazing variety of corn grows in the fertile expanses of the country and enhances local dishes. Two very popular drinks are made from purple corn: *chicha morada* and its fermented and alcoholic counterpart, *chicha de jora*. *Choclos* (corncobs) are sometimes eaten with a spicy cheese sauce. *Chicharrones con mote* is boiled corn on the cob served with pork.

Regional Cuisine

The Mountains

In the Sierra, dishes are typically based on meat, potatoes and corn. Chicken, pork and beef are prepared in various ways. *Anticuchos* is a traditional Inca meal consisting of marinated and barbecued beef heart brochettes. *Cau cau* is a mixture of tripe and potatoes cooked in tomato sauce. *Cuy*, another Andean specialty, is a spit-roasted guinea pig. *Rocoto relleno* is, as its Spanish name indicates, a red bell pepper stuffed with meat, potatoes and eggs. *Pachamanca* ("Mother Earth" in Quechua) is a preparation of meat and vegetables cooked over low heat in a stone-covered pit.

Lake Titicaca and its surrounding area are renowned for trout (*truchas*) and *pejerrey* fishing. The latter fish is specific to the region.

The Amazon Basin

Amazonian cuisine is the product of the region's numerous waterways and luxuriant tropical vegetation. Many delicious meals are prepared from a fusion of fruits, vegetables and a variety of local fish, including *pirañas* and *paiches*, huge catfish threatened by extinction due to overfishing. Fish is usually grilled and garnished with *palmitos* (palm hearts), cassava and fried bananas. Another popular dish in the Amazon is *sopa de motela*, or turtle soup.

The Coast

The Costa is washed by the waters of the Pacific Ocean and, as expected, a huge variety of fish and seafood figure prominently on menus in this region. *Cebiches* (or *ceviches*, depending on the place) are deliciously prepared by most restaurants in the Costa. Peruvians and Ecuadorans both claim to have invented this tasty, traditional dish of fresh, lighlty-cooked seafood or fish (usually *corvina*, or sea perch) marinated in an acidic mixture of onion and lemon and often accompanied by corn. *Tiradíto* is almost identical to *cebiche*, except that strips of fish are used and onions omitted. Be careful, though, since the lightly-cooked fish in these dishes can contain parasites that a tourist's digestive system simply cannot handle. Fish lovers can also feast on delicious *escabeche de pescado*, fried fish served cold and covered with hot sauce; *camarones* (shrimp); *calamares* (squid) and *chorros* (mussels). Note that "*a lo macho*" dishes are served with a spicy seafood sauce.

Another delicious dish, *chupe de camarones*, is a cream of shrimp soup with simmering peppers, onions, potatoes and eggs. Its close relation, *chupe de pescado*, is a creamy fish-based soup with peppers, vegetables and cheese.

Beside fish and seafood, La Costa also offers a variety of meat dishes. *Ají de gallina* is a blend of *ají mirasol* and white chicken meat covered with sauce, served over boiled potatoes. *Seco de cabrito* is roast kid served with rice and beans. A specialty in the coastal town of Chiclayo, *arroz con pato a la chiclayana* is composed of duck and rice.

Desserts

Your mouth will water at the sight of Peru's *postres* (desserts). The most popular are *churros*, fritters with a honey or blancmange (milk, sugar and almond custard) centre; *arroz con leche* (rice pudding) and *yucitas*, fried and sugar-coated cassava balls.

Vegetarian Cuisine

If you follow a macrobiotic diet, you'll have to put it on hold while in Peru. If your diet is based on milk products, however, you shouldn't have any trouble. Large cities like Lima, Cuzco and Trujilo have vegetarian restaurants. Occasionally the definition of vegetarian is somewhat softened to include fish and chicken dishes. In more remote villages, even if the menu does not list vegetarian dishes, it is usually possible to politely make a special request. Some useful expressions are: *Yo soy vegetariano* (I am vegetarian), *Yo no como carne* (I don't eat meat).

Non-Alcoholic Beverages

You will be able to enjoy plenty of exotic fruits during your stay. An extraordinary variety of fresh fruit is available all year round. Oranges, *murucayás* (passion fruit), papayas, bananas and watermelon are just a few examples. These fruits, of course, also make delectable juices. Peruvians also quench their thirst with herb teas: *mate de coca* is a reviving infusion of coca leaves, and *manzanilla* is camomile tea. Try Inca Cola, which is like Coca Cola, except for its lemon-yellow colour. *Chicha morada* is a refreshing purple-corn drink that is sometimes sweetened with sugar, and is enjoyed with lunch and dinner.

Lastly, coffee lovers will be disappointed with the rather mediocre brew served in Peru. In fact, the country exports almost all of its modest crop. If you order a coffee anyway, don't be surprised if you get a glass of hot milk and a small jar of instant coffee. In most establishments, you have to add the coffee crystals to the hot milk yourself.

Alcoholic Beverages

Though in no way comparable to European beers, several local brands are brewed including Cristal, Cusceña and Pilser. Similar to beer and more popular with Peruvians, *chicha de jora* is a whitish alcoholic drink made from fermented corn.

Pisco Sour is the undisputed favourite drink of Peruvians and foreigners who have sampled this delicious national cocktail. Named after the port city from which it originates, *Pisco* has been a well-known marc brandy in Peru since the 16th century. Today, *Pisco* is mixed with a blend of egg white, sugar, lemon juice, bitters and cinnamon to make *Pisco Sour*.

Pisco is also used to make *algarobina*, an aperitif blended with carob, milk and egg white, and sprinkled with cinnamon.

Another alcoholic drink, *aguardiente*, is made from sugar cane and spices.

Unfortunately, wine lovers might return home empty-handed. Peru is neither a great wine-growing country nor a big consumer of the grape's nectar. The best wines are produced in the Ica region (see p 132).

A Few Peruvian Recipes

Pisco Sour (6 glasses)
1 egg white
15 g sugar
1 cup of *Pisco*
Juice of 6 limes
Crushed ice
Bitters (optional)

Beat the egg white and sugar in a blender. Add *Pisco*, lime juice, ice and a dash of bitters (if desired). Mix and pour.

Ceviche de Corvina
1/2 kg fillet of *corvina* (sea bass), finely diced
8 lemons
3 garlic cloves, minced
1 red onion, finely diced
1 yellow pepper (*ají amarillo*)
1 head of lettuce
2 sweet potatoes
2 corn cobs, cut into thin slices
Salt and pepper to taste
Fresh coriander (optional)

Place the diced fish in a large bowl, then add the lemon juice and garlic. Marinate for 15 to 30 minutes, then season with salt, pepper and chili (coriander optional). Serve on a bed of lettuce and garnish with onions, boiled sweet potatoes and corn.

Lomo Saltado (traditional beef dish)
1 kg fillet of beef, cut in strips
3 yellow peppers (*ají amarillo*), chopped
3 red onions, sliced in rings
4 tomatoes, quartered
Soya sauce
Balsamic vinegar
1 kg rice
1 kg fried potatoes

Sauté the peppers and beef strips in oil until beef is browned. Set aside. In the same pan, saute the onions and tomatoes. Add soya sauce and balsamic vinegar, and let simmer for a few minutes. Fry the potatoes. Mix the peppers, beef and potatoes into the onion-and-tomato mixture. Serve on a bed of rice.

Papas a la Huancaína (8 servings)
10 medium-size potatoes
500 g cheese (feta or Mexican-style)
2 hot peppers
250 ml unsweetened condensed milk
125 ml vegetable oil
2 garlic cloves, minced
8 soda crackers
5 g prepared mustard
Salt and pepper
Lettuce
3 hard-boiled eggs
Black olives

Peel and cook potatoes. Set aside. In a blender, whip the cheese, peppers, condensed milk, oil, garlic, crackers and mustard. Season with salt and pepper. The sauce should be thick; if not, add more crackers. To dilute, add a little milk. Place the potatoes on a bed of lettuce and cover with sauce. Garnish with halved hard-boiled eggs and olives.

Small Gastronomical Glossay

Aji: very spicy condiment
Ajo: garlic
Almuerzo: lunch
Arroz: rice
Bon provecho: enjoy your meal
Café sin leche: black coffee
Café con leche: coffee with milk
Camarones: prawns
Carne: meat
Cerveza: beer
Cena: supper
Chancho: pork
Chifles: fried banana chips
Chivo: kid (goat)
Chuleta: cutlet
Comida: food
Cuy: whole guinea-pig on a spit, slow-cooked over an open fire
Chifa: Chinese restaurant
Desayuno: breakfast
Empanadas: small, cooked corn patties stuffed with onions, meat, chicken or vegetables
Encocado: fish mixed with coconut milk
Huevos revueltos: poached eggs
Huevos fritos: fried eggs
Huevos duros: hard-boiled eggs
Hornado: suckling-pig
Jugo: juice
Leche: milk
Legumbres: vegetables
Llapingachos: potato, cheese and corn dish
Locro: potato- and milk-based soup
Mantequilla: butter
Pimienta: pepper
Palta: avocado
Pato: duck
Pavo: turkey
Pollo: chicken
Postre: dessert
Queso: cheese
Res: beef
Sal: salt
Seco: fried meat
Tallarines: pasta

PRACTICAL INFORMATION

Tamal: beef, chicken or vegetables in a corn pattie
Ternera: veal
Verde: dried banana chips
Vino: wine
Zanahoria: carrot

 SHOPPING

Native Markets

Peru has a rich tradition of crafts that has been passed down for generations. These creations can be found in the public markets of villages along the Andean cordillera. These markets are the social gathering places of the Andean people. During the day, clothing, mats, fruit, flowers and animals liven up the streets, offering a picturesque show unique to Latin America. The prices are better here than in boutiques. However, if you are searching for bargains, check the quality of the products and beware of ever-present pickpockets.

These countless markets attract scores of craftspeople, farmers, shoppers and tourists who come to sell and buy a multitude of different goods. Besides the traditional craft items like mats, ponchos, scarves and other exotic clothing and accessories, you'll find all sorts of local animals, living and dead, here to satisfy the most eccentric of consumers. The treatment of certain animals may seem cruel and shocking to travellers; just remember that you are in a foreign country where the established practices and norms differ from those of another cultural context. If this disparity bothers you and you don't want to be shocked, simply avoid this part of the market, which on the whole will surely prove most fascinating.

The Major Markets

Chincheros

Chincheros (Sunday) Market
A more traditional and less touristy market than the one in Pisac. Discover the lost art of bartering with the merchants and admire the original Inca mural that stands in the middle of the central market place.

Cuzco

Cuzco Market (every day)
This central market is *the* place for artwork, pottery, clothing, books and secondhand goods.

Pisac Sunday Market
Located some thirty kilometres from Cuzco, Pisac makes way for a big Sunday market renowned for its wide selection of handicrafts such as pottery, textiles and silverware. Note that items are sometimes more expensive and of lesser quality than elsewhere in the country. Try to get here early as this market draws busloads of tourists during peak season. You'll be charmed by the surrounding landscape brightened up by the multicoloured garb of the *campesinos* (countryfolk), whose hats are shaped according to their town of origin.

Junín

Huancayo (Sunday) Market
This market is spread over several blocks and sells regional wares as well as highly renowned handicrafts from Central Peru.

Lima

Art, Handicraft and Antique Markets (Saturday and Sunday)

These very popular markets are held at the Parque Central and Parque Kennedy and display paintings by local artists, as well as sculptures and pottery. Antiques are the most coveted items.

Bargaining

Bargaining is part of the fun of visiting the markets. More often than not, a cheaper price can be negotiated. Remember, however, that natives depend on the sale of their goods to survive. If you have no intention of buying something, don't bargain just to see how low you can go. Furthermore, some people don't realize that they may actually be haggling over what amounts to a couple of dollars, a nominal sum for a tourist, but quite a lot of money to a local vendor.

A Few Souvenir Ideas

Cuzco or Puno felt hats for hat lovers.

Woolens, for those not allergic to wool.

Alpaca woolens are better for sensitive skin, because they are much finer than lamb's or even llama's wool.

Baby alpaca woolens are even finer than their adult counterparts.

If you are looking for an original travel trophy to make your home more exotic, you can by either a Puno carnival mask, an Ayacucho retable, a Selva blowpipe, a Cuzco *manta vieja*, or a Pucará *torito*.

FESTIVALS AND PUBLIC HOLIDAYS

Peruvians' incredible zest for life is evident in the myriad holidays marked on their calendar. Many of these are religious celebrations through which the devout express their faith in prayers, processions and pilgrimages. The people of each town and village honour their patron saint with pious and lavish festivities at Christmas, Easter and All Saints' Day. In addition to the deeply ingrained Catholicism, Andean beliefs preceding the Spanish conquest still persist. Peruvians still observe Inti Raymi, the Solstice Festival, with reverence and celebration. Both religious and secular occasions are marked with traditional feasts, dances and songs that have been passed down from generation to generation.

Below is as complete a list as possible of holidays and festivals in Peru. To avoid inconveniences, confirm the exact dates of local events in remote areas with a tourist office.

National Holidays

January 1:	New Year's Day
February:	Carnaval
April:	*Semana Santa* (Holy Week)
May 1:	Labour Day
June 29:	Saint Peter and Saint Paul
July 28-29:	Independence Day
August 30:	Battle of Angamos

PRACTICAL INFORMATION

November 1:   All Saints' Day

December 25: Christmas Day

Other Festivals
Across the Country

January

Ancash

Festival Patronal de la Virgen
Chiquinquira: January 19
Popular dances and handicraft sale.
There are firework displays at night.

Huancavelica

Festival del Niño Perdido
January 13 to 16
A popular festival whose main attraction is a theatrical performance of the Adoration of the Baby Jesus. Several places host dancing competitions.

La Libertad

National *Marineras* Dance Competition
January 24 to 31
One of the most beautiful festivals celebrating northern Peru's folklore. Hundreds of couples of all ages vie for the prize of *El pañuelo de oro* (golden scarf) in Trujillo. The Marineras queen is crowned as part of the closing ceremony which takes place in the Gran Chimú coliseum.

Lima

Lima's Anniversary Week
January 15 to 20
A ceremony commemorates the city of Lima`s founding on January 18, 1535. A cultural exhibit and popular festival mark the event.

Piura

Epiphany
January 5 to 31
During this holiday, all kinds of social and cultural activities and entertainment take place. The *Festival del Arroz* (rice festival) and the International Festival of Music and Dance are also held during this time.

February

Ancash

Carnaval de Huaráz
Third and fourth weeks of February
A traditional festival with a procession of allegorical floats in Huaraz and its surroundings.

Arequipa

Carnaval de Arequipa
Third and fourth weeks of February
The whole city shows up for the crowning of the carnival queen, the procession of allegorical floats, and the folk dancing competition.

Cajamarca

Carnaval de Cajamarca
Third and fourth weeks of February
Everyone takes part in this special event, during which *unshas* (trees decorated with fruits and presents) are set up and then knocked down in time to the rhythms of the dance. A large procession, singing competition and selection of the carnival queen also take place.

Piura

Carnaval de Bajo Piura
Third and fourth weeks of February
A large procession of dancers of different origins files through the city's carnival ambiance. On Ash Wednesday, brightly costumed men and women

perform the *yunza*, a Peruvian dance in which couples dance in a circle around a tree and hit it with their machetes until it topples. Legend has it that a year of happiness lies ahead for the couple that succeeds in felling the tree. If the woman is not married, she will become engaged before long.

Puno

Fiesta de la Virgen de la Candelaria
February 8 to 14
A highly traditional festival in honour of the patron saint Mamita. People come from all the provinces to take part in this majestic, colourful festival with music, singing and costumed dancers.

Carnaval
February 24 to 27
The whole city takes part in this festival during which groups dancing to the rhythms of traditional music wind through the streets.

March

Ica

International Grape Harvest Festival
March 4 to 14
The most beautiful Inca woman is crowned harvest queen and presides over the ceremonies celebrating the successful grape harvest. She is flanked by American and European harvest queens.

True to its motto "Grapes are marriage; wine is love", Ica extends a warm welcome to visitors, offering them wine and *cachina*, as well as *pisco* to drink. Popular dances, a wine fair, a special local wine-tasting contest, a procession of allegorical floats and a show of *caballos de paso* (Peruvian trained horses) are held during the festival.

April

Semana Santa (Holy Week)
The dates of the *Semana Santa* change every year.

Easter 1999: April 4
Easter 2000: April 23
Easter 2001: April 15
Easter 2002: March 31
Easter 2003: April 20

Ancash

Semana Santa
Several processions celebrate the Passion of Christ, the most lavish and colourful of which is on Easter Sunday.

Arequipa

Semana Santa
Religious fervour characterizes these grandiose celebrations. Barefoot men and women wearing purple cowls walk in a solemn procession. Churches are visited and the Holy Sacrament is displayed. On Good Friday, you can see a figure of Christ being carried through the streets before it is laid to rest by the devout, who are dressed in mourning. The week finishes on Easter Sunday with a colourful procession to Yanahuara, where Judas' testament is read derisively, followed by the burning of his effigy.

Ayacucho

Semana Santa
A week of festivities that includes a staging of the Passion of Christ and nocturnal processions in which the whole city participates, begins on Palm Sunday. On Easter Saturday, people sing and dance through the night on the Acuchimay hillock to usher in Easter Sunday. There are also a bullfight and horse races.

Cuzco

Semana Santa
Take in the famous procession of *Señor de los Temblores* (patron saint of Cuzco) on Maundy Thursday, and stop to savour the regional cuisine.

Junín

Semana Santa
There are religious festivals as well as craft and agricultural fairs that give you the chance to sample some of the region's beverages. The streets are strewn with flower petals for the nightly processions that take place throughout the *Semana Santa*.

Lima

The National Peruvian *Caballos de Paso* Competition
First and second weeks of April
The exhibition and equestrian competition of the *caballos de paso* are attended by horse trainers from around the world.

Piura

Semana Santa
The *Semana Santa* begins on Palm Sunday with Christ's arrival on a donkey. The Last Supper is re-enacted in the cathedral's portico. A huge dance is held in the Plaza de Armas on Easter Sunday. Handicrafts made by artisans from northern Peru are also on display.

May

Arequipa

Festival Patronal de la Virgen de Chapi
May 1 to 5
A legion of theatre troupes come to pay homage to the virgin. There is a pilgrimage to the sanctuary. This is a good opportunity to sample the region's food and beverages.

Cuzco

Cruz Velacuy
May 2
A festival to celebrate the vigil and Adoration of the Cross. The church crucifixes are veiled. Groups perform traditional folk dances to Peruvian music.

Junín

Señor de Muruhuay
May 1 to 30

The devout make pilgrimages to the *Santuario del patrono* (sanctuary of the patron saint) throughout the month, joining in with the processions along the flower-strewn streets. Fireworks, craft exhibits and concerts are among the activities.

Lima

Feria de Acomuc
Third and fourth weeks of May
A large exhibition and competitions of handicrafts made in the countryside.

Puno

Feria de Las Alasitas
First week of May
Exhibition of miniature handicrafts, among which the *ekekos* (small idols of prosperity that are given for good luck) are especially interesting.

Cuzco

Festival de Raqchi
June 16
Come celebrate this holiday during which regional dance troupe performances, a bovine and agricultural fair, and a traditional cooking competition are held.

Festival del Dios
June 21
One of the most beautiful traditional religious celebrations, marked by the *Entrada de los Santos* (entry of the saints) and an impressive procession. There is singing and folk dancing.

Inti Raymi (Solstice Festival)
June 24
Inti Raymi, the most spectacular festival of the Inca Empire, takes place on the summer solstice on the esplanade of the Sacsahuamán fortress. Here, the sun-worship ceremony practised by the Incas is re-enacted. An Inca is carried in the ceremonial procession by a retinue of guards, and costumed dancers from the mountains perform traditional dances. A fire is then lit, and a llama sacrifice to the Sun is simulated in front of the temple's altar. Thousands of visitors from Peru and abroad come to see the week-long festivities every year. It is therefore a good idea to reserve your hotel room long in advance.

Huancavelica

Festival del Espritu Santo
First week of June
A traditional festival celebrated throughout the town. Popular dances bullfights and traditional musical performances.

Iquitos

Iquitos Tourist Week and
FICA Songs Festival
Third week of June
The week's events: a procession of allegorical floats, handicraft exhibit, folklore festival and crowning of the festival queen.

The International Festival of Songs in Amazonia (FICA) attracts participants from all over the world.

Puno

Regional Folklore and Aboriginal Dance Competition
June 24
About 50 dance groups come from all over the country to take part in this prestigious competition.

July

Ancash

Ancash Regional Fair
July 20 to 29
The political founding of Huaráz is celebrated with cultural and recreational activities and a large fair featuring crafts, agricultural, industrial and commercial products.

Cajamarca

Agricultural and Crafts Fair
July 25 to 30
Handicrafts made locally and in northern Peru are displayed and sold here. There are also cultural and recreational activities.

Cuzco

Festival de la Virgen del Carmen
July 15 to 17
The entire population confirms its faith in the Catholic religion. Folk dancers add music and colour to the celebration.

Lambayeque

Fexticum
July 22 to 31
This cultural fair is very traditional, so you can admire handicrafts of all kinds as well as traditional performances.

Festival Regional de la Santa Cruz de Motupe
July 25 to August 14

This venerable festival dating from the last century is celebrated twice a year: first, from February 1 to 8, and again from July 25 to August 14 (the second celebration is the more important one). Hundreds of pilgrims from Peru, Ecuador, Chile, Brazil, Colombia and Venezuela crowd this place of worship every year. There are a craft exhibit, a parade of *caballos de paso*, and open-air concerts and performances.

Madre de Dios

Madre de Dios Regional Agriculture and Craft Fair
July 27 to 31

Products from the surrounding region and from the jungle are exhibited. Variety of performances.

Pasco

Pozuzo Tourist Week
July 27 to August 3

This festival commemorates the arrival of the first colonizers on July 28, 1859. Folk and Tyrolean dancing and cockfights are among the events.

Peru

Independence Day
July 28 and 29

Various events and festivities take place throughout the country during this holiday which celebrates Peru's Independence.

August

Amazonas

Virgen Asunta
August 8 to 16

Everyone enjoys this festival, which celebrates the cult of the virgin Asunta.

The most important day is the 15th. There are a craft fair, traditional performances and various cultural activities.

Ancash

Festival Patronal de Chiquian
August 30

Musicians and dancers perform in the religious celebrations honouring Santa Rosa de Lima. There are also craft fairs, bullfights and fireworks.

Arequipa

Tourist Week
August 13 to 19

A festival commemorating the Spanish foundation of the "white city", to which all Peruvians, as well as the artists from other Latin-American countries are invited. Among the attractions are a huge traditional show, a *Festidanza* (Dance Festival), bullfights, craft exhibitions, processions of allegorical floats and a military parade.

Ayacucho

Festival of the Virgin of the Snows
August 5

Ayacucho honours its patron saint in a traditional manner with the colourful *diablada* dance, and with religious and cultural festivities.

Ayacucho Tourist Week
August 24 to 31

Discover the city with guided tours of the main attractions, explore the Wari-Quina archeological zone (also a village of craftspeople), and take in the traditional, cultural and sports events.

Cajamarca

Cajamarca Tourist Week
August 5 to 12

There are many interesting tourist activities: Latin-American music and folklore, exhibits of pre-Colombian ceramics, the crowning of the festival queen and a Peruvian film festival.

Cuzco

Warichacuy
August 25
Wara, the famous Inca rite where boys wear special clothing symbolizing their passage from puberty to adult-hood is staged on the spectacular Saqwaywaman esplanade. In this cere-mony, thousands of young people dressed in multicoloured Inca costumes demonstrate their physical agility and prowess.

Huánuco

Huánuco Tourist Week
August 11 to 17
Huánuco invites tourists to help cele-brate its Spanish founding with a large craft and agriculture fair.

Junín

Commemoration of the Glorious Battle
August 6
A military and civic ceremony takes place at the foot of the monument in Junín Pampa. Popular fairs.

Lima

Cañete Tourist Week and *Festival de Arte Negro* (Afro-Peruvian Art)
Fourth week of August
Renowned festival of Afro-Peruvian music and dance. Among the various events are the *folklore negro* show which features the best local artists, and the crowning of the festival queens.

Santa Rosa de Lima
August 30
Religious ceremonies honouring the patron saint of the Americas.

Pasco

Oxapampa Tourist Week
August 26 to 31
Celebrations in honour of Santa Rosa de Lima, patron saint of Oxapampa. Among the festivities are fairs and outdoor dance performances, cock-fights, Tyrolean dancing and regional cuisine.

Piura

National *Tondero* Competition
Fourth week in August
Several brightly-clad couples perform the *tondero*, Piura's traditional dance, in the hopes of winning the competi-tion.

Puno

Departmental *Zampoña* Competition
Dates vary
This competition lets the best musi-cians demonstrate their talents on the *zampoña* (panpipes), an aboriginal wind instrument native to Puno.

Tarapoto

Tourist Week
August 25 to 30
Folkloric celebrations, sports and cul-tural events are held during this week.

Tacna

Anniversary of Tacna's Reintegration
August 25 to 30
The main day of this huge patriotic celebration is the 28th. The many activ-ities include a youth offering, a flag procession, a military-civic parade, agricultural, commercial and craft fairs, national and international folk dancing groups, plays and a tourist photo ex-hibit.

Tumbes

Tumbes Tourist Week
Dates vary
Tourists can make the most of guided visits, as well as cultural and sports activities and popular fairs.

September

Ancash

Ancash Tourist Week
Fourth week in September
A mix of cultural and recreational activities, craft exhibits, folk competitions, and sale of traditional food and beverages.

Ica

Festival de Pisco
September 1 to 8
Pisco province commemorates the arrival of Argentinian general José de San Martín in Paracas in 1820 by organizing popular fairs, craft exhibits and parades.

Nazca Tourist Week
First week of September
A fairground featuring craft, commercial, industrial and agricultural exhibits. Take part in the popular celebrations, the crowning of the Nazca festival queen, cockfights and the *cabellos de paso* show.

Ica Tourist Week
Fourth week of September
Guided tours are offered, and food fairs and a variety of cultural and recreational activities are held. There is a big neighbourhood celebration.

Huancavelica

Huancavelica Tourist Week
September 20 to 26
Cultural, folkloric and sports activities, an agricultural and craft fair, and the crowning of the festival queen.

Huancayo Tourist Week
September 9 to 16
Cultural and recreational activities, a craft exhibition, the crowning of the festival queen, and guided tours.

La Libertad

International Spring Festival
Third and fourth weeks of September
Trujillo resounds with music and singing during these two weeks of festivities. Song and dance competitions are held, as well as folk performances, bullfights, *caballos de paso* performances and a race of *caballitos de totora*, small reed boats used for fishing since Inca times. There is also a spectacular procession of the festival queen, who is accompanied by beauty queens from America and Europe.

Puno

Festival Nuestra Señora de las Mercedes
September 22 to 28
A religious festival in honour of the patron saint of the city of Juliaca. There are a big commercial fair and folk and religious performances.

October

Arequipa

Arequipa Tourist Week
Dates vary
Fairs display crafts and agricultural products. There are a traditional food competition and sports and cultural events. Fireworks, folk dancers, the

crowning of festival queens, a procession of allegorical floats and various other festivities also take place.

Cuzco

Cuzco Tourist Week
Second week of October
Various exhibitions of arts and crafts, industrial products, and floral arrangements. Crowning of Cuzco's tourist queen. There are also fashion shows.

Huánuco

Tingo María Tourist Week
Octobre 13 to 19
Major exhibition of handicrafts from the jungle, an agricultural fair, a procession of festival queens, and folk dancers.

Festival del Señor de Burgos
Octobre 28 to 29
Devout Catholics organize a major procession in honour of the king and patron saint of Huánuco. There are also popular fairs.

Ica

Festival del Señor de Luren
Octobre 7 to 20
Religious festival in honour of the Inca patron saint. Thousands of pilgrims form a procession, carrying images of Señor de Luren. There is also a festival fairground.

Chincha Tourist Week
Fourth week in October
All sorts of artistic and cultural events, including an agricultural fair, crowning of the festival queen, and a procession of allegorical floats.

Lima

Festival del Señor de los Milagros
October 18 to 28
Peru's Indigenous people are devoted to the Señor de los Milagros, whose likeness was originally painted on a wall by a black slave in 1650. Since 1746, many pious followers clothed in purple robes have carried the canvas picture of him. Today, an enormous wooden platform decorated with gold and silver serves as the sacred image and is carried in the procession of nearly half-a-million people which passes through the streets of Lima. Much of the folklore found in the country's main regions pays tribute to this occasion, which is why the international bullfighting competition is held in Rimac.

Moquegua

Festival de la Santa Fortunata
October 14
The citizens of Moquegua celebrate this day to commemorate the discovery of Santa Fortunata's body by Brother, Tadeo Ocampo, in October 1976. There are popular fairs and fireworks as well as religious and folk festivities.

Oxapampa - Pasco

Villa Rica Tourist Week
October 7 to 14
Crowning of the coffee queen, equestrian events, cockfights, agricultural and commercial fairs, and popular dances.

Piura

Piura Tourist Week
First week of October
Cultural activities, processions, crowning of the tourist queen, aquatic competitions and under-water fishing events.

Tacna

Tacna Tourist Week
Second week of October
Many events take place during the week: the crowning of the tourist queen, traditional Latin-American folk

song and dance performances, a traditional cooking competition , a procession of allegorical floats, sports competitions and a craft exhibition.

Ucayali

Political Anniversary of the Founding of Pucallpa
October 13 to 21
Pucallpa's anniversary is celebrated with a variety of popular activities.

November

Ayacucho

All Saints' Day
November 1 to 3
On the second day of this important religious festival, people gather at the cemetery to honour the dead and share a traditional meal, including the well-known festive bread baked in the shape of a child or a horse.

Cerro de Pasco

Tourist Week
November 23 to 29
The anniversary of the department of Cerro de Pasco is marked with patriotic ceremonies, agricultural and craft fairs, cultural activities and processions.

Cuzco

All Saints' Day
November 1 to 3
This festival is celebrated differently in each town and village, according to local traditions.

Lima

Pacific International Fair
Third and fourth weeks of November
Countries from all five continents participate in this major fair to display their technological and industrial innovation.

Visitors can attend various shows and taste the cuisine of the different participating countries.

Moquegua

Moquegua Anniversary and Tourist Week
November 25
This day celebrates the city's founding by the Spanish in 1541 and its many tourist attractions and cultural events.

Puno

Jubilee Week
First week of November
A week of traditional celebrations commemorates the founding of the city of Puno. The legend of Manco Capac and Mama Ollo, who emerged from the waters of Lake Titicaca to found the Inca Empire, is re-enacted. A handicraft exhibition and song and dance competition are held.

Trujillo

International Ballet Festival
November 20 to 30
An annual festival which attracts renowned ballet dancers from Peru, America and Europe.

December

Ayacucho

Latin-American Liberty Week
December 9
The battle of Ayacucho is commemorated. During the week, you can visit craft exhibits, cultural events and history lectures, or take part in the fairground festivities in the evening.

Identity and Culture Shock

Before going on vacation, we prepare our luggage and get the necessary vaccinations and travel documents, but rarely do we prepare for culture shock. The following text explains what culture shock is and how to deal with it.

In a nutshell, culture shock can be defined as a certain anxiety that may be experienced upon arriving in another country where everything is different, including the culture and language, making communication as you know it very difficult. Combined with jetlag and fatigue, the strain of orienting yourself in a new cultural context can lead to psychological stress that may throw you off track.

Culture shock is a frustrating phenomenon that can easily turn travellers setting out with the best of intentions into intolerant, racist and ethnocentric ones – they may come to believe that their society is better than the new, and seemingly incomprehensible, one. This type of reaction detracts from the whole travel experience.

People in other countries have different customs and lifestyles that are sometimes hard for us to understand or accept. We might even find ourselves wondering how people can live the way they do when their customs run contrary to what we deem to be "normal". In the end, however, it is easier to adapt to them than to criticize or disregard them.

Even though this is the era of globalization and cultural homogenization, we still live in a world of many "worlds", such as the sports world, the business world, the worlds of different continents, suburbia, and the world of the rich and the poor. Of course, these worlds intersect, but each has its own characteristic set of ideas and cultural values. Furthermore, even if they are not in direct contact, each has at least an image of the other, which might be distorted and wrong, or accurate, but in either case is ultimately nothing more than an image. If a picture is worth a thousand words, then our world contains million upon millions of them. Sometimes it is hard to tell what is real and what isn't, but one thing is certain: what you see on television about a place is not the same as when you travel there.

When people interact with each other, they inevitably make sense of each other through their differences. The strength of a group, human or animal, lies in its diversity, whether it be in genetics or ideas. Can you imagine how boring the world would be if everyone were the same?

Travelling can be seen as a way of developing a more holistic, or global, vision of the world; this means accepting that our cultural fabric is complex and woven with many different ethnicities, and that all have something to teach us, be it a philosophy of life, medical knowledge, or a culinary dish, which adds to the richness of our personal experience.

PRACTICAL INFORMATION

Remember that culture is relative, and that people's social, technological and financial situation shape their way of being and looking at the world. It takes more than curiosity and tolerance to be open minded: it is a matter of learning to see the world anew, through a different cultural perspective.

When travelling abroad, don't spend too much energy looking for the familiar, and don't try to see the place as you would like it to be – go with the flow instead. And though a foreign country might be difficult to understand and even seem unwelcoming at times, remember that there are people who find happiness and satisfaction in life everywhere. When you get involved in their daily lives, you will begin to see things differently – things which at first seemed exotic and mystifying are easily understood after having been explained. It always helps to know the rules before playing a game, and it goes without saying that learning the language will help you better understand what's going on. But be careful about communicating with your hands, since certain gestures might mean the opposite of what you are trying to say!

Prepare yourself for culture shock as early as possible. Libraries and bookstores are good places for information about the cultures you are interested in. Reading about them is like a journey in itself, and will leave you with even more cherished memories of your trip.

Written by Jean-Étienne Poirier

Cuzco

Santa Ranticuy Popular Festival
December 24
Exhibition and sale of regional handicrafts. Several items bear the image of the *Niño Emmanuel* (Baby Emmanuel), which is this city's representation of the Baby Jesus.

All of Peru

Christmas Day
December 25
The big Christmas celebration begins with midnight mass, followed by a late-night feast.

Tumbes

8th of December Regional Fair
First and second weeks of December
This event is held in the province of Zarumilla.

Other Popular Events

Bullfights
Dates vary
Bullfights are held mostly in October, November, December and March.

Rimac

On Sunday, the most famous toreros arrive on the Plaza de Acho to contend for the prestigious golden cape of Señor de los Milagros. The Plaza de Acho is found in Rimac, one of Lima's historic districts, and is the oldest arena in America. In fact, except for the arena in Seville, Spain, it is the oldest in the world.

Some Advice

All too often in a developing country, the traveller wearing flashy clothes sticks out like a sore thumb. Sometimes even his or her behaviour, physical appearance or way of referring to people can draw unfavourable attention. Don't carry America as your identity card: it's too diverse and you will hear all kinds of negative remarks about your country which don't necessarily apply to you. If you want people to see you for what you really are, be open-minded and talk about yourself and your personal experiences without any formalities.

Drugs in your luggage?

If you have packed medication, make sure you have a copy of your prescriptions for them in case your baggage is checked. Never leave your backpack or suitcase anywhere unattended: not only can it be stolen, but someone can also put drugs in your bags to try and retrieve them later so you can get arrested and thrown in prison instead of them.

MISCELLANEOUS

Religion

The majority of Peruvians consider themselves Roman Catholic (about 95%). In essence, as in many Latin American countries, Catholicism has occupied a very important place in the history of Peru, from colonial times to the present day. Today, however, there are fewer and fewer of practising Catholics in the major cities, though the religion continues to inspire a vibrant tradition and remains popular in rural and Andean regions. During certain of the traditional religious holidays, Holy Week for example, all economic activity can come to a halt.

Taking Pictures

From stunning landscapes to colourfully clad villagers, Peru is full of great photo-opportunities. Ask people to take their picture first. It is normal for them to ask you for some money in return. If you don't feel like paying, politely decline. Don't just go around snapping shots of them like they are animals in a zoo: remember, they are human, too, and should be treated with the same respect you or I expect. Developing your film in Peru is not recommended; wait until you get back home.

Electricity

Electrical appliances run on an alternating current of 220 volts (60 cycles), just as in North America. European travellers will need both a converter and an adapter with two parallel flat pins for any appliances they plan to bring along. In the city of Arequipa, the current is 220 volts, but 50 cycles.

Drugs

If you are travelling with prescription drugs, bring the prescription in order to justify their presence in your luggage.

Drugs are easy to find in Peru. If you plan on enlivening your trip with a bit of hashish or marijuana, or some other illicit substance, we would like to remind you that many North Americans and Europeans with the same idea now languish in the humid cells of prisons in Puno and other unpleasant locations. This would definitely put a damper on your trip, so think twice.

N.B. If you would like to pay a visit to these unfortunate detained souls who are always happy to receive visitors, bring along some reading material, food and toiletries (soap, toothpaste, sanitary napkins, etc.).

Hora Peruaña

No, the following is not about time zones, but to warn you that Peruvians are not big on punctuality. If your excursion is delayed because the driver or guide hasn't shown up yet, you will know why. Arrange to meet with someone in a restaurant or café so you don't end up waiting somewhere impatiently for hours.

Time Zones

Peru is five hours behind Greenwich Mean Time. There is, however, no daylight savings time. Consequently, in the spring and summer, Peru is one hour behind the east coast of North America, two hours ahead of the west coast, six hours behind continental Western Europe and five hours behind the United Kingdom. The rest of the year, the country is on the same time as North America's east coast, three hours ahead of the west coast, seven hours behind continental Western Europe and six hours behind the United Kingdom.

Weights and Measures

Officially, Peru uses the metric system. The following conversion table may be useful, especially since many products, such as gasoline, are sold by Imperial measures.

Weights
1 pound (lb) = 454 grams (g)
1 kilogram (kg) = 2.2 pounds (lbs)

Linear Measure
1 inch = 2.2 centimetres (cm)
1 foot (ft) = 30 centimetres (cm)
1 mile = 1.6 kilometres (km)
1 kilometres (km) = 0.63 miles
1 metre (m) = 39.37 inches

Land Measure
1 acre = 0.4 hectare
1 hectare = 2.471 acres

Volume Measure
1 U.S. gallon (gal) = 3.79 litres
1 U.S. gallon (gal) = 0.83 imperial gallon

Temperature
To convert °F into °C: subtract 32, divide by 9, multiply by 5
To convert °C into °F: multiply by 9, divide by 5, add 32.

OUTDOORS

Peru's natural landscapes are so stunning that they will take your breath away. The Andean Cordillera is furrowed with slopes that are ideal for hiking or mountain climbing. Plant and animal life abounds in La Selva's national parks. The Manu reserve and Tambo Pata national Park harbour natural treasures within their dense, tropical vegetation. In short, this Andean country is home to such rich and diversified environments, that it is inevitably associated with "ecotourism". Unfortunately, no universal definition for this word exists, and people seem to make it mean whatever they want it to.

In order to preserve its rich ecological heritage for the generations to come, it is very important not to spoil or destroy the biodiversity of this magnificent Andean country. The discovery of oil in Amazonia has already had a considerable adverse effect on the forest and the environment. Several plant and animal species have disappeared since people arrived here, while others have ben pushed to the verge of extinction. Indigenous groups have become reduced to quaint tourist attractions for tourists with no regard for human dignity in their quest for the exotic.

Protecting nature also means preventing destructive modifications and thoughtless habits that are sometimes made. At the risk of seeming terribly moralizing, we must remind visitors that it is very important, if not imperative, to obey certain rules:

• Do not discard trash or garbage, because it pollutes the environment.

• Do not make fires in parks or nature reserves because they destroy the forest.

• Do not feed the animals.

Ecotourism, or Green Tourism

Not so long ago, ecologists were thought of as a group of dreamers in search of the Holy Grail. Today, the word "ecology" is on everyone's minds and is referred to in many fields, including tourism. Thus, for some years now, tourism in general has been making way for ecotourism.

Ecotourism, or "Green Tourism", if you prefer, is becoming more fashionable all over the world. Exotic images spring immediately to mind: animal photo safaris; hiking through luxuriant forests crisscrossed by streams, where the flora and fauna are so spectacular, they almost seem unreal. Though ecotourism is synonymous with "respect for nature", it means, above all, getting off the beaten path.

• Do not buy souvenirs made from animal skin or feathers, because it encourages poaching.

• Do not hunt animals. If a guide suggests a meal be made from an animal he will kill, refuse categorically.

• Out of respect, ask permission before taking photographs of people.

• Bring as few plastics bags as possible, because more often than not they are forgotten; and whether they remain buried forever underground or are left on the surface, they are not biodegradable.

• Use biodegradable soaps and shampoos.

You will no doubt have the time to take part in some outdoor activities during your stay in Peru. Be aware that some of Peru's attractions are in remote and hard-to-reach locations and require specialized equipment or involve complicated logistics. Specialized travel agencies can therefore be extremely helpful. Some areas are nearly impossible to reach if you don't go through one of these companies, even if you are an experienced traveller, setting out on your own. For more information about travel agencies, see p 62.

Here is an overview of the main outdoor activities available.

PARKS AND NATURE RESERVES

Peru is dotted with numerous parks and reserves, most of which are difficult to visit. Some are traversed by trails, allowing you to discover the rich and varied flora and fauna. The major parks are described in this guide are:

Parque Nacional Manu (see p 290) and Parque Nacional Huascarán (see p 221).

Most parks are only accessible if you go with a guide. If you are thinking of visiting one of these places, be careful, since many non-qualified people pose as guides or representatives of specialized agencies.

If you visit a national park or reserve, make sure that the guide has a valid certificate and is associated with an agency that has a permit to enter the park.

OUTDOOR ACTIVITIES

Hiking and Climbing the Andes

Peru is crossed by majestic mountain chains, making it a dream spot for anyone who wants to climb to their summits. The Callejón de Huaylas has the highest mountains in Peru, whose jagged snow-covered peaks draw a large number of visitors each year. With a 6,634-metre summit, the Huascarán is undeniably the ruler of this world of mountains and ice, and will appeal to experienced climbers looking for a challenge.

In recent years, increased interest in climbing in the Andes has led to a proliferation of tour companies and mountain guides. Be careful! Many of these people are simply not qualified to do this type of work. To attract customers, they offer expeditions at ridiculously low prices. However, they have no knowledge of safety practices in mountain climbing, don't know how to use the necessary equipment, and wouldn't know how to react if a problem should arise along the way. They can barely be counted on to know the correct route to get to the top of the mountain. Unfortunately, the inexperience of these pseudo-guides causes accidents, some fatal.

If you are seriously interested in conquering the majestic summits of the Andes, it is recommended that you contact the **Casa de Guías** *(Huaráz, Parque Ginebra 28-G aparto 123, ☏721-811, ⇌722-306)*. La Casa de Guías is an association of professional guides well-known in the area and can be extremely useful to help you prepare for your ascent or to work out all the details, including porters, food, tents, etc. These guides can also tell you which areas to avoid, depending on which level of difficulty you prefer.

Numerous fatal accidents have occurred in the country's high mountain ranges since the beginning of the century. For your own safety, consult a specialized tour company to obtain the services of an experienced guide. Be wary of so-called guides who can't prove their competence or aren't recommended by a reputable company. For a short list of recommended companies and guides, see p 62.

The best-known hiking route in Peru, and perhaps in all of South America, is the Inca Trail. This section of the network of highways that once connected all the empire's cities with Cuzco, its centre. In addition to spectacular scenery, the trail is also famous for where it leads: Machu Picchu (see p 199).

Bird-Watching

The huge variety of bird species draws many ornithologists to Peru's prime bird-watching areas every year. More than 2,000 species have been spotted in La Selva alone.

Rafting

In Peru, the rivers flow from high Andean peaks through magnificent canyons to verdant tropical forests. In recent years, rafting has become more and more popular with tourists visiting Peru. The rivers range from Class I to Class V levels. Before setting off on an excursion like this, take the time to choose a serious, competent company. Don't forget that a good reputation is often synonymous with safety, and your life may depend on the compe-

OUTDOORS

tence of your guide. November to May are the best months to shoot the rapids.

Snorkelling and Scuba-Diving

Snorkelling equipment is really quite simple: fins, a mask and a snorkel. With no required course, snorkelling is still one of the most interesting of all outdoor activities, allowing everyone access to the beauty of the underwater world. The best place for snorkelling and scuba diving is on the northern coast, near Tumbes, where the water is warmer. Contact the Mundo submarino boutique *(Lima, San Isidro, Avenida Conquistadores 791, ☎441-7602)*.

Downhill Skiing

You can definitely hit the slopes in Peru! Some summits around the Callejón de Huaylas are covered in snow year-round. Of course, there is no infrastructure in place to take skiers to the top, but several travel agencies in Huaráz, or even the Casa de Guías, can give you more information about how to get there.

Surf- and Sail-Boarding

Beginners who want to enjoy these two sports to the fullest will find some windswept bays on the Pacific coast in the vicinity of Puerto Chicama (see p 247).

Deep-Sea Fishing

Most of the large, coastal tourist centres, like Cabo Blanco, offer deep-sea fishing excursions. It's a nice way to get out onto open water and enjoy the beauty of the ocean, even if it is somewhat expensive. It's also a good way of getting to know the different types of fish that are caught in Pacific waters. Equipment and advice are furnished on board. For a more picturesque experience, ask a local fishing boat to take you along.

Cycling

The roads in Peru are not ideal for cycling. Given that the highways have no bicycle lanes and the secondary roads are strewn with potholes, a mountain bike would be the most practical. Extreme caution is necessary, because the drivers go fast and don't always obey traffic laws. Nevertheless, if you have the time and are well-equipped, cycling can be a very pleasant way of seeing the country. Remember that the landscape quickly becomes hilly when you get to the Andean Cordillera.

Horseback Riding

In certain regions of the country, particularly in the high Andean plateaus, the inhabitants get around on horseback more often than otherwise. Since the roads are narrow and unpaved, it is a most convenient means of transportation. Visitors can sample the pleasures of riding too, because many hotels and tour companies offer excursions on horseback.

Swimming

The beaches on the Pacific coast cannot compare to the white sandy beaches of the Caribbean. However, some of the former are very nice for swimming and relaxing. The beaches north of Chiclayo are not yet very developed, but are nonetheless interesting. The temperature of the water is also warmer here.

Soccer or *Fútbol*

Fútbol is, without a doubt, the most popular sport throughout Peru. The young, and the not so young, play it with passion. You can attend weekend *fútbol* matches in Lima at the national stadium *(Lima, Paseo de la República)*.

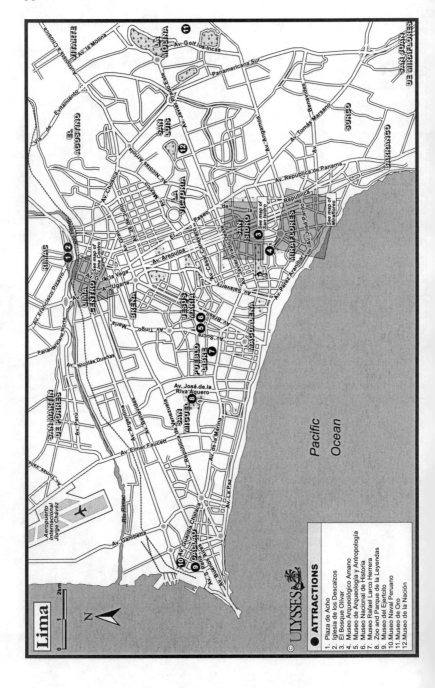

Lima

0   1   2km

N

© ULYSSES

● ATTRACTIONS

1. Plaza de Acho
2. Iglesia de los Descalzos
3. El Bosque Olivar
4. Museo Arqueológico Amano
5. Museo de Arqueología y Antropología
6. Museo Nacional de Historia
7. Museo Rafael Larco Herrera
8. Zoo and Parque de la Leyendas
9. Museo del Ejército
10. Museo Naval Peruano
11. Museo de Oro
12. Museo de la Nación

Pacific

Ocean

Aeropuerto
Internacional
Jorge Chávez

Plaza San Martin, built in 1921, 100 years after the general declared the nation's independence.
- *Alain Legault*

The eye-catching balcony of the Archiepiscopal Palace – a masterpiece of craftsmanship with 5,000 finely worked pieces of Nicaraguan cedar.
- Tibor Bognar

Construction of the Iglesia de la Compañía de Jesús was begun in
1570 and completed in 1670. - T. B.

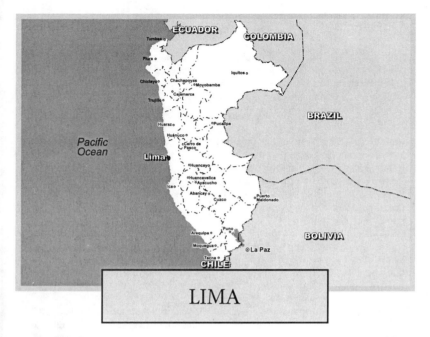

LIMA

Lima was once one of those dazzling Spanish cities that aroused a great deal of envy. Magnificent colonial buildings lined its streets, presenting the kind of harmonious view that the eye drinks in effortlessly, pausing only to admire the even more splendid buildings on certain street corners. It was here that San Marcos, the oldest university in the New World, was founded in 1551, and the famous French writer Jules Verne dedicated his first novel, *Martín Paz*, to the city.

Lima, whose name is a corruption of the Spanish translation of a Rimac Indian term meaning "talkative", grew rapidly amidst the vestiges of the millennia-old cultures that had once thrived throughout the region. Over the following centuries it was coveted, attacked, besieged, plundered, mutilated, sacked and partially destroyed. Today, it is a sprawling city bustling with some nine million inhabitants –

nearly half the population of Peru. Bereft of its former splendour, Lima is now a gigantic urban jungle enveloped nine months out of the year in an ochre-coloured fog known as the *garúa*. There are no Inca ruins to be found, and vehicles of all different sorts career through the streets, filling the air with a nonstop cacophony of blaring horns. Despite these drawbacks, however, Lima still manages to spark the imagination of nostalgic visitors, who enjoy strolling through old neighbourhoods haunted by ghosts of the colonial era, a prosperous time that is long-gone. This is reason enough why UNESCO added the city's historic centre to its list of World Heritage Sites. Furthermore, Lima boasts the best museums, hotels and restaurants in the country and knows how to throw a good party now and again to celebrate its rich history.

Located on the right bank of the Río Rimac, Lima is sometimes referred to as

---

The *Garúa*

The *garúa* is a thick fog that blankets the coast around Lima when the cold Humboldt Current encounters the warm, seasonal current known as El Niño. From April to December, the days are a little colder and damper and, though it never rains, the climate is not as pleasant as it is during the rest of the year.

---

the "City of Kings". It was on Twelfth Night, January 5, 1535, that the bloodthirsty Spanish conquistador Francisco Pizarro drew up the first plans for Plaza de Amas, using a checkerboard pattern; the town was officially founded that same year on January 18. Therefore, Lima was in effect founded by Pizarro. As the saying goes, he who lives by the sword dies by the sword: a few years later, in 1541, Pizarro was assassinated by the Almagrists on the steps of his palace. His death was followed by over 470 years of historic events, tradition and, unfortunately, bloody conflicts. Sadly, Lima's past is marked by such clashes, whose outcome was decided solely by violence – the flash of the sword, the crack of the harquebus and the blade of the knife.

Thirty-four years after being founded, Lima became a viceroyalty governed by Francisco de Toledo. At the time, all Spanish colonies were divided into viceroyalties, each ruled by a viceroy representing the king of Spain. Lima grew rapidly, and its residents prospered - so much so that the city became one of the richest in the New World, as well as the political, religious and commercial hub of Spanish South America. Unfortunately, Lima's wealth and glory did more than simply dazzle artists and aristocrats. Just as the gold of the Incas had attracted the Spanish conquistadors, the riches of the Spanish colonists who subsequently settled in the area attracted the attention of the brigands and pirates who combed the shores and inspected the galleons

laden with gold sailing full-speed toward Spain.

The Spanish thought of the famous English corsair Sir Francis Drake as nothing but a pirate. In February 1579, he earned his reputation by sacking the port of Callao. After this bitter setback, a decision was made to encircle the town with ramparts – a project which would not be completed until 100 years later (1687).

Catastrophe struck Lima again in 1746. This time, it was a natural disaster: a violent earthquake reduced most of the town to rubble. Of some 3,000 houses, only about 20 remained standing. Efforts to rebuild the City of Kings and restore its former glory and prestige proved futile. Toward the end of the 18th century, Spain accorded greater powers to the viceroyalties of Buenos Aires and Bogotá. Lima was on the decline and remained in a slump for over a century. In the meantime, on July 28, 1821, an Argentinean by the name of José de San Martín marched into Lima unhindered and declared the country independent. In 1851, work was begun on a road linking the port of Callao to the Andean peaks, which had been found to contain all different sorts of rich ore. This vital artery was completed in 1870.

At the beginning of the 20th century, Lima experienced a population explosion. By the 1970s, it had nearly 3,300,000 inhabitants, up from barely 275,000 in 1930. Due to the sluggish

The Hostage Crisis

The city of Lima was thrown into a terrible state of turmoil on December 17, 1996, when a revolutionary group known as the Túpac Amarú took over the Japanese embassy. Some 500 people were taken hostage, then released a few at a time. This crisis, which lasted several months, sent shockwaves through Lima and the world. A climate of incertitude once again settled over the City of Kings. The terrorists demanded the immediate liberation of some 450 comrades rotting away in Peruvian prisons. President Fujimori categorically refused to give in to blackmail, even though his mother and brother were among the hostages. Instead, he came up with a strategy to get into the embassy, based on the concept of the tunnels of the ruins of Chavín in Huantar (see p 226). To prepare the troops for a rescue mission, he ordered the immediate construction of a replica of the Japanese embassy. For over two months, the best soldiers in Peru studied the terrorists' every move and trained around the clock. Of the 500 original hostages, only 72 remained. Noisy army helicopters flew over the embassy, filling the air with noise, while the Peruvian soldiers broke through earth and rock, clearing a 120-metre-long, 1.5-metre-wide tunnel leading to five different spots inside and outside the embassy. On April 22, 1997, 126 days after the terrorists besieged the building, the soldiers burst out of the tunnel to free the hostages. All the terrorists, one hostage and one soldier were killed in the course of the operation. Later, a number of international humanitarian organizations harshly criticized the Peruvian government's expeditious methods. The terrorists, as it turned out, had been prepared for any eventuality: they had an impressive military arsenal, complete with grenades, bulletproof vests, Uzis and rocket-launchers. Things are now back to normal, and visitors can safely explore Miraflores, San Isidro, Barranco and Lima Centro.

economy in the hinterland, many Native Americans have been coming from the mountains and the coast to Lima over the last 30 years to seek a better life in the populous capital city and land of opportunity for some. Unfortunately, their hopes are often dashed when they find themselves faced with the harsh economic realities of modern life. As more and more of them settled on the outskirts of town, *pueblos jovenes* (the term for new communities that are quickly becoming sprawling, over-crowded shanty towns) formed, bloating the city to the east, the north and the south. Most of these new arrivals are doomed to live in the most unpleasant conditions imaginable.

In the 1980s, the city was the scene of repeated attacks by the Shining Path (Sendero Luminoso) terrorist group. Bombs exploded all over and a number of assassinations took place. Alberto Fujimori's ascension to power coincided with the arrest of Shining Path leader Abimaël Guzmán, and was followed by a lull in that sort of urban terrorism and a return to a state of relative calm.

 FINDING YOUR WAY AROUND

Area code: 01

Most tourists who fly into Peru arrive at Aeropuerto Jorge Chávez, located 16 kilometres west of Lima Centro, the city's historic district. Several bank branches, as well as a currency exchange office, a post office, a

Aeropuerto Jorge Chávez

Lima's Jorge Chávez Airport was named after a young aviation pioneer. Born in France to Peruvian parents, Chávez made flying history on July 23, 1910, at the tender age of 23, when he took off on a small airplane in the Swiss village of Brigue and flew over the 2,000-metre-high Simplon Pass. Thus, he became the first person to fly over the Alps. Sadly, when landing in Domodossola, on the Italian side, he lost control of his aircraft and died in the ensuing crash.

restaurant, a Telefónica del Perú and a tourist agency with a hotel reservation service can be found at the airport. Going through customs can be a lengthy and unpleasant process, and the police often check people's baggage. Smuggling drugs is illegal, and if you are caught with them in your possession, you can easily spend a long time in a dank Peruvian prison.

Getting to Lima by Bus from the Airport

We might as well tell you up front: taking the bus is not your best option. It is complicated and somewhat dangerous, especially at night. However, if you're absolutely determined to do so, here's how: when you leave the airport, walk straight ahead to the exit with a frenzy of vehicles zipping around in front of it. Some of these are *micros* and *colectivos*; look at the stickers on their windshields to see where they are headed, and cross your fingers. The odds that one of these vehicles will drop you off near your hotel are slim. The ride will cost you about 40¢.

Getting to Lima by Taxi from the Airport

Taking a taxi is definitely the simplest option, though not the cheapest. Upon exiting the airport, you will be greeted by a swarm of cabbies eagerly offering you their services. Some drivers belong to a group called *Taxis seguros* and

guarantee reliable service, but they charge more. Depending on your bargaining skills, the current fares are in the following range:

Airport to Lima Centro: $7
Airport to San Isidro: $10 to $15
Airport to Miraflores: $15 to $25

Self-employed drivers can charge a little less, but they often wait until they have a few passengers to make it worth their while. If you don't speak Spanish, you might have a hard time figuring out what's going on, but there's no reason to be alarmed.

If you speak some Spanish, don't have much baggage and feel sure of yourself, you can go to the airport exit road, hail a taxi and try to negotiate a better fare than what the drivers at the exit offer. For your own safety, however, don't try this after dark.

Getting Around Lima by Bus

With nearly nine million inhabitants fighting their way as best they can around this gigantic and, well, disorganized city, many visitors to Lima feel frightened and bewildered. The buses may be slow, but they are the cheapest way to get around. There are two kinds of buses: standard **buses**, familiar to all, and **combis**, nicknamed *los combis de la muerte*, or the *combis* of death, because the inevitable sometimes occurs while they are weaving their way at high speeds through the dense traffic on the major arteries. Fortunately, accidents don't happen every day, but the fact that they are so common should give you an idea of how chaotic the traffic is in Lima.

Combis are smaller than buses. The fare is always 40¢, no matter where you are going. In addition to a driver, there is an assistant who stands in the doorway and calls out to potential clients on the sidewalk. If you want to climb aboard, wave your arm and the *combi* will pull over just long enough to let you jump on. When we say just long enough, we mean it: like buses, *combis* usually don't come to a complete stop, but simply slow down for a moment before tearing off again. When you want to get off, a simple *"aqui lomas"* will prompt the driver to put on the breaks long enough for you to make your way safely back to solid ground.

There are several ways to get from Lima Centro to Barranco by public transportation. The best-known and most direct route, via San Isidro and Miraflores, is to take Tacna (from Lima Centro), which becomes Garcilaso de la Vega, then Avenida Arequipa, then Avenida Larco (from Miraflores), which becomes El Libertador in Barranco. El Paseo de la República also links Lima Centro with the neighbourhoods of San Isidro, Miraflores and Barranco, but there aren't many buses along it. The buses and *combis* that take these routes usually have a sticker reading *Todo Arequipa* on their windshield. A bus ticket costs about 40¢.

Bus Stations

Strange as it may seem, Lima has no central bus depot, or *terminal terrestre*.

Each of the many bus companies that serve the capital has its own station.

Buses North

Cruz del Sur: Jr. Quilca 531, Lima Centro, ☎423-1570.

Ormeño: Av. Tómas Zavala 177, Lima Centro, ☎427-5679.

Trans-Olano: Av. Grau 617, Lima Centro, ☎427-3519.

To the Central Andes

Expreso Molina Unión: Jr. Ayacucho 1141-1145, Lima Centro, ☎428-0617.

Buses South

Cruz del Sur: Jr. Quilca 531, Lima Centro, ☎423-1570.

Ormeño: Av. Tómas Zavala 177, Lima Centro, ☎427-5679.

Oltursa: Av. Grau 617, Lima Centro, ☎427-3519.

Getting Around Lima by Taxi

Taxis in Lima don't have meters. Ask the driver how much he's going to charge you at the start of the trip, since anyone can turn his car into a makeshift taxi and there are no official fare regulations. Real taxis have a coloured sticker on their windshield with the word *Taxi* clearly printed on it. Depending on your destination, a ride will generally cost you between $1 and $3.

LIMA

The following companies offer round-the-clock service:

Taxi Miraflores
Av. República de Panamá 5581, Miraflores, ☎446-3953 or 446-4336.

Taxi Fono
Aramburú 965, Of. 101, San Isidro, ☎422-6565 or 422-6527.

Getting Around Lima
by *Colectivos*

Some taxis, commonly known as *colectivos*, have a fixed route and also serve as public transportation. As indicated by their name, they carry as many passengers as they can. They are cheaper than taxis, but a bit more expensive and faster than the bus.

Getting Around Lima by Car

We strongly advise you not to drive in Lima. The traffic is chaotic, basic rules of driving are ignored, roadsigns are often missing and the city has developed without any regard for urban planning. Some people say that if you can drive in Lima, you can drive anywhere. If, in spite of all these warnings, you are determined to get behind the wheel, we wish you the best!

Here is a short list of car-rental agencies:

Avis Rent-a-Car
At Jorge Chávez Airport; ☎565-1637.

Av. Javier Prado Este 5235, Camacho, La Molina, ☎434-1111, ⇌437-7813.

Budget Rent-a-Car
At Jorge Chávez Airport, ☎575-1674.

Carnaval and Moreyra 724, San Isidro, ☎442-8703, ⇌441-4174.

PRACTICAL INFORMATION

Tourist Information

Promperú
Calle Uno Oeste - Edificio Mitinci, Ministerio de Industria, Comercio, Turismo y Integración URB, CORPAC, San Isidro, 14th floor, ⇌442-9280, www.rcp.net.pe/promperu.

Promperú is a governmental organization that was created to promote tourism in Peru. However, its offices are a bit far from the city's hotels and attractions, so it is best to take a taxi there or communicate with the staff by fax or e-mail.

Info tour
Jr. De la Unión (Belen) 1066, Of. E-2, ☎/⇌431-0117.

Much more centrally located than Promperú, Info tour is right near Plaza San Martín and is definitely one of the best sources of free tourist information in Lima. It is run by a friendly woman named Bertha Quezada Guzmán, who speaks French and English in addition to Spanish and organizes all sorts of tours of Lima and its surroundings.

South American Explorer's Club
Av. Républic de Portugal 146 and Breña, ☎425-0142, montague@amauta.rcp.net.

The South American Explorer's Club is an excellent source of information if you don't mind paying a small fee. It is a non-profit organization that was founded in Lima in 1977. Though it also has an office in Quito, Ecuador, the headquarters are now in Ithaca, New York. The club's mission is to help anyone interested in exploring South America, whether it be as a sportsperson, for cultural purposes or simply as a means of broadening one's horizons. Annual memberships cost $50 per person or $70 per couple and entitle you to receive the club's quarterly magazine and enjoy access to a wealth of information, including topographical and road maps, travel reports written by members and other documents available at the club library. Members can also store their belongings at the club's office and receive letters and e-mail there. Non-members are welcome to take a quick look around, but out of respect for members are politely requested not to linger too long. The staff is young, friendly and helpful.

In Quito, Ecuador:
Jorge Washington 311 and Leonidas Plaza, ☎/≈702-225-228, explorer@saec.org.ec.

There is a small **tourist information booth** in the middle of Parque Kennedy, in Miraflores.

Guided Tours

Even if you are planning to travel on your own, there are certain advantages to enlisting the services of a tour operator, which is sometimes the only way to get to remote places like the tropical forest or the high peaks of the Andes. Furthermore, if you want to learn more about the local architecture, history or neighbourhoods, these agencies are the best places to turn. Those listed below offer a variety of guided tours of Lima and its environs, as well as numerous other excursions in the rest of the country.

Coltur
Av. José Pardo 138, Miraflores, ☎241-5551, ≈446-9392 or 446-8073, www.coltur.com.pe, postmaster@coltur.com.pe.

Condor Travel
Amando Blondet 249, San Isidro, ☎442-7305, ≈442-0935, condortravel@mcimail.com.

Giulia
San Martín 751, Miraflores, ☎444-210 or 444-420, ≈447-9478, giula@amauta.rcp.net.pe.

Tudor
Av. Benavides 470, Of. B, Miraflores, ☎444-9362 or 447-1643, ≈447-1650.

Post Offices

Pasaje Piura, right near the Palacio del Gobierno; Monday to Saturday, 8am to 8pm, Sunday 8am to 2pm.

At Jorge Chávez Airport

DHL: Los Castaños, San Isidro, ☎954-4345.

Telephone

Telefónica del Perú

South of Plaza San Martín, in the Edificio Sud America 933, on Augusto N. Wiesse, Lima Centro.

Diez Canseco, at the corner of Avenida La Paz, Miraflores.

Internet Access

Phantom Café Internet
Av. Diagonal 344, 2nd floor, Miraflores, ☎/≈446-5423, www.phantom.com.pe.

LIMA

At the South American Explorer's Club (see p 102).

Police

Dial 105

Tourist Protection Service
Salaberry 1156, Jesús María, ☎471-4313.

Embassies and Consulates

American Embassy
La Encalada Cdra. 17 s/n, Monterrico, ☎434-3000, ≈434-3037.

Australian Embasssy
Gertrudis Echeñique 420, Santiago, Chile, ☎(56-2) 2285065, ≈2081707.

Belgian Consulate
Av. Angamos 392, Miraflores, ☎241-7566, ≈241-6371.

Bolivian Consulate
Los Castaños 235, San Isidro, ☎/≈422-8231.

Brazilian Consulate
Av. José Pardo 850, Miraflores, ☎421-5650 or 421-5660, ≈445-2421.

British Embassy
Natalio Sánchez 125, Piso 4, Lima Centro, ☎433-8923 or 431-5314, ≈433-8922.

Canadian Embassy
Libertas 130, Miraflores, ☎444-1145, ≈444-4347.

Chilean Consulate
Av. Javier Prado Oeste 790, San Isidro, ☎221-2817 or 221-2818, ≈221-2816.

Colombian Consulate
Av. Jorge Basadre 1580, San Isidro, ☎441-0530 or 442-9648, ≈441-9806.

Ecuadoran Consulate
Las Palmeras 356, San Isidro, ☎442-4184, ≈422-0711.

Dutch Embassy
Avenida Principal 190, Piso 4, Santa Catalina, La Victoria, ☎475-6537 or 476-1069, ≈475-6536.

German Embassy
Av. Arequipa 4210, Miraflores, 422-4919, ≈422-6475.

Irish Consulate
Santiago Acuña 135, Urb. Aurora, Miraflores, ☎445-6813, ≈242-3849.

Italian Embassy
Gregorio Escobedo 298, Jesús María, ☎463-2727 or 463-2728, ≈463-5717.

Spanish Embassy
Av. Jorge Basadre 498, San Isidro, ☎221-7704 or 221-7207, ≈440-2020.

Swedish Embassy
Camino Real 348, Piso 9, Torre Le Pillar, ☎421-3400 or 421-3421, ≈442-9547.

Swiss Embassy
Av. Salaberry 3240, Orrantia, San Isidro, ☎264-0305, ≈264-1319.

Airlines

Aero Condor
Jr. Juan de Arona 781, San Isidro, ☎441-1354.

AeroContinente
Av. Larco 123, Piso 2, Miraflores, ☎445-0535.

Javier Prado Oeste 640, San Isidro, ☎221-3449 or 221-3349.

AeroPerú
Av. José Pardo 605, Miraflores, ☎447-1990.

Garcilaso de la Vega 870, Lima Centro, ☎433-1341.

Aeropuerto Jorge Chávez, Callao, ☎574-7078.

Air Canada
Lord Nelson 128-A, Miraflores, ☎442-4541.

Air France
Av. José Pardo 601, Of. 601, Miraflores, ☎444-9285.

Aeropuerto Jorge Chávez, Callao, ☎574-5748 or 574-5750.

American Airlines
Juan de Arona 830, Piso 14-15, San Isidro, ☎442-8555.

Aeropuerto Jorge Chávez, Callao, ☎575-1806.

Avianca
Centro Comercial Boulevard Los Olivos, Av. Paz Soldán 225, Of. C-5 Mezzanine, San Isidro, ☎221-7530, www.avianca.com.

British Airways
Andalucía 174, Miraflores, ☎422-6600.

KLM
José Pardo 805, Piso 6, Miraflores, ☎242-1240.

Lufthansa
Jorge Basadre 1330, San Isidro, ☎442-4455.

Saeta
Andalucía 174, Miraflores, ☎442-4466.

Lan Chile
José Pardo 805, Piso 5, ☎241-5522.

Banks and Foreign Exchange Offices

Banco de Credito
Avenida Lampa 499, at the corner of Schell, Miraflores.

LAC Dollar
Jr. Camaná 779, Lima Centro.

Avenida La Paz 211, Miraflores.

Casa de Cambios Le Olivar
La Pinta 192, San Isidro.

There are a few **banks** and one **currency exchange office** at the airport.

Laundrettes

They charge by the kilo or by item.

Lavaquik
Av. Benevides 604, Miraflores.

Burbujitas
Porta 293, Miraflores.

 EXPLORING

Most travellers only spend two or three days in Lima before setting off for Cuzco, Nazca, Arequipa or Lake Titicaca. That isn't really long enough to explore the capital, because the various points of interest are spread far apart. The city is divided into many neighbourhoods, some older, some newer, but each with its own distinct character; the very best and the very worst are sometimes right next to each other. Lima Centro, San Isidro, Miraflores and Barranco are likely to be of greatest interest. You might also want to spend half a day visiting

LIMA

El Señor de los Milagros

Generations are born and die and the years and centuries roll past, but some things never change. Every year, on the 18th of October, millions of pilgrims in mauve-coloured ceremonial garb, candles and incense-burners in hand, have been coming to venerate and render thanks to the Señor de los Milagros, just as they have been doing since 1746. This cult actually dates as far back as 1655, the year an Angolan slave painted Christ on one of the walls of the Iglesia la Nazarenas. This was one of the few churches left standing after the earthquake of 1746, and its survival was hailed as a miracle.

Pueblo Libre and San Borja, home to the finest museums in Lima.

Lima Centro

The major tourist attractions are all located of the historic district of Lima Centro. Most of the churches in the old city date from the 17th century, and are among the few building left standing after the great earthquake of 1746. Though many of its historic structures have been destroyed, Lima Centro has still made it onto UNESCO's list of World Heritage Sites. In 1995, the municipal government launched a program to revitalize the historic centre, and the results have been encouraging so far. Most points of interest are clustered around Plaza de Armas and Plaza San Martín.

Plaza de Armas and Plaza San Martín

When it was first laid out, **Plaza de Armas** was a beautiful square where the viceroy and the municipal and religious authorities all had their seat of power. Since then, earthquakes and the massive increase in the city's population have taken their toll on this symbol of Spanish colonization, which is now considerably less impressive. Even so, Plaza de Armas is still of great historical interest. The presidential palace, cathedral and municipal government buildings surround it.

The huge baroque façade of the **Palacio del Gobierno ★**, on the north side of Plaza de Armas, was completed in 1938. The official residence of the current President of the Republic, Alberto Fujimori, is at the back, under heavy guard. Francisco Pizzaro once lived at this same location, and it was in front of the first building erected here that he was assassinated in 1541. Today, the changing of the guard is solemnly carried out in front of the palace from Monday to Saturday, at about 11:45am.

The **Catedral ★★** was designed by architect Francisco Becerra, who modelled it after the cathedral of Jaén, in Spain. Its enormous, ostentatious silhouette, distinguished by its huge twin towers, soars up into the sky on the east side of Plaza de Armas. Though it was consecrated in 1645, its architecture features a mixture of relatively modern styles, since it has been damaged repeatedly by earthquakes. In fact, just over a century after its inauguration, the cathedral was largely destroyed by Lima's first major earthquake. Its interior with three naves and a whole series of small side chapels is extremely austere. The first chapel on the right contains the remains of Francisco Pizarro himself. The cathedral also

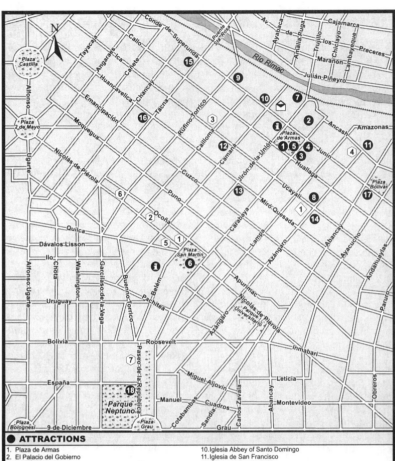

● ATTRACTIONS

1. Plaza de Armas
2. El Palacio del Gobierno
3. Catedral
4. Archbishop's Palace
5. Bronze Fountain
6. Plaza San Martín
7. Casa Aliaga
8. Palacio Torre Tagle
9. Casa de Osambela
10. Iglesia Abbey of Santo Domingo
11. Iglesia de San Francisco
12. Iglesia de San Agustín
13. Iglesia and Convento de la Merced
14. Iglesia de San Pedro
15. Iglesia de Santa Rosa de Lima
16. Iglesia de Las Nazarenas
17. Museo de la Casa de la Inquisición
18. Museo de Arte Italiano

◯ ACCOMMODATIONS

1. El Gran Hotel Bolívar
2. Familia Rodríguez
3. Hostal Europa
4. Hostal Roma
5. Hostal San Martín
6. Hotel Crillón
7. Hotel Sheraton

◇ RESTAURANTS

1. L'Eau Vive

Lima Centro

0   300   600m

LIMA

©ULYSSES

Los Balcones Limeños (The Balconies of Lima)

The splendid openwork balconies of the City of Kings are of Muslim and Mudejar (the Spanish version of Muslim art) design. Similar balconies can be found in Cairo and on Tenerife, the largest of the Canary Islands. Their main function was to protect their owners from the sweltering heat, but they also served the other, much subtler purpose of enabling women to watch what was happening on the street without being seen.

---

has a small museum of sacred art at the far end, on the left.

The **Archiepiscopal Palace ★★★**, right next to the cathedral, is sure to catch your eye. Its magnificent openwork balcony is worth a closer look, since it is made up of nearly 5,000 pieces of Nicaraguan cedar, held together without a single nail.

The **bronze fountain ★** in the centre of Plaza de Armas is the oldest structure on the square, dating all the way back to 1650.

Plaza de Armas is linked to **Plaza San Martín ★** by the narrow, crowded Jirón de la Unión. Plaza San Martín was built in 1921, some 100 years after General San Martín's declaration of independence. A bust of the general gazes at passersby from atop a column in the centre of the square, which is surrounded by neoclassical buildings.

Colonial Houses

From Plaza de Armas, head north on Jirón de la Unión, alongside the Palacio del Gobierno. You'll soon find yourself in front of the **Casa Aliaga ★★** *(Jr. de la Unión; visits must be arranged by Lima Tours, which has exclusive touring rights; ☎424-5110)*, built in honour of Jerónimo de Aliaga, one of Francisco Pizarro's comrades. Descendants of the original owners still live in this splendid example of colonial architecture, which

contains some elegant vestiges of the past, including what some claim to be the oldest ceiling in Lima.

The **Palacio Torre Tagle ★★★** *(Mon to Fri 9am to 5pm; Ucayli 358)*, south of Plaza de Armas, is a lovely specimen of colonial architecture that now serves as the Ministry of Foreign Affairs. Its façade is adorned with two ornately carved wooden balconies. The palace also has a lovely Andalusian-style courtyard, which the security guards posted at the entrance might let you have a peek at if you ask nicely. The building was completed in 1735 and was the home of José de Tagle y Bracho, a gentleman from northern Spain upon whom Philip V bestowed the title of Marquis.

Though it is not open to the public, the **Casa de Osambela ★★★** *(Conde de Superunda 298)*, sometimes referred to as the Casa Oquendo, is another fine example of late 18th-century Spanish colonial architecture, thanks to the five magnificent, finely worked balconies adorning its exterior walls. This was once the home of General San Martín.

Churches

The **Abbey of Santo Domingo ★★** *($3; Jr. Camaná; Mon to Sat 9am to 1pm and 3pm to 5pm)*, a block from the Plaza de Armas, stands on a piece of land granted to a Dominican friar named Valverde by Francisco Pizarro.

Valverde was a member of the expedition that captured Atahualpa in Cajamarca. Begun shortly after Lima was founded and completed toward the end of the 16th century, the church has three naves and an octagonal, rococo-style tower. Also noteworthy is its statue of Santa Rosa de Lima, the first New World saint and the patron saint of Lima. The monastery is among the oldest in town. The parlour has a magnificent coffered ceiling dating from the Renaissance, and the cloister is decorated with *azulejos* illustrating the life of St. Dominic.

The **Iglesia de San Francisco ★★★** *($2; every day 9:30am to 5:30pm; Jr. Lampa, at the corner of Ancash)* was designed by the Portuguese architect Constantino de Vasconcellos, except for the side portal, which is the work of Manuel de Escobar. Begun at the end of the 16th century and completed in the mid-17th, this church was one of the few to survive the earthquakes of 1687 and 1746.

Unfortunately, its elegant baroque façade, enhanced by two lovely stone towers rising proudly into the sky, has been tarnished by a large number of pigeons that make their nests there. This church is nonetheless one of the city's finest examples of 17th-century architecture and contains a number of ornately worked retables and paintings dating from colonial times. The galleries of the monastery, built in the 17th century, are decorated with *azulejos*. Most fascinating of all, however, are the gloomy catacombs that make up the crypt. Discovered in 1951, these passages are believed to contain the bones of some 70,000 people. Not for the claustrophobic! We strongly recommend taking the guided tour, which lasts about 45 minutes and will give you a good overview of the history and architecture of the church.

Founded in 1592, the **Iglesia de San Agustín ★** *(changing schedule; Ica and Camaná)*, west of Plaza de Armas, is distinguished by its superb **Churrigueresque façade ★★**, which is in fact its only attraction, since the rest of the original structure has been destroyed by earthquakes. The current, rather uninspired building dates from the late 18th century.

The **Iglesia y Convento de la Merced ★** *(changing schedule; Jr. Unión, at the corner of Huancavelica)* is where residents of the newly founded city of Lima celebrated Mass for the first time. Its baroque façade, as finely carved as a retable, is well worth seeing. The monastery contains a large number of religious paintings.

Built in 1624, the **Iglesia de San Pedro ★** *(every day 7am to 1pm and 4pm to 8pm; Jr. Ucayali)* was occupied by the Jesuits until they were expelled from the continent. Completed in 1638, this elegant baroque structure has a single nave and a number of small side chapels.

The unobtrusive **Iglesia de Santa Rosa de Lima ★** *(9:30am to 6pm; Jr. Tacna)* would be of little interest if it hadn't been built right near the house where Santa Rosa de Lima was born in 1586 (she died 31 years later, in 1617). Canonized in 1671, she was the first New World saint and is the patron saint of the Peruvian capital.

The **Iglesia de Las Nazarenas ★** *(Jr. Tacna, near the corner of Huancavelica)* is more noteworthy for its historic past than for its architecture. Small as it is, this church is very important to Peruvians, for whom it is inextricably linked with the annual *Señor de los Milagros* (see inset) procession.

LIMA

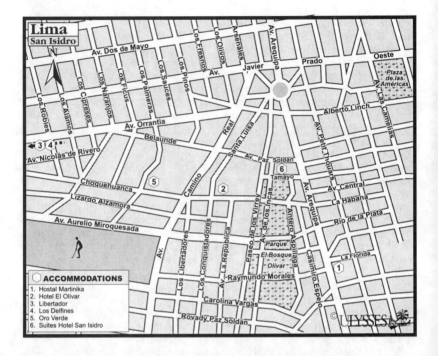

```
Lima
San Isidro
```

ACCOMMODATIONS
1. Hostal Martinika
2. Hotel El Olívar
3. Libertador
4. Los Delfines
5. Oro Verde
6. Suites Hotel San Isidro

Museums

Morbid curiosity attracts large numbers of visitors to the **Museo de la Casa de la Inquisición** ★★ *(free admission; Mon to Fri 9am to 1pm and 2:30pm to 5pm; Plaza Bolívar)*. The house was built when the Inquisition reached Peru. It used be home to sinister individuals who inflicted gruesome tortures on their victims, most of whom did not even know why they were being punished. A quick glance at the archaic instruments of torture displayed throughout makes it all too easy to imagine the sort of suffering they endured. The Inquisition began in Europe before spreading to South America, where it ushered in a very dark chapter in Peru's already tragic history. During this period of religious intolerance, it was common practice to force people to convert to Christianity. On your way in the museum, make sure to take a look at the magnificent panelled ceiling in one of the rooms on the right.

Who would have thought that you could find an Italian museum in a former Spanish colony? The **Museo del Arte Italiano** ★ *($1; Paseo de la República, ☎423-9932)*, located near Plaza San Martín, displays a large number of paintings by artists from Italy and elsewhere in Europe in a building with a lovely neoclassical façade.

Rimac

Though the city of Lima was founded in this neighbourhood in 1535, few interesting monuments have survived here.

Though you might not agree with certain local customs, bear in mind that bullfighting has deep roots in Peruvian culture and that corridas are part of the country's colonial heritage. It is every matador's dream to wave his cape at a bull in **Plaza de Acho** ★, the oldest bullfighting ring in the Americas, while a crowd of spectators cheer and shout *Viva*!

El Paseo de Agua is a lovely, tree-lined, cobbled street that leads to the **Iglesia de los Descalzos** ★, founded in the late 17th century. The baroque interior is decorated with a number of paintings by members of the *escuela cuzceña*.

San Isidro

San Isidro is a fairly modern neighbourhood with few real tourist attractions to speak of. One notable exception is **El Bosque Olivar** ★, a grove of majestic trees planted around 1560.

The **Museo Arqueológico Amano** ★ *(Retiro 160, ☎441-2909)* is a small, private museum containing pre-Inca artifacts, most notably objects made by Chancay Indians. By appointment only.

The **Huaca Pucllana** *($2; Tue to Sun 9am to 5pm, near Avenida Arequipa)* is a poorly restored pre-Inca adobe structure, which some say resembles a toad. If you use your imagination, it can look like just about anything!

Miraflores

The city's shopping malls, cafés, bars, theatres, cinemas and best restaurants are concentrated in this posh, lively neighbourhood located just under 10 kilometres from Plaza de Armas.

With its trees, flowers and giant statue of two lovers entwined in each other's arms, **El Parque del Amor** ★ looks like a big Spanish garden, with a view of the sea. Surprise, surprise, it is a very popular refuge for couples seeking to escape the hubbub of the city for a little while. A "longest kiss" contest is held here every year on Valentine's Day. Apparently, the official record is just over an hour.

The **Museo Enrico Poli** ★ *(Lord Cochrane 466, ☎422-2437)* is a small, private museum displaying pre-Columbian crafts. By appointment only.

Pueblo Libre

Pueblo Libre is not very interesting in and of itself, but it does have a few museums devoted to Peru's rich ancestral heritage, as well as something rarely found in urban areas these days: a zoo.

The **Museo de Arqueología y Antropología** ★★★ *($2; Tue to Sat 9am to 6pm; Plaza Bolívar, ☎463-5070)* covers Peruvian history from its origins to the modern era. Its various galleries enable visitors to familiarize themselves with the numerous cultures that gradually intermingled over the ages to form modern-day Peru. Almost 95% of the pieces on display are original; these include the famous Raimondi stela, the Tello obelisk (see p 227), intriguing, well-preserved mummies from Nazca, sumptuous Paracas fabrics, magnificent Moche and Chimú pottery and various Inca crafts. Also on exhibit are numerous models of pre-Columbian archaeological sites, including one of Machu Picchu. It is well worth paying a visit to this fascinating museum before exploring the historic sites of Peru.

The nearby **Museo Nacional de Historia** ★ *($1; Tue to Sat 10am to 6pm)*, set up inside the former home of

LIMA

● **ATTRACTIONS**

1. Parque del Amor

○ **ACCOMMODATIONS**

1. El Doral
2. El Pardo
3. Holiday Inn
4. Hospedaje Varnes
5. Hostal La Casa de los Sánchez

6. Hotel Colonial Inn
7. Hotel Residencial Huaychulo
8. Las Américas
9. Miraflores Park Plaza
10. Youth Hostel

◇ **RESTAURANTS**

1. Bircker Berner
2. Café Café
3. Café de la Paz
4. Café Haiti
5. El Rincón Gaucho

6. Govinda
7. La Costa Verde
8. La Rosa Nautica
9. Las Brujas de Cachiche
10. Tiendita Blanca

Simón Bolívar, displays paintings, furniture and clothing from the colonial era.

The **Museo Rafael Larco Herrera ★★★** *($5; Tue to Sat 9am to 6pm, Sun 9am to 1pm; Av. Bolívar, ☎461-1312)* has an impressive collection of *huacos*, a generic term for terracotta pottery. In all, some 80,000 pieces have been discovered during excavations – both authorized and unauthorized – in the many pre-Inca cemeteries throughout the coastal desert. Most are from the Mochica and Chimú eras. The objects on display reveal a remarkable attention to detail and offer a vivid glimpse of the day-to-day life of a forgotten era. The pottery comes in all different shapes, and some have a very distinctive, erotic quality that attracts visitors' attention.

The **zoo** *($2; every day 9am to 5pm; Parque de la Leyendas, ☎452-6913)* is a traditional facility with few areas where the animals can move about freely. It has a large number of animals from the Selva and the Sierra. If you won't be visiting Amazonia, you might want to take a look at a few snakes and other denizens of that dense, damp habitat. Unfortunately, the cages are not always well kept, and the health of

their occupants sometimes suffers as a result.

Callao

Thanks to its nearby military and industrial port, Callao, Lima is the only Andean capital on the shore. Located a few kilometres north of Lima, Callao has quite a history. During the prosperous years of colonization, the merchandise that Spanish galleons brought back to Spain passed through this port. Repeated pirate attacks led to the construction of imposing fortifications. Today, aside from a few museums and typical restaurants, there is nothing picturesque about Callao, whose streets are rather prowled by sailors and businessmen of dubious character.

Cameras and video cameras are not permitted inside the **Museo del Ejertcito ★** *($1; Mon to Sat 9am to 2pm; ☎290-532)*, where you can see a replica of the façade of the still extant colonial house in Arica where, during the Pacific War, Francisco Bolognesi told the Chileans that he would keep fighting until the bitter end, knowing full well that the battle was not going

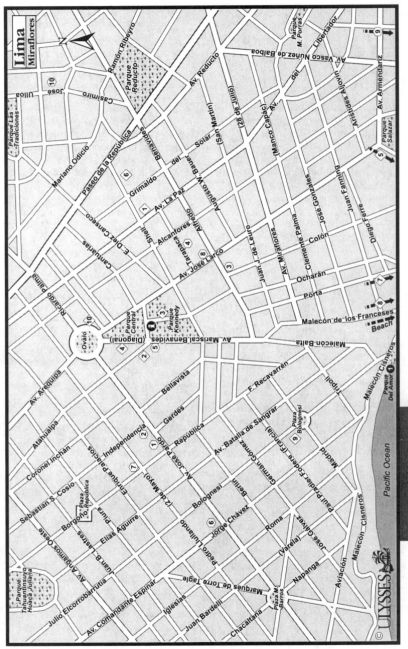

LIMA

Pacific Ocean

his way. An assortment of tanks, cannons, sabres and knives is also on display.

Other Attractions

Though its name means the Gold Museum, the **Museo de Oro** ★★★ *($5; every day noon to 7pm; Avenida de la Molina, ☎435-0791)* has a collection composed mainly of silver objects, since most gold items were melted down and shipped off to Spain to fill the royal coffers. This private museum is nonetheless impressive, and a guided tour is well worth your while, since it will help you understand the cultural and historic significance of the countless objects on display. There are a large number of Moche and Chimú crafts, as well as some sumptuous Paracas, Chancay and Inca fabrics. The museum is a perfect example of the systematic pillaging carried out by the *huaqueros* for over a century, since the vast majority of the items on exhibit were purchased from these despicable grave-robbers. The ground floor is devoted to an impressive and somewhat unsettling collection of weapons of all different sorts dating from all different periods, from the colonial era to the age of the Samurai to the World Wars.

Like the Museo de Arqueología y Antropología, the **Museo de la Nación** ★★★ *($4; Tue to Fri 9am to 5pm, Sat and Sun 10am to 5pm; Av. Javier Prado Este 2465, San Borja, ☎476-9890)* focuses on early Peruvian history. Its collection is much the same as that of the Museo de Arqueología y Antropología, only many of the pieces are copies. It also has models of various pre-Columbian archaeological sites (including a lovely one of Machu Picchu), which are fun to look at. In 1997, the museum added a fascinating gallery devoted to the tomb of the

Señor of Sipán. A must for anyone who won't have a chance to visit the north coast.

Barranco

Come nightfall in the seaside neighbourhood of Barranco, there is a certain je ne sais quoi in the air that piques the imagination of romantic souls and lends a mysterious quality to the nocturnal activities of local artists and performers.

El Puente de los Supiros ★, a wooden bridge spanning a small street, will charm romantics – and anyone else willing to play along. According to local custom, you have to hold your breath and make a wish when you cross it.

 # ACCOMMODATIONS

Most travellers on a limited budget stay in one of the many small, inexpensive hotels in the historic district, **Lima Centro**. Generally speaking, most places around Plaza San Martín and Plaza de Armas are noisy, and unsavoury characters sometimes lurk about on the neighbouring streets. When the city was swept by a wave of terrorism, visitors fled to **Miraflores**. Over the past few years, luxury hotels have been sprouting up left and right in the posh residential neighbourhood of **San Isidro**, and most business travellers with big expense accounts stay in these establishments.

Lima Centro

The **Familia Rodríguez** *($10; sb; Nicolás de Piérola 730, ☎423-6465)*, right near Plaza San Martín, is an inexpensive option for backpackers. The rooms are basic but relatively clean and the staff is friendly and helpful.

The **Hostal España** *($10; pb, sb, ℜ; Jr. Azángaro 105, ☎428-5546)*, located a block from the Hostal Europa (see below), is backpacker central. The rooms are generally quite clean and safe, and are laid out around a lovely courtyard that summons up images of the city's glorious past. Old paintings hang on the walls, the occasional bird flies overhead, and the atmosphere is always lively. The rooms get snapped up quickly, so it is wise to make reservations.

The **Hostal Europa** *($10; pb, sb; Jr. Ancash 376, ☎427-7576)*, located right next to the Iglesia de San Francisco, caters mainly to travellers on a shoestring budget. Some of its rooms are on the gloomy side, others inviting, and a number have their own bath. Those at the front are the best; some even have a balcony. The friendly staff will be glad to help in any way they can.

Located near the Iglesia de San Agustín, the **Hostal Roma** *($15; sb; Ica 326, ☎427-7576)* is another good choice if the places listed above are full. It costs a few dollars more, but the rooms are clean and decent and the service is friendly.

A bit more expensive but also a bit more comfortable, the **Hostal San Martín** *($30; Nicolás de Piérola 882; pb, 5; ☎428-5337)* is located just steps away from Plaza San Martín. The rooms are simply decorated, but the place is spotless. Good value for this category of accommodations.

Also near Plaza San Martín, the **San Agustín Riviera** *($80; ctv, pb, hw, ℜ; Av. Garcilaso de la Vega 981, ☎424-9438)* celebrated its 30-years

anniversary with a facelift during our stay in Lima. It is a six-story building with about 300 well-appointed rooms.

El Gran Hotel Bolívar *($115 bkfst incl.; pb, ℜ, hw, tv, ◯; Plaza San Martín, ☎428-7672 or 428-7673, ⌐428-7674)*, which faces onto Plaza San Martín, was the first luxury hotel to be built in Lima. Once the finest hotel in Peru, it was hard hit by terrorism, which forced its clientele to find somewhere else to stay. Its lobby is undeniably impressive, with its high ceilings and immense stained-glass dome, but most of the rooms off its long hallways have seen better days. Only the suites offer a view of Plaza San Martín. In spite of all that, the hotel restaurant has managed to maintain its excellent reputation and serves a delectable *pisco sour*.

The **Hotel Crillón** *($130; pb, hw, tv, ℜ; Av. Nicolás de Piérola, ☎428-3290, ⌐426-5920)* celebrated its 50th anniversary in November 1997, but it looks like it is stuck in the 1970s. The 500 rooms on 20 stories, have not aged well and are in serious need of some freshening up. On the bright side, there is a lovely terrace with a panoramic view of the city on the top floor.

From the outside, the **Hotel Sheraton** *($180; pb, hw, ctv, ℜ, ≈; Paseo de la República 170, ☎433-3320, 800-325-3535 within the USA or Canada, ⌐433-5844, www.ittsheraton.com)* looks more like a prison than a hotel. Ironically, the municipal jail once stood on this very site, full of prisoners waiting to be tried across the street in what is still the Courthouse. Inside, however, there are few faults to be found with the 300 rooms in this 19-story building. The high rates are justified by a whole slew of amenities, including a casino, a Japanese restaurant, an international restaurant, three tennis courts, a pool and a fitness centre.

Miraflores

The **Youth Hostel** *($10; cb; Casimirio, Ulloa 328, ☎446-5488)* is located near the Paseo de la República and offers the cheapest accommodations you're likely to find in Miraflores. It has shared rooms and tends to attract a rather bohemian clientele. Perfect for anyone travelling on a shoestring.

The **Hospedaje Varnes** *($35; pb, tv; Jr. Tarata 256, ☎242-7850 or 444-0850)* has only seven rooms, which are small but clean, safe, well-located and inexpensive by Lima standards.

The **Hotel Residencial Huaychulo** *($60 bkfst incl.; pb, hw, ℜ, ctv; Av. 2 de Mayo 494, ☎241-3130)*, just steps away from Avenida Larco, has quiet, simple rooms and a friendly staff.

🏖 For the same amount, you can stay at the **Hostal La Casa de los Sánchez** *($60; tv, hw, pb, ℜ; Av. Oscar Benavides 354, ☎241-7642 or 446-4944, ⌐445-2738)*, which faces onto Parque Kennedy near the Ovalo de Miraflores and has cozy, comfortable rooms. Some have a balcony, but they're a bit noisier.

🏖 With its old windows and balconies, the yellow and white façade of the **Hotel Colonial Inn** *($70; pb, tv; Comandante Espinar 310, ☎241-7471, ⌐445-7587, www.alignet.com/colonialinn)* evokes the glorious past of the City of Kings. Its 40 rooms, of various sizes, are clean and safe but not as elegant as the façade.

The **El Doral** *($90 bkfst incl.; pb, hw, ℜ, ≈; Av. José Pardo 486, ☎447-6305, ⌐446-344)* has a great location but is a bit dated. It has clean, comfortable, safe, well-equipped, nondescript rooms and a small rooftop pool and terrace.

If you don't mind loosening your purse strings a bit, opt for the year-old **Boulevard** *($120 bkfst incl.; pb, hw, ctv, ℜ, ≈; Av. José Pardo 771, ☎444-6564, ⌐444-6602)*. It offers more or less the same level of comfort as the nearby El Doral but is much newer and more modern and also has a small fitness centre to stay in shape.

The **Holiday Inn** *($150 bkfst incl.; Av. Benavides 300, at the corner of Colón, ctv, hw, pb, ☎242-3200, ⌐242-3193)* is a symbol of the American invasion of Peru. It has 15 floors with a total of about 150 clean, modern rooms decorated in an unimaginative fashion. A good choice for those who don't want to feel too far out of their element.

The **El Pardo** *($165; pb, hw, ctv, ℜ, ≈; Independencia 141, ☎447-0283 or 444-2236, ⌐444-2171, postmaster@pardohot.com.pe)* is conveniently located right in the centre of Miraflores and has functional, modern facilities, including a pool, conference rooms, a whirlpool bath, a nonsmoking floor and a local travel agency. The courteous staff scores high points with guests.

The **Las Américas** *($195; pb, hw, ctv, ℜ, ≈; Av. Benavides 415, ☎445-9494, ⌐444-1137)* was designed specifically for business travellers, and its rooms and amenities are those of a high-end hotel. Courteous, attentive service.

🏖 If you've got the money to spend, treat yourself to a stay at the **Miraflores Park Plaza** *($220; hw, ctv, pb;*

Av. Malecón de la Reserva 1035,
☎*242-3000,* ≈*242-3393,*
www.mira-park.com), a luxurious hotel
complex whose rooms all offer a view
of the sea. Upon entering the hotel,
you'll find yourself in front of a huge
and impressive spiral staircase, which
forms a lovely visual ensemble with the
vast library. Next to the reception desk,
there is an English bar with panelled
walls and a pool table overlooking the
room.

San Isidro

If you want to stay in San Isidro
without breaking your budget, head to
the **Hostal Martinika** *($40, ctv, pb, hw;
3701 Av. Arequipa, at the corner of
Florida,* ☎*221-4785,* ≈*422-3094,
martink@telematic.edu.pe),* which is
one of the best deals in town in its
category. Built about two years ago, it
is located about 10 minutes by foot
from Miraflores, right near the French
consulate. Its rooms are of various
sizes but are all spotless, safe and well-
appointed, with comfortable beds and
good showers. The hotel also offers
24-hour room service, something you
won't find often in *hostales* in this
category. If you feel like spending a bit
more, you can stay in the suite, which
is very spacious and has a whirlpool
bath and a small balcony. The friendly
staff will be happy to help you in any
way they can. On the down side,
Avenida Arequipa is a busy street, and
the noise of the traffic might bother
you if you're a light sleeper. Then
again, peace and quiet is hard to come
by in Lima.

La Posada del Inca *($125 bkfst incl.;
ctv, hw, pb, ℜ; Av. Libertadores 450,
www.posadas.com.pe),* the newest
luxury hotel in Lima, has 50 large,
comfortable, well-appointed rooms.

As indicated by its name, the
9-story **Suites Hotel San Isidro** *($140;
ctv, hw, ℜ, ≈, △; Av. La Paz Soldán
167,* ☎*221-1108 or 221-2209,*
≈*221-1107, suites@amauta.rcp.net.pe)*
is an all-suite hotel. All 54 units are
elegant, immaculate and equipped with
a kitchenette. Guests have their choice
of pillows – feather, water,
hypoallergenic, etc. Foreign newspa-
pers are available, and the hotel will
even print the cover page of your favourite newspaper from the Internet
and slide it under your door before you
wake up. The staff is extremely well-
trained.

Tastefully furnished with antiques, the
lobby of the **Libertador** *($150; pb, hw,
ctv, ℜ; Los Eucaliptos 550,*
☎*421-6666,* ≈*442-3011,
www.libertador.com.pe)* is absolutely
charming. Don't get your hopes up too
high, though: the rooms are clean, safe
and decently furnished, but you'd expect more for the price.

Just over five years old, the **Hotel
El Olívar** *($220; ctv, hw, ℜ, ≈; Pancho
Fierro 194, El Olívar,* ☎*441-1454,*
≈*434-4434, ventas@elolivar.com.pe)*
was named for the olive trees in the
park in front of it, some of which were
planted a century ago. Unlike other
luxury hotels, the El Olívar is low and
wide rather than high and narrow.
That, along with the unparalleled gra-
ciousness of its staff, will make you
forget all about the chilly atmosphere
and snobbism that generally characterize high-end hotels. Its amenities, however, are those of a top-rate hotel: a
fitness centre, a whirlpool bath, a
sauna, a pool, a bar and a large terrace
can all be found on the top floor, and
the spacious, impeccably appointed
rooms are all equipped with a modem
hookup for guests with laptop comput-
ers. The clientele consists mainly of

scurrying businesspeople, cell phone in one hand, briefcase in the other.

Diagonal to the Libertador, the **Los Delfines** *($220; ctv, hw, ≈, ℜ, ◁; Calle Los Eucaliptos, ☎442-9750, ⇨421-3448)* is one of the city's newest luxury hotels. It was named after the two friendly dolphins who have been frolicking about in its giant aquarium since late 1997. Their captivity has been the cause of a great deal of controversy, but the issue should be resolved soon. As for the hotel itself, it has an excellent staff, 207 rooms on 13 floors, and a fitness centre.

The luxurious **Oro Verde** *($220; hw, ctv, ≈, ℜ, ◁; Centro Empresarial Camino Real, ☎421-4400, ⇨421-4422, peov@ibm.net)* is one of the recent additions to Lima's hotel strip. With its three panoramic elevators, two non-smoking floors, Italian restaurant, Swiss restaurant, café, bakery, fitness centre, outdoor pool and attentive staff, who will do everything in their power to make your stay as pleasant as possible, this is definitely one of the finest hotels in Peru. There is a piano bar where guests can relax while nibbling on a sandwich and sipping an excellent *pisco sour*. Business travellers will also find everything they need here: computers, faxes, etc. The rooms are impeccable: bright, spacious, charming and well-appointed.

RESTAURANTS

Lima boasts the finest restaurants in Peru. Fish and seafood naturally get top billing, but dishes to suit other tastes are also available. Though most of these places are very expensive, you can always find one within your budget. Generally speaking, the best restaurants in Lima, which attract large numbers of tourists, are in San Isidro

and Miraflores. There are a few in other parts of town as well, and if you have a little time to spare they are well worth the trip.

Lima Centro

L'Eau Vive *($; Ucayali 370, ☎427-5612)*, across from the Palacio Torre Tagle, is definitely one of the most interesting restaurants in Lima. The food is freshly prepared by French nuns, who sing *Ave Maria* every night at 10pm. There is an inexpensive *menu du jour*, and the profits go to charity.

It isn't hard to guess what's on the menu at the **Pizzeria Americana** *($; 520 Nicolás de Piérola)*. You got it: pizza, pizza and more pizza, prepared in a variety of ways. Young clientele and laid-back atmosphere.

Despite its rather unsettling name, **Buena Muerte** *($-$$; Jr. Paruro, ☎427-3576)* is a simple restaurant that serves excellent *ceviches*.

Wa Lok *($-$$; Paruro 864, ☎427-2656)* serves good, affordable Asian cuisine. If you're just looking for a quick snack, a wide assortment of desserts and pastries is also available.

La Bodega Queirolo S.A. *($$; Calle Camana 900, ☎425-0421)*, located near Plaza San Martín, is a picturesque bar and restaurant where local residents come to eat simple Creole dishes. Countless bottles of alcohol are displayed on the walls and two fans spin lazily overhead on humid days.

San Isidro

Black and white is the theme of the decor at **C'est si bon** *($;*

Av. Comandante Espínar 663, ☎446-9310), which serves tasty crêpes and excellent cakes. Friendly service.

If you're hankering for some ice cream or sorbet, head straight to **Dolce Freddo** *($; Av. Comandante Espínar 800, ☎447-0689)*, which also serves milkshakes and other sweets.

🦐 **Govinda** *($; Schell 630)*, located a few steps away from the Bircker Berner (see below), has an unpretentious decor, a relaxed atmosphere and a menu that changes daily. Though the Hare Krishnas' religious views don't appeal to everyone, their tastes are hard to dispute when it comes to vegetarian cuisine. Unpretentious decor and relaxed atmosphere.

Right near the Hostal Martinika, **Herber Baruch** *($; Av. Petit Thouars 3798)* is a small, well-lit café with a modern decor, which serves sandwiches, empanadas, cakes and, of course, coffee.

🦐 The **Bircker Berner** *($-$$; Schell 598, ☎444-4250)*, set up inside an old house, is the best health-food restaurant in Lima. It has an affordable *menu du jour*, and the à la carte menu includes a number of tofu-based vegetarian dishes. There is also a small shop that sells health-related products on the premises.

🦐 The **Café Café** *($-$$; Calle Martín Olaya 250)* is a lively, modern place that caters to a young clientele who comes here to practice the art of conversation to the sounds of trendy music. On the menu: milkshakes, a large selection of coffee, and alcoholic beverages like whisky and cognac.

🦐 The **Café de la Paz** *($-$$; Calle Lima 351, ☎241-6043)* faces onto Parque Kennedy. It has a prix fixe menu that changes from day to day and serves an excellent, potent *pisco sour*. At the end of your meal, you'll get a bookmark with a message of peace written on it.

The **Café Haiti** *($-$$; Diagonal 160)*, located next to the Pacifico cinema, is a pleasant place that welcomes a non-stop stream of customers from morning to night. The food is simple and the service unpretentious. The terrace is the perfect place to start off or finish the day.

The **Café Manolo** *($-$$; Av. Larco 608)* is a long, narrow place with a few tables looking right out onto the street and a counter displaying all different kinds of hearty sandwiches.

🦐 The **Café Olé** *($-$$; Pancho Fierro 115)*, a few steps from the Hotel El Olívar, opens at 7am for breakfast, which you can eat inside in relatively modern surroundings or outside in the shade of a big parasol. The café also has a standard à la carte lunch and dinner menu.

The **News Café** *($-$$; Santa Luisa 110, ☎421-6278)* doesn't open until noon. Its glass façade displays a wide selection of delicious cakes for sale, which you can wash down with a good *café con leche*.

The **Tiendita Blanca** *($-$$; Av. Larco 111, ☎445-9797 or 445-1412)*, a Swiss café with a cozy decor, stands at the edge of the Ovalo de Miraflores. You can linger over a slice of cake or a soup, followed by a cup of coffee, or sit outside on the pretty little terrace and sip a glass of wine or write a postcard.

LIMA

If you're looking for delicious fish or seafood, **Alfresco** *($$; Santa Luisa, ☎422-8915)* is just the place. The food is always fresh and carefully prepared. If you like a little variety in your diet, order one of the restaurant's pasta dishes, which makes a wonderful accompaniment to the seafood specialties that form the bulk of the menu.

The **Casa de Don Martín** *($$; Av. Jorge Chávez 400; Jorge Chávez is the continuation of Comandante Espinar; ☎444-5887 or 445-6550)* is an old colonial house with a small terrace. This friendly restaurant has a fixed-price menu ($13 per person) that includes an appetizer, a main dish, a dessert, a *pisco sour* and coffee. *Lomo saltado*, *arroz con mariscos* and *arroz con pato* all appear on the menu.

You can relive the past at **El Gato Pardo** *($$; Pardo 547, ☎421-2222)*, where the jukebox plays old hits at random. The menu consists of a variety of pasta, meat and fish dishes.

Norky's *($$; Cuadra 2 of Av. Pardo, ☎242-7652)*, located just steps away from the Ovalo de Miraflores, is a huge, well-lit, modern restaurant that serves a variety of meat specialties. A number of traditional Peruvian dishes appear on the menu, including an excellent *lomo saltado*. You can top off your meal with a slice of homemade cake. Professional service.

The **Chifa Fungkuan Garden** *($$; 802 Av. Los Conquistadors, ☎441-0181)* is located on busy Avenida Los Conquistadors. You can eat inside or outside on the inviting, sheltered patio in the courtyard. One of the specialties of the house is *las bolitas de langostinos molidos*, a dish consisting of puréed scampi balls sautéed with vegetables and served in oyster sauce. The soups are excellent, and the Chinese noodle dishes are delectable. Polite, unpretentious service.

Astrid et Gaston *($$$; Cantuarias 175, ☎444-1496)* combines delicious French recipes with local Peruvian flavours. The *conchas negras*, *magret de canard* and steak tartare all come highly recommended. For a sweet finish, make sure to try one of the elegantly presented desserts, like the sorbet. The service is impeccable and the food consistently excellent.

El Rincón Gaucho *($$$; Parque Salazar, ☎447-4778)* is a favourite with carnivores. You can choose your own piece of meat from a selection of precut beef, lamb, pork and chicken, or an assortment of sausages that the chef will grill for you. This restaurant might move to another space right nearby, a little closer to the sea.

El Señorio de Sulco *($$$; Malecón Cisneros 1470, at the end of Av. Pardo, ☎441-0389)* is our favourite restaurant in Lima, and scores equally high in all categories – ambiance, decor, cuisine and service. A giant quipu, masks representing the various cultures of modern-day Peru, dried flowers and peppers hanging from the ceiling, wooden chairs with leather seats, colourful wooden dishes, live piano music to accompany your meal of unparalleled Creole cuisine, and a view of the sea that stretches all the way to the horizon (weather permitting)... this restaurant has all the right ingredients for a real feast that will delight all the senses.

I Vitrali *($$$; Pancho Fierro 194, El Olívar, ☎441-1454)*, in the Hotel El Olívar, cooks up excellent, homemade, four-cheese and mushroom lasagna as well as a slew of local specialties, including *ceviches* and *sancochados*, served with a smile by its invariably friendly staff.

🦀 **José Antonio** *($$$; Calle Bernado Moneagudo 200, ☎264-0188 or 264-3284)* caters mainly to businesspeople, who come here to enjoy traditional dishes like *anticuchos de corazón* and *papas rellenas*. In many people's opinion, this wonderful restaurant serves the best Creole cuisine in town. The decor is plush, the service professional and the food excellent – and you pay for what you get.

🦀 In many connoisseurs' opinion, **La Costa Verde** *($$$; on the beach, ☎441-4084)* is the finest restaurant in Lima. It has managed to maintain the same level of excellence for over 25 years now. Located on the beach, it serves a lavish – and lucrative ($60 per person) – buffet that deserves to win the world record for the widest selection of dishes. Just the place for visitors with deep pockets who are seeking a memorable gastronomic experience.

🦀 Who would have thought you could find a bit of Switzerland in a city like Lima? Swiss chalet-style **La Fondue** *($$$; Centro Empresarial Camino Real, ☎421-4400)*, is located in back of the Oro Verde, a German-Swiss hotel. The cheese fondue naturally comes highly recommended, but you should also make sure to try the *raclette*, a Valais specialty. The wine list is extensive, and you'll even find a few bottles from the cantons of Vaud and Valais.

La Rosa Náutica *($$$; on the beach, ☎447-0057)*, on the waterfront near La Costa Verde, is built on piles, with a long footbridge leading to it. The emphasis, naturally, is on fish and seafood, and you can gaze out at the roll-

ing waves through the big picture windows while savouring some *pescado a la plancha*, *ceviche* or *langostina*. Perfect for an intimate dinner for two.

🦀 **Las Brujas de Cachiche** *($$$; Av. Bolognesi 460, ☎444-5310)* is a magnificent old house that has been converted into one of the finest restaurants in town. The imaginative menu consists of a variety of local specialties, which are served by a discreet, efficient staff. *Lomo Saltado*, *tiraditos*, *lenguado* and *arroz con mariscos* are just a few of the dishes you can sample here.

For innovative, attractively presented cuisine served in a traditional decor, head to the **Royal** *($$$; Av. Prescott 231, ☎421-0874 or 422-9547)*, which has a buffet ($30 per person) as well as an à la carte menu with all sorts of Asian specialties, such as *el tofo frito al aji*, *el pato saltado con verduras* and *las unas de cangrejo*. The prices here shouldn't turn you off.

Barranco

🦀 Located right near the Puente de los Supiros, **El Otro Sitio** *($$; Jirón Sucre 317, ☎477-2413)* is laid out inside a magnificent colonial house, and the owners have put a lot of work into the decor. Windows adorned with stained glass, pastel-coloured walls and magnificent, original fabric made by the Paracas, a pre-Colombian culture, are among the decorative elements. One room has tables, chairs, ashtrays, bottles, glasses and a "floor" on its ceiling! If you're in the mood to dine alfresco, you can sit on the lovely terrace, which is shaded by two big umbrellas. The menu includes *ceviche*, *aji de gallina* and various other succulent local specialties.

LIMA

Pueblo Libre

🦐 Before visiting the Museo Arqueológico, stop by the picturesque **Antigua Taberna Queirolo** *($$; Gral Vivanco, at the corner of San Martín)*, a long, narrow place where you can enjoy simple food made with the freshest ingredients. It's best to show up early: once the day's dishes run out, there isn't much to eat here.

If you've been stuffing yourself with fish before coming to Lima, you might want to try the **Granja del Abuelo** *($$; Av. Salaberry 3580, Magdalena, ☎264-2016 or 264-0233)*, which specializes in *pollos a la Brasa*. Take a seat on the terrace, where you can watch the chickens on the spit slowly turning over the fire until they are roasted to perfection.

🦐 **Shiac** *($$; Calle Pablo Bermúdez 252, Jesús María, ☎423-5172 or 431-3990)* means "fish", so no need to wonder what's on the menu. The restaurant has about 10 wooden tables in a well-lit but cramped space, where guests enjoy delicious seafood and tasty fish prepared in the manner of their choice. After sampling the excellent *ceviche*, try the *leche de tigre*.

  ENTERTAINMENT

When you hear a name like **Delirium** *(near Parque Municipal, Barranco)*, you can't help but think of loud music and a raucous crowd in a smoky atmosphere, and that's exactly what you get here.

If you'd like to have drinks while gazing out at the sea, head to **El Alcantilado** *(near the Puente de los Supiros,*

Barranco), whose pretty balcony is the perfect place for a quiet conversation. Retro music and laid-back atmosphere.

El Ekeko *($5; Avenida Grau 266, Barranco)*, near Plaza Municipal, is the perfect place to have a drink or sip a cup of coffee while enjoying some live modern Latin music.

Johann Sebastian Bach *(Av. Grau 687)* has a clientele of regulars – an intellectual crowd that comes here to talk and philosophize about everything under the sun to the sounds of classical music.

La Estación *(Pedro de Osma 112, Barranco)* attracts a motley crowd of young Peruvian students and tourists.

Set up inside a colonial house, **La Noche** *($5; Calle Bolognesi 307)* hosts live shows and shows videos. Tourists come here to exchange travel stories over a pitcher of beer.

Las Brisas del Titicaca *($10; near Plaza Bolognesi)* is a lively *peña* that presents folk dancing performances from the various regions of Peru.

If you want to overcome some inhibitions, head to **Metropolis** *(Av. 2 de Maya 1545, San Isidro)* for a night of karaoke.

A young, energetic crowd packs into **The Edge** *($10; Avenida Larco)* to dance to pop music.

Theatre

El Teatro Municipal *(Ica 300, ☎428-2303)* and **El Teatro Segura** *(Huancavelica 261, ☎427-7427)* present classic and contemporary plays.

Movie Theatres

Alcazar:
Santa Cruz 814, Miraflores,
☎422-6345.

El Pacífico:
Avenida José Pardo, Miraflores,
☎445-6990.

Jockey Plaza, Moterrico.

SHOPPING

If you miss the big, modern shopping malls back home, head to the **Jockey Plaza** *(Monterrico)*, which could hold its own any day against its North American and European counterparts. Its stores sell international brands and it has four modern movie theatres.

The **Mercado Indio** *(Av. Petit Thouars 5495, Miraflores)* has a large assortment of wooden and metal handicrafts, as well as all sorts of knickknacks, colourful woolen clothing, scarves and a whole slew of other interesting travel trophies to bring back home.

Bookstores

La Casa Verde
(Pancho Fierro 130, right near the Hotel El Olívar). Latin American literature and beautiful art books.

Libreria Epoca
(Av. Pardo 399, Miraflores, ☎447-8907). Small selection of travel guides.

The South American Explorer's Club (see p 102) Good selection of used travel guides.

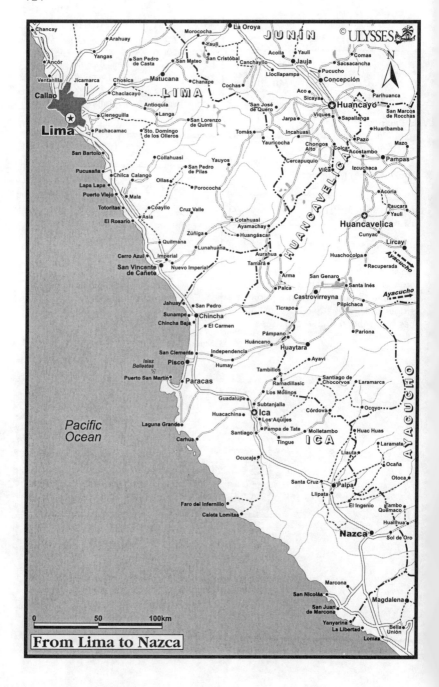

From Lima to Nazca

0   50   100km

LIMA TO NAZCA

Before flying to Cuzco, the former capital of the Inca Empire, some visitors travel south of Lima to learn more about the fascinating pre-Inca civilizations that have contributed to making Peru what it is today.

In the coastal region south of Lima, the silence is broken by the wind which seems to transmit the mysteries of the forgotten civilizations of Paracas and Nazca. After passing the last *pueblos jovenes* on the southern limits of Lima, the Pan American Highway comes to a roadsign indicating the way to the sacred ruins of **Pachacamac**. Then it runs along a strip of beaches which are very popular with Peruvians but not with tourists, particularly during the summer months, from October to January. These beaches don't have much in the way of facilities, but are notable for the high cold waves that crash relentlessly against the shore. A few people drown here every year, underestimating the force of the undertow.

The Pan American Highway continues to round the beaches as it makes its way through the arid and desolate landscape. Farther south, it cuts through the desert to the small village of **Pisco**, and then **Paracas**, which is where boats leave the jetty for the offshore **Islas Ballestas**. If you stay a few more days, you can visit the **Reserva Nacional Paracas**. The southbound highway then passes a series of oases, sand dunes and lunar landscapes, ultimately reaching **Ica**. Vineyards and a very interesting local museum exhibiting the cultural riches of the Paracas and Nazca civilizations make a brief stop here worthwhile. Ica lies in the middle of a wine-growing region that produces the country's national beverage, *Pisco Sour*, a drink that is in certain respects similar to Pinot des Charentes. An absolute must farther south is **Nazca**, a town primarily known for its mysterious geoglyphs etched on a giant scale in the coastal desert. Nazca is the last stop after Pisco, Paracas and Ica, on a standard tour heading south from Lima. The highway continues farther south through the small villages of Chala and Camana before leading inland to the city of Arequipa.

FINDING YOUR WAY AROUND

Pachacamac

By Bus

Buses leave Lima for Pachacamac from Avenida Montevideo, at the corner of Ayacucho. The fare for the one-hour trip is about 60¢.

Pucusaña and San Vincente de Cañete

By Bus

There are frequent departures from Lima to Cañete, via Pucusaña. The two-hour trip to Cañete costs about $2.

Chincha and Pisco

By Bus

The buses that travel to Pisco stop at Chincha, and most of them take just under 3 hours to make the complete trip. Note, however, that some buses drop passengers off by the Pan American Highway, far from the village of Pisco, and proceed south without entering the village itself. The fare is approximately $5.

Paracas

By Bus

Some buses take passengers directly from Lima to Paracas, while others drop them off in Pisco. Several buses travel from Pisco to Paracas; the trip takes a little under 30 minutes for the modest sum of 40¢.

Ica

By Bus

All the buses that travel from Lima to Nazca stop at Ica. The trip takes about 6 hours for the sum of $6.

Nazca

By Bus

Many buses go from Lima to Nazca. The trip lasts about 7 hours and costs $6 to $7.

Huacachina

By Bus

Buses run from Plaza de Armas, in Ica, to Huacachina for the modest sum of 45¢.

PRACTICAL INFORMATION

Pisco

Telecommunications

There is a telephone on Plaza de Armas.

Bank

The Banco de Credito is located on Plaza de Armas. Visa credit card holders can obtain cash advances here.

Excursion Agencies

A few agencies on Calle San Francisco near the *Ormeño* bus terminal offer excursions to the Islas Ballestas for about $7 per person.

Paracas Tours
San Francisco 257, ☎533-630 or 665-547.

Ica

Bank

The Banco de Credito is on Plaza de Armas. Visa credit card holders can obtain cash advances here.

Nazca

Bank

The Banco de Credito is located at Jr. Lima 495. Visa credit card holders can obtain cash advances here, as well.

Post Office

The post office is located at Jr. Lima 816, near the Banco de Credito.

Internet Access

The Hotel Alegría (see p 140) Has one computer hooked up to the Internet, which you can surf for a few dollars.

Excursion Agencies

Alegría Tours
Jr. Lima 168, ☎522-444, ⇋523-775, alegriatours@hotmail.com.

Alegría Tours organizes conventional excursions in the Nazca region, as well as some around Ica and Paracas. The owner has his own fleet of small planes and flies passengers over the Nazca lines. The agency also takes clients to the Chauchilla cemetery, the aqueducts and the *Paredones*. Tours visit the Museo Regional and the vineyards in the Ica region, and the Islas Ballestas and the Reserva Nacional Paracas around Paracas. The agency also organizes excursions to the Reserva Pampas Galeras and the Ronquillo hot springs. The staff is competent and speaks several languages, including English. The agency belongs to the owner of the Hotel Alegría (see p 140) in Nazca, and has been in operation for a long time.

EXPLORING

Pachacamac

The Pachacamac ruins lie about 30 kilometres from Lima and consist of some 15 terraced adobe pyramids, most of which are in bad shape or half

The Sea Otter and the Penguin

The sea otter has smaller ears, better defined pectoral flippers and a longer neck than the seal. Weighing in at 200 kilograms, the dominant male marks his territory, mates with many females who live there and generally lords it there until he is vanquished by a stronger male.

The black-and-white-feathered penguin is a loveable little web-footed bird that can reach 40 centimetres in height. This flightless species swims quickly and gracefully through the cold currents of the Pacific. The sea otter, the seal and the penguin all inhabit the Islas Ballestas.

engulfed in sand. The visit to the ruins will probably appeal most to people who are interested in ancient civilizations, because the site itself is fairly dull and rather disappointing. To fully appreciate the tour, it is best to be accompanied by a guide, because the religious significance of the ruins requires a thorough explanation. Pachacamac roughly translates as "Reformer of the Earth". The site was an important place of pilgrimage before the arrival of the Spanish.

One of the only pyramids that can be explored is the Temple of the Sun, named by the Incas, who were the last people to reside here before the Spanish conquest. This temple consists of four tiered terraces facing west, three of which are discernible and afford magnificent views of the sea and the islands that loom up off shore.

Like other Peruvian attractions, a very romantic legend is associated with these islands. Long, long ago, a nobleman fell in love with a beautiful young woman who refused to marry. One day, he decided to disguise himself as a beggar and hide in a tree under which the young woman had stopped for a moment. A fruit (*lucuma*) suddenly dropped at her feet; she picked it up and ate it. Some time later, she became pregnant. When the news broke, the young woman's father insisted on knowing who the future child's father was. After the woman gave birth, her father gathered the young men of the village together, including the man disguised as a beggar, so that the son could identify his father. The son unexpectedly ignored all the fine-looking men and stopped before the beggar. His mother, blushing with shame, picked her son up in her arms and dashed off into the sea. The beggar raced after them removing his old rags, but was never to reach them, for mother and son were magically transformed into a large island that can now be seen on the horizon.

The **Templo de la Mama**, or Templo de la Luna can also be seen in the distance. This temple was built by the Incas and stored the vestals.

A Brief History

After overthrowing Atahualpa in Cajamarca in 1533, Francisco Pizarro chose his half bother, Hernando, to lead an expedition to Pachacamac to seize its treasures. After several long days' march south along the coast, the Spanish finally reached Pachacamac. However, the priests saw what they were coming for and refused them entry to the main temple where the supposed treasures were. Pizarro was hardly in the mood to let a few bold priests turn him away. In a show of diplomacy, he drew his sword and, holding his head up high, slashed everything in is way to enter the precinct. He and his men were greatly disappointed, however, to find nothing but a wooden idol, Pachacamac, "Reformer of the Earth", which stood in the middle of a foul-smelling dark room used for sacrifices. Pizarro and his men may not have found gold, but they did seal their reputation as bloody conquerors by slaughtering all those in their path and sacking everything they could lay their hands on.

Pucusaña

Pucusaña is a picturesque cliffside fishing village off the beaten path, about sixty kilometres south of Lima.

San Vincente de Cañete

Located about 150 kilometres south of Lima, San Vincente de Cañete was named after the Marquis de Cañete, who founded this small town in 1557. Nothing spectacular to see aside from the beaches popular with the locals.

Chincha

A little over 50 kilometres south of Cañete along the Pan American Highway is the little village of Chincha. Beside a former hacienda converted into a hotel just outside the village, there are few tourist amenities here. Chincha is like a slice of Africa in the Peruvian desert. This region is mostly populated by descendants of African slaves who worked on Spanish cotton plantations. This heritage is most in evidence in late February when the village celebrates *verano negro* to the musical blend of Peruvian and African beats.

Pisco

Pisco is a large coastal town of about 100,000 inhabitants, 230 kilometres south of Lima. Founded in 1640, it gave its name to the national drink known as *Pisco Sour*. Though there are few attractions aside from its church, Pisco is of historical importance, for it was here that Argentine General San Martín and his troops landed on September 7th, 1820 to liberate the country from the Spanish. It is no coincidence that a statue of this historic figure stands in the middle of Plaza de Armas to honour his memory.

Travellers generally stop here before visiting Paracas bay, which is 15 kilometres farther south, and the point of departure for boats to the Islas Ballestas or the Parque Nacional Paracas.

The **Iglesia de la Compañia** *($1; varying schedule)* was built by the Jesuits in the late 1600s, and was completed around 1730. Behind its lovely baroque façade, a few paintings of the *escuela cuzqueña* hang on the walls, though three of them were unfortunately stolen in 1997. The church also has three lovely baroque *altares* covered in gold leaf.

Paracas ★★★

Just follow your nose to the small village of Paracas: several fish-processing plants line the road from Pisco to Paracas and release a repulsive odour into the air. You'll have to bear the smell, though, because the village is the starting point for the

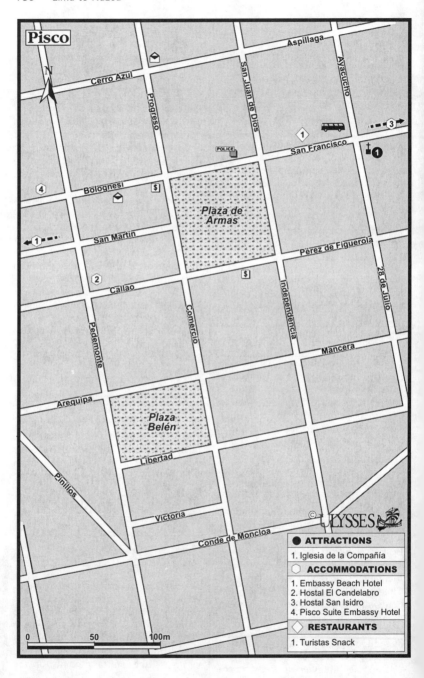

Pisco

ATTRACTIONS
1. Iglesia de la Compañía

ACCOMMODATIONS
1. Embassy Beach Hotel
2. Hostal El Candelabro
3. Hostal San Isidro
4. Pisco Suite Embassy Hotel

RESTAURANTS
1. Turistas Snack

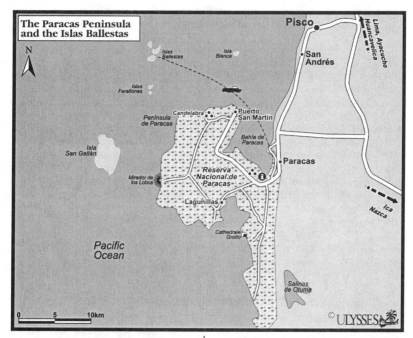

The Paracas Peninsula
and the Islas Ballestas

Pisco

Lima, Ayacucho
Huancavelica

N

Islas
Ballestas

Isla
Blanca

San
Andrés

Islas
Farallones

Candelabra

Peninsula
de Paracas

Puerto
San Martín

Bahía de
Paracas

Isla
San Gallán

Paracas

Mirador de
los Lobos

Reserva
Nacional de
Paracas

Lagunillas

Ica
Nazca

Pacific
Ocean

Cathedrale
Grotto

Salinas
de Otuma

0   5   10km

© ULYSSES

Reserva Nacional Paracas and sea excursions to the Islas Ballestas.

The Paracas Culture

Paracas is the Quechua word for the sand storms that hit the peninsula of the same name every August, and is also the term used to designate the pre-Inca civilization that inhabited this coastal region from roughly 1200 BC to AD 100. It is divided into two phases: **Paracas Cavernas** and **Paracas Necrópolis**.

In 1925, Julio C. Tello discovered several underground burial sites he referred to as **Paracas Cavernas**. Each of these tombs is reached via a long narrow passage that first leads to a fairly large chamber about ten metres below where about thirty mummified bodies are laid out with ritualistic objects meant to accompany the dead on their journey of no return. These chambers usually contained deceased workers and their families, and another passage that descends to a second chamber where the mummified bodies of more important people were preserved. This procedure is similar to that used by the Ancient Egyptians to prevent the royal tombs from decaying. These tombs were further protected from erosion by the very dry climate of the coastal desert. As a result, numerous trepanned skulls, cranial deformations and ceramics were discovered intact. Paracas pottery is more utilitarian than aesthetic, though it does bear feline symbols, undoubtedly inspired by Chavín culture (see p 227).

The **Paracas Necrópolis** is also a Tello find. This royal burial site contained a total of 429 mummies. The body was wrapped in plain white linen, and the underlying fabric, the richly coloured *fardo*, is considered the finest in preColumbian textile art. These figurative embroideries with polychromatic check-

The Nazca Lines

These arcane lines were accidentally discovered in 1939 by American-born Paul Kosok as he flew over the region while working on the aqueducts. Eighteen animal figures were identified, including a monkey, a spider, birds, a lizard and a dog. Some lines even span valleys and mountains, including the odd "owl man" or extraterrestrial being. These colossal drawings have managed to stand the test of time due to their location in the middle of the arid desert, which receives very little or no precipitation. Since the Nazca lines are only visible from the air, one major question arises: how and why were they built? Rome wasn't built in a day, and neither were the perfectly symmetrical Nazca lines, some of which measure up to 50 by 300 metres in dimension. Thus, these shapes called for some careful planning. One possible theory suggests that surface stones were carefully removed, forming furrows lined with some of the rocks put back to accentuate their reliefs. Many have tried to solve the mystery behind these strange geoglyphs, but so far, no one has succeeded, leading some to believe that they are the work of UFOs! Thus, the Nazca lines continue to fascinate tourists and perplex historians. Their message may be inscribed in the ground, but the desert still refuses to divulge their secrets.

erboard patterns depict either anthropomorphic, zoomorphic or supernatural beings, or deities.

The Islas Ballestas ★★★

The Islas Ballestas consist of three islands and many islets off the Pacific coast of Peru. They can be thought of as a kind of "ersatz-Galapagos Islands", since great numbers of sea lions and sea birds, such as penguins, similar to those on the in the Galapagos Islands off the coast of Ecuador, make their nests in the jagged cliffs here. Unfortunately, unlike the Galapagos Islands, visitors can only see this spectacular sight from afar, because only authorized *guano* collectors are allowed on the island. Nevertheless, the scenery is spectacular. It is best viewed from aboard a large boat since the smaller ones may make you seasick, especially if the sea is rough. On the way to the *islas*, you will be able to see the colossal **Candelabro** etched into one of the islands' sheer cliffsides. This enigmatic geoglyph is about 200 metres long and 60 metres wide, and was carved by the Nazcas. Its significance is still unknown, but historians believe that it was probably some kind of landmark for boats. You may also be lucky enough to spot a few friendly dolphins frolicking in these surging Pacific waters. The sea can get choppy, so it is advisable to bring a raincoat or waterproof clothing.

La Reserva Nacional Paracas (see p 138).

Ica

Founded around 1560, Ica is an oasis in the middle of the arid Peruvian coastal desert, 70 kilometres south of Pisco and 300 kilometres from Lima, on both banks of the Rió Ica. *El Niño* almost wiped it off the map in 1998 with torrential rains. Ica is the main town of the department of the same name and is primarily known for its choice *bodegas* (vineyards). Although Peru's

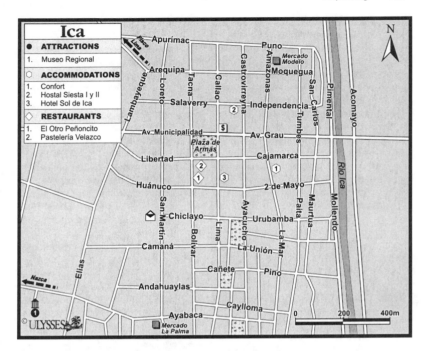

Ica

● ATTRACTIONS
1. Museo Regional

○ ACCOMMODATIONS
1. Confort
2. Hostal Siesta I y II
3. Hotel Sol de Ica

◇ RESTAURANTS
1. El Otro Peñoncito
2. Pastelería Velazco

© ULYSSES

national drink is named for Pisco, its nectar has been produced in Ica since colonial times. It was dispatched to Lima from the port of Pisco — hence its name, *Pisco Sour*.

A bustling town where "motorbike taxis" rule the streets, Ica is blessed with intense sunshine all year round. The nights, however, are cool, due to its proximity to the sea. The climate is favourable to winegrowing, and a few *bodegas* have emerged that are worth visiting to sample their latest harvest. Among these are Vista Allegre, (☎231-432) and Bodega Alvárez, about ten kilometres outside Ica.

The modest but very interesting **Museo Regional** ★★*($1.50; Mon to Sat 8am to 6pm, Sun 9am to 1pm; outside town)* is also worth a visit. It contains artefacts from the Nazca and Paracas cultures, including mummies, trepanned skulls, sumptuous Paracas textiles,

cranial deformations, a few beautiful pieces of Nazca pottery and many other interesting objects.

Huacachina

In the mid-20th century, Huacachina was a sort of spa for the *Limeña* bourgeoisie. It is a palm-lined lagoon whose green sulphurous waters once had curative properties. Today, the lagoon is visibly polluted, and has lost much of its charm through neglect.

Nazca ★★★

Before the discovery of the mysterious Nazca lines, this town was merely a quiet, secluded little village, in the coastal desert 140 kilometres south of Ica. Every year more and more curious people fly over the region to get a look at the enigmatic Nazca lines. These are geometric designs or outlines of stylized anthropomorphic figures and animals etched on the desert soil, and can be up to 300 metres long. The southern coastal region, including Nazca, was hard hit by the violent earthquake of 1996. Fortunately, the earthquake shook the town late in the morning, when most children were in school. This meant that many homes were empty, so the number of casualties was significantly reduced.

In the middle of Plaza de Armas is an object of curiosity and excitement: a television set perched atop a column, broadcasting *fútbol* matches and the news, until it is shut off for the night.

Nazca Culture

The Nazca culture arose during the decline of the Paracas culture around 200 BC. Since many people only associate Nazca culture with the enigmatic lines scoring the desert floor, other important achievements are overlooked. For example, the Nazcas engineered aqueduct networks that made the desert bloom. They painted birds, serpents, trophy heads and supernatural beings on their pottery using ten different colours and many more shades. They devised mathematical and astronomical formulas to build adobe pyramids and draw geometric lines and numerous animals and anthropomorphic figures in the desert with extraordinary precision. The culture vanished around AD 600.

Size of some of these figures:

The whale: 70 metres long
The monkey: 90 metres long
The "owl man" or extraterrestrial: 32 metres long
The pelican: 285 metres long

How to view the Nazca lines?

There are not many ways to see these lines in all their glory. The best way is also the most expensive: chartering a small plane for a 45 minute flight over the desert. Try to go very early in the morning to take in as much as you can and avoid the air turbulence in the afternoon. Don't eat too much before setting out, or you may experience digestive problems such as nausea. The small planes fly slowly over the desert, then suddenly dip and tilt from side to side so that all of the passengers can see the various drawings on the ground. Several agencies sell tickets for the flight, priced at $40 to $50.

If you cannot afford this, you can get a sense of some of the drawings, including the four-finger hand and the tree, from atop the small metal **mirador** (observation post) located about 30 kilometres north of Nazca.

North of the observation post is a small **museum** *($1; every day 8am to 5pm)* that was inaugurated a few years ago in honour of Maria Reiche (see p 136). The room that she occupied before living at the Nazca Lines hotel is on view here. There are also Nazca books, photographs and drawings.

Chauchilla

Visiting a cemetery may sound spooky to some, but the one in Chauchilla is definitely worth the trip. This ancient cemetery is located in the middle of the desert some 20 kilometres south of Nazca, and strewn with skulls, full heads of hair, bones and even whole skeletons as well as a few shards of pottery. All these remains were exposed by the *huaqueros* who looted and desecrated the graves. Note the skulls' perfect teeth, which suggest

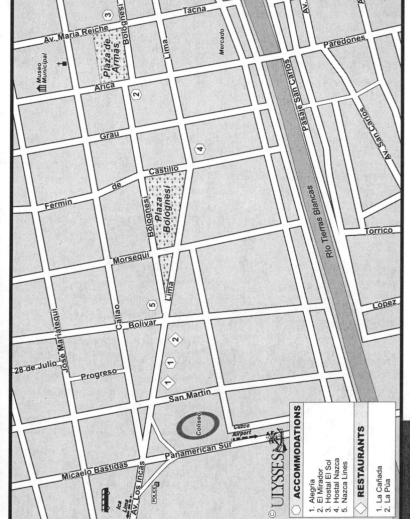

Nazca

N

Tarapacá

Tacna

Av. Maria Reiche

Paredones

Plaza de Armás

③

Bolognesi

Lima

Mercado

Av. San Carlos

Av. Zarumilla

Museo Municipal

Arica

②

Pasaje San Carlos

Grau

Av. San Carlos

④

Castillo

de

Bolognesi

Plaza Bolognesi

Fermín

Morsequi

Torrico

Rio Terras Blancas

Lima

López

⑤

Callao

Bolívar

②

José Mariátegui

①

28 de Julio

①

Progreso

San Martin

Cuzco

Coliseo

Airport

Nazca Lines

Micaelo Bastidas

Panamerican Sur

Av. Los Incas

Ica
Lima

POLICE

© ULYSSES

0   50   100m

⬡ **ACCOMMODATIONS**
1. Alegria
2. El Mirador
3. Hostal El Sol
4. Hostal Nazca
5. Nazca Lines

◇ **RESTAURANTS**
1. La Cañada
2. La Púa

Maria Reiche

Maria Reiche's name is inextricably linked to the Nazca Lines. Born in Dresden in 1903, this German mathematician arrived in Peru in 1932, worked for the German consul in Cuzco and, seven years later, became Paul Kosok's assistant. Reiche soon became fascinated with the lines and completely devoted herself to them. Indeed, she spent some thirty years of her life studying, publicizing and trying to preserve this rich heritage. At first, the locals thought she was simply mad. They saw this strange woman venture into the desert alone with a small broom to clear the lines and compile data from dawn to dusk. She theorized that these lines are closely related to the position of certain stars and represent some sort of astrological calendar. She tirelessly pursued her research and gave seminars at the Nazca Lines hotel, where she stayed before retiring in Lima. In 1989, Reiche was severely stricken by the dreadful Parkinson's disease. Soon after, glaucoma robbed her of sight. Maria Reiche celebrated her 95th birthday in May 1998.

that the Nazcas' diet was devoid of sugar. Another interesting detail is that most of the mummies have their mouths wide open, though they were certainly not buried that way. The *huaqueros*, greedy for gold and silver, pried their jaws open to check for hidden spoils.

The Aqueducts

Nazca culture is best known for its mysterious desert lines, but its people also made significant achievements that allowed them to develop as a civilization despite the arid and rather inhospitable environment in which they lived. The aqueducts are an important legacy of the Nazca people. Following the examples of the Moche and Chimu peoples on the north coast, the Nazcas managed to divert the water running down mountains, thereby creating coastal oases and enabling cultivation where it collected. Though somewhat the worse for wear, some aqueducts are still in use, testifying to the ingenuity of this unknown people.

The *Paredones*

The Paredones are the adobe ruins of a former checkpoint between the Costa and the Sierra a few kilometres east of Nazca. Wari (or Huari), Nazca and Inca influences are evident here. The one-way taxi fare is about $2.

San Juan de Marcona

San Juan de Marcona, almost 25 kilometres southeast of Nazca, was quickly transformed from a tiny fishing village into a mining town in 1953 when an American company managed to open a mine after only three months. Some fifteen years later, the government decided to nationalize it before selling it to Chinese interests about five years ago. The village has neither tourist facilities nor attractions.

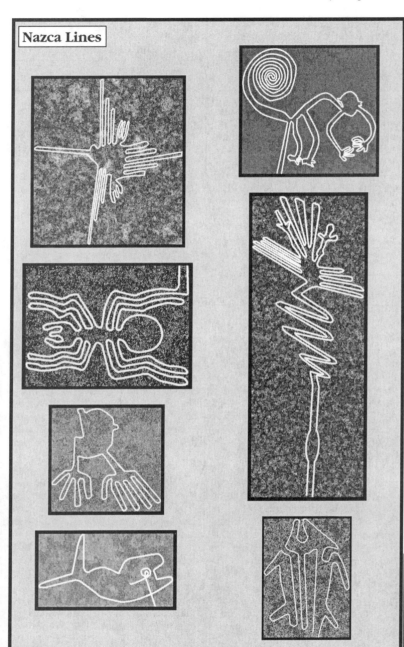

Nazca Lines

PARKS

 ACCOMMODATIONS

La Reserva Nacional Paracas

The Reserva Nacional Paracas was established in 1975 and is the only nature reserve in the country with access to the sea. In fact, only 117,406 of its 335,000 hectares are on dry land while 217,594 hectares extend into the sea. The reserve encompasses a small museum and two picturesque fishing villages, and is home to numerous winged, land and marine species, including the brown pelican and the pink flamingo.

Reserva Pampas Galeras

The Reserva Pampas Galeras is 98 kilometres from Nazca, on the road to the Andes alongside which you can see some *Puya de Raymondi* bromeliad flowers in season. The reserve rises in tiers from 3,800 to 4,100 metres, covers a surface area of 3,100 hectares and shelters the greatest number of *vicuñas* (type of llama) in Peru; about 5,000 of them. Despite this impressive number, vicuñas only travel in small groups of seven or eight and usually stay out of sight for visitors. The best time to observe them is on June 24, when they are rounded up to be sheared. The site is hard to reach; you have to take a desert road that is in rather bad condition. It is best to visit the reserve on a guided tour.

Chincha

There are a few inexpensive places around Plaza de Armas if you are on a tight budget and not too fussy: **La Rueda** *($10)* and **Residencial Majestic** *($10)*.

Hostería San José *($65 bkfst incl.; pb, hw, ℜ, ≈; outside town)* is a former hacienda that has been converted into a hotel. The rooms are clean and charming, and some face the swimming pool. You can rent a horse here and explore the surrounding area. Obliging hosts.

Pisco

Travellers on a limited budget should check out the **Hostal San Isidro** *($10; sb; San Clemente)*. It is located two minutes' walking distance from the *Ormeño* bus terminal, and has modern, clean and safe rooms. The very friendly staff can help you organize an excursion to the Islas Ballestas. Perks include laundry service and free morning coffee.

Two hotels near Plaza de Armas offer roughly the same kind of accommodation for about the same price: the **Pisco Suites Embassy Hotel** *($25; pb, hw, tv; Avenida San Martín 202, ☎532-040, ⌐532-252)* and the **Hostal El Candelabro** *($25; pb, hw, tv; Jr. Callao, at Pedemonte, ☎532-620, from Lima: ☎435-2156)*. Both establishments have relatively clean and simply decorated rooms.

The **Embassy Beach Hotel** *($65; pb, hw, ≈, ℜ, ⊛; Avenida San Martín 1119, ☎532-568, ⌐532-256, from Lima:*

☎472-3525) is a recent addition to Pisco's somewhat drab hotels. With a modern glass façade, it does not really look like a hotel from the outside. But once inside, you will be convinced that this is the best hotel in town. Each of of the impeccable rooms faces the pool, and is equipped with a mini bar as well as a fan.

Paracas

Located about twenty minutes' walking distance from the jetty, **El Mirador** *($30; pb, ℜ; on the way into the village, for reservations contact ☎445-8496 in Lima)* rents out simple but clean rooms.

In a superior category, the **Hotel Paracas** *($78 - $95, around $15 less on weekdays; pb, hw, tv, ℜ; ☎221-736, from Lima: ☎446-5138 or 446-5079, ⌐447-6548)* is the best and, of course, the most expensive hotel in town. On the premises are a badly kept mini-golf course, a children's playground and a small museum that features a few pieces of Nazca pottery. The hotel also has boats that take guests to the Islas Ballestas (about $20 per person). If you want to get away from the city, it is worth staying here provided it fits your holiday budget.

Ica

The sparsely decorated rooms of the small **Confort** *($10; sb; La Mar 251)* hotel will suit those with limited budgets. The establishment is a two minutes' walk southeast of Plaza de Armas.

Two *hostales* run by the same owners are located right near Plaza de Armas: **Hostals Siesta I & II** *($10; sb; Independencia 160 and 192)*. The

rooms are nothing to rave about, but will do for seasoned travellers.

The **Hotel Sol de Ica** *($30; pb, tv, ℜ, ≈; Jr. Lima 265, ☎236-168)* offers very good value for your money. The rooms are clean, safe and well-equipped. There are a laundry service and an outdoor swimming pool on site.

Las Dunas *($60; pb, hw, ≈, ℜ; Avenida La Angostura 400, ☎231-031, ⌐231-007, from Lima: ☎421-470 or 423-091, ⌐424-180)* is the most stylish hotel in town, and also the most expensive. Comfortable and spacious, with well-equipped rooms. The pool terrace is just the place to read and relax. Guests can also rent horses and bicycles, and play tennis and golf. The hotel has its own landing strip and organizes flying excursions over the Nazca lines. Take an early morning flight because of afternoon turbulence.

Nazca

The **Hostal El Sol** *($10; sb; Plaza de Armas)* offers modest and inexpensive rooms.

Located near the Alegría Tours agency, the **Hostal Lima** *($10; sb; Jr. Lima 56)* rents out very basic rooms popular with globetrotters.

The **Hostal Nazca** *($10; sb; Jr. Lima 438, ☎522-085)* will also suit travellers seeking discount accommodation. The friendly staff provides tourist information.

For a little more comfort, **Hotel El Mirador** *($20; pb; Plaza de Armas)* offers clean, though somewhat drab, rooms with wall-to-wall carpeting.

The **Hostal Las Lineas** *($20; pb; Arica 299)* faces Plaza de Armas and offers modest but clean rooms.

The **Hotel Alegría** *($10 to $35; pb, hw, ℜ; Lima 168, ☎522-702, ▰522-444, alegriatours@hotmail.com)* is globetrotter central. The best rooms are in the main building, and are clean, safe and well-equipped. More spartan rooms for budget-conscious travellers are in the building in back. Since the hotel belongs to the Alegría Tours agency, you can take part in various excursions in the region organized by the very obliging staff. The hotel also offers guests access to the Internet.

The **Hotel Borda** *($60; pb, ⊛, ≈; ☎522-750, from Lima: ☎440-8430, ▰442-6391)* is reached via a bumpy, unlit road. It is a former hacienda converted into hotel with some 30 bungalows, each equipped with a fan, most of which face the lovely swimming pool.

La Maison Suisse *($60; pb, ⊛; ☎/▰522-434, www.peruhot.com/nazcaline)* is across the street from the small local airport and has some 30 clean and safe bungalows with fans. The hotel is affiliated with Aeroica, so you can reserve tickets to fly over the famous Nazca lines. Camp sites are provided for budget-conscious travellers.

🏅 The award for the best hotel in town goes to **Nazca Lines** *($80; pb, tv, ℜ; Jr. Bolognesi, ☎/▰522-293)*, a two minutes' walk from Plaza de Armas. This former *hotel de turistas* offers impeccably clean, safe and charming rooms bordering a large swimming pool lined with palm trees. This is where Maria Reiche (see p 136) stayed during the thirty years she spent carrying out tireless research in the desert. Her room remains intact and her furniture and

several personal effects have been reverently preserved. The service is attentive and the hotel restaurant (see p 141) is the best in town.

RESTAURANTS

Pisco

Turistas Snack *($; Jr. San Francisco 256)* is a small eatery right next to the *Ormeño* bus terminal. As its name indicates, this is a simple place where you can stop for a quick sandwich or a glass of freshly squeezed orange juice.

Paracas

The are many small **restaurants on Malecón** *($)* that offer roughly the same low-priced menu that varies according to what the sea brings in.

The best restaurant in town is that of the **Hotel Paracas** (see p 139). Fresh, delicious and, of course, rather expensive local and international cuisine are served.

Ica

For fresh bread or a pastry to satisfy your sweet tooth, head to **Pastelería Velazco** *($; Plaza de Armas)*.

Located two blocks south of Plaza de Armas, the restaurant **El Otro Peñoncito** *($; Bolívar 255)* is a clean and pleasant place that serves simple but delicious dishes at reasonable prices. The menu features sandwiches, chicken, meat and fish. Remember to sample their *Pisco Sour*.

For a little luxury, head to the restaurant of the **Hotel Las Dunas** *($$-$$$)*, where you can savour a few fish and seafood specialties, including *ceviche de pescado* or *mixto* and *pescado a la plancha*, in a refined yet relaxed ambiance.

Nazca

La Púa *($; Jr. Lima)* is a pizza lover's delight. In addition to pizza, the menu features à-la-carte dishes such as seafood and pasta. The service is friendly and the *ceviches* delicious.

El Griego *($; Bolognesi 287)* offers a simple but hearty Creole fixed menu for the modest sum of 5 *soles*.

Should you have a sudden craving for meat, the chef at the small Argentine restaurant **Portón** *($; Jr. Lima 235)* cooks up delicious *parilladas*.

Another good and inexpensive place to savour *ceviche* is **Mister Tiburón** *($; San Martín)*. Minimal decor; simple family fare.

Not to be confused with Canada, **La Cañada** *($; Jr. Lima 160)* offers a low-priced daily menu. Family fare with local flavours.

For fine dining, try the restaurant of the **Nazca Lines** hotel *($$; Jr. Bolognesi, ☎522-293)*. The menu features numerous local and international specialties such as the traditional *ceviche*, *lomo saltodo* or *pollo a la milanesa*, the whole washed down with *Pisco Sour* and served in a dining room with a classic decor and a relaxed ambiance.

Chala

The restaurant of the **Hoteles del Sur** *($)* prepares excellent seafood dishes. Try the *corvina a la plancha*. A half-litre of orange juice costs a mere 5 *soles*. Lovely view of the sea.

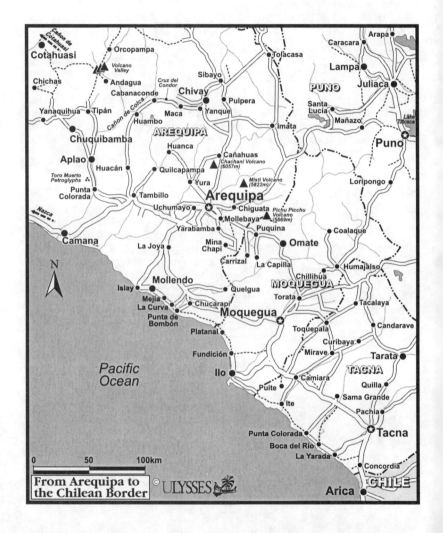

From Arequipa to the Chilean Border

AREQUIPA TO THE CHILEAN BORDER

After Nazca, the Pan-American Highway forges ahead into the luminous coastal desert and runs alongside jagged cliffs, where you might spot the distinctive silhouette of a condor. At the village of Camaná, it heads inland toward the Andes, to the lovely colonial town of Arequipa. Located only 2,400 metres above sea level, Arequipa is a pleasant place to stop on your way south, not just to see the sights, but also to get acclimatized to the altitude before travelling any higher, whether it be to the lofty plateaux of Lake Titicaca or to Cuzco. Furthermore, this arid, mountainous area has some fascinating geographical and geological features. Two canyons, the Cañon del Colca and the Cañon de Cotahuasi, cut deep chasms into the Andean rock, forming a strange and spectacular landscape.

After staying in this area, most travellers head to Cuzco or Lake Titicaca. Some, however, make their way slowly back down the mountains, to Moquegua then on to Tacna and the Chilean border.

👉 FINDING YOUR WAY AROUND

Arequipa

By Plane

Aeroperú and Aerocontinente both offer daily service from Lima to Arequipa. The flight takes nearly an hour and a half, and the fare is about $80. The Aeroperú and Aerocontinente flights from Juliaca to Arequipa take 30 minutes and cost about $40. Arequipa is also just a short flight from Cuzco. The trip takes approximately 45 minutes and will cost you about $45.

By Bus

There is frequent bus service to Arequipa from Lima, Cuzco, Juliaca, Puno, Moquegua, Nazca and Tacna. The ride from Lima takes 20 long hours. Needless to say, it's an exhausting and uncomfortable trip; on the other hand, at somewhere between $10 and $20, depending on the quality of the bus, it is substantially cheaper than taking the plane.

There is regular bus service from Cuzco to Arequipa. The trip takes 12 to 16 hours and costs about $12.

There is daily bus service between Arequipa and Puno, via Juliaca. The trip takes approximately 10 hours and costs about $11.

It takes nearly three hours to get from Moquegua to Arequipa by bus. The fare is about $4.

There is daily bus service from Nazca to Arequipa. The trip takes 10 hours on average and costs $10.

The bus ride from Tacna to Arequipa takes four to five hours and costs about $5.

By Train

The train is definitely **not** the best way to get to Arequipa. There are frequent breakdowns, and mechanical problems often prevent the trains from leaving the station. The bus is a much better choice.

There is train service from Puno to Arequipa, by way of Juliaca, which serves as a rail hub between the towns of Cuzco, Arequipa and Puno.

We recommend the Pullman class, which costs a bit more than the budget classes but has more comfortable seats. Furthermore, the risk of theft, which unfortunately must always be taken into consideration, is lower in this section. Be sure to cover up: the nights are cool in the mountains.

Tickets are available the day before the trip, and the schedules can vary. It is common for trains to be late, and often they never even leave the platform for some obscure reason or another.

Puno - Juliaca - Arequipa: $20

There are four trains per week from Puno to Arequipa; on Tuesday, Wednesday, Thursday and Sunday. It's a night trip and takes about 12 hours.

Cañon del Colca - Chivay - Yanque - Cruz del Condor - Cabanaconde

By Bus

Buses shuttle between the Cañon del Colca and the Arequipa and Cabanaconde terminals, travelling via Chivay, Yanque and Cruz del Condor. The trip from Arequipa to Chivay takes about four hours and costs about $4. The schedules are irregular, so you are better off going through a tour operator (see p 147).

These three places are hard to get to, so it is wise to consult a local tour operator (see p 147).

Mollendo

By Bus

The bus ride from Arequipa to Mollendo takes approximately three hours and costs around $3.

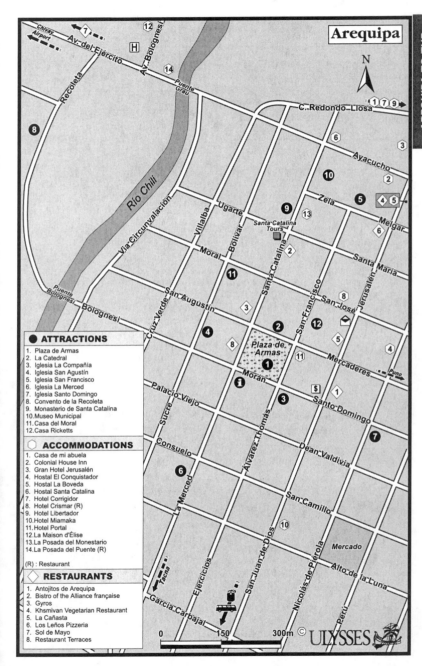

Map labels:

Chivay Airport · Av. del Ejército · Recoleta · Río Chili · Vía Circunvalación · Puente Bolognesi · Bolognesi · Av. Bolognesi · Puente Grau · C. Redondo–Llosa · Ayacucho · Zela · Melgar · Santa María · Ugarte · Villalba · Bolívar · Moral · Santa Catalina · San Augustín · Cruz Verde · Santa Catalina Tours · San Francisco · San José · Jerusalén · Mercaderes · Plaza de Armas · Morán · Palacio Viejo · Sucre · Álvarez Thomás · Santo Domingo · Puno · Dean-Valdivia · Consuelo · La Merced · San Camillo · Ejercicios · San Juan de Dios · Nicolás de Piérola · Perú · Mercado · Alto de la Luna · Tacna · García-Carbajal · Peru

Arequipa

N

AREQUIPA TO THE CHILEAN BORDER

● **ATTRACTIONS**

1. Plaza de Armas
2. La Catedral
3. Iglesia La Compañía
4. Iglesia San Agustín
5. Iglesia San Francisco
6. Iglesia La Merced
7. Iglesia Santo Domingo
8. Convento de la Recoleta
9. Monasterio de Santa Catalina
10. Museo Municipal
11. Casa del Moral
12. Casa Ricketts

◻ **ACCOMMODATIONS**

1. Casa de mi abuela
2. Colonial House Inn
3. Gran Hotel Jerusalén
4. Hostal El Conquistador
5. Hostal La Boveda
6. Hostal Santa Catalina
7. Hotel Corrigidor
8. Hotel Crismar (R)
9. Hotel Libertador
10. Hotel Miamaka
11. Hotel Portal
12. La Maison d'Élise
13. La Posada del Monestario
14. La Posada del Puente (R)

(R) : Restaurant

◇ **RESTAURANTS**

1. Antojitos de Arequipa
2. Bistro of the Alliance française
3. Gyros
4. Khsmivan Vegetarian Restaurant
5. La Cañasta
6. Los Leños Pizzeria
7. Sol de Mayo
8. Restaurant Terraces

0   150   300m   © ULYSSES

Moquegua

By Bus

The bus ride from Arequipa to Moquegua takes just under four hours and costs about $4.

Ilo

By Bus

For the modest sum of $1, you can ride the bus from Moquegua to Ilo, which takes just under two hours.

Tacna

By Plane

Aeroperú and Aerocontinente both offer daily service from Lima. The flight takes about two hours and costs about $90 one-way.

Aeroperú and Aerocontinente also offer daily service from Arequipa for about $40 one-way. Travel time: 40 minutes.

By Bus

The bus ride from Arequipa to Tacna takes nearly four hours and costs about $4.

There is daily bus service from Lima to Tacna. The trip costs $30 per person and takes 25 hours on average. The bus ride from Nazca to Tacna takes 11 hours and costs about $10.

PRACTICAL INFORMATION

Arequipa

Tourist Information

There is a small tourist information office on the Plaza de Armas, across from the cathedral.

Tourist Police

The local Proteción de Turista office is located at Jerusalén 317.

Bus Station *(Terminal Terrestre)*

Unlike other Peruvian towns, Arequipa has a central bus station. It is located at the south end of town, right behind the train station.

Train Station

The train station is located at the south end of town.

Banks

There is a Banco de Credito at the corner of Santo Domingo and Jerusalén.

The Banco Latino, also located on Santo Domingo, at an angle to the Banco de Credito, will give you a cash advance on your MasterCard or American Express card.

Post Office

The post office is located diagonally across from the Hotel Crismal, at Moral 118.

Internet Access

Internet access is available at the university, on Santa Catalina, right near the Plaza de Armas.

Laundry

Lavandería Rapida: Jerusalén 404, ☎266-437. It costs about $3.50 to have one load washed and dried.

Tour Operators

There is a whole slew of tour operators in Arequipa. Though they offer more or less the same excursions, the service varies greatly from one outfit to another. A few of the more reputable agencies are listed below:

Santa Catalina:
Santa Catalina 204,
☎/≈216-994.
This agency, which also has a branch in Cuzco, offers all sorts of excursions in the area, including city tours, trips to the Cañon del Colca, rafting trips in the Cañon del Colca and tours of the Cañon de Cotahuasi and Toro Muerto (petroglyphs). If you call in advance, they can arrange for you to be picked up at the airport, bus station or train station. Excellent service.

Coltur:
San Francisco 206,
☎281-510,
☎/≈239-159,
www.coltur.com.pe.
This agency, which has branches in both Lima and Cuzco, organizes stan-

dard city tours and trips to the Cañon del Colca and the Cañon de Cotahuasi, as well as excursions to more faraway parts of the country.

The *Casa de mi abuela* (see p 159), a hotel, has its own little agency that offers traditional tours of local points of interest.

Moquegua

Telephone

There is a telephone on Plaza de Armas.

Post Office

The post office is on the Plaza de Armas.

Bank

There is a Banco de Credito three blocks from the Plaza de Armas, on Jr. Moquegua, at the corner of Tarapaca. Cash advances on Visa cards.

There is a Banco de la Nación on Jr. Tacna, at the corner of Jr. Lima.

Tacna

Bank

There is a bank on the Plaza de Armas.

Bullfights

Though they might seem cruel and archaic to some visitors, bullfights have always been part of Arequipa's festive traditions.

EXPLORING

Arequipa ★★

Situated about 1,000 kilometres from Lima and bounded by the luminous coastal desert to the west and the steep foothills of the Andes to the east, the lovely city of Arequipa is surrounded by three magnificent volcanoes: Misti (5,822 m), Pichu Picchu (5,669 m) and Chachani (6,057 m). Many of its buildings are made of *sillar*, a white volcanic rock, earning it the nickname *Arequipa la Blanca*, or Arequipa the White. It is also known as the *Ciudad de Eterna Primavera*, or the City of Eternal Spring, for it enjoys a spring-like climate year-round, thanks to its location at an altitude of 2,400 metres. The second largest city in Peru after Lima, Arequipa has nearly 1,000,000 inhabitants.

Nearly every town or village in Peru has a legend about its origins, and Arequipa is no exception. According to oral tradition, *are* means "O.K."; *quipa*, "we're stopping here". The Spanish conquistadors levelled the ancient Inca city that once occupied this site, then decided to rebuild it stone by stone, founding it anew on August 15, 1540.

Plaza de Armas

Arequipa's Plaza de Armas is the bustling hub of the city. It is here that you will find the cathedral as well as scores of shops sheltered by arcades. To get a quick overview of the city, stop by one of the second-story restaurants along the square's west side.

The **Catedral ★★** was one of the first churches to be built in the early 17th century, but has been remodelled several times since. Its imposing façade takes up the entire north side of the plaza.

The **Iglesia de la Compañía ★★** (Morán, at the corner of San Francisco), adjacent to the Plaza de Armas, was completed in 1698 and has three naves. It went up in flames in 1844 and was seriously damaged by an earthquake 22 years later. Its façade is a beautiful example of mestizo architecture, while its austere interior features a pretty wooden pulpit.

The **Iglesia de San Agustín ★** *(San Agustín, at the corner of Sucre)*, the **Iglesia de San Francisco ★** *(Zela 103, one street west of the cathedral)*, the **Iglesia de La Merced ★** *(La Merced 303, between Tristán and Consuelo)* and the **Iglesia de Santo Domingo ★** *(Santo Domingo, at the corner of Nicolás de Perola)* are all good places to sit for a little while and gather your thoughts.

The **Convento de la Recoleta ★★** *($2; Mon to Sat 9am to 5pm)* was founded by the Franciscan Order in 1647, and is the only religious building on the other side of the Río Chili. It has a library containing nearly 25,000 priceless old books, as well as a small museum that displays a large number of stuffed and mounted Amazonian animals.

Monasterio de Santa Catelina ★★★

The **Monasterio de Santa Catalina** *($4; every day 9am to 4pm; Santa Catalina*

Monasterio de Santa Catalina

301) is the uncontested jewel in the city's crown of tourist attractions. Founded in 1579, it remained under a shroud of monastic silence until 1970, when it finally opened its doors to the public. A real little city within a city, it is a remnant of the colonial era right in the middle of modern-day Arequipa. Covering an area of 20,426 square metres, this walled-in enclosure has five streets (Granada, Sevilla, Córdoba, Málaga and Burgos) which lead to old chapels, the novices' rooms, three cloisters, the cemetery, the kitchens and various other buildings. The nuns who lived here devoted most of their waking hours to prayer and contemplation. They came from wealthy families who made generous donations to the convent so that their daughters would be admitted. Ironically, a feminist named Flora Tristán claimed that these nuns who had supposedly taken a vow of silence and dedicated their lives to prayer, actually lived in the lap of luxury in the 17th century – they had servants, and spent much of their time playing music. When the Church got

wind of these questionable practices, it sent someone to bring the nuns into line.

The nuns now occupy only about 5,000 square metres of land (a quarter of the area once covered by the convent) and have been living semi-cloistered since the Pope visited in 1985. Even though they have been authorized to do so by the Pope, some of the older nuns still refuse to leave the convent walls.

The convent's architecture is somewhat unusual. It features a juxtaposition of various 17th-, 18th- and 19th-century styles, because the numerous earthquakes that rocked this region over the years, forced the nuns to make numerous repairs on the buildings.

As you wander about, you'll find yourself transported back in time to a glorious, forgotten era.

Arequipeños

It is difficult to categorize Arequipa as either an Andean or a coastal city, and Arequipeños revel in their unique status, describing themselves a particularly proud and perhaps even pretentious lot. They have even created their own passport and currency. Though none of this is really serious, it is fairly indicative of the local residents' pride.

We strongly recommend taking a guided tour, which will give you a greater understanding of what you are seeing. Multilingual guides are available at the entrance. Though they offer their services for free, they naturally expect to receive a well-deserved tip at the end of the two-hour tour.

Museums

At the **Museo de Altura-UCSM** ★★★ *($2; Mon to Sat 9am to 5pm, closed 1pm to 3pm; Samuel Velarde 305, ☎/≈252-554, jchavezc@ucsm.edu.pe)*, you can see the frozen body of a young Inca woman known as Juanita (see p 152), which was found at the top of the Ampato volcano and is displayed in a refrigerated glass case.

The **Museo Municipal** *(75¢; Mon to fri 9am to 5pm; across from the Iglesia de San Francisco)* displays antique furniture, old photographs of the city, historic documents, paintings and pre-Columbian pottery.

Colonial Houses

The **Casa del Moral** ★★ *($2; Tue to Sun 8am to 5pm; Moral 318)*, located two blocks from the Plaza de Armas, was built during the second half of the 18th century. It takes its name from an old tree that was planted in the middle of its courtyard some 200 years ago.

The **Casa Ricket** *(San Francisco 108)*, a pretty colonial house, is now a branch of the Banco Continental.

Around Arequipa

You can take all sorts of day-trips from Arequipa. The **Cañon del Colca** ★★★ and the **Cañon de Cotahuasi** ★★, two magnificent natural sites carved into the Andes, are among the most spectacular places to go. You can also explore the fascinating **Volcano Valley**, climb the El Misti volcano, check out the petroglyphs at Toro Muerto or visit the colonial houses at the edge of town. With all these things to do, you're sure to find something that appeals to you. Because of their somewhat unusual geographic location, most of these sites are hard to get to. Though you can take public transportation, we recommend going with a tour operator. Not only will they get you where you want to go with fewer headaches, but they will also give you an exhaustive tour so that you can fully appreciate what you're seeing. Of course, you'll have to spend a bit more, but when you consider that public transportation rarely runs on schedule and that a tour operator will supply a guide and stop the bus from time to time so that you can take pictures (something no public bus is going to do), you are far better off putting yourself in the hands of professionals.

A Novice's Life

Being the second child in a family of noble lineage was not always an enviable fate in previous times. The eldest male child would enter the military; his younger brother, the priesthood. The eldest daughter would be married off, while the second daughter would become a nun – not because she had a calling, but in adherence to family tradition. At the tender age of 10, she would be sent to a convent, where she would embark on a four-year novitiate in strict silence to determine whether or not she would become a nun and devote her life to God. Imagine, for an instant, the tremendous pressure weighing on the frail shoulders of these young girls just as they were entering adolescence: four years to decide whether or not they would be willing to sacrifice their future for God. If, once the four years had passed, the girl decided not to become a nun, she would be considered a disgrace to her village and her family, which would turn their backs on her. More often than not, therefore, the novice would resign herself to the fate tradition had assigned her, hoping to sanctify her soul and contribute to the salvation of the world.

Yanahuara

You can take a trip to Yanahuara to visit its pretty white baroque church, which was built around 1750 and offers a lovely view of the surrounding mountains.

La Casa del Fundator ★★

La Casa del Fundator *($2; every day 9am to 5pm)* was named in honour of the city's founder, Don Garcí Manuel de Carbajal. A charming colonial house, it is decorated with period furniture that evokes images of the colonial past. Unfortunately, there are no guides on hand to tell you about what you're seeing.

El Molino de Sabandia ★

Built around 1621, **El Molino de Sabandia** *($1.75; every day 9am to 5pm)* is still in operation. This old mill is located just under 10 kilometres from Arequipa in a peaceful, pleasant landscape where different members of the

camelidaes family can sometimes be seen roaming about.

Yura

Located about 30 kilometres from Arequipa, Yura is a quiet little village set against the backdrop of the Chachani volcano. Overlooked by most tourists, it livens up when Peruvians come here to relax in the hot springs scattered about the area.

Misti ★★

Rising up 5,822 metres into the sky, Misti stands out even in this spectacular setting, thanks to its majestic shape and splendid snow-capped summit. If you're in good shape and in the mood for a real challenge, the best way to explore the volcano is to go on a two-day hike with an experienced guide. This is not the kind of outing to embark on on a whim; it is physically demanding and requires more effort than, say, the Inca Trail. Make sure to bring along a tent, a sleeping bag, a change of clothing, provisions and most impor-

La Juanita

In September 1995, the city of Arequipa made international headlines when the remains of a young woman were discovered in the eternal snows on a nearby volcano, Ampato, at an altitude of about 6,000 metres. *La Dama de los Hielos de Ampato* (Ice Lady of Ampato), nicknamed "La Juanita", had been frozen there for centuries until 1995 when Sabancaya, the volcano beside Ampato, suddenly started spewing out lava, melting parts of the snowy cap of Ampato. In an extraordinary combination of circumstances, some mountaineers who were climbing Ampato that day happened across the incredibly well-preserved body of a young Inca woman wrapped in sumptuous cloth. It was one of the most important ethnographic discoveries to take place in Peru in the 20th century. Historians believe that La Juanita was about 14 years old when she was sacrificed some five hundred years ago. The Incas had the utmost respect for volcanoes, which they viewed as divine powers that could punish or reward them. This young victim was no doubt selected from a group of children to make this voyage of no return. It is believed that a very solemn religious ceremony was held, during which she was drugged. Once she was in a semi-unconscious state, she was killed by a sharp blow to the skull, then offered up as a sacrifice to the volcano gods. Though it might sound cruel, the young woman might very well have been delighted and honoured to be the person chosen to appease the anger of the gods. The bodies of two other children were discovered nearby in subsequent excavations.

tantly, an ample supply of water, since you won't find any potable water on the mountain. You will need a minimum of three litres of water per person, some of which will be used to prepare your meals.

There are a number of trails on the mountain; where you start depends on your guide. Some set out from the cemetery, at an elevation of 3,000 metres; others a little higher, at 3,600 metres. In the former case, you'll leave the cemetery at around 5:00 or 6:00 in the morning. On the first day, you'll walk for about eight hours. At first, it's a fairly easy hike across an arid, hilly plain that runs past the *piedra grande* (big rock). Misti is visible in the distance, while Chachani rises up in all its glory to an altitude of 6,059 metres to your left. The climb gets a little harder as you cross a steep, windswept section of the mountain where the vegetation is sparse. Watch your step:

it is easy to slip on the small volcanic rocks rolling underfoot. At around 1pm or 2pm, you'll reach the base camp known as the Eagles' Nest, which is the perfect place to pitch your tent, have something to eat, then admire the sunset and the lights of Arequipa glittering in the distance. At dawn the next day, you start the leg of the hike that takes you to the top of the mountain. It is likely to be colder, and you might see some snow. The temperature warms up as the sun rises. The terrain gets very uneven, and you have to climb over big rocks, always taking care not to slip on loose stones. The first day is hard on the legs; the second is hard on the lungs. Don't be surprised if you have to stop every 10 steps to catch your breath. It takes three hours to reach the Line of Rocks, which is located nearly 5,200 metres above sea level and screens the summit. After that, it's just two to three more hours to the 10-metre metal cross at the top of the mountain, where you can take in a sweeping view of the valley and the volcano's enormous crater. It will take you about an hour to walk back down to the base camp, then another three to four hours to reach the cemetery. The trip down is made that much easier by the bed of volcanic stones underfoot, which makes it feel like you're sliding, or even skiing, down the mountain. It is best to leave the summit before 2pm, since it is not a good idea to be in the cemetery after dark, when taxis are scarce and you run a greater risk of being robbed. Climbing Misti is well worth the effort and courage required, if only to see this unparalleled landscape from a new angle.

Cañon del Colca ★★

The geography of the Peruvian Andes is remarkably varied. Located northwest of the city of Arequipa, the Cañon del Colca is a huge chasm in the mountain plateau. Descending about 3,400 metres, it is twice as deep as Arizona's Grand Canyon. There are all sorts of hiking expeditions to be available here, as well as some exciting rafting opportunities. Several local tour operators organize excursions that last two days or longer.

To get to the Cañon del Colca from Arequipa (2,400 metres), you have to take a poorly maintained paved road that slowly climbs the mountainside, then, at nearly 3,900 metres above sea level, runs alongside the Reserva Nacional Salina y Aguada Blanca, where vicuñas are bred. These charming silken-fleeced creatures are quite wild and will run off if you try to get too close. Buses usually make a brief stop at 4,200 metres, where you can sample a *maté de coca* at a little restaurant (if it can be called that) in the middle of nowhere. The road continues to climb gently, to an altitude of about

4,700 metres, where the wind whips the ground, the grass is sparse and the sun pounds down on the rocky soil. Then it winds down to the village of Chivay. It's a bumpy ride down, but the scenery is spectacular.

Chivay ★

Located approximately 140 kilometres from Arequipa, at an elevation of about 3,700 metres, Chivay is the gateway to the Cañon del Colca. The capital of the province of Caylloma, it has the most extensive infrastructure of any town in this isolated Andean region and has been welcoming more and more tourists.

Los Baños La Calera ★★ *($2; every day 5:30am to 6pm)* are located four kilometres northwest of Chivay. In addition to the hot springs, there is a thermal pool where visitors can go for a dip before or after a day of exploring.

Yanque ★

Located just under 10 kilometres from Chivay, Yanque is a picturesque village surrounded by terraced land. Its baroque church dates from the 17th century.

The Cruz del Condor ★★

The canyon's most popular attraction is the Cruz del Condor where, as you may have guessed, condors can often be seen gliding overhead. These birds are the undisputed masters of the heavens. It would be hard not to be impressed by the sight of these vultures, with their enormous wings outspread, sillhouetted against the sky.

Vicuñas

Cabanaconde ★★

Perched at an altitude of 3,300 metres, Cabanaconde is a small town with potholed, dusty streets where cows, llamas, dogs, donkeys and other friendly animals, both wild and domesticated, wander around unfinished adobe houses. The hustle and bustle of modern life doesn't seem to have caught up with this remote Andean town.

Lately, however, more and more visitors have been coming here to take one of the many paths leading to the narrow, winding trail that runs 1,500 metres downhill to a luxuriant oasis at the bottom of the Cañon del Colca. If you plan on making this trip, be aware that there are no restaurants or other tourist facilities along the way. Also, you can't take a taxi back up. Though it is not hard to get to the oasis, don't forget that you are at a fairly high altitude, and spectacular as the trip down may be, the inevitable climb back up is likely to be less pleasant and might leave you with slightly more painful memories... Don't overestimate your strength; you are better off being careful and taking your time. Bring along some fruit, a sandwich and

a sufficient supply of water. The trip down takes about three hours, the trip up a few hours more, depending on what kind of shape you're in.

Toro Muerto ★

Toro Muerto is another little-known Peruvian archaeological site. Located off the beaten track, it is poorly protected and may soon be lost to pillaging if something isn't done soon. So, you're probably asking, just what exactly is Toro Muerto, anyway? It's a group of rock paintings and mysterious petroglyphs drawn the Wari on some rocks strewn on the ground in the middle of nowhere. Sure to be of interest to archaeology buffs, this site is hard to get to, and we strongly recommend enlisting the services of a tour operator.

Volcano Valley ★★

Discovered only at the beginning of the 20th century, Volcano Valley is a silent witness to the ages. This series of about 30 volcanoes, dozing with half-closed eyes beneath sunny skies, is found in a grandiose setting whose

rocky, desert-like, untamed landscape might remind you of the moon. Like Toro Muerto, Volcano Valley is off the beaten tourist track, so you'll have to contact a tour operator in Arequipa to get there.

Cotahuasi

The remote village of Cotahuasi is as picturesque as can be, but has only basic tourist amenities. Over the past few years, however, its name has been popping up in tourist brochures, because it is becoming more and more popular as a jumping-off point for excursions to the canyon that bears its name.

Cañon de Cotahuasi ★★

Some claim that the Cañon de Cotahuasi plunges to a depth of some 3,450 metres, making it deeper than the Cañon del Colca or even the Grand Canyon in Arizona. Though the canyon is a formidable natural obstacle, this hasn't prevented people from settling nearby. In fact, the area is dotted with modest villages that seem to have existed since time immemorial, and whose residents go about their business peacefully, as yet undisturbed by the outside world. You can go hiking or rafting here, but you are strongly advised to enlist the services of a reputable agency in Arequipa before setting off on an adventure in the wilderness. This site is still virtually undeveloped for tourism, and many dangers lie in

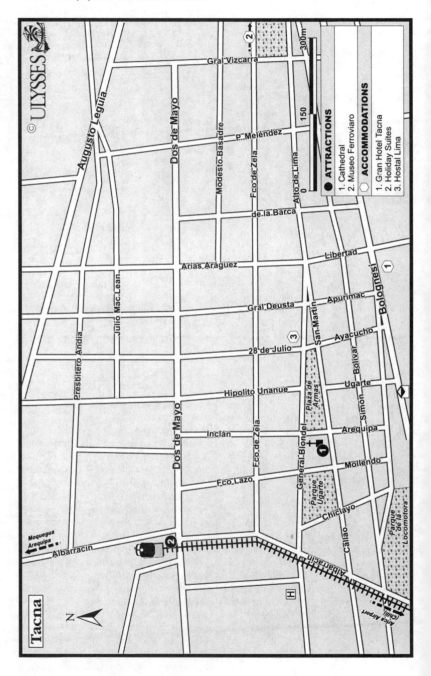

Tacna

N

© ULYSSES

ATTRACTIONS
● 1. Cathedral
2. Museo Ferroviaro

ACCOMMODATIONS
⬡ 1. Gran Hotel Tacna
2. Holiday Suites
3. Hostal Lima

Gral Vizcarra

P. Meléndez

de la Barca

Libertad

Arias Aráguez

Apurímac

Gral Deusta

Ayacucho

28 de Julio

Hipolito Unanue

Plaza de Armas

Inclán

Arequipa

Mollendo

Fco Lazo

Chiclayo

Parque de la Locomotora

Callao

Albarracín

Moquegua
Arequipa

Dos de Mayo

Augusto Leguía

Modesto Basadre

Fco de Zela

Alto de Lima

Julio Mac Lean

Presbítero Andía

Fco de Zela

General Blondel

San Martín

Bolívar

Simón

Ugarte

Bolognesi

Parque Ugarte

Arica Airport
(Chili)

Albarracín

0   150   300m

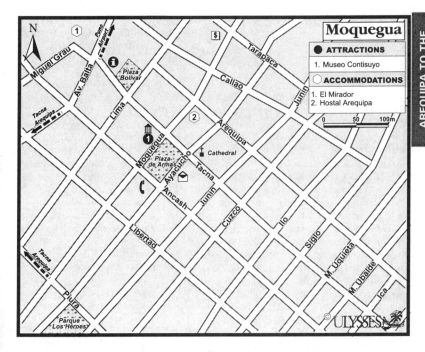

Moquegua

● **ATTRACTIONS**
1. Museo Contisuyo

○ **ACCOMMODATIONS**
1. El Mirador
2. Hostal Arequipa

wait for the ill-prepared or slightly fool-hardy excursionist.

To the Coast and the Chilean Border

The road leading down the mountains from Arequipa forks at the little village of La Joya. One branch heads southeast to Mollendo, the other towards Chile.

Mollendo

Most people who come to the peaceful little seaport of Mollendo are simply passing through on their way to the Sanctuario Nacional de las Lagunas de Mejía, home to numerous species of aquatic birds.

Mejía

The little village of Mejía lies just under 10 kilometres from Mollendo. Located within its boundaries is the Sanctuario Nacional de las Lagunas de Mejía, a group of large lakes surrounded by greenery and teeming with birds. The total area of the wildlife sanctuary is nearly 700 hectares.

Ilo

This little seaport attracts few tourists, for the simple reason that it has nothing of interest to offer them. The copper ore mined in Toquepala is shipped out through here.

Bolivia, which, as you may remember, lost its access to the sea after the Pacific War, has obtained permission from the Peruvian government to use the port of Ilo without having to pay any taxes.

Moquegua

Moquegua, whose name means "silent place" in Quechua, lies about 215 kilometres from Arequipa, at an altitude of just 1,437 metres. The capital of the department of the same name, it is a quiet coastal town on the banks of the Río Moquegua. Usually overlooked by tourists, Moquegua is drenched in bright sunshine year-round and enjoys a hot, dry climate. It has decent amenities for tourists wishing to make a brief stop here before continuing on to Tacna. Most local activity revolves around the town's pretty Plaza de Armas, which is shaded by old trees.

The **Museo Contisuyo** *($1; changing schedule; The Plaza de Armas)*, located inside the Iglesia de la Matriz on the Plaza de Armas, has a small collection of Inca and Wari-Tiahuanaco artifacts.

Tacna

Located just under 500 kilometres from Arequipa, in the middle of the dazzling coastal desert, Tacna is the last Peruvian town before the Chilean border, which lies about 30 kilometres away. At the end of the Pacific War, Bolivia lost its access to the sea, while Peru had to surrender the towns of Arica and Tacna. The latter was returned to Peru in 1929, but Arica has become a permanent part of Chile.

The cathedral which faces the local Plaza de Armas was supposedly designed by the famous French engineer Gustave Eiffel.

The town's main attraction is the **Museo Ferroviaro** ★ *($1; changing*

schedule; 2 de Mayo, at the corner of Albarracín), which displays a fascinating assortment of locomotives in the train station.

Crossing the Border

There are a number of ways to cross the border. There are three trains per week, which leave the station in the late afternoon on Mondays, Wednesdays and Fridays. The fare is only $1.50. There is regular bus service to the border as well. Your last option is to take a taxi, which is more expensive but also faster and more comfortable.

The border station opens every day at 9am and closes around 10pm.

When you get to Chile, don't forget to set your watch forward an hour.

 # ACCOMMODATIONS

Arequipa

All classes of accommodations are available in the Arequipa area. There are a number of hotels near the Plaza de Armas, a convenient location for exploring the town and organizing daytrips. Several luxury hotels lie outside the city, and it is also possible to find chic, comfortable lodgings near the centre of town.

The **Hostal La Boveda** *($8; Jerusalén 528, ☎281-685)* is located above the little vegetarian restaurant Khsmivan (see p 162); take the stairs in the courtyard. Basic, affordable rooms, some of which have a small balcony overlooking Jerusalén Street.

The **Hostal Santa Catalina** *($8 cb, $12 pb; Santa Catalina 500,*

☎243-705) is great for tight budgets. The top-floor rooms are sunnier and drier than those on the ground floor. You can wash your clothes on the terrace.

The **Colonial House Inn** *($12; pb, hw, ℛ; Puente Grau 114, ☎223-533, casos@mail.interplace.com.pe)* has six rooms with very high ceilings. Breakfast is served in the courtyard under shady trees. Laundry service.

The **Hotel Miamaka** *($30 bkfst incl.; pb, hw, tv, ℛ; San Juan de Dios 402, ☎241-496 or 243-160, ⌐227-906, hotel_miamaka@mail.interplace.com.pe)* has about 20 clean rooms, each with a modern bath with skylights that let in the sun, lending a soothing radiance to the predominantly blue and white walls. The reception desk is on the second floor. Friendly service.

From the outside, there is no way of guessing what awaits you at the **Casa de mi abuela** *($33; pb, hw, tv, ℛ, ≈; Jerusalén 606, ☎241-206, ⌐242-761, lperezwi@ucsm-edu.pe)*, surely one of the most unique hotels in town. Its owners have bought up a series of houses and connected them. The rooms vary in size but are all clean, quiet and safe. There are two large courtyards (one in front and one in back) where birds swoop amid the trees and flowers surrounding the pool. The hotel operates its own little tour agency for guests who want to explore the area.

The **Hotel Corregidor** *($35; hw tv, ℛ; San Pedro 139, ☎288-081, ☎239-803, hotel***@unsac.edu.pe)*, situated outside the downtown area, is appealing for its peace and quiet. It has about 20 clean, modern, safe rooms on three floors. Internet access.

The **Hostal El Conquistador** *($40; hw, tv, pb, ℛ; Mercaderes 409, ☎212-916, ⌐218-987)*, located four blocks from the Plaza de Armas, has clean, well-equipped but rather plain rooms. The lobby and dining room summon up memories of the colonial era. Pleasant staff.

The **Hotel Crismar** *($40 bkfst incl.; pb, hw, ctv, ℛ; Moral 107, ☎215-290, ⌐239-431, www.crismar.com.pe)* is just steps away from the Plaza de Armas, right near the Monasterio de Santa Catalina. Having undergone renovations in 1997, it offers spacious, safe, charming, well-appointed rooms, each with its own modern bathroom. Its restaurant has a good reputation (see p 162) as well. Impeccable service. A bargain for this class of accommodations.

The **Gran Hotel Jerusalén** *($60; pb, hw, tv, ℛ; Jerusalén 601, ☎244-481 or 235-001, ⌐288-347)*, right near the Casa de mi abuela, is a four-story building with 86 clean, modern, well-appointed rooms, which were recently renovated.

The **Posada del Monasterio** *($60; pb, ctv, hw, ℛ; Santa Catalina 300, ☎215-705, ⌐283-076)*, across from the Monasterio de Santa Catalina, is one of the newest hotels in town and tastefully combines the old and the new. The reception area, restaurant and part of the ground floor bear witness to the building's colonial past, while the rooms are more modern and functional. Gracious staff.

La Maison d'Élise *($70; pb, hw, ctv, ≈, ℛ; Av. Bolognesi 104, ☎256-185 or 253-353, ⌐271-935)*, on the other side of the bridge, is run by a friendly French-Peruvian couple who named the place after their daughter, emphasizing its homey character. Though there are a few rooms in the main building where the reception desk is located, those in the group of colourful little bungalows near the pool in the back are much more inviting.

The **Posada del Puente** *($70; pb, hw, ctv, ℜ; Avenida Bolognesi, ☎253-132, ⌨253-576)* is thus named because it also lies on the other side of the bridge *(puente)*, on the banks of the Río Chili. The rooms are all spotless, safe and equipped with a minibar, and some offer a view of the river. The hotel restaurant (see p 162) has a good reputation in town.

The best thing about the **Hotel Portal** *($80; ctv, pb, hw, ≡, ℜ; Portal de Flores 116, ☎215-530, ⌨234-274)* is its location on the Plaza de Armas. The rooms are clean and have wall-to-wall carpeting, but are overpriced. The bar and restaurant look like they are straight out of the sixties or seventies. The hotel has a rooftop terrace and a pool so tiny it could pass for a big bathtub.

🏨 The **Hotel Libertador** *($100; pb, hw, ctv, ≡, ℜ; ☎215-110 or 282-550, ⌨241-933, www.libertador.com.pe)* is a little far from the Plaza de Armas. The town's former *hotel de turista*, it now belongs to a small local hotel chain. Far from the downtown hubbub, it is just the place for travellers who want to stay in Arequipa but would also like some peace and quiet. The rooms are bright and well decorated, the restaurant has a good reputation and the service is excellent. A good choice if you want to pamper yourself.

🏨 A similar place, but even farther from the action, right near the Molino de Sabandia (see p 151), the **Hotel Holiday Inn** *($100 bkfst incl.; ctv, pb, hw, ℜ; ☎448-383, ⌨448-344,*

holiaqp@lared.net.pe, from Lima, ☎/⌨221-1650) might sound like a place to avoid if you're looking for local colour. That would be a mistake, however, since this member of the well-known American chain doesn't look anything like its drab North American counterparts. It is built near a lagoon, with the snow-capped volcanoes in the background. Those travellers willing to give it a chance won't be disappointed. The lobby is decorated in warm hues with local handicrafts, while the 52 rooms are spacious, bright and charming. Some have a lovely view of the mountains. The staff is helpful and will do everything possible to make sure you have a wonderful stay.

Chivay

Travellers on a tight budget can stay at the **Hostal Plaza** *($6; sb)* or the **Hostal y Cafetería Corpeli** *($5 sb, $7 pb)* two modest and very affordable *hostales* on the Plaza de Armas.

La Posada del Inca *($20 bkfst incl.; pb, hw, ℜ; Avenida Salaverry 325, ☎/⌨521-108, from Arequipa ☎254-996)*, just north of the Plaza de Armas, has clean, safe, reasonably priced rooms. Friendly service.

🏨 If you're looking for the best place in town, head straight to the **Hotel Rumillaqta** *($35; pb, ℜ; Huayna Capac, ☎/⌨521-098)*. Rumillaqta means "stone village" in Quechua, and the place is aptly named, for it is a group of little stone bungalows with thatched roofs. Though hardly luxurious, the rooms are spotless, bright and charmingly decorated.

Roman Catholic holidays are a time of pilgrimage, procession and prayer.
- *Patrick Escudero*

Colourful Inca and other art are on display at the Museo de
Arquelogía de Cuzco. - *T. B.*

Yanque

The **Colca Lodge** *($35 bkfst incl. or $60 for four people; to make reservations contact Calle Zela 212, ☎245-199, ✉242-088 in Arequipa)* is about half an hour from Chivay, on the banks of the Río Colca. Surrounded by magnificent terraces, this place will appeal to anyone wishing to relax in a peaceful, bucolic setting. Aside from the gas stove in the kitchen, everything here runs on solar energy. You can rent a horse and explore the area at your leisure. The hotel has its own hot springs, where you can relax and bask in the mild afternoon sun.

Cabanaconde

The **Hostal Valle del Fuego** *($5; cb; from Arequipa ☎425-985)*, a small family-operated hotel, has about 25 relatively clean rooms with absolutely no frills. The father and son double as tour guides and can provide you with all sorts of information on the region.

The **Hostal la Virgen del Carmen** *($6; cb)* has bright, clean, safe rooms.

Moquegua

The little **Hostal Arequipa** *($10; Jr. Arequipa)*, right near the Plaza de Armas, is fine if you're not too demanding.

El Mirador *($30; tv, pb, hw, ≈, ℜ; Alto de la Villa s/n, ☎761-765, ✉761-895)*, located right near the airport, strives to be the best hotel in the area. It has 12 rooms, 12 bungalows and a pretty swimming pool.

Tacna

Travellers on a tight budget can find shelter at the little **Hostal Lido** *($10; San Martin 876)*.

The well-located **Hostal Lima** *($20; ℜ, pb)* offers simple accommodations.

The **Holiday Suites** *($45; pb, hw, tv, ℜ; Alto de Lima)* has clean, safe, quiet rooms.

The **Gran Hotel Tacna** *($65; pb, tv, hw, =, ℜ; Av. Bolognesi 300, ☎724-193, ✉722-015)*, located right near the Plaza de Armas, is the most stylish hotel in town. It has about 70 well-appointed, clean, bright rooms.

 RESTAURANTS

Arequipa

Arequipa has a wide assortment of restaurants, and the local cuisine is as varied as it is delicious. The regional specialties are *cuy chactado*, *rocoto relleno* and *camarones d'agua dulce* (freshwater shrimp farmed in the Arequipa area).

If you visit the Monasterio de Santa Catalina in the late afternoon, stop by the bistro run by the **Alliance française** *($; Santa Catalina 208)*, which opens at 1:30pm and serves delicious, made-to-order crêpes. The menu also includes sandwiches, coffee, *pisco sour* and various other alcoholic beverages.

Speaking of garish decors, the emphasis is on pink at **Antojitos de Arequipa** *($; San Juan de Dios 108-A)*. But don't be put off: this unpretentious little restaurant opens at 6:30am and serves a good choice of fresh juices and homemade yogurts.

As indicated by its name, **Gyros** *($; Santa Catalina 105, ☎282-006)*, just steps away from the Plaza de Armas, serves tasty Greek *gyro* sandwiches, as well as crêpes.

You can always count on the Hare Krishnas who run **Govinda** *($; Jerusalén 505)* for a simple, nutritious meal. This small vegetarian restaurant is filled with the scent of burning incense. Breakfast, lunch and dinner.

Right nearby, on the same street, the **Khsmivan Vegetarian Restaurant** *($; Jerusalén 402)* is located in the courtyard of the little Hostal La Boveda (see p 158). The *menu del día* is both nourishing and affordable. The restaurant also sells homemade bread and a few other natural products.

La Cañasta *($; Jerusalén 115, ☎214-900)* is a small bakery where you can buy fresh bread and empanadas, which are perfect for a quick snack.

If you're craving sweets, treat yourself to some mouthwatering chocolates at **La Iberica** *($; Av. Juan Vidaurrazaga M. 131, ☎215-670)*.

Los Leños Pizzeria *($; Jerusalén 407)* looks a bit like the Berlin Wall. Its concrete walls are covered with graffiti and messages scribbled by globetrotters. Pizza baked in a wood-burning oven.

Little **Pizza Presto** *($; Morán 108, ☎212-374)* serves up pizza at reasonable prices. With its flashy red and white decor, it looks like it's backed by Coca-Cola.

The restaurant at the **Hotel Crismar** *($-$$; Moral 107, ☎239-431)* serves remarkably fresh, delicious and affordable food, as well as good, fresh fruit juices. The menu usually consists of a variety of beef, chicken and pasta dishes. Friendly, efficient service.

If you want to grab a bite to eat while watching the action on the Plaza de Armas, take a seat outside at one of the **restaurants with terraces** ($-$$) on the west side of the square. There are three or four of them, all serving more or less the same fare at similar prices. Ask for the *menu del día* and pick the one that strikes your fancy.

Sol de Mayo *($-$$; Jerusalén 207, Yanahuara, ☎254-148)*, on the other side of the bridge, prides itself on the fact that it has been open since 1897. It has changed with the times, of course, and wins our vote for the best restaurant in town. It serves a vast assortment of attractively presented dishes in the courtyard of a colonial house. You're sure to find something that tempts your palate, since this place does its utmost to maintain the highest standards of Peruvian dining. The kitchen is open to the public and inspires confidence, since you are welcome to have a look at it before ordering your meal. *Ocopa con queso frito*, *corvina en salsa de camarones* and *cuy chactado* are just a few of the dishes on the menu.

If you want to have a good meal in a chic, muted atmosphere, try the restaurant at **La Posada del Puente** *($$-$$$; Av. Bolognesi, ☎253-132)*. The menu is varied, the food fresh and the service unpretentious. Of course, quality of this kind comes at a certain price...

Moquegua

For a quick meal in a simple setting, head to **Chifa Chino** *($; Jr. Tacna, southeast of the Plaza de Armas)*, which serves inexpensive Chinese food.

Tacna

If you'd like to cool off with a scoop of ice cream, stop by **Helados Piamonte** *($; Av. Bolognesi, near the Gran Hotel Tacna)*.

El Viejo Almacén *($; Jr. San Martin 577)*, two blocks east of the Plaza de Armas, serves pasta and meat dishes in an uninspiring decor.

If you're in the mood for a good meal, opt for the restaurant at the **Gran Hotel Tacna** *($-$$; Av. Bolognesi 300, ☎724-193)*, which has a varied menu and a friendly staff.

 ENTERTAINMENT

Arequipa

Arequipa is not the most exciting place as far as nightlife is concerned. Though it does have a few nightclubs, they are relatively quiet during the week.

Among the more popular hangouts, the **Blues Bar** *(San Francisco 319)* seems to be the number-one place in town to go for drinks and listen to all different kinds of music. Live shows on weekends.

Diego's Video Pub *(Moral 305)* is both a bar and a small restaurant, where you can grab a quick snack and watch some videos.

Chivay

For drinks and a good mix of music, head to little **Pub Witite** *(José Gálvez, near the Plaza de Armas)*, which has a small dance floor.

 SHOPPING

Arequipa

If you've got money to spend and are looking for a top-quality alpaca sweater, stop by Alpaga 21 *(Tenda 15, in the cloister of the Iglesia de la Compañia)*.

You just might happen upon that special something at the local market, where clothing and all sorts of other handicrafts are sold.

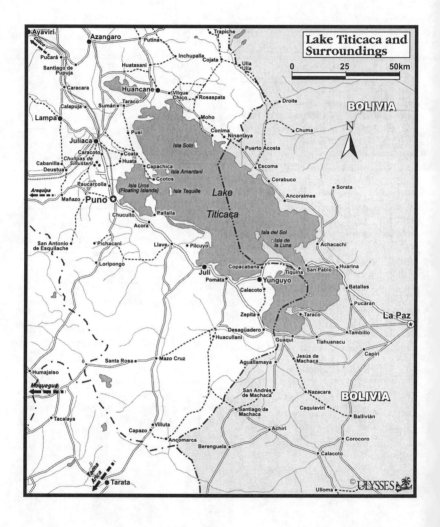

Lake Titicaca and Surroundings

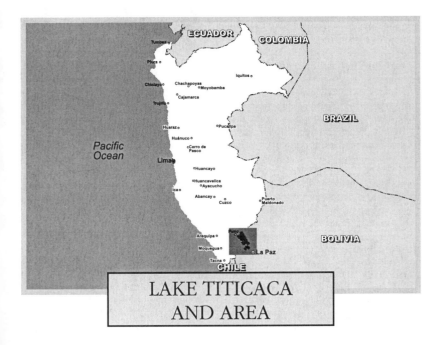

LAKE TITICACA
AND AREA

L it by a blazing sun, surrounded by towering mountains and inhabited by people from a forgotten era, Lake Titicaca looks like a small inland sea. Strewn across its azure waters are about 40 islands with flocks of birds swooping overhead. Some of these are not real islands but rather are floating masses of tortora, a robust, lacustrine plant with big, bamboo-like stems.

Because Lake Titicaca itself is so impressive, visitors tend to overlook the picturesque little towns along its shores. Travellers who make it up to these lofty plateaux usually visit Isla Taquile, Isla Amantani and the floating islands inhabited by the Uros Indians, before making a brief stop at the Chullpas de Sillustani. From here, they generally continue on to Cuzco or head to the Bolivian border to check out Copacabana, Isla del Sol and Isla de la Luna on their way to the highest capital in the world, La Paz, Bolivia. However,

those who take the time to spend a few days exploring these sleepy little villages will be amply rewarded.

The sacred connotations of the waters of Lake Titicaca hold a certain fascination for travellers. According to an old legend, the famous lake was created when the god Viracocha, venerated by the Tiahuanacos, shed a tear. The Tiahuanacos were a pre-Inca civilization that flourished on the Bolivian shores of Lake Titicaca around 200 BC, before it mysteriously vanished around the 12th century. A few large-scale monoliths still bear witness to its existence, including the famous Puerta del Sol, located 70 kilometres from La Paz. This gigantic piece of stone, three metres high and four metres wide, has an anthropomorphous figure at its centre; this is Viracocha, with his arms outstretched and a baton signifying his royal and divine power in each hand. Viracocha appears often in the various Andean cultures, though in different forms – on the stela at Chavín and the monoliths of Pucará, for example.

According to another Inca legend, Manco and his sister, Mama Ocllo, sprang forth from the waters of the sacred lake one day, and went to a previously unknown place where they founded a city named Cuzco, which later became the capital of the Inca empire.

The Spanish were not impressed by the myths associated with the lake, but did give some credence to the legend that a huge gold chain weighing over two tons, which had once belonged to the Inca Huáscar, lay somewhere at the bottom of the lake. Their repeated efforts to find it proved futile, however.

Much later, in 1968, the French scientist and explorer Jacques Cousteau searched the lake himself with a bathyscaph. Though he didn't find any sunken treasures, he did come across a giant female frog measuring a full 60 centimetres when fully extended!

Travellers will have no trouble picturing tutelary gods gazing at their reflections in these waters, which, at 4,000 metres above sea level, form the highest navigable lake in the world.

Lake Titicaca is shared unequally by Peru (65%) and Bolivia (35%). Because its geographic location makes it hard to get to, the lake remains shrouded in mystery even today.

FINDING YOUR WAY AROUND

Juliaca

By Bus

There are lots of buses from Puno to Juliaca. You can catch one at the corner of Avenida Titicaca and the railroad. The trip takes about an hour and costs 50¢.

By Plane

There are regular flights to Juliaca from Arequipa, Cuzco and Lima.

Aerocontinente offers daily service from Lima. The fight takes about two hours and 10 minutes and costs $80. Aeroperú also offers daily flights from Lima for about $90.

Aerocontinente and Aeroperú both offer daily service from Cuzco and Arequipa to Juliaca for about $45. Travel time: 45 minutes.

Pucará

By Bus

There is regular bus service from the Plaza de Armas in Juliaca to Pucará, a 50-minute trip. The fare is about $1.

Lampa

Buses for Lampa depart regularly from the Plaza de Armas in Juliaca. The trip takes 20 minutes and costs about 70¢.

Cañon de Tiahuani

You're better off going through an agency (see p 168).

Sillustani

By Bus

The buses from Puno to Sillustani depart daily from the corner of Jr. Tacna and Jr. Melgar at around 2pm. The trip takes 45 minutes and costs about $1.

Puno

By Plane

There are no direct flights to Puno. You have to fly to Juliaca then take a bus or train to Puno. There are regular flights to Juliaca from Arequipa, Cuzco and Lima (see above).

By Bus

The bus ride from Arequipa to Puno takes nearly 10 hours. The fare is about $8.

There is daily bus service from Cuzco to Puno, by way of Juliaca. The trip takes 11 hours on average and costs $8.

The bus ride from Lima to Puno takes 30 long hours, with a stop at Arequipa. The fare is about $20.

By Train

Taking the train is definitely not the best way to get to Puno. There are frequent breakdowns, and trains are often stuck at the station because of mechanical problems. The bus is more reliable and travels through the same scenery.

There is train service from Cuzco and Arequipa to Puno, by way of Juliaca, which is the rail hub between the three towns.

The railway line between Arequipa and Puno runs through some magnificent scenery. Unfortunately the train leaves the Arequipa station after sunset, so you can't see much. The trip takes nearly 11 arduous hours. When you make your reservations, you can choose a $9, $12 or $18 seat. The extra $9 buys you a more comfortable ride and decreases your chances of being robbed, which, unfortunately, is a factor that must be taken into consideration. Cover up well: the nights are cool at high altitudes.

In principle, the train from Cuzco to Puno (by way of Juliaca) departs from the Huanchac station four times a week, on Monday, Wednesday, Friday and Saturday morning at around 8am. Tickets may be purchased the day before, and the schedule can vary. It is common for trains to be late, and often, for some obscure reason or another, they never even leave the platform. If this happens, make sure to get reimbursed for your tickets. Sometimes, locals charter a bus and drive as many passengers as they can get to Juliaca or Puno. Of course, they charge more than the standard bus fare. The road from Cuzco to Puno (by way of Juliaca) follows the railway line, so you can see the same scenery that you would on the train. On the down side, because of the delay, you'll end up getting to Puno much later, even though the trip takes about the same time by bus as by train (between 10 and 11 hours). A one-way ticket for the *tren de turismo* costs about $23; for a chartered bus, about $19.

LAKE TITICACA AND AREA

Lake Titicaca (Isla Taquile, Isla Amantani and the Floating Islands)

By Boat

If you go to the pier at Puno, you will be swarmed by boatmen offering to take you to the islands. Of course, they usually wait until their boat is full before setting out.

The Uros Islands: There are departures for the Uros Islands from 7am to about 10am. If you want to go after 10am, you'll have no trouble finding a ride if you can round up 10 passengers. The trip to the islands and back takes a total of two hours and costs about $4.

Isla Taquille: Same schedule as for the Uros Islands, but the trip takes a total of eight hours and costs about $10.

Isla Amantani: About $11 for the nine-hour return trip.

Given how long it takes to get to the islands, you might want to consider staying with a local family so that you can make the most of your visit.

Tour Operators (see below).

Chucuito, Acora, Llave, Juli, Pomata and Yunguyo

By Bus

Buses to Yunguyo depart from Avenida Tacna, near the railway tracks, and pass through Chucuito, Acora, Llave, Juli and Pomata along the way.

Copacabana and La Paz (Bolivia)

There are lots of buses from Puno to La Paz, Bolivia, by way of Copacabana. They depart from the corner of Avenida Titicaca and Avenida Tacna. The trip to La Paz takes six hours and costs about $7. If you're only going as far as Copacabana, the three-hour ride will cost you just over $3.

Several tour operators (see below) offer bus service from Puno to La Paz, with a stop at Copacabana. Their buses are faster and more comfortable than public transportation; of course, they are also a bit more expensive.

PRACTICAL INFORMATION

Puno

Tourist Information

There is a small and not always reliable Infotour office on Jr. Lima, at the corner of Jr. Deustua. You're better off contacting a tour operator (see below).

Bank

The Banco de Credito at the corner of Jr. Lima and Grau will give you a cash advance on your Visa card, but you might have to wait in line.

Telecommunications

There is a telephone on Jr. Lima, at the corner of Grau.

Tour Operators

León Tours:
Jr. Libertad 176,
☎352-771,
≈351-316,
leontiticaca@protelsa.com.pe;
León Tours offers standard tours of the Chullpas de Sillustani and the various islands in Lake Titicaca. It sets itself

apart from the other agencies in that it also organizes excursions to destinations that are off the beaten track, like little-known villages and sites north of Lake Titicaca. The agency also offers trips to Bolivia and can even make plane reservations for you. Outstanding service.

Solmatour:
Arequipa 140,
☎352-901,
≈351-654;
Solmatour organizes traditional tours of the Chullpas de Sillustani and the islands.

Laundry

Lavandería Don Marcelo: Jr. Ayachucho 651, ☎352-444; About $1.50 per kilo.

 EXPLORING

From Cuzco, the road to Lake Titicaca leads through Pucará and Juliaca and past the Chullpas de Sillustani on its way to Puno, which lies on the western shore of the lake.

Pucará

Located just over 100 kilometres northwest of Puno, Pucará is often overlooked by tourists who are pressed for time. Lesser known than the Inca and Tiahuanaco cultures, Pucará civilization dates back to 800 BC and is distinguished by its strange-looking monoliths, whose central figure resembles the Tiahuanaco god Viracocha.

The town of Pucará is divided into two sections, Pucará pueblo and Pucará estación. Pucará pueblo is the old town, while Pucará estación developed when the railway arrived and people

decided to build their houses near the train station.

The **Iglesia de Santa Isabel**, a single-nave baroque church, dates from the 17th century. The most interesting thing about it is that it only has one tower. Apparently, the monks didn't have enough money to finish the second one. Behind the church is a trail leading to a pre-Inca ceremonial centre that is typical of the Pucará culture. It consists of a series of platforms rising up in three tiers to a decrepit stone temple where some Pucará monoliths once stood. The village craftsmen are renowned for their distinctive *torrito* sculptures (elaborately decorated bulls with enormous features).

LAKE TITICACA AND AREA

Lampa

Known as *La ciudad rosa* (The Pink City) because of its many pink buildings, Lampa lies about 30 kilometres northwest of Juliaca. Its most noteworthy attraction is its **church ★★**, which contains a flawless replica of Michelangelo's famous *Pietá* and a crypt made up of about 4,000 skulls. The church has a somewhat unusual feature – a nearly 35-metre-high Tuscan-style tower that stands about eight metres from the main body of the building.

Juliaca

Juliaca is a long, narrow, predominantly Amerindian town located nearly 4,000 metres above sea level. Though it is the region's capital, the town is poor and has no tourist attractions to speak of. It is known as the "Taiwan of the Altiplano" because a huge amount of merchandise of all different sorts passes through here in transit. Juliaca owes its development to the railway line between Cuzco and Puno (though

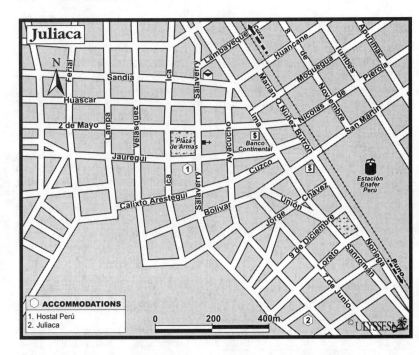

the trains are not always reliable) and to its airport, which connects it to Cuzco and Lima by air. It is a depressing, quiet town that livens up a bit on Mondays, when the weekly market is held. It attracts few tourists, and those who do come here only stay long enough to catch a plane or train headed somewhere else. If you take the train, watch out for thieves.

Cañon de Tiahuani ★

The Cañon de Tiahuani is not a real canyon. Located at an altitude of just over 4,000 metres, it is another of those strange-looking places, common in Peru, which suddenly appear before your eyes like a mirage. It is actually a group of huge, odd-looking rock formations whose ochre hue might remind you of the Grand Canyon. They have been carved by nature into amorphous shapes which, like clouds, can "be" whatever your imagination wants them to be. We spotted a mushroom, a Native American woman with a papoose and a medieval castle.

The Chullpas de Sillustani ★★

There are *chullpas* all around Lake Titicaca, but the most famous are the Chullpas de Sillustani, an ancient cemetery some 34 kilometres northwest of Puno. Perched at an altitude of 4,000 metres, this "city of the dead" consists of a group of cone-shaped towers up to 12 metres high, overlooking the Laguno Umayo. These are made of enormous stones, which are bigger at the top than at the bottom. There are about 45 towers in all, the successive legacies of the Pucarás, Collas, Tiahuanacos and Incas, who buried important members of their communi-

Puno's Fiesta Jubilar

The Fiesta Jubilar, a theatrical presentation of the legend of Manco Cápac and Mama Ocllo, is held in Puno every year from November 3 to November 9. Manco Cápac and Mama Ocllo arrive by boat at the local pier, where they are welcomed by the townspeople, who solemnly carry them on a litter to the centre of town, where the party gets into full swing. Aymara and Quechua dances play a central role in the festivities, drawing everyone into the fun.

ties here. The Pucará and Colla *chullpas* are cruder and made with much rougher stones than the Tiahuanaco and Inca tombs, which are carefully finished by comparison.

It is best to visit the *chullpas* early in the morning to avoid the hordes of tourists who usually arrive in the afternoon, the only time when public transportation to the site is available. If you want to escape the crowds, you'll have to go through a tour operator.

Puno

You're likely to be disappointed when you get to Puno. It doesn't take long to see that the town has lost a great deal of its charm over the years. Perched at an altitude of 3,825 metres, Puno is not only whipped by the powerful winds of the lofty Andean peaks, but is also pounded by the sun. Aside from its Plaza de Armas, the town has no real attractions to speak of. It does, however, serve as the jumping-off point for tours of the islands of Lake Titicaca and the handful of little towns along the shore. After sunset, the daytime heat evaporates and night falls swiftly. The temperature sometimes plunges below 0°C, so be sure to dress warmly.

The Laykakota silver mines put Puno on the map, but the area had been inhabited by the Aymaras long before that. The viceroy Conde de Lemos founded San Juan Bautista de Puno in 1668. The town was renamed San Carlos de Puno in honour of King Charles II of Spain. The railway line between Puno and Arequipa was completed in 1870, the same year steamships first appeared on the lake, earning it the title of the highest navigable lake on the planet.

Plaza de Armas is the town's sole attraction. It is surrounded by the cathedral and a few buildings that still bear witness to the colonial era.

Built in 1757, Puno's cathedral has a pretty baroque façade with decorative elements inspired by the flora and fauna of Peru. Its interior, however, is remarkably austere. While most Peruvian churches are adorned with gold and other precious materials, this cathedral is so simple that it almost looks bare.

A statue of Francesco Bolognesi stands on a pedestal in the middle of the plaza.

The **Museo Municipal** *($1.50; schedule varies; Conde de Lemos)*, right next to the Plaza de Armas, has a small collection of pre-Inca (Nazca, Moche, etc.) pottery, as well as a few mummies.

The **Arco Deustua** *(at the end of Jr. Independencia)* is a small monument to the soldiers who fought in the Battles of Ayacucho and Junín.

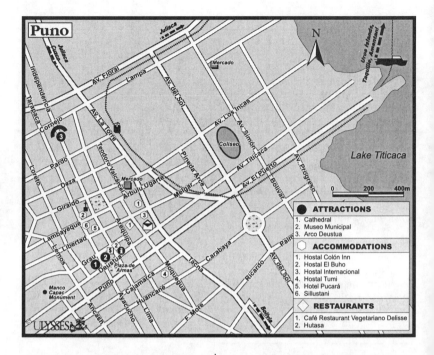

Lake Titicaca ★★★

Everyone has heard of Lake Titicaca, whose distinctive name, a mixture of Quechua and Aymara meaning *puma de piedra* (stone puma), has a way of sticking in your memory. For some people, "Titicaca" is simply a funny word; for others, it is fraught with folkloric associations. In any case, this legendary lake is up to 280 metres deep and stretches lazily across 6,900 square kilometres on the border of Peru and Bolivia. Located at an altitude of 3,182 metres, it is known as the highest navigable lake in the world. Actually, there are other, smaller, lesser-known lakes that could make the same claim, but international celebrity has its rewards!

Lake Titicaca topped the list of the world's highest navigable lakes in

Taquileños

Taquileños still adhere to ancestral traditions and a strict code of ethics. They are not allowed to lie, steal or be jealous, and pay careful attention to their dress, which reflects their values and civil status. For example, married men wear red hats, while single men looking for wives wear white hats. What's more, a man cannot get married if he doesn't know how to weave!

1870, when a steamboat was assembled on its shores after being carried by mules piece by piece from thePeruvian coast, a perilous (and some might say crazy) undertaking.

Lake Titicaca

Today, thousands of tourists ascend to Lake Titicaca each year, eager to explore its islands and local points of interest.

The Uros Islands ★

There are about 40 Uros islands in Lake Titicaca. Uros islands are not real islands, made of earth and stone, but rather are dense tangles of a hardy lacustrine plant known as tortora. The first time you set foot on one of these islands, you'll feel like you are walking on a water bed. Most inhabitants of the Uros Islands are descendants of Uros Indians, about whom little is known aside from a legend that they had black blood. The Uros have died out; their descendants are part Uros and part Aymara. They use tortora to build their houses and oddly shaped boats, as well as for fuel. Some islanders eat the plant; others grow vegetables in it. Stalks of tortora piled on top of each other form a substratum that serves the same purposes as soil.

The Uros Islands are a mere shadow of what they were in the not-so-distant past. The incessant flow of tourists to the area has wiped out all traces of their original character, leaving them overcommercialized. Unfortunate as that may be, the sad truth is that the residents of these islands are very poor, and rely heavily on tourism, as well as fishing, for their survival. When you arrive on the islands, you will be greeted by a swarm of children with tousled hair, cheeks reddened by the sun and the cold, torn clothing and a pleading look in their eyes, holding out their hands in the hope that you will give them some money or sweets. It is truly a pitiful sight, and few people are able to simply turn away. For mercy's sake, avoid giving them sweets, since they develop a taste for them and have probably never even seen a tube of toothpaste. The only way to help these children is to buy one of their little tortora boats or a piece of clothing made by their parents. The islanders are also in the habit of asking people who want to take their picture for a few *soles* in return.

The Formation of One of the Highest Navigable Lakes in the World

Lake Titicaca is what remains of Lake Ballivian, a huge body of water that once stretched all the way to Lake Poopó and the Salar de Uyuní, in present-day Bolivia. Over the centuries, Lake Ballivian gradually dried up because of temperature changes. Little remains of Lake Poopó, which is now surrounded by a vast, clayey desert, while the Salar de Uyuní is nothing but a 9,000-square-kilometre expanse of desolate land covered with salt deposits, making it the biggest *salar* (saltpan) in the Andes.

Isla Taquile

Located four hours by from the Puno pier by boat, Isla Taquile has an area of 11 square kilometres and attracts more visitors than any other island off Peruvian shores. A flight of over 500 stairs awaits visitors on the island. It's an arduous climb, but your efforts will be amply rewarded by the magnificent panoramic view at the top. You'll see mountains all around you, and terraces like giant steps that lead all the way down to the lake. Nearly 350 families live on the island in adobe houses with no electricity or running water. We recommend staying overnight to get a real feel for the place. A hotel, to be run by island residents, was under construction at press time. Your other option is to stay with a local family.

In 1540, the island belonged to Emperor Charles V, who decided to sell it to Marquis Pedro González de Taquila. Over the years, the name of the island became "Taquile". During the same period, the islanders developed a weaving technique which was so unique that wealthy Spaniards began coming here to purchase their highly coveted textiles. Much later, between 1919 and 1931, the island served as a penal colony.

Isla Amantani ★

Amantani is farther from Puno than Taquille and thus attracts fewer visitors. If you have a taste for the picturesque and the exotic, you will fall in love with this place. Unlike the Uros Islands, Amantani has not yet been overrun by tourists. It also has some unique archaeological remains.

Chucuito

This sleepy little village of adobe houses has two churches and some pre-Inca ruins. Next to the **Iglesia de Santo Domingo** are the remains of a temple dedicated to phallic worship, as evidenced by the evocatively shaped sculptures found throughout. No rational explanation has been found for this temple's construction. Some people think it was built as some sort of joke, while others claim that it is a pre-Inca site. Pregnant Native women often come here to pay tribute to the god of fertility in the hope that he will bless them with a beautiful child.

The village's other church, La Asunción, was built by Dominicans in the 16th century and has a raised porch supported by a stone arch. A type of sundial set atop a pedestal sits out front.

Charles V

The son of a German king and a Spanish princess, Charles V (1500-1558) was once the most powerful monarch in Europe. Thanks to a series of inheritances, he found himself at the head of a gigantic empire, which encompassed the Netherlands, Franche-Comté, the kingdoms of Castille, Naples and Sicily, and the Spanish colonies in America. Wishing to expand his realm even further, he was more concerned with defeating France and fighting infidels (Turks and German Protestants) than colonizing a little island in Lake Titicaca.

Acora

What sets this picturesque little village apart is its colourful Saturday market where you can watch locals trading and selling horses, llamas, cows and donkeys. Acora also has one of the oldest Dominican churches in the region.

Llave

Another sleepy, picturesque mountain village, Llave lies 56 kilometres east of Puno. The atmosphere livens up a bit during the Sunday market.

Juli ★

In the 16th century, Juli was considered the Rome of America, thanks to its splendid churches and buildings whose beauty rivalled that of the most famous architectural creations of the time. Founded in 1565, it became a missionary centre for Jesuits devoting their lives to educating Native Americans before the order was expelled from South America. Afterward, the churches they had built were left to crumble, though four have survived to this day: San Juan, San Pedro, Santa Cruz and La Asunción.

The best-preserved of the group is the **Iglesia de San Juan ★★**. A veritable museum, it contains some remarkable paintings from the Cuzqueña School, including a few by Bernardo Bitti. Its windows are not made of stained-glass but rather of pieces of *piedra de Huamanga*, a translucent rock that lets the light filter through. The rock was quarried near the town of Ayacucho, in the central Andes, and had to be carried here by men and llamas, which should give you an idea of how rich and powerful the Jesuits were back then.

Facing onto the Plaza de Armas, the **Iglesia de San Pedro** was the first church the Jesuits built in Juli.

Pomata

Pomata is a quiet little village on the shores of Lake Titicaca, 35 kilometres east of Puno. The road forks as it leaves Pomata. To the left, it leads to Yunguyo; to the right, to Desaguadero.

Crossing the Bolivian Border

South of Lake Titicaca are two roads leading to the Bolivian border. Most people take the one that passes through the Peruvian village of Yunguyo, since the other one, which passes through Desaguadero, is in poor condition.

The Jesuits

The Jesuits arrived in Lima in 1569 and then were sent to the shores of Lake Titicaca to educate and convert the Aymaras and other native groups in the region to Catholicism. The task was arduous, and many physical and cultural obstacles had to be surmounted before they succeeded in establishing themselves in Juli, which became their base. The Jesuits taught the natives about music, wood sculpting, and painting. Their primary objective, however, was to save souls. At their peak, the Jesuits had a strong presence in Bolivia, Argentina, Brazil and Paraguay, and their flourishing missions began to overshadow their rival cities, including Cuzco, Arequipa and Lima. Meanwhile, the king of Spain was not pleased about their growing wealth and power, which was at his expense. Thus, he expelled the Jesuits from the continent in 1767. An excellent movie called *The Mission* by Roland Joffé gives a good overview of the Jesuits, and is available on video.

Make sure you have your *tarjeta de turista*, which proves that you entered Peru legally. If you have lost it or forgotten it somewhere, you'll have to pay $5. The border station is open every day from 8am to 5pm. The customs officers sometimes ask tourists to pay a special tax that doesn't really exist. Be firm but polite, and you won't get caught in their little trap.

Don't forget that Bolivia is an hour ahead of Peru.

Yunguyo

Yunguyo is the last Peruvian village before the Bolivian border and the road to Copacabana, and the only reason tourists come here is to convert their dollars to bolivianos at the little currency exchange office on the Plaza de Armas. Though the rates are not particularly good, it is not a bad idea to exchange a small amount of money so you don't arrive in Bolivia empty-handed. Once you get to Copacabana or La Paz, you can exchange a larger amount.

Copacabana (Bolivia) ★★

Nestled between two mountains in the bend of a windy bay on Lake Titicaca, Copacabana lies barely 15 kilometres from the Bolivian border and is the first town you'll reach after leaving Peru. A pleasant town perched at an altitude of nearly 4,000 metres, it serves mainly as a stopping-off place for travellers on their way to La Paz from Isla del Sol and Isla de la Luna.

Isla del Sol ★★ and Isla de la Luna (Bolivia) ★★

These two islands are indistinguishable, and both play an important role in Inca folklore, since the founders of the Inca dynasty, Manco Cápac and Mama Ocllo, supposedly came from here. Túpac Yupanqui ruins can be found on Isla del Sol.

La Paz ★★★

Located at an altitude of 3,636 metres, La Paz is the highest capital city in the world. It owes its name to the period of relative calm, then peace, which followed a long period of incessant fighting between the Almagrists and the Pizzarists. The Spanish used to stop on these lofty plateaux on their way to the rich silver mines of Potosí. The land on which the town now stands belonged to the Chuquiago Indians before their arrival.

During the Mexican struggle for independence, the residents of La Paz followed suit, attempting to overthrow the local Spanish authorities on July 16, 1809. The viceroy at the time, whose seat of government was Lima, would hear of no such thing and sent a small army to quash the rebellion. Six months later, all the insurgents were executed. This bloody setback paved the way for independence, however. Fifteen years later, on December 9, 1824, General Antonio Sucre and his men finally succeeded in defeating the Spanish in Ayacucho.

Today, La Paz is not only considered the highest capital in the world, but also one of the safest in Latin America. The narrow streets of the colonial district are lined with churches and museums that bear witness to the glorious but not forgotten past.

La Paz is a jumping-off place for exploring the ruins of Tiahuanaco, the Valle de la Luna, the Yungas and, of course, Lake Titicaca.

 ACCOMMODATIONS

Generally speaking, local accommodations are quite basic. Besides Puno, where the few higher-end establishments are located, the area does not have the infrastructure necessary to provide tourists with lodgings that meet modern standards of comfort.

Lake Titicaca's islands have neither electricity nor running water, and, except on Taquile where a small hotel was about to go up in at press time, the only available accommodations are in private homes. If you wish to stay with a local family, contact a tour operator, who will find you a place to spend the night. If you plan to find your own accommodations on Taquile or Amantani, start at the pier in Puno, where a horde of boatmen will offer to take you to the island of your choice. Ask them if they know a family that would be willing to let you spend the night in their home, then negotiate a price. The going rate for frugal lodgings and three simple meals is about $4.

Juliaca

Travellers on a tight budget can stay at the **Hostal Perú** *($10; hw, cb; Braceso 409, ☎321-510)*, which offers basic, relatively clean rooms and friendly service.

The **Hostal Royal** *($10; sb; San Ramón 158)* is another inexpensive option for travellers who aren't too fussy.

The **Hotel Samari** *($20; pb, hw, ℛ; Jr. Noriega 325, ☎321-670, ≈321-852)* has 24 decent, reasonably clean rooms.

The best hotel in town is the old *hotel de turistas*, known today as the **Juliaca** *($65; pb, hw, ctv, ℛ; Jr. Manuel Prado 335, ☎/≈327-270, dcarloshos@tci.net.pe)*. It was being remodelled during our stay and should now offer all the amenities you would expect to find at a high-end hotel.

Puno

If you're looking for a cheap place to stay, head to the **Hostal Tumi** *($15; pb,* hw, tv; Cajamarca 152, ☎353-270), which has decent, relatively clean, unadorned rooms.

The **Hostal Internacional** ($20; pb, hw, ℜ; Jr. Libertad 161, ☎352-109, ⇌355-632) has about 10 no-frill rooms on three floors.

🏅 A newcomer on the local hotel scene, the **Hotel Pucará** ($40 bkfst incl.; pb, hw, tv; Jr. Libertad 328, ☎/⇌368-448 or 622 141) has that brand-new smell about it. It is nice to see a fresh face among Puno's hotels, which are somewhat outdated on the whole. Inaugurated in 1997, the Pucará has 14 clean, carpeted rooms on four floors. You have to go up one floor to reach the reception area, whose walls are decorated with a huge model of the village of Pucará.

The rooms at the **Hostal El Buho** ($45; pb, hw, ctv; Jr. Lambayeque 142, ☎/⇌351-409 or 366-122) are bright, clean, well-ventilated, and were being renovated at the time of our visit. This place also has its own little tour agency, which organizes excursions in the area and can make plane reservations for you.

The **Hostal Ferrocarril** ($45; pb, hw, tv; Avenida La Torre 185, ☎351-742), in front of the train station, rents out clean but somewhat spartan rooms.

🏅 The **Hostal Colón Inn** ($50; pb, hw, tv, ℜ; Jr. Tacna 290, ☎351-431, colon@cosapidata.com.pe) boasts one of the few colonial façades with balconies in Puno, and is the best hotel in the area, hands down. It also has the area's best restaurant (see p 180). The rooms are well-appointed, sparkling clean, safe and equipped with individual heating units. Some also have a small balcony. Solar-heated water is available on all three floors. The hallway walls

are decorated with local handicrafts, and the reception desk is next to a glassed-in courtyard, where you'll find a pretty fountain surrounded by greenery and birds flying about. If you want some peace and quiet, head up to the bar on the top floor, where you can sip a drink to the sounds of well-known classical music. The hotel is run by a friendly Belgian named Christian, who worked all over Latin America before settling down here.

The **Hostal Hacienda** ($50; pb, hw, tv; Jr. Duestua 297, ☎/⇌356-109), located one block from the Plaza de Armas, has 13 clean rooms, each with its own little heating unit, laid out around two pretty, bucolic courtyards.

Though they look worn-out and are decorated in an outmoded style, the rooms at the **Sillustani** ($50 bkfst incl.; pb, hw, tv; Jr. Lambayeque, at the corner of Tarapaca, ☎351-431, ⇌352-641, htl-sill@unap.edu.pe) are clean and safe.

The **Isla Esteves** ($120; pb, hw, ctv; on Isla Esteves; ☎367-780, ⇌367-879, www.libertador.com.pe), a big block of concrete with doors and windows carved into it, looks like it was plopped down on the island for the sole purpose of ruining the landscape. Its 121 clean, safe rooms are equipped with individual heating units and offer a lovely view of the lake and the surrounding area, but you would expect much more for the price. The staff is very efficient, however, and the restaurant (see p 180) has a good reputation. The hotel is located approximately five kilometres from downtown Puno; the taxi ride costs about $2.

Copacabana

Backpackers can stay at the little **Hostal Emperador** *($8; cb; Murillo, at the corner of Manuel Meijia)*, which offers basic accommodations at low rates.

The **Hotel Rosario** *($30; pb, ℜ; Parades, between Avenida 16 de Julio and Avenida Costanera, ☎316-156, turisbus@wara.bolnet.bo)* belongs to the same owners as the Hostal Rosario in La Paz, who can reserve you a room at either place and also run a tour agency that organizes excursions all over Bolivia.

Our vote for the best hotel in town goes to **La Cúpula** *($30; pb, hw, ℜ; Michel Pérez)*, which has charming, spacious rooms, a friendly staff and a restaurant that serves excellent vegetarian dishes.

The **Playa Azul** *($40 ; pb, hw, ℜ; 6 de Agosto, ☎320-068)*, right next to Plaza Sucre, has clean, safe but rather spartan rooms.

La Paz

Travellers on a shoestring budget can choose between the **Austria** *($5-$8; Yanacocha 531)* and the **Tambo de Oro** *($10; Armentia 367, near the train station)*.

The **Hostal Rosario** *($20 sb, $30 pb; hw, ℜ; Illampu 704, ☎316-156, ⇌375-532, turisbus@wara.bolnet.bo)* has about 30 safe, clean rooms, most of which are laid out around a pretty courtyard. The hotel also runs its own travel agency. Friendly service.

If you're looking for slightly more luxurious accommodations, try the **Libertador**

($60; pb, tv, hw, ℜ; Obispo Cárdenas 1421, ☎351-792), which has spacious rooms and good service.

If you've got money to spend, opt for the **Plaza** *($125; pb, hw, ctv, ℜ; Avenida 16 de Julio 1789, ☎378-317, ⇌343-391)* or the **Presidente** *($125; pb, hw, ctv, ℜ; Potosí 920, at the corner of Sanjines, ☎368-601, ⇌354-013)*, both of which are fully equipped to satisfy the needs of business travellers. Trivia buffs might be interested to know that the Presidente is the highest luxury hotel on the planet.

 RESTAURANTS

Juliaca

If you're looking for a quick, simple meal, head to the **Trujillo** *($; Plaza San Martín)*, an unpretentious restaurant with an affordable daily menu.

The best restaurant in town is the old *hotel de turistas*, now known as the **Juliaca** *($$; Av. Arequipa 1381, ☎/⇌715-241)*, whose menu includes of a variety of fish, beef, chicken and pasta dishes.

Puno

Así es mi perú *($; Jr. Libertad 172)* is the perfect place to go for *ceviche de pejerrey*, steamed or fried trout, or chicken dishes.

The **Café Restaurant Vegetariano Delisse** *($; Jr. Moquena 200)* is a small place that doesn't look like much but serves simple, inexpensive breakfasts.

Across from the Banco de Credito is a simple little restaurant named **Hutasa** *($; Lima 521)*, an Aymara word meaning "our house". The menu consists of empandas, homemade cakes and beer. Friendly service.

 The restaurant at the **Hostal Colón Inn** *($-$$; Tacna 290, ☎351-431)* is without a doubt the best in the region. It has two rooms decorated in more or less the same way. In the first, there is a wood-burning oven. Twenty or so pizzas are featured on the menu, and the one you choose will be baked right before your eyes. The second room is reserved for hotel guests, who, if they aren't in the mood for pizza, can order from a menu of local and international cuisine. The pasta is excellent; the meat is tender and the fish is always fresh. Efficient, friendly service.

As its name suggests, the **International** *($-$$; Jr. Libertad 170)* serves local and international cuisine. A few Chinese selections even appear on the menu, along with various chicken, trout and pasta dishes. You can get the daily special (soup and and entrée) for the modest sum of about $2.

 Located in a colonial house just over a block from the Plaza de Armas, **La Casona** *($-$$; Conde de Lemos 128, ☎351-425 or 351-108)* serves local

specialties like *anticuchos de alpaca*, *cuy* and *chicharonnes de chancho*. The restaurant at the **Isla Esteves** *($$-$$$; on Isla Esteves, ☎367-780, www.libertador.com.pe)* offers a whole slew of dishes, which you can savour while admiring the view of Lake Titicaca. Courteous, attentive service.

Copacabana (Bolivia)

Whether you're looking for a good meal or simply a quick snack, **Sujna Wasi** *($-$$; Jaurequi 127, ☎0862-2091)* is an excellent choice. The paella is delicious, the menu varied and the service as friendly as can be.

ENTERTAINMENT

Puno

To find out why Puno is the folklore capital of Peru, stop by **Nayjama Danzas** *(starting at 7pm, Tue to Sat; Av. La Torre 658, ☎368-137)*, where all sorts of traditional dances are performed, including the *diablada* and the *marinera*.

CUZCO AND AREA

All roads lead to Cuzco, a Quechuan word meaning "centre of the universe". This Mecca of Peruvian tourism has many Inca ruins, several picturesque villages and interesting excursions. Nowadays, the main problem for travellers arriving in Cuzco is deciding which tourist sites to see and which roads to take to visit them.

It takes at least three or four full days to really discover the city with its churches, museums and relics from the Inca era, including the incredible, cyclopean fortress of Sacsahuamán. Make sure, though, that you set aside your first day to rest and get used to the altitude. Also, expect to take a few days to visit the Machu Picchu ruins, which are undeniably the region's star attraction, and stay overnight in Aguas Calientes. Hikers will certainly not want to miss the chance to follow in the footsteps of the Incas by taking the most popular trail in South America, the Inca Trail, to Machu Picchu.

You can also get off the beaten track and visit the excavation sites of Tipón and Moray or the salt marshes of Maras. Cuzco can serve as home base for treks to the smaller surrounding villages, deeply recessed in the mountains, such as Chinchero, Pisac, Ollantaytambo or Andahuayllas, or even fly to Puerto Maldonado, which is the starting point for the road to Manu Reserve, an exceptional nature reserve, one of the most pristine in the world.

Cuzco is surrounded by high, snow-capped mountains. As it melts, the snow flows down in torrents to the rivers where rafting enthusiasts happily practice this fun but potentially dangerous aquatic sport. Most agencies (see p 189) organize rafting excursions on the Río Urubamba and Río Apurimac.

A Brief History

Because the Incas could not write and the Spanish were far too busy conquering them than to be concerned with their story of the founding of Cuzco, the event has been passed down only through oral tradition. Although there is no historical evidence to confirm it, the tale is very romantic and worth telling.

This city's origin is lost in the mists of time, an obscure time – where mysterious and contradictory myths were born. Very long ago, Inti the Sun God found that there was not enough light and life on this arid and desolate planet we now call Earth. So he decided to send his son, Manco Capac, and his sister, Mama Ocllo, to explore new lands where they could procreate and build a better world. One fine day, the divine couple sprang forth from the sacred waters of Lake Titicaca, and went to the place where Manco planted his enormous golden staff to claim the territory and found the city of Cuzco. They both settled down into the traditional roles of the couple: Manco taught men how to work the earth and make war, and Mama Ocllo taught the women how to sew and cook. Together, they are the ancestors of the Inca people.

The version told by historians and archeologists is much more prosaic. They all agree that the Incas appeared in the Peruvian Andes somewhere around the 11th or 12th century AD. The first Inca was called Manco, and was the forerunner of a dynasty of 11 Inca emporers. The Inca empire did not really expand until the ninth emperor, Pachacutec, came to power. A man of vision, often compared to Alexander the Great by historians, he made Cuzco his capital and, with the help of his son, built a vast empire which, at its apogee, extended north to Chile and south to modern-day Columbia, encompassing Bolivia, Peru and Ecuador. Because of its continuous expansion, the empire was becoming too large to govern. Around 1525, it was split between the governorate of the city that later became Quito, Ecuador, and that of Cuzco. Less than 10 years later, a fratricidal war broke out between the two governorates, and Atahualpa, the victor, inherited an enormous kingdom which was more or less reunified, but again became difficult to rule.

Upon landing in South America in the 16th century, the Spanish, led by Pizarro, took advantage of the enfeebled state of this huge empire and began its destruction by capturing and executing its leader, Atahualpa. After this shocking victory of the Spanish conquistadors over the Incas, the road was clear to conquer the entire Inca Empire. Indeed, Pizarro and his men only had to follow the Inca-built roads that linked the cities to Cuzco, which they took almost without a fight on November 15, 1533. Although the invaders were at first dazzled by Cuzco's architectural beauty, they were persistent in their quest for gold and turned a blind eye to the culture they came across. And so the great treasures of Cuzco were quickly looted, the city was pillaged and anarchy reigned. To prevent another war to determine who would succeed Atahualpa from occurring, Pizarro appointed a puppet Inca ruler, Manco, the half-brother of Huáscar, who temporarily filled the power void and calmed the ire of the people. Manco quickly realized that the Spanish were not the least bit interested in respecting the glory and prestige of the Incas – what they really wanted was the people's gold. In the end, Manco was caged like a wild animal and forced to submit to humiliation and scorn; his guards even raped his concubines in front of him, while uri-

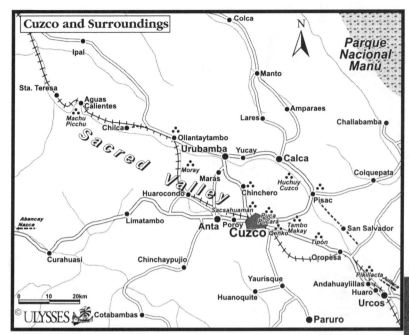

Cuzco and Surroundings

nating on him. Manco managed to escape from his torturers and went into hiding to mount a rebellion. Three years later, on May 6, 1536, Manco and his men laid siege to Cuzco, which suffered repeated attacks by the Incas. During this time, Pizarro was peaceably developing the foundation of Lima, but failed in his attempt to mobilize from the coast to help the besieged Spaniards in Cuzco.

By pure chance, Diego de Almagro and his men, who were on their way back to Lima from a disastrous expedition in Chile, passed through the Cuzco region and came to the assistance of those under siege. Cuzco became the scene of a bloody battle of epic proportions from which the Incas again had to flee, this time to Vilcabamba, taking along their gold and riches. While preparing for another uprising against the conquistadors some time later, Manco was stabbed to death a traitor. Manco's

son, who was only 10 years old, was proclaimed Emperor of the Incas. Naive, he made a deal with the Spanish; in exchange for his neutrality and conversion to Christianity, he was left to govern in peace. A few years later, he suffered a bout of food poisoning under suspicious circumstances and died. Faced with another power vacuum, another of Manco's many sons, Titu Cusi, replaced his brother. He rebelled against the Spanish, but in vain – he ended up being assassinated.

In 1572, another of Manco's sons, Túpac Amarú, considered to be the last of the Inca rulers, rallied his people against the Spanish. But his plans would fail: his rebellion was quashed and he was captured, humiliated, and then drawn and quartered in the middle of the Plaza de Armas in Cuzco. In the decades to follow, the Spanish made a point of building palaces and churches on the Inca foundations.

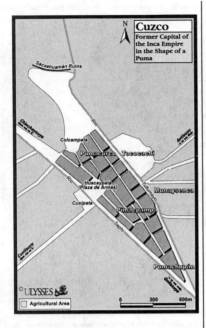

In 1650, a strong earthquake shook the entire Cuzco region. Ironically, most of the Spanish churches were destroyed, but the Inca foundations remained intact, even to this very day.

In 1780, about 200 years after Túpac Amarú's failed rebellion, José Gabriel Condorcanquí, a Jesuit-educated mestizo who was unable to ignore the cruel and merciless exploitation of the Amerindians by the Spanish, took the name of one of his distant and most illustrious ancestors, Túpac Amarú. Then, fueled by patriotism, he went to war against the ruling Spanish. A wave of revolt quickly spread through the surrounding areas, and he managed to rally the people to his side. The Spanish, feeling threatened, decided to show Condorcanquí the same fate as his mentor, Túpac Amarú. He was captured and tortured, and then executed on January 18, 1781 in Cuzco's Plaza de Armas.

Today, over two centuries after these bloody and unfortunate events, Cuzco is visited by thousands of tourists who walk its narrow streets that are filled with a secular past where the Inca and Spanish cultures are ever present.

FINDING YOUR WAY AROUND

Cuzco

By Plane

Aeroperú serves Cuzco from La Paz, Bolivia every day of the week, except Sundays. Most flights from Lima, Arequipa or Juliaca arrive early in the morning to avoid sudden changes in temperature and storms arising over the Sierra, which generally occur in the afternoon. From Lima, a one-way flight costs approximately $75 and takes about an hour. There are three Aeroperú and Aerocontinente flights a day, every day, beginning at 5:30am. From Arequipa, Aeroperú or Aerocontinente leave 25 minutes later for around $35. Aeroperú also offers regular 45-minute flights between Cuzco and Puerto Maldonado for $40.

From the Airport to Downtown Cuzco

The airport is located about 4 kilometres from downtown. Most deluxe hotels have their own reservation counter and provide free shuttle service to the airport terminal. However, if you do not have a reservation, you will be met by a number of taxi drivers anxious to offer you their services once you leave the airport. As a general rule, they charge about three or four dollars to take you to your hotel. If you do not have the budget for such an expense, go directly to the Avenida del Sol exit to hop a bus to the Plaza de Armas.

You should know, however, that you will probably have to walk a ways from the bus stop to your hotel, and that the bus has practically no room for luggage. This trip only costs 40¢, but make sure you have the right change on you.

You can also hail one of the cabs running along the Avenida del Sol and try to bargain a better fare than you get at the airport.

By Bus

A large number of buses run from Lima, Arequipa, Juliaca and Puno to Cuzco. Lima is approximately 40 very long hours by bus from Cuzco with an obligatory 8-hour stop at Arequipa. It goes without saying that this trip is very uncomfortable and exhausting, but far cheaper than taking the plane: expect to pay between $25 and $30. Buses leave regularly from   Arequipa for Cuzco. The trip costs around $15 and takes 14 to 16 hours. Daily buses link Cuzco to Puno via Juliaca. The trip takes about 12 hours and costs approximately $10. Though it is long, the trip should be cut down by several hours when the road between Puno and Cuzco is completely repaved before the end of 1998.

To date, Cuzco does not have a *terminal terrestre*, a central bus depot for the departures and arrivals of the various bus companies serving the city. Instead, each company has its own bus depot. There are many reputable bus companies in Cuzco offering safe and reliable service. Here are just a few:

Ormeño
Plaza Túpac Amarú 114B,

Cruz del Sur
Avenida Pachacutec 510,

Transportes Civa
Avenida Pachacutec 420,

Cristo Rey
Avenida Pachacutec 312.

By Train

In Peru, the train is one of the slowest and least effective means of transportation. The engines are outmoded, sometimes break down in the middle of nowhere, and in some instances the train stays at the station for no apparent reason. The only reliable train service runs between Cuzco and Aguas Calientes – this is the route that serves Machu Picchu. There are two train stations in Cuzco: the train travelling to Machu Picchu leaves from the **San Pedro Station**, and the one going to Juliaca and Puno departs from **Huanchac Station**.

The train serving Puno via Juliaca usually leaves the Huanchac Station four times a week on Monday, Wednesday, Friday and Saturday mornings around 8:00am. Tickets go on sale the day before, and schedules are subject to change. It is normal for the train to be late or, for some reason, not to move from the station. If this happens, you can get your ticket reimbursed at the booth. Sometimes people charter a bus for a large number of people to a specific destination, such as Juliaca or Puno. Charter buses cost more than regular buses. The road linking Cuzco and Puno via Juliaca runs along the railway. Therefore, you can enjoy the same scenery as you would from the train. The disadvantage is that because of the time spent chartering the bus, you will leave later and arrive in Puno a lot later than if you had taken the train, although the trip takes about the same amount of time, between 10 and 11 hours.

CUZCO AND AREA

Inca Ruins in the Surrounding Areas

By Bus

Board one of the buses leaving Cuzco on Calle Huáscar 128, and travelling to the village of Pisac. Ask the driver to drop you at the Tambo Machay ruins. Departures every half hour. The 15-minute trip costs 40¢.

On Foot

Physically fit people who are not in a hurry can take the hour-long walk to the ruins. From the Plaza de Armas, go to Tuourmán Street and turn left on Pumacurco. We don't want to sound paranoid, but it is best to make this trip in a group.

Guided Tours

Almost all agencies (see p 189) in Cuzco organize excursions to the surrounding ruins in conjunction with a brief tour of the city.

Poroy

By Bus

Buses to Chinchero go through the small town of Poroy. They leave Cuzco on Avenida Tullumayo. The trip takes under 20 minutes and costs about 40¢.

Maras and Moray

These two sites are off the beaten path and difficult to reach, especially in the rainy season. The best way to get there is by bus from Urubamba. Buses run on an irregular schedule, and will drop you at an intersection. From here it's only a 3-kilometre or 7-kilometre walk to Maras and Moray respectively. The Kantu Agency (see p 189) organizes visits to these two sites.

Chinchero

By Bus

Buses leave Cuzco from the Avenida Tullumayo for Chinchero following an irregular schedule, but do not go into the village itself; they will drop you on the road, about a 5-minute walk into town.

Pisac

By Bus

From Cuzco, the bus trip departs from Avenida Tullumayo and takes approximately 25 minutes and costs just under a dollar. To get to the Pisac ruins, you must trek 7 kilometres along a bumpy road north of Plaza de Armas. If you are physically fit, it should take you about 1.5 hours to walk there. You can also take a taxi for $2 to $3, depending on your bargaining skills, or rent a horse to get there; ask about this service near the church.

Yucay

By Bus

From Cuzco, the trip takes 1.5 hours and costs approximately 75¢. Buses regularly depart from Avenida Tullumayo.

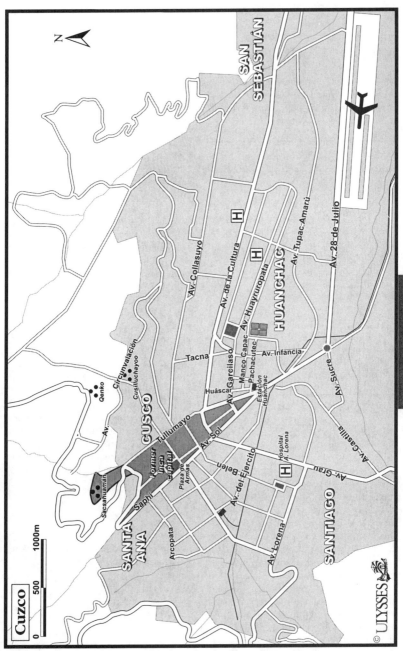

Urubamba

By Bus

Many buses leave regularly from Avenida Tullumayo to Cuzco. The trip takes approximately 2 hours and costs about $1.50.

Ollantaytambo

By Bus

It is difficult to find a bus that goes directly to Ollantaytambo. Go to Urubamba first, and get on a bus to Ollantaytambo from there.

By Train

The train for Cuzco leaves early in the morning from the San Pedro Station, with a stop in Ollantaytambo 2 hours into the journey. Expect to pay between $5 and $6.

Aguas Calientes - Machu Picchu

By Helicopter

If you are in a hurry and if money is no object, why not visit Machu Picchu by helicopter? HeliCusco ensures daily flights between Cuzco and Aguas Calientes, from where a bus will take you to to the ruins. The breathtaking flight from Cuzco takes about 25 minutes and costs approximately $80 per person for a one-way trip ($150 for a round trip). For reservations, contact the company at Triunfo 379, 2nd floor, ☎/≈227-283 or 243-555, or in Lima, Paseo de la República 5663, Miraflores, ☎01-447-104 or 447-110, ≈467-197. The chopper leaves Cuzco at 8:30am

and returns from Aguas Calientes at 3:30pm.

By Train

Remember: there are **two** railway stations in Cuzco. To reach Machu Picchu, go to the **San Pedro Station**.

Two classes of train serve Machu Picchu. First, there's the "autowagon", also known as the *tren de turistas,* which leaves the San Pedro Station every morning around 6am, stops in Ollantaytambo and finally arrives in Aguas Calientes about 3.5 hours later. It costs about $60 for a round trip. Then there's the local train which, as you'd expect, carries lots of local people and a few less well off tourists. You will pay about $12 for a round trip. You should know that the risk of being robbed is real and it is always best to travel at least in pairs so you can watch your bags at all times. The local train leaves San Pedro station approximately an hour later than the *tren de turistas* and costs less than half the amount, about $12 for a round trip. Once you have reached the Aguas Calientes Station on either train, a bus will take you to the ruins in 15 minutes for about $2. On your way back, the "autowagon" for Cuzco leaves around 3:30pm, and the local train an hour later.

On Foot

You can reach Machu Picchu by taking the Inca Trail (see p 204).

Pikillacta

By Bus

This site is difficult to access, but you can always take the bus for Andahuaylillas and ask the driver to drop you off at the 1.1-kilometre-long road to the ruins. It is easier to go through an excursion agency (see below).

Oropesa

By Bus

Take the bus for Andahuaylillas and get off at Oropesa.

Tipón

By Bus

Tipón is another site that's difficult to access. Take the bus going to Andahuaylillas and ask the driver to drop you off near the road leading to the terraces. It is a 4-kilometre walk along the road to the terraces. As with Pikillacta, it is better to take a taxi or go through an excursion agency.

Andahuaylillas

By Bus

For about $1.50, buses will leave you at the entrance of the city. This trip will take 45 minutes.

PRACTICAL INFORMATION

Cuzco

Tourist Information Offices

Cuzco's tourist office is located in front of the Iglesia de la Merced. Manta 111, ☎263-176.

Tourist Police Service

If you want to lodge a complaint against an agency, hotel or guide, go to the *policia de turista,* beside the Iglesia de la Compañía.

Organized Tours

Although it can be interesting to travel with no set schedule or itinerary, you should visit certain sites with a travel agency. There are just too many agencies in Cuzco to list, and all vary in terms of quality, but here are a few which you may find useful during your stay:

Coltur *(Maruri 316, ☎222-511, ≈234-950, www.coltur.com.pe)* has been offering tourists traditional excursions for many years now, such as city tours, visits to the markets of Pisac and Chinchero or the Ollantaytambo ruins, and of course, to Machu Picchu. Coltur also organizes excursions to other parts of the country.

Kantu *(Avenida Ricardo Palma L-8, ☎221-381 or 232-021, ≈233-155, kantupe@mail.cosapidata.com.pe)* offers traditional tours throughout the country, but sets itself apart from other agencies by organizing trips off the beaten path, such as horseback rides to the surrounding ruins, whitewater raft-

CUZCO AND AREA

ing, motorcycle trips, Amazon excursions and Inca Trail hikes. The service is excellent.

Santa Catalina (Procuradores 50, ☎235-579, ≈233-536, jorge.guzman@rocketmail.com) is a small but dynamic travel agency that organizes all kinds of excursions, including city tours, whitewater rafting, not to mention the traditional Inca Trail hike, all at reasonable prices. This agency also has an office in Arequipa.

Cuzco is an excellent point of departure for organzed trips to the Amazon Forest in southern Peru. A few agencies even have offices here to better serve visitors.

Pantiacolla Tours (Plateros 360, ☎238-323, ≈252-696, pantiac@mail.cosapidata.com.pe) has earned high praise from travellers who have gone with this agency. Facilities are rustic, but the staff is very competent and will go out of their way to make your stay as pleasant as possible.

Pantiacolla Tours USA
29856 Quail Run Drive, Agoura Hills, CA 91301, USA, ☎/≈500-674-1457.

Pantiacolla Tours The Netherlands
Singel 417, Netherlands, 1012 WP Amsterdam, ☎31 20 62 58 455, ≈31 20 63 87 894.

Las Touristik
Elsenstr. 62, 12059 Berlin, Germany, ☎/≈49 30 688 5314.

Manu Nature Tours
(582 Avenida del Sol, ☎224-384, ≈234-384, postmaster@mnt.com.pe) has the only lodge in Manu National Park. Its facilities are perfect for anyone who wants to visit the Amazon and enjoy a certain level of comfort.

Peruvian Safaris (365 Plateros, ☎235-542) has a lodge in the Reserva Tambopata-Candamo, about 60 kilometres and 3 hours south-east of Puerto Maldonado by boat; it has simple, but comfortable cabañas.

Mail and Telecommunications

Telefónica del Perú
Medio, between Espinar and the Plaza de Armas.

386 Avenida del Sol, near the Iglesia Santo Domingo and Koriancha.

Internet

Telefónica del Perú
Medio, between Espinar and the Plaza de Armas, telser@telser.com.pe. It costs 40¢ for 10 minutes.

Avenida del Sol. About $2 for an hour of use.

Banking

Banco de Credito
Avenida del Sol.
You can obtain cash advances on your VISA credit card here.

Interbank
Avenida del Sol.
Another bank where you can obtain cash advances on your VISA credit card.

Post Office

Avenida del Sol, at the corner of Avenida Garcilaso.

Laudromats

Lavanderia Procuradores
Procuradores 351.
It will cost you approximately $1.50 for one load (1 kilo) of clothing.

Lavamatik
Procuradores 341.
It will cost you approximately $1.50 for one load (1 kilo) of clothing.

Language Courses

Taking courses at a Spanish language school is an interesting way to learn a foreign language and experience the culture at the same time. There are many different programs, lasting from one week to several months.

Amauta
Procuradores 50, ☎/≠241-422, amautaa@cosapidata.com.pc.

Airline Offices

Aeroperú
317 Avenida del Sol.

Aerocontinente
179 Portal Comercio, on Plaza de Armas.

Pisac

Telephone

Immediately to the right after crossing the bridge.

Urubamba

Telephone

Beside the Parque Principal.

Ollantaytambo

Telephone

Across from the Parque Central.

Aguas Calientes

Telephone

Near the railway, next to the Plaza Manco Capac.

 EXPLORING

Cuzco ★★★

With a population of approximately 300,000 inhabitants, perched at an altitude of about 3,400 metres, the prestigious city of Cuzco, former capital of the Inca Empire, is breathtaking and astounding. Although it has undergone many changes over the centuries, its old quarter still contains precious and wonderful relics of the past. Once the hub of Inca culture, Cuzco, whose name, as you'll remember, means "centre of the universe" in Quechuan, extended out in all directions. To understand the remarkable atmosphere that prevails in this city, wander through the maze of narrow streets lined with churches and houses built on ancient Inca ceremonial sites. You'll hear conversations held in a mix of Spanish and Quechua, and see how the two cultures contributed to Cuzco's long development. Nowadays, it is hard for tourists to leave Cuzco out of their travel plans, especially since you have to pass through this city to visit the incredible Inca ruins which make this region even more interesting.

CUZCO AND AREA

Inca ceramics

The **Plaza de Armas** is built in the centre of the city and on the former Inca ceremonial site of Huacaypata, which was considered "centre of the universe". Today, the spirit of Túpac Amarú still seems present here. It is on this very spot that this unfortunate Inca, and the man who honoured his memory a century later, were drawn and quartered in front of their weeping people for having risen up twice within 100 years against the Spanish oppressor.

The Plaza des Armas is lined by the Cathedral and the Iglesia de la Compañía, as well as porticos of the various restaurants, cafés, hotels, souvenir shops and travel agencies.

The imposing and typically baroque **Catedral** ★★★ *(Mon to Sat 2:30pm to 5:30pm)* dates back to the 17th century and is still the Catholic religious centre of Cuzco. It is located on the northeastern side of the Plaza de Armas and was built on the base of the ancient Inca temple Huacaypata, which had originally been built for the Inca ruler Viracocha. This temple has three naves that are supported by Roman-style arches. The reason for this somewhat unusual mix of styles is that it took almost a century to complete the cathedral. Indeed, construction began in 1559, and only ended in 1653. It contains more than 350 paintings from the *escuela cuzqueña*, some of them by the master Diego Quispe Tito. The main altar is surrounded by Doric columns and covered in silver from Cuzco and Potosí. It weighs almost 1,200 kilograms! The lateral naves house several chapels, one of them contains the *Señor de los Temblores*, a sculpture of Christ. During the 1650 earthquake, this sculpture was removed from the Cathedral to appease the anger of the gods – and it seems to have worked! Today, it is blackened by the smoke of the candles constantly burning in front of it. The *Cuzqueños* bring it out during Easter celebrations to pay thanks to divine providence. Another unusual part of the church is found in one of its towers: a bell made of an alloy of silver, bronze and gold, over 300 years old and weighing more than a tonne.

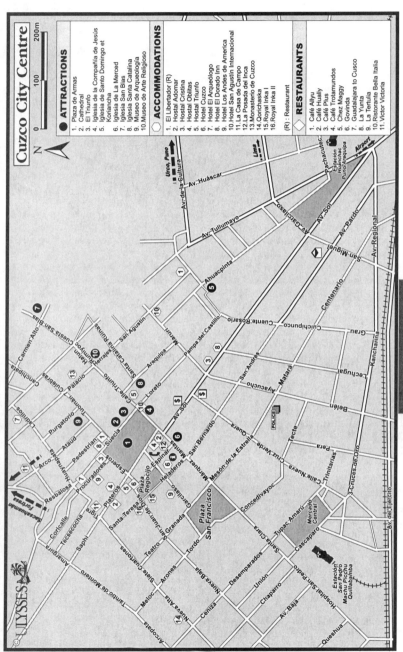

Cuzco City Centre

N

0   100   200m

● **ATTRACTIONS**

1. Plaza de Armas
2. Cathedral
3. El Triunfo
4. Iglesia de la Compañía de Jesús
5. Iglesia de Santo Domingo et Koriancha
6. Iglesia de La Merced
7. Iglesia San Blas
8. Iglesia Santa Catalina
9. Museo de Arqueología
10. Museo de Arte Religioso

◇ **ACCOMMODATIONS**

1. El Libertador (R)
2. Hostal Adomar
3. Hostal Cristina
4. Hostal Oblitas
5. Hostal Triunfo
6. Hotel Cuzco
7. Hotel El Arqueólogo
8. Hotel El Dorado Inn
9. Hotel Los Andes de America
10. Hotel San Agustín Internacional
11. La Casa de Campo
12. La Posada del Inca
13. Monasterio de Cuzco
14. Qorichaska
15. Royal Inka I
16. Royal Inka II

(R) : Restaurant

◇ **RESTAURANTS**

1. Café Ayllu
2. Café Hually
3. Café Plus
4. Café Trotamundos
5. Chez Maggy
6. Govinda
7. Guadalajara to Cusco
8. La Yunta
9. La Tertulia
10. Ristorante Bella Italia
11. Victor Victoria

CUZCO AND AREA

Boleto de Turista

If you are planning to visit a lot of churches, ruins and museums, it may be worth buying a *boleto de turista*. This two-week pass costs $10 and includes admission to the following places: the cathedral, El Convento de Santa Catalina, Iglesia San Blas, the Museos de Arte Religioso, the Museo de Historia Regional, and the ruins at Pisac, Tambo Machay, Kenko, Sacsahuamán, Puca Pucará and Chinchero. The pass does not include admission to Machu Picchu. The pass is sold at various agencies in the city (see p 189).

According to the *Cuzqueños*, it can be heard from 40 kilometres away.

Next to the Cathedral, **El Triunfo ★★★** is the oldest Catholic church in Cuzco and was built to recall the resounding and almost miraculous victory of the Spanish over the Incas during the siege of the city in 1536. In fact, this is where the Spanish hid during the siege, between the Suntur Wasi, the stone walls built by the Incas. The Inca threw fiery objects on the straw roof, which immediately burst into flames. By chance, the fire went out. According to the Spaniards' pious version of this story, a saint on horseback appeared to extinguish the fire... A more credible version tells of the Spanish ordering their slaves to climb onto the roof to put it out.

El Triunfo is also the final resting place of the mestizo writer Garcilaso de la Vega. Although he died in Spain in 1616, he was buried in Peru. After entering this sanctuary, you will see a painting from the *escuela cuzqueña*, to your right which shows the city of Cuzco in ruins after the devastating earthquake of 1650.

Towering over the southeast side of the Plaza de Armas, the **Iglesia de la Compañía de Jesús ★★★** *(variable hours)* is another example of Spanish domination over the Inca people. Built in 1570, and completed in 1670, it stands on the very site of the Palace of the Inca Huayna Cápac, father of Atahualpa and Huáscar. Its a superb baroque façade with Corinthian columns includes a single nave under which a series of chapels lead to a magnificent baroque main altar.

The **Iglesia de Santo Domingo ★★★** *($1; every day 9am to 5pm)* was built in 1534 by the Dominicans on the most sacred Inca religious site in Cuzco, the "Sun Temple", known as Koricancha. Built by Pachacutec, this temple was very important to the Incas because it was here that they worshipped their main gods: Viracocha, the supreme God; Inti, the Sun God; Quilla, the Moon God; Chaska, the Star God; Illapa, the God of Thunder and Lightning; and K'uychi, the Rainbow God. The craftmanship involved in the stonework is superior to that of the walls of Machu Picchu. When the Spanish divided Cuzco among themselves, Koricancha became the property of Hernando Pizarro. Unfortunately for him, he lost his life during the Battle of Sacsahuamán. Koriancha was then left to the Dominicans, the first religious order to establish itself in Cuzco.

The church cloister is worth a visit for the paintings in its upper and lower galleries that illustrate Dominican life.

The **Iglesia de La Merced ★** *($1; every day 9am to 5:30pm)* was built in 1534, but was redesigned in the late 17th century after the major earth-

Inti Raymi

Every June 24, the Ancient Inca Empire comes to life with dazzling splendour for a lavish religious and cultural ceremony called Inti Raymi. This festival takes place in Cuzco's Plaza de Armas and in Sacsahuamán, the ancient Inca military fortress on the outskirts of the city. During this ceremony, actors dressed in splendid costumes inspired by the dress of Inca nobility give their best performance to reproduce the beauty and tradition of centuries of Inca civilization. Today, this traditional Inca festival is also called the Fiesta del Sol (Celebration of the Sun), since it takes place during the summer solstice, the longest night of the year in the southern hemisphere.

quake of 1650. It has three naves with stone arches, and its numerous lateral chapels contain a few ornaments from the colonial era.

From the outside, the **Iglesia San Blas** *(Tue to Sat 2pm to 5pm)* appears sober and unassuming. However, this church, made of adobe and painted white, houses an authentic masterpiece from the colonial era: a **pulpit ★★★** carved out of a single piece of wood, a glorious baroque triumph. Like so many of the artists who worked at the time of colonization, its creator remains unknown to this day.

The **Iglesia Santa Catalina ★** *($1; Mon to Thurs 9am to 6pm, Fri 9am to 6pm, Sat 8pm to 5:30pm)* was built a few years after the earthquake in 1650 at Acclahuasi, where the Incas kept the Sun vestals. Today, the church has been converted into a religious art museum, and displays different paintings by the *escuela cuzqueña*. About 20 cloistered nuns still live here and rarely leave the premises.

The **Museo de Arqueología ★** *($2; Mon to Fri 8:30am to 5:30pm, Sat to Sun 9am to 2pm)* is just two steps away from the Plaza de Armas and has a small, but interesting collection of mummies, ancient tools for carving stone and other Inca arts and crafts.

Built on the foundations of Inca Roca, the ancient Inca temple, the **Museo del Arte Religioso ★** *($2; Mon to Sat, 9am to 6pm)* takes up almost 40% of the Archbishop's Palace and has some beautiful paintings of the *escuela cuzqueña*. There are also altars with gold-leaf, Gothic-style windows and azulejos

Surrounding Inca Ruins

Puca Pucará ★

Puca Pucará *(7:30am to 5:30pm)* means "red citadel". These Inca ruins are the remains of an ancient guard tower, surrounded by terraces where the *chasquis* used to deliver messages to Inca soldiers, who in turn handed them to their intended recipients. Apparently, Puca Pucará guarded access to Cuzco and Tambo Machay.

Tambo Machay ★

Tambo Machay *(7:30am to 5:30pm)* is an ancient resting place where Incas would relax and bathe. These ruins are a 25-minute walk southeast of Puca Pucará, and blend in perfectly with the countryside. There are three gravel terraces from which water flows into several basins once reserved for the

Inca ruler. Although its source hasn't been found, the water is pure and safe to drink. Indeed, the stones from which the water flows are smooth; if the water contained even the slightest amount of minerals, the stone would be rough. Female natives attribute special properties to this source and believe that by drinking it, they will give birth to twins or triplets.

Qenko ★

A fifteen-minute walk from Sacsahuamán, Qenko (7:30am to 5:30pm), sometimes called Kenko, means "labyrinth". Completely buried by the Spanish who tried to destroy every place of Inca worship, this site was only discovered in the early 20th century. Upon entering it, you will see the table carved in rock where llamas were sacrificed with the *tumi*. During this ceremony, the entrails of the llamas were removed to read the future, which would be told to an eager crowd gathered around the semi-circle of rock erected at the entrance of the site.

Sacsahuamán ★★★

The megalithic ruins of Sacsahuamán (7:30am to 5:30pm) are three kilometres north of Cuzco, and they have managed to stand the test of time. However, the question remains: is Sacsahuamán a fortress or a religious site? Though no one knows for sure, Sacsahuamán most probably played a religious role before the Spanish conquest, since there is evidence that different gods were worshipped here. Giant zig-zagged walls surround three terraces, prompting some people to believe that it was built for the God of Thunder and Lightning. When the Spanish arrived, Sacsahuamán's role suddenly changed, and these walls were used to protect the Incas against the

invaders. Whatever its original purpose, Sacsahuamán certainly saw its share of armies pass its secular walls, and gave refuge to many soldiers.

Some historians believe that Sacsahuamán was built during the reign of Túpac Yupanqui, while others claim that it was founded much earlier. Either way, you will definitely be impressed and fascinated by this puzzling cyclopean structure. The ruins are spread over three terraces, and it is hard to understand how the gigantic rocks of these ruins could fit so perfectly together. Some of the boulders that form the lower terrace are almost 9 metres high and weigh approximately 360 tonnes! Many stones from the Sacsahuamán ruins were shipped to Cuzco by the Spanish to build monuments there. Of course, they left the bigger stones! This is where Juan Pizarro died after being mortally wounded by a sling shot.

If you enjoyed visiting the Sacsahuamán ruins, wait until you see the Machu Picchu ruins!

If you were to look at the city from above, you would see that Cuzco and its surroundings were built in the shape of a giant puma whose head is the Sacsahuamán fortress.

Poroy-Maras-Moray-Chinchero

Poroy

The road which winds west of Cuzco passes through the village of Poroy before slowly making its way up to Chinchero, Maras and Moray. The story of how Poroy got its name is more interesting than the sparse attractions this small village has to offer. After the Spanish executed Atahualpa in Cajamarca, they decided to stop here for the day before continuing on to Cuzco. Francisco Pizarro halted his horse, raised his arm and addressed his men by shouting *"Basta por hoy!"* which means "Let's call it a day". Upon hearing this, the Incas, who had closely observed the Spanish, named the place Poroy.

Chinchero ★

Located approximately 25 kilometres from Cuzco at an altitude of 3,762 metres, the quiet and picturesque village of Chinchero livens up a bit with its **Sunday market** where bartering is still practised. Its **church** (*sometimes closed*), built on the central square of these ancient Inca ruins, is another example of the cultural hegemony imposed by the Spanish on the people they subjugated during the conquest. Inside, paintings of the *escuela cuzqueña* adorn its walls, while attractive frescos that line its façade illustrate the rebellion of Matéo Pumacawa, a mestizo who, after working for the Spanish, rose up against them in 1700. Upon leaving the church, you will see some interesting **Inca wall vestiges** and beautiful **terraces** rising along the side of the mountain on your right.

Maras ★

Maras has over 40,000 shallow clay shafts that are fed by an unknown source of water which becomes salty after infiltrating the moderately salt-filled sediment layer. Not long ago, the Incas mined salt from these shafts, which they transported to Cuzco. The salt here is iodine-free.

Moray ★★

Located at an altitude of 3,100 metres, off the beaten track and close to Maras, Moray is simply fascinating. It looks like a forgotten amphitheatre in the middle of nowhere. It is made up of several terraces complete with filtration canals which allow water to drain off. They become wider as they extend farther from the centre. A large quantity of starch was found here, which leads certain people to believe that potatoes were grown here. Apparently, Incas planted potatoes at the back of the terraces where they would freeze overnight. The next day, the sun would rise and warm the frozen potatoes. That evening, the potatoes were planted in a higher terrace; this exercise was repeated until the last terrace was reached. The end result was dehydrated potatoes that the Incas could pack in their bags and use as food during war. What's more, the *moraya* is one of the many varieties of Peruvian potatoes. During the rainy season, it is difficult to access this site, as is Maras.

The Sacred Valley

Pisac ★

From Cuzco, the road to Pisac gradually rises to 3,700 metres before winding downwards 30 kilometres later to the small village of Pisac. Hemmed in by the mountains, Pisac is known for its **Sunday market** and incredible **ruins ★★** *(7:30am to 5:30pm)* in terraced rows along the mountain which can be seen from afar by travellers. The Pisac market has lost much of its authenticity as it and the village became overrun with busloads of tourists. Similar wool goods and other handicrafts can be found for the same prices in Cuzco. A smaller Thursday market is also held. If you come here on an excursion from Cuzco, a visit to the market will probably not leave you much time to see the ruins, which are far more interesting and are the main reason tourists come here.

CUZCO AND AREA

The Pisac ruins are another good example of Inca architecture, and overlook the village of the same name. Although they are smaller and less spectacular than those at Machu Picchu, they have been excellently preserved. Their strategic position overlooking the entire region suggests that they were probably built as an ancient watch tower. A path leads to the edge of a ravine behind which lies one of the largest Inca cemeteries. Although the cemetery is difficult to access, some of the burial sites can be seen in the mountainsides (later desecrated by the *Huaqueros*).

Yucay ★

Yucay is a small, peaceful village which Sari Túpac, son of the Inca Manco, made his home around 1558, before he was poisoned under rather strange circumstances a few years later. There is not a lot to see here, but the village comes alive on Pisac market days when

tourists lunch here as part of organized tours in the area.

Urubamba

The village of Urubamba perches at an altitude of approximately 2,900 metres and, like Yucay, rarely attracts tourists except during market days, when groups of tourists dine at the Valle Sagrado de los Inkas hotel.

Ollantaytambo ★★

A charming little village at an altitude of nearly 2,800 metres, Ollantaytambo is very picturesque with its old, narrow stone streets lined with sunken aqueducts which carry pure mountain water all year long. The slow and relaxed pace of this ancient village has unfortunately been disturbed by droves of tourists who visit the ruins and the famous *andenas* (terraces) which give the village its charm. Instead of sleeping in Cuzco, some travellers spend the night here in order to leave the next morning on the train for Machu Picchu.

In 1536, Ollantaytambo was the scene of the last battle between the Inca and the Spanish. On the way back from a futile expedition in Chile, the Spaniard Diego de Almagro and his army stopped in the besieged city of Cuzco to liberate their compatriots. Thus Inca Manco and his men were forced to lift their siege and flee to Ollantaytambo, where they put up a fierce fight against the Spanish. The Inca could not resist, however, and were forced to flee again, this time to the village of Vilcabamba.

This temple, which now lies in ruins, is attributed to the Inca Pachucatec. However, because of the Spanish conquest and the Inca fratricidal dynastic war, this structure and the terraces surrounding Ollantaytambo were never

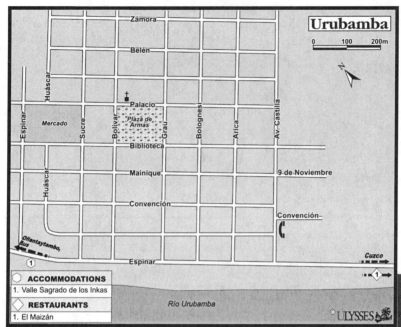

finished. Given their size, it is thought that these buildings had served both religious and military purposes. You can access the ruins by climbing a series of superb terraces, from which you can enjoy an incredible view of the surroundings.

Apparently, the name "Ollantaytambo" comes from Ollantay, a warrior from the proletarian class who fell hopelessly in love with the sister of the Inca Pachucatec.

Aguas Calientes

Aguas Calientes, also called "Machu Picchu Pueblo" because it is so close to these famous ruins, is a small simple town hidden deep in the mountains, along the Río Urubamba. The small village of Aguas Calientes owes its name, which means "hot water" in Spanish, to the **thermal baths** *($2; 5am to 8pm, at the end of the Calle Princi-*

pal) which can still be enjoyed by residents and visitors. Like the hotels and restaurants, most houses are found along the *río* up to the train station.

Machu Picchu ★★★

Sometimes, something is so great that words cannot express our amazement at the the greatness of a place. This is the case with Machu Picchu, which has been described as the most spectacular archeological site in South America. Spectacular? Make that superb, magnificent, sublime, wonderful, dazzling...!!! The list of adjectives is endless, and it is better to admire this monumental witness to a people obliterated by the lust for gold, power and glory in silence. Apart from Tikal in Guatemala, Machu Picchu is the only site in Latin America to be classified by Unesco as both a cultural and natural heritage site.

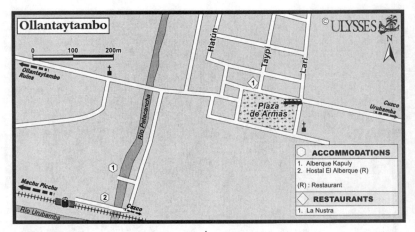

Though the words are hard to find, we will describe this wonderful site as best we can. Sitting atop a rocky outcrop overlooking the Río Urubamba and surrounded by breathtakingly high peaks lost in the mountain mist, the ancient village of Machu Picchu is as irresistibly charming and powerfully bewitching, as it was at the height of the Inca empire.

With the discovery of Machu Picchu in 1911, American explorer Hiram Bingham unlocked a treasure trove. Considered to be the eighth wonder of the world (and with good reason), this vast site is a mix of oddity and beauty that testifies to the architectural genius of the Incas.

Machu Picchu remained unknown to the Spanish, because it was hidden by the high surrounding mountains. As a result, it is indeed one of the few Inca sites that the Spanish did not destroy. In fact, it is so well hidden that more ruins were only recently discovered, while others have yet to be found. Since the time of its discovery, some of the mystery surrounding Machu Picchu has been resolved, but, despite the relentless efforts of historians and archeologists, it is still unknown why exactly it was built. Though several

hypotheses have been put forth by experts trying to solve the puzzle to these ruins, none is conclusive. Bingham mistakenly thought Machu Picchu was Vilcabamba, the last refuge of Manco. Others have postulated that this was where the Incas kept the Sun vestals, because of the large number of women's bones on site. However, further research has proven this false.

Since the Incas did not have a written language, they did not leave any documents explaining what was involved in building this lost village. Thus, Hiram Bingham made it his life's work to find the names of each ruin. However, although Bingham was a great explorer, he was not a professional archeologist. Bingham's names, which are now used by tour guides and listed in books on the ruins, have become commonly accepted, although modern historians contest their validity. This is another reason why, to this very day, Machu Picchu remains a mystery.

A Bit of History...

A graduate of Yale University, the American Hiram Bingham arrived in South America in 1909 looking for Vilcabamba, the last refuge of the Inca

Manco and his army. Two years later, in 1911, a native took Bingham to the ruins of Machu Picchu. At that time, the ruins were known only to a few people in the area who took care of the terraces and had baptized the place Machu Picchu, which means "old peak", although they had no idea of its importance. Sure that he had finally found the lost city of Vilcabamba, Bingham convinced everybody about his discovery. Over the next few years, Bingham continued his research and excavated other Inca ruins which make up what is known as the "Inca Trail" today. Bingham also discovered the ruins at Vitcos, which he realized were related to, but considered to be less important than, those at Machu Picchu. As it turns out, these ruins are located just before the lost city of Vilcabamba, which Bingham had searched for in vain, and are now called Espíritus Pampa.

The Ruins of the Lost City

Unless you take the Inca Trail, the bus will leave you in front of the modern Machu Picchu Ruinas hotel. From here you can follow a path straight to the ruins. **Machu Picchu** *($10; if you decide to come back the next day, it's only $5; 7am to 5:30pm)* is divided into two sectors, the rural and urban. Access the ruins by the rural sector, where you can admire a set of stepped mountainside terraces which were cultivated by the local inhabitants up until the time when Bingham made his discovery.

Take the terrace path, then climb up the steps to your left to see the splendid view from the **Casa del Vigilante**. A little higher up, a path leads to the **Inca Bridge**. Of course, this bridge was reconstructed and now serves as a walkway, but the impressive original stonework is still visible.

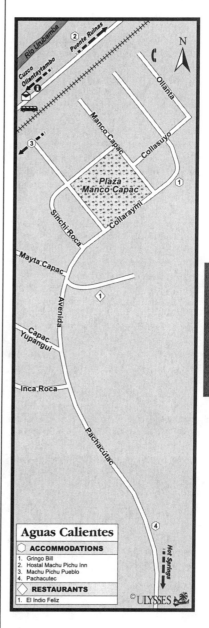

Aguas Calientes

○ **ACCOMMODATIONS**
1. Gringo Bill
2. Hostal Machu Pichu Inn
3. Machu Pichu Pueblo
4. Pachacutec

◇ **RESTAURANTS**
1. El Indio Feliz

© ULYSSES

CUZCO AND AREA

Retrace your steps back to the terrace path, and turn right to see the **Fuentes Sagradas**, a collection of 16 terraced ceremonial baths with a waterfall similar to the one in Tambo Machay (see p 195). From there, you can see the **dungeons**, trapezoid recesses where, according to Bingham, the prisoners stood while the recesses were filled.

Returning to the centre of site, climb the stairs and turn right to the **Royal Sector**, named for the fineness of its stones which are cut very differently from the other stones, leading people to believe that this structure was built for royalty. Go back to the stairs and you will find yourself right in front of the **Torreón** or "Sun Temple", similar to the Korinancha in Cuzco. Use the trapezoid door, whose base is riddled with holes that probably once contained pieces of gold, to access this semicircular building. If by chance you are there early in the morning on June 21, the summer solstice, you will witness an incredible sight: one of the windows aligns perfectly with the rays of the rising sun, and bisects them. The effect produced here and at similar sights demonstrates that the builders of Machu Picchu, like their Mayan counterparts, had acquired a profound knowledge of astronomy. In addition, the inside walls of the Torreón contain recesses into which offerings were probably placed. Bingham believed that the Incas raised snakes here.

Just below the Sun Temple is an interesting monolithic grotto called the **Royal Tomb**. Since no funereal remains have ever been found, this name is questionable.

Go back to the stairs and turn left to *las canteras*, the quarry. This is where the Incas would look for stones to build their houses. It is easy to see how the stones were cut: they were heated and quickly sprayed with cold water. In the fissures that this process created, a moist piece of wood would be inserted, which would then expand and break the stone.

A little further on is the **Templo de las Tres Ventanas**, or "Temple of the Three Windows", so named for its three trapezoidal windows through which the sun shone when it was at its zenith. These windows probably represented the Incas' conception of the world, which was divided into the Hanan Pacha, the spiritual world; the Kay Pacha, the physical world; and the Uhu Pacha, the world of the dead. Next to the Templo de las Tres Ventanas is a building called the "**Sacristy**", recognizable by its door made up of a **stone** which apparently has 32 corners. If you're up to it, try to find all of them.

From there, a small set of stairs takes you to one of the main attractions of this site: **Intihuatana**. According to legend, the Incas could "capture" the sun here, as it is the highest point of the ruins. Intihuatana is a smooth monolith that reaches towards the heavens. The protruding part was supposedly used as a sundial.

Further still, your eyes will be drawn to a very high peak called the **Huayna Picchu**, meaning the "young summit". Before the path that leads to Huayna Picchu is the **Roca Sagrada**. It is believed that this "sacred rock" was an altar used to sacrifice animals, and perhaps even humans. This holy place was probably used by the Pachamama cult which worshipped a goddess called "Mother Earth", because the blood of the victims ran onto the ground, and thus into her. Some say that this stone radiates energy through human touch. From this site, an hour's walk on a very narrow and straight path leads to the summit of Huayana Picchu, from which you will have an incredible, unforgettable view of the site and its surround-

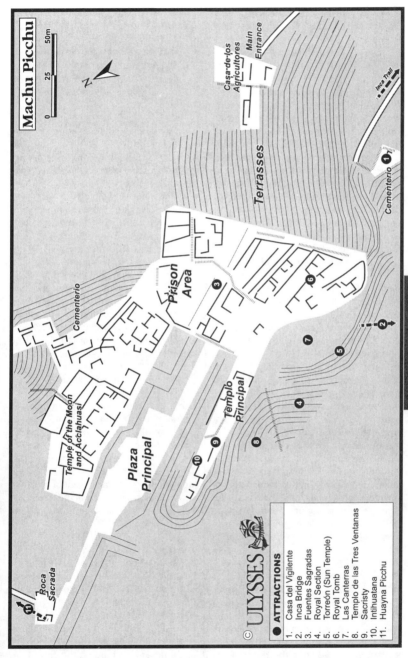

Machu Picchu

0 25 50m

N

Casa-de-los Agricultores

Main Entrance

Inca Trail

Cementerio

Terrasses

Cementerio

Prison Area

Temple of the Moon and Acclahuasi

Plaza Principal

Templo Principal

Roca Sacrada

© ULYSSES

CUZCO AND AREA

● **ATTRACTIONS**

1. Casa del Vigilente
2. Inca Bridge
3. Fuentes Sagradas
4. Royal Section
5. Torreón (Sun Temple)
6. Royal Tomb
7. Las Canterras
8. Templo de las Tres Ventanas
9. Sacristy
10. Intihuatana
11. Huayna Picchu

ings. At press time, the path was closed due to a devastating forest fire.

The Inca Trail

For people who did not use the wheel, the Incas designed an incredible network of paths extending over 30,000 kilometres, crossing Peru in all directions – to Bolivia and northern Chile in the south, and Ecuador and southern Colombia in the north. A true feat of civil engineering, this network stretched across the mountainous Andean Cordillera, bridging chasms, ravines and *ríos*. One of the sections still in existence is the Inca Trail, which leads to Machu Picchu and has become famous because of this prestigious site.

A Few Tips Before Taking the Inca Trail

Hiking the Inca Trail can be an unforgettable experience. But not being prepared for the altitude, the cold, insects and no-frills lodging can turn the trip into a nightmare. Although you can follow the Inca Trail on your own, we strongly recommend that you go with an agency (see p 189) to prevent problems arising on the trail, such as being robbed. Moreover, it may be worth spending a few dollars more to go with one of the better agencies, as these tend provide a greater level of comfort and expertise. Be wary of agencies whose prices seem too good to be true. The trip is generally a four-day walk on a 33-kilometre-long rugged path.

The price charged by the agencies is approximately $65 per person, which includes a tour guide (for at least 6 people), meals and camping equipment, but not sleeping bags or personal walking gear. You will also have to pay an additional $20 for the right to use the Inca Trail. This fee also covers a

visit to the Machu Picchu ruins, however.

- Make sure that you have become accustomed to the altitude by spending a few days in Cuzco or other places at about the same elevation.

- Make sure you are in good physical condition.

- Bring a compass.

- You should hire a porter to carry your sleeping bag, clothing and any travel equipment that could load you down. They charge between $25 and $30 per person; it's a worthwhile investment.

- The best season to take the Inca Trail is between May and late October. There are fewer tourists between November and April, but the conditions are also not as pleasant since it rains often.

A Brief Summary of the Trip

The hiking trip starts at Kilometre 88, just after the village of Ollantaytambo. From there, the path runs along the Río Urubamba, crosses the Llaqtapata ruins, climbs, then descends into the Cusíchaca valley, and reaches the village of Huayllabamba, where you can purchase supplies. Huayllabamba is the only village you will pass through during your hike.

The second day is by far the most difficult, since it starts at 3,400 metres where the air is thinner, and hikes up 800 metres to the Warmiwañusqua Pass before slowly descending into the Pacamayo Valley. Warmiwañusqua means "dead woman"; hikers who get there will understand its meaning. The sharp descent is hard on the calves and knees; look out for falling rocks – you

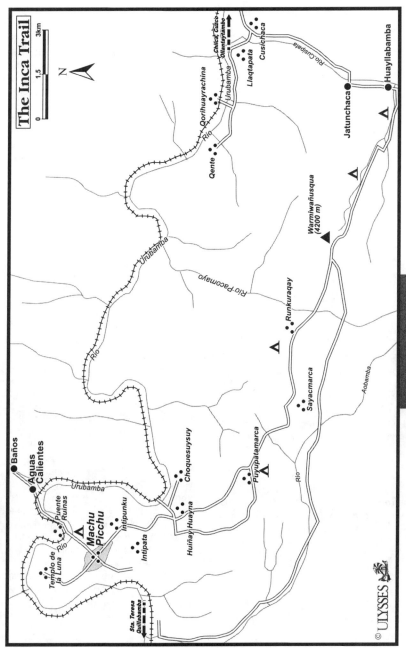

The Inca Trail

N

0   1.5   3km

Chilca, Cuzco
Ollantaytambo

Llaqtapata

Cusichaca

Qorihuayrachina

Rio Cusipata

Rio Urubamba

Huayllabamba

Qente

Jatunchaca

Warmiwañusqua
(4200 m)

Rio Pacomayo

Runkuraqay

Urubamba

Rio

Sayacmarca

Rio

Aobamba

Baños

Aguas
Calientes

Urubamba

Choquesuysuy

Puente
Ruinas

Intipunku

Machu
Picchu

Huiñay Huayna

Puyupatamarca

Intipata

Templo de
la Luna

Rio

Sta. Teresa
Quillabamba

© ULYSSES

could trip on them. At nightfall, your legs will be sore from the cold and fatigue, but you should have no problem falling asleep.

The third day begins early once again to confront the last difficult ascent to 3,860 metres. On the way, you will briefly pass Runkuraqay, the "Moon Temple", before arriving at the camp.

On the last day, rise and shine is at 4am to admire the breathtaking sunrise, illuminating the Machu Picchu site. Most people visit the site, then take the bus down to Aguas Calientes to relax in the thermal baths, which give the village its name. Masochists can walk down instead of taking the bus, but this takes a gruelling 1.5 hours.

Southeast of Cuzco

Tipón ★★

Tipón is another site that is off the beaten track and difficult to access. This village is about 20 kilometers from Cuzco. It is another example of the Inca's ingenuity: they built a set of 12 immense terraces irrigated by a network of aqueducts, whose water source is in the mountains. There is also a purification bath similar to the one found at Tambo Machay (see p 195). Tipón is located four kilometres from the road, on a bumpy trail which passes a few horses, barking dogs, grazing sheep and wild pigs. There are no hotels or restaurants. If you plan to visit this village on your own, make sure to take some water and a sandwich with you.

Pikillacta ★

For some mysterious reason, Pikillacta means "city of fleas" – Piki means

"flea", and llacta means "city". These ruins of an ancient, pre-Columbian Wari city lie just over 30 kilometres from Cuzco and might have been abandoned due to a famine or because of the invading Incas. The city is surrounded by an eroded wall, but the amazing urban planning of these people who lived around 900 BC is still evident. The roads and homes are perfectly aligned in a grid-like pattern. A few houses with straw roofs have been restored, but are not very spectacular. The site is 1.1 kilometres off the main road, and is difficult to reach. To visit this site, it is best to go with an agency or take a taxi. The site keeper is often absent.

Oropesa

Oropesa has little to see, except for its simple, sober adobe church. The town is a major bread producer, and most of its products are sold in Cuzco.

Andahuaylillas

Almost 40 kilometres east of Cuzco, Andahuaylillas boasts a rare jewel – a colonial **church ★★★**. Known as the "Sistine Chapel of South America", it was built in the 17th century by the Jesuits who settled here to convert the natives to Catholicism. Proudly rising over the Plaza de Armas, the church alone is worth the visit to Andahuaylillas. It may not look like much from the outside with its decaying façade in need of restoration work, but the sumptuous interior will leave you awe-struck. Its walls are richly covered with paintings by the *escuela cuzqueña*, and a number of illuminations are covered in gold-leaf.

Huaro

By walking three kilometres further up the road, you will come across the small village of Huaro and its church full of pretty frescos, which is worth a stop.

 # ACCOMMODATIONS

Cuzco

You won't find better prices elsewhere than those at the small *hostal* with the unpronunciable name, the **Qorichaska** *($8 sb, $12 pb; 458 Nueva Alta)*. The run-down, unventilated rooms will do for tourists short on cash. The place is popular with backpackers.

The **Hostal Suecia** *($10; sb; 332 Suecia)* is located near the Plaza de Armas and offers cheap, simple, dormitory-style rooms.

The **Hostal Triunfo** *($12; sb, hw, ℜ; 350 Triunfo, ☎232-772)* is also just a few steps from the Plaza de Armas and, as you might have guessed, right beside Iglesia El Triunfo. The austere but relatively clean rooms will suit travellers on a limited budget.

Rooms at the **Hotel El Arqueólogo** *($15 sb, $20 pb; 425 Ladrillos, ☎232-569)* are not luxurious, but comfortable, relatively clean and cheap.

In the busy Calle Plateros, close to the Plaza de Armas, the **Hostal Oblitas** *($25 pb, 15 cb; hw; 358A Plateros, ☎223-871)* has twenty rooms, some with wall-to-wall carpeting.

Right beside the Coltur agency, the **Hostal Wasichay** *($30 bkfst incl.; pb, hw, ℜ; 312 Maruri, ☎231-529)* rents out seven small, clean but unimagina-tively decorated rooms on three floors. Rooms on the 2nd and 3rd floors are quieter. Friendly staff.

Just a five-minute walk from the Plaza de Armas, **La Casa de Campo** *($30 bkfst incl.; pb, hw, ℜ; 296B Tandapata, San Blas, ☎244-404 or 262-345, ⌐241-422, amautaa@cosapidata.com.pc)* has 20 big, comfortable, immaculate, bright rooms laid out in terraces up the side of the mountain and generally occupied by globetrotters. Visitors can have breakfast in the hotel's restaurant (see 211). Without a doubt, this place is one of the best deals for this price. The establishment is owned by the same people who run the La Tertulia café and the Amauta language school (see p 191) This place is very convenient if you want to take a Spanish class while staying in Cuzco. The staff speaks English, German, Dutch, and, of course, Spanish. They will also pick you up from the airport.

Hostal Cristina *($40 bkfst incl.; pb, hw, ℜ; Avenida del Sol, ☎/⌐227-251, hcristina@protelsa.com.pe)* is another pleasant place to stay. This hotel is located on the bustling Avenida del Sol, not far from the Plaza de Armas, and has clean and adequately furnished rooms, as well as friendly staff.

The **Hostal Santa Catalina** *($40 bkfst incl.; pb, hw; 366 Santa Catalina, ☎228-471, ⌐241-254)* is in an old colonial house. The clean, safe rooms have high ceilings, and some also have a balcony.

The **Hostal Adomar** *($50 bkfst incl.; pb, hw, ℜ; 128 Portal Mantas, ☎232-249, ⌐232-507)* has a good location, only two steps away from the Iglesia de la Compañía. Its 10 small rooms are clean, safe and bright. Some have a view of the Plaza de Armas. The only thing it is missing is an elevator, so you will have to walk up two flights of stairs to get to the lobby. This might be inconvenient for anyone not yet accustomed to the climate.

🌴 One of the newest hotels in Cuzco, the **Hotel Los Andes de America** *($70 bkfst incl.; pb, hw, ℜ, heating; 234 Garcilaso, ☎223-058, ⌁222-253, andeame@mail.cosapidata.com.pe)* is located near the Plaza Regocijo. There are thirty clean, stylishly decorated rooms around an inner courtyard. Some rooms have small balconies. The staff is very helpful.

🌴 The **Royal Inka I** *($80; pb, hw, ℜ, tv; 299 Plaza Regocijo, ☎222-284 or 233-037, ⌁234-221)* is on the Plaza Regocijo and has 34 clean, safe and well-furnished rooms. Some look out onto a pastoral inner courtyard.

Larger than its namesake, the **Royal Inka II** *($90; pb, hw, ℜ, tv; 335 Santa Teresa, ☎222-284 or 231-067, ⌁234-221)*, is near the Royal Inka I and offers a similar standard of accommodation. Its 65 rooms are simple, but warm. Luxury services are available, including a whirlpool and sauna.

🌴 On the busy Avenida del Sol, the **Hotel El Dorado Inn** *($90 bkfst incl.; pb, hw, tv, ℜ; 395 Av. Del Sol, ☎231-135 or 231-232, ⌁240-993, from Lima ☎421-393, ⌁413-347, doratur@mail.cosapidata.com.pe)* offers its guests a free breakfast buffet. It has 60 rooms along vaulted hallways. All of them are furnished differently: some have antiques, while others have waterbeds or balconies.

The **Hotel San Agustín Plaza** *($90; pb, hw, tv, ℜ; Avenida del Sol, ☎245-774*

or 238-121, ⌁237-7375, from Lima, plaza@telematic.edu.pe)* has 26 clean, safe, but unimaginatively decorated rooms, some of which face Koricancha.

The large lobby of the **Hotel Cuzco** *($90; pb, hw, ℜ, tv; 150 Heladaros, ☎224-821 or 222-832)* is next to a huge common room with enormous fireplaces that heat up the cool Andean nights. Two staircases lead up three floors to the 125 differently decorated rooms. The place needs to be renovated, and the service is a bit cold.

🌴 Located half a block away from the Plaza de Armas, **La Posada del Inca** *($90; pb, hw, ctv, ℜ; 351 Espinar, ☎232-829, ⌁231-548, reservations from Lima, ☎422-4345, www.posadas.com.pe)* is a former refuge for backpackers that has been beautifully renovated and deserves its reputation as one of the best hotels in Cuzco. You will be served coca tea when you arrive, and can have as much as you like during your stay. Just take some from the thermos right next to the fireplace where the logs crackle; both are sure to warm you up. The rooms are ultra-clean, roomy, comfortable and have their own thermostats. Some have small balconies facing the front of the hotel. The hotel's restaurant also has a good reputation, and its staff is most helpful. Basically, this is one of the best places to stay for the price.

Despite its charming façade and its superb wooden balconies, the **Hotel San Agustín Internacional** *($102 bkfst incl.; pb, hw, tv, ℜ; 346 Maruri, ☎231-001, ⌁221-174, from Lima, plaza@telematic.edu.pe)* is not as good a deal as La Posada del Inca, even though it is larger and more expensive. It has about 70 clean and safe rooms, but the decor is inconsistent and the prices are too high.

The **Holiday Inn Hotel** *($140; pb, hw, ctv, ℜ; 602 Avenida del Sol, ☎226-207 or 224-457, ⊷241-375)* offers 50 modern, secure but sterile rooms that overlook noisy Avenida del Sol. A good place to stay if you want something a little more upscale, and aren't on a tight budget.

How would you like to stay in a 300-year-old monastery that has been transformed into a deluxe hotel? You can at the **Monasterio de Cuzco** *($160-$320 bkfst incl.; pb, hw, ctv, ℜ, 140 Palacio, ☎241-777, ⊷237-111, from Lima ☎221-0826, ⊷421-8283, www.peruhotel.com)*. Most rooms are situated around three inner courtyards. They are spacious, with a pastel decor and modern bathrooms. A relaxing lounge with a high ceiling is located next to the lobby. Travellers can sip *maté de coca* in this antique-filled room at any time of the day. Since it was originally a monastery, there is also a splendid private chapel whose walls are adorned with several paintings by the *escuela cuzqueña*.

Diagonally across from Korianacha is Cuzco's luxury hotel *par excellence*, **El Libertador** *($190; pb, hw, ctv, ℜ, 400 San Agustín, ☎232-601, ⊷231-961)*. Part of the building was built on an ancient Inca stone base, and the bright lobby is decorated with antiques and paintings by the *escuela cusqueña*. The rooms are impeccable, modern and spacious, and some even look out onto an old interior courtyard. The hotel's restaurant (see p 212, 257) is probably one of the best in the region. A luxurious place priced accordingly.

Yucay

If you cannot afford to stay at La Posada del Inca (see p 208), try the

Hostal Y'llary *($20; pb, hw, ℜ, right next to La Posada del Inca, ☎201-112)*, which rents out clean, simple rooms.

Across from La Posada del Inca (see p 208), **La Posada del Libertador** *($45; pb, hw, tv, ℜ; ☎342-567, ⊷324-834)* is in a colonial house, that can accommodate up to 30 guests. Apparently, Simón Bolívar stayed here; hence the hotel's name.

The **Hostal Antigua Misión San José de la Recoleta** *($35; pb, hw, ℜ; on the road to Yucay, directly to your right before Urubamba, ☎201-263, ☎/⊷201-004)* has kept a few traces of its past, as attested to by the slightly shaky façade and a few arches in the inner courtyard. The coutryard is surrounding by eight clean and very simple rooms. There are 12 slightly larger and more modern in the other building.

The **Posada del Inca** *($120; pb, hw, tv, ℜ; Plaza Principal, ☎234-842, ⊷213-263)* was built on the foundations of an ancient Franciscan monastery. The 14 rooms overlook the oldest part of the building; a pleasant inner courtyard. The best rooms are in the front, and some have a balcony. Room 111 is supposedly haunted by the ghost of a priest who killed himself for moral reasons. The older part of the hotel houses a small, private museum, which displays Nazca, Moche and Wari ceramics. The rooms behind the main building are surrounded by trees and flowers, and are quite a bit larger and more modern, but have managed to preserve their colonial charm. The floors are made of hardwood, as is most of the building. Some of these rooms also have balconies. There is also a small, modern chapel decorated in pastel colours on the premises. The hotel bar has a pool table, and sometimes plays videos. You can go hiking through the surrounding mountainside on the trails behind the building, or rent a bicycle. On market days, the place is pretty busy, since many tourists come to dine at the restaurant (see p 212).

Urubamba

Just a short distance from the Plaza de Armas, the **Hostal Urubamba** *($10; sb; Bolognesi)* has spartan, cheap rooms.

Standing proud at 2,850 metres, the **Valle Sagrado de los Inkas Hotel** *($110; pb, hw, ℛ; on the main road, ☎201-117, ⇌201-071)* is no doubt the city's luxury hotel. There are a total of sixty well-equipped bungalows with attractive views of the surrounding area.

Ollantaytambo

Consider **Hostal Miranda** *($10; pb; Plaza de Armas)* if you are on a tight budget.

Just before the El Albergue (see below), the **Albergue Kapuly** *($30; pb, hw, ℛ)* offers simple, clean and safe rooms.

Across from the railway, the **Hostal El Albergue** *($30; pb, hw, ℛ)* is run by Wendy Weeks, a friendly American who has lived in Peru for the past 25 years. She rents out seven clean and comfortable rooms.

Pisac

Directly across from the market, the **Hotel Pisac** *($20 sb, $26 pb; hw, ℛ; ☎/⇌ 203-062)* offers service with a smile, and has 10 simple, clean rooms, generally rented by backpackers.

Nearly 800 metres east of the village of Pisac, the **Royal Inka Pisac Hotel** *($80; pb, hw, ctv, ℛ, ≈, ⊛, ◯; ☎203-065 or 203-066, ⇌203-064)* is off the beaten track and away from the noisy market. Opened in late 1997, this luxury hotel has 76 rooms, some of which have their own fireplaces. There are also a tennis court with night lighting, a sauna, a whirlpool, a massage service, a beauty salon and a large heated indoor pool.

Aguas Calientes

The **Hostal Machu Picchu Inn** *($10; sb; on the railway)* is alright for backpackers. Rooms are small, simple and a bit noisy.

A small, affordable inn just to the left of the road leading to the baths, the **Pachacutec Hotel** *($15; pb, hw)* has silghtly outmoded rooms, which are nevertheless clean and safe.

With a name like **Gringo Bill** *($15 to $25; pb, hw, tv, ℛ; ☎223-147, ⇌211-375)*, you may have guessed that this inn is quite popular with adventurers. The rooms are spread over three floors and are furnished differently, so it is a good idea to ask to see a few of them before making up your mind. There is on-site laundry service. They will also keep your bags for you for a few days and change your dollars and travellers' cheques.

The **Machu Picchu Pueblo Hotel** *($180; pb, hw, tv, ℛ; on the railway, ☎231-425, ⇌221-121, www.peruhotel.com)* is undeniably the region's luxury hotel. Built with the scenery in mind, its bungalows blend in harmoniously with the large stones and trees which delimit the hotel's territory. There are approximately 55 bright, spacious and very clean bungalows, 18 of which have a fireplace. All have large and comfortable beds, with alpaca mattresses. Also, though orchids usually bloom only once or twice a year, the close to 160 varieties found here can be seen in bloom year round thanks to the favourable climate.

The concrete **Machu Picchu Ruinas Hotel** *($190; pb, hw, tv, ℛ; ☎221-082, ⊯440-619)* lacks charm and does not fit in with the area. Its only advantage is that it is located right near the Machu Picchu ruins, so you can get there before the rush of tourists arrives. The rooms have a magnificent view of the area, but are ordinary in themselves. They are clean and safe, but quite overpriced for what they offer.

 | RESTAURANTS

Cuzco

Many restaurants serve daily specials for about $2 per person, which include soup, *el secundo* (the main dish: usually pasta) and a drink (usually *maté de coca* or juice). You will probably find many restaurants of this type along the Calle Plateros or Calle Procuradores. If this doesn't appeal to you, you can also order à la carte.

Despite its shabby decor, the **Café Hually** *($; 363 Plateros)* attracts globetrotters with its simple and cheap family cooking.

Govinda *($; 128 Esperos)* is a small health-food restaurant run by the tireless Hare Krishna. It offers simple, nutritious and cheap meals at any time of day.

Tiny but pleasant, **Naturalia** *($; 351 Procuradores)* is another place in Cuzco that serves nutritious meals.

A small, unpretentious restaurant, **Victor Victoria** *($; 130 Tigre)* serves simple and affordable dishes that vary from day to day.

Café Allyu *($-$$; 208 Portal de Carnes)* opens its doors at 7am (around 6am during the high season) to serve you a hearty breakfast to classical music.

Near Café Allyu, **La Yunta Restaurant** *($-$$; Portal de Carnes)* is a good place for breakfast, lunch and dinner. In addition to the continental breakfast there is a daily menu, including spaghetti, at reasonable prices. Sit by the window for a view of the Plaza de Armas.

Located upstairs, the small but pleasant "café-restaurant" **La Tertulia** *($-$$; 4450 Procuradores, ☎241-422)* has the same owners as the Casa de Campo and the Amauta language school. This place is very popular with tourists and is known for its breakfast buffet. Early in the morning, classical music wakes you up. Crepes, pizzas, sandwichs and cakes are also on the menu.

The **Café Trotamundos** *($-$$; 177 Portal Comercio, upstairs, ☎232-387)* is a comfortable café with a small balcony where tourists can drink cappuccino or hot chocolate while watching all the action on the Plaza de Armas.

The **Bagdad Café** *($-$$; Portal de Carnes, beside the Cathedral)* is another café with a balcony overlooking the Plaza de Armas. The service is a bit slow, but if you are not in a hurry, this is a good place to enjoy a coffee and write a postcard in the sun, weather permitting. The specials are cheap and there is a good selection of pizza.

Café Plus *($-$$; 151 Portal de Panes, upstairs, ☎232-763)* is a good place to have coffee on a balcony overlooking the Plaza de Armas. Relaxed atmosphere and friendly service.

If you want to try something new and are in the mood for Mexican cuisine, go for the **Guadalajara to Cusco** *($$; 392 Procuradores)*. Burritos, tacos, guacamole, enchiladas – everything is on the menu, to be washed down with tequila, of course.

The **Chez Maggy Restaurant** *($$; 339 Plateros)* has a crowded room with a few picnic tables close to the wood stove where a wide variety of pizza is baked. The location is very popular with tourists and sometimes hosts musicians, who are passing through town and stop to liven up the night with their songs.

Owned by the same people as Chez Maggy, **Chez Maggy II** *($$; 344 Procuradores, ☎344-365)* is unlike the original and serves only pasta, prepared to your liking, in a small, picturesque room decorated with horse saddles and ceramics.

The **Chifa El Dragón** *($$; 215 Portal Belén, upstairs)* has a balcony overlooking the Plaza de Armas. The menu features a variety of Oriental specialties, such as soups and dishes with Chinese noodles and vegetables.

Right next to the Iglesia de la Compañía, the **Ristorante Bella Italia** *($$; 258 Portal Carrizos, ☎263-457)* prepares tasty dishes inspired by succulent Italian recipes. A large choice of pasta and excellent espresso. Be sure to try the prosciutto.

The **José Antonio Restaurant** *($$$; 356 Santa Teresa, ☎241-364)* has a large room with a lavish Peruvian buffet served during folklore shows. The breakfast buffet is served between noon and 3pm, and costs $12 per person, while dinner is served between 7:30pm and 11pm and costs $16.

The **El Truco Restaurant** *($$; 261 Plaza Regocijo)* and **La Taberna del Truco** *($$$)* are connected and are owned by the same people. The food is good in either place, and the menu features Peruvian specialties such as *rocoto relleno* or *cuy al horno*. The real difference lies in the decor. The ambiance of El Truco is far more relaxed, and the food is slightly cheaper.

At **La Posada del Inca Restaurant** *($$$; 351 Espinar, ☎232-829)* you can try some local specialties while enjoying a good view of the city's rooftops. The menu offers a combination of traditional Peruvian fare and international dishes: *lomo saltado*, *cuy*, fresh pasta, chicken and fish. The staff is friendly and attentive.

The mission of the restaurant in **El Libertador Hotel** *($$-$$$; 400 San Agustín, ☎232-601)* is to seduce your tastebuds. The menu has a variety of fresh dishes, including both international and local specialties. On weekends, musicians lead everyone in dances while singing folk songs.

Pisac

The **Samana Wasi** *($; southwest of the Plaza de Armas)* is a small, unpretentious restaurant, which serves trout prepared to your taste.

Close to the Samana Wasi is a small **local bakery** *($)* which bakes fresh bread every day in a wood stove.

For a quick, cheap bite, try the restaurant in the **Hotel Pisac** *($; facing the market, north of the Plaza de Armas)*, which serves pizzas and sandwiches. Simple decor and friendly staff.

Yucay

There are only a few reasonably priced places to eat at in Yucay. The **Mini Market Don Bosco** *($; 200 Avenida San Martín, ☎623-695)* sells cheese, honey, strawberry jam and ham.

The restaurant of **La Posada del Inca Hotel** *($$; Plaza Principal)* is quiet during the week, but comes to life with tourists on the weekends. The menu offers meat plates, such *lomo saltado* or *pollo a la milanesa*, as well as pasta and fish.

Urubamba

The **El Maizal Restaurant** *($$; on the main road)* is quiet during the week, but livens up on weekends when groups of tourists come to savour its buffet shaded by parasols.

Ollantaytambo

La Nusta *($; northwest of the Plaza de Armas)* serves simple, cheap meals.

You can have breakfast or lunch at **El Alberque** *($; across from the railway)* by informing the owner ahead of time.

Near Machu Picchu

At the entrance to the path leading to the Machu Picchu ruins is a **small fast food counter** *($)* that sells cheese and meat empanadas as well as softdrinks

and alcohol. You can enjoy a splendid view from under the colourful umbrellas on the terrace.

The restaurant at the **Machu-Picchu Ruinas Hotel** *($$-$$$)* almost has a monopoly over the other resturants around the ruins. Therefore the food is good and definitely overpriced.

Aguas Calientes

Several small restaurants line the railway and offer daily menus at reasonable prices.

A small, unpretentious vegetarian restaurant, **Govinda** *($; near the Plaza Manco)* carefully prepares simple, nutritious dishes at very reasonable prices. Relaxing environment and friendly staff.

La Choza *($; facing the railway)* offers unpretentious family cooking.

Chez Maggy's *($; Pachacutec)* serves pizza and pasta in a relaxing, friendly atmosphere.

Run by a friendly Frenchman who has travelled throughout the world, and his equally friendly Peruvian wife, **El Indio Feliz** *($-$$; Lloque Yupanqui Lote 4 M-12, ☎211-090)* is unquestionably our favourite restaurant in the region. Charming, simply decorated and warm, it is the ideal place for an enjoyable fresh meal. Patrick, the chef, has a flair for international cuisine. While waiting for your table, sit near the huge wood stove and try a swig of beer or sip delicious espresso, which is rare in this area. Everyone leaves this place with a full stomach. A poster on the restaurant's back wall describes the atmosphere here: "Welcome Tourists and Extraterrestrials". At press time, Patrick was planning to add on a few rooms to transform his establishment into a B&B – something to watch for.

 The restaurant at the **Machu Picchu Pueblo Hotel** *($-$$)* is made almost exclusively out of eucalyptus wood. Bright and airy, it opens out onto a beautiful terrace, where you can enjoy your meal while watching the Río Urubamba flow by. The predictable menu offers quality meat, fish and pasta dishes, although it is a bit expensive.

 ENTERTAINMENT

Cuzco

Ukuku's Pub *(316 Plateros)* shows subtitled American films on Thursday and Friday evenings. The place gets going around 10pm, when a well-dressed clientele show up to socialize or dance.

Up Town *(302 Sucia)* is a dance bar where a young, energetic clientele comes to get down to a variety of music.

At the **Kamikaze** *(Plaza Regocijo)*, the clientele squeezes into an art-deco room which opens up onto a huge balcony. There are shows on weekends.

As you may have guessed, the **Cross Keys Pub** *(Plaza de Armas)* is a British pub. Tourists come here to drink, chat or play pool. Happy hour is between 6pm and 9pm. Pizza is also served. It's a great place to begin your evening.

Mama Africa *(upstairs, 135 Plateros)* attracts a young energetic clientele which comes to party to the sound of reggae and popular music.

At **Tumi's Vidéo Café** *(next to La Yunta restaurant)* you can choose a video from the list, and reserve one of the two rooms to watch it in.

 SHOPPING

Cuzco

Cuzco has a lot to offer shoppers: colourful crafts, ponchos, wool hats, bright alpaca sweaters, and other original items. Bargaining makes shopping fun, but don't do it if you have no intention of buying anything. The difference of a couple of dollars may be insignificant to us, but it is not so for the vendor.

If, after a few hours of walking and shopping, you still have not found anything to your liking because you cannot find the right size or colour, and if you have some time on your hands, you can always buy some material, such as cloth, wool, etc., and talk to a merchant about tailor-making an item for you.

There are many boutiques and street vendors selling their wares around the Plaza de Armas and Plaza Recocijo.

If you are looking for some wonderful antique *mantas* and money is no object, visit **Josefina Olivera** *(501 Santa Clara)*.

Want to warm up in an alpaca wool sweater? **Alpaga Llampu** *(Ruinas)* is the place to go.

You can find a small but good **store** that sells handmade T-shirts at the end of Calle Procuradores on the right *(394 Procuradores, ☎221-948)*.

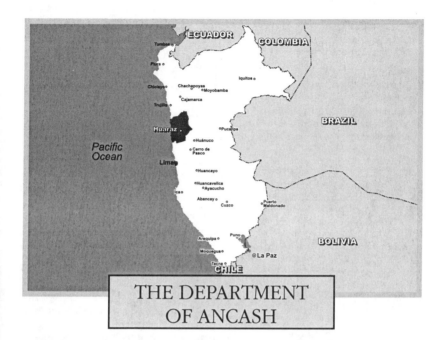

THE DEPARTMENT OF ANCASH

T ravelling north on the Pan American Highway from Lima, the road passes through scatterings of *pueblos jovenes*, little fishing villages, the Chimú ruins of Paramonga and a barren, lunar countryside like that found south of the capital. A few kilometres further, the highway leaves the Department of Lima and enters Ancash, which encompasses a portion of the northern coast as well as part of the Andes. The Ancash coastline does not have much in the way of attractions, but it is dotted with villages that serve as departure points for journeys up the western flanks of the Andes to the Callejón de Huaylas, a favourite destination of mountaineers.

The most developed city in the Callejón de Huaylas is Huaráz, and it functions as base camp for enjoyable mountain hikes, treks and climbs. This isolated Andean setting features superb mountains with breathtaking summits that, in the case Huascarán, reach heights of

up to 6,634 metres and amaze even the most indifferent visitor. This isolated, at times inhospitable region also harbours the remains of the first Peruvian civilization to develop a theocratic society, the Chavín culture, so there is plenty for archeology buffs to explore. The most beautiful, picturesque and spectacular route to the Callejón de Huaylas unfortunately leaves from the commercial port of the least interesting coastal city – Chimbote.

 FINDING YOUR WAY AROUND

Barranca

By Bus

Barranca is about three and a half hours from Lima. Budget a little over $3.

Paramonga and the Chimú Ruins

By Bus

Buses from Lima do not go all the way to the ruins, so travellers must first go to Paramonga, where buses to the archeological site leave regularly from south of the village.

Casma and Cerro Sechin

By Bus

Buses take almost six hours to reach Casma from Lima. The fare is about $5. In Casma, buses to the Sechin ruins leave frequently from the market for the modest fare of 60¢.

Chimbote

By Plane

Chimbote is less than one hour by air from Lima. AeroCondor has flights between these two cities every day for about $55.

By Bus

The bus trip between Lima and Chimbote takes close to six hours and costs about $10. From Huaráz, budget about $7 for a trip of eight hours.

Cañon del Pato

By Bus

Unfortunately, the road between Chimbote and Huaráz is sometimes closed, and some buses only make the trip after dark. Some Transportes Moreno *(Jr. Gálvez 1178)* buses travel from Chimbote to Huaráz via Cañon del Pato. Budget about $8 for close to 10 hours of travel.

Caraz

By Bus

Buses travel from Lima to Caraz via Huaráz. Foresee 12 hours of travel for a fare of $9. From Huaráz, buses reach Caraz in two hours for a fare of slightly over $2.

Yungay

By Bus

Several buses leave Huaráz regularly for Yungay. It costs a little over $1 for a one-and-a-half-hour trip.

Huaráz

By Plane

There is no airport in Huaráz, but there are occasional flights from Lima to the small village of Anta.

By Bus

Many buses leave Lima and arrive seven hours later in Huaráz. Budget about $9.

Chavín de Huantar

By Bus

Chavín de Huantar lies 100 kilometres southeast of Huaráz. Buses travel south from Huaráz and then fork east to the

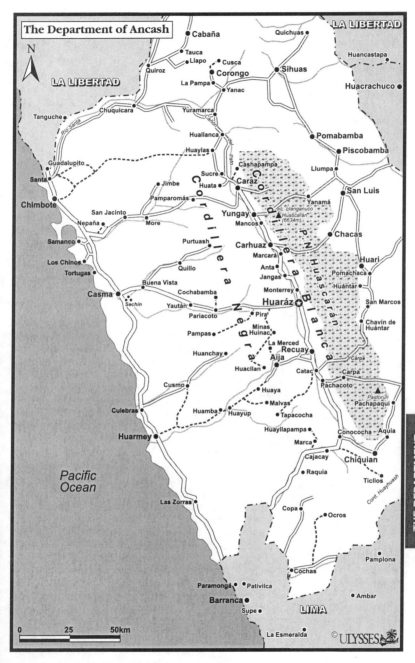

The Department of Ancash

N

LA LIBERTAD

LA LIBERTAD

Cabaña
Quichuas
Huancastapa
Tauca
Llapo
Cusca
Quiroz
Corongo
Sihuas
Huacrachuco
La Pampa
Yanac

Tanguche
Chuquicara
Yuramarca
Pomabamba
Piscobamba
Huallanca
Huaylas
Guadalupito
Cashapampa
Llumpa
Santa
Sucre
Caraz
San Luis
Chimbote
Jimbe
Huata
Yanamá
Pamparomás
Yungay
Huascarán (6634m)
San Jacinto
Mancos
Chacas
Nepaña
More
Samanco
Purtuash
Carhuaz
Los Chinos
Quillo
Marcará
Huari
Tortugas
Anta
Pomachaca
Buena Vista
Jangas
Huántar
Casma
Cochabamba
Monterrey
San Marcos
Sechín
Yaután
Huaráz
Pariacoto
Chavín de Huántar
Pira
Pampas
Minas Huinac
Carpa
Huanchay
La Merced
Recuay
Aija
Huacllán
Catac
Carpa
Cusmo
Pachacoto
Huaya
Pastoruri
Culebras
Huamba
Huayup
Malvas
Tapacocha
Pachapaqui
Huarmey
Huayllapampa
Conococha
Aquia
Marca
Cajacay
Chiquian
Raquia
Pacific
Ocean
Ticllos
Cord. Huayhuash
Las Zorras
Copa
Ocros
Pamplona
Cochas
Paramonga
Pativilca
Ambar
Barranca
Supe
LIMA
La Esmeralda

Cordillera Negra
Cordillera Blanca
P.N. Huascarán
Río Santa
Cañón del Pato

0 25 50km

© ULYSSES

small village of Catac. From here they slowly climb the mountainsides along a rough road, round Laguna de Queros, climb back up again to an altitude of 4,300 metres, and enter the dark tunnel of Kawish in the Cordillera Blanca. Finally they descend a spectacular, slightly dangerous, winding road that might thrill or scare you to reach the archeological site at Chavín de Huantar.

From Huaráz, the 100-kilometre trip takes close to four hours and costs about $3.

Many agencies organize excursions to the Chavín ruins (see p 219).

PRACTICAL INFORMATION

Chimbote

Banking

The Banco de Credito is located on Calle Bolognesi at the corner of Avenida José Gálvez. It offers Visa credit card cash advances.

Telecommunications

The telephone booth is on Calle Tumbes between Haya de la Torre and Bolognesi.

Caraz

Banking

The Banco de Credito is located at Jr. Daniel Villar 217.

Telecommunications

The telephone booth is on Plaza de Armas.

Huaráz

Banking

The Banco de Credito is on Avenida Luzuriaga.

Trekking Services

La Casa de Guías *(Parque Ginebra 28-G, aparto 123, ☎721-811, ⁓722-306).*

The Callejón de Huaylas is the setting of some of the most beautiful mountains in Peru and constitutes an ideal locale for anyone who dreams of conquering the Andes. **Warning:** Before setting off for these snowy peaks, it is recommended to consult the professional guides at La Casa de Guías. These guides have a broad knowledge of the region and can help you prepare for your climb with porters, food, tents and the like.

These guides can also inform visitors of areas to avoid, according to their climbing experience.

The best time of year for hiking and climbing in the Andes is from May to late September; meaning outside the rainy season, which extends from October to the end of April.

La Casa de Guías also houses a small restaurant and a large dormitory that can accommodate up to 40 people.

Lobo Adventure Shop *(Avenida Luzuriam 557, ☎/⁓721-833)* sells camping and mountaineering equipment.

Tour Agencies

Huaráz is swarming with agencies, all of which organize basically the same types of excursions, including standard city tours, outings to the enigmatic ruins at Chavín de Huantar and excursions to the Pastoruri glacier and Lagunas de Llanganuco. The quality of service varies from one agency to another. The following companies are recommended:

Chavín Tours
Avenida Luzuriana 502, ☎721-578.

Montrek
Avenida Luzuriana 646, ☎721-124.

There is also an agency at Hostal Andino (see p 230).

 EXPLORING

Barranca

Barranca is a little village less than 10 kilometres from the ruins of Paramonga and has a few services for tourists.

Paramonga

The adobe **ruins** *(about $2; every day)* of Paramonga dominate the coastal landscape approximately 200 kilometres north of the nation's capital and three kilometres from the port of Paramonga, in the Department of Lima. This site was once the most southerly settlement of the Chimú nation. Historians are undecided about what function it might have served. Some hypothesize that it was a fortress built for protection against Inca attacks, while others believe it was a ceremonial centre because the walls do not have parapets.

These theories leave room for several interpretations, but it is presumed that the settlement's function changed over time. The building's coastal setting towers over the sea and would have been an excellent lookout. Unfortunately, like many other undervalued archeological sites, the Paramonga ruins are poorly maintained and in shabby condition.

Casma

Casma is a small, modern village, of no interest to tourists, that was severely damaged by the famous earthquake of 1970. Visitors generally stop here briefly on the way to the ruins of Sechin.

The Ruins of Sechin ★ ★

The incongruous ruins at Cerro Sechin, just outside the village of Casma, were discovered in 1937 by Peruvian archeologist Julio C. Tello, who is also credited with finding the Chavín and Paracas ruins. The Sechin site is unusual because the buildings here were made of granite, a rarity on the coast where most buildings are made of adobe. The history of this lost civilization is traced on its surviving walls in rather mysterious, complex engravings that depict macabre warrior scenes. Aside from these disquieting images of agonized humans staring blankly into eternity, little is known about this civilization. However, archeologists do know that, like many other cultures, it inexplicably vanished in about the 4th century BC. Some of the structures found here were built around 1,500 BC, much earlier that the Chavín ruins.

THE DEPARTMENT OF ANCASH

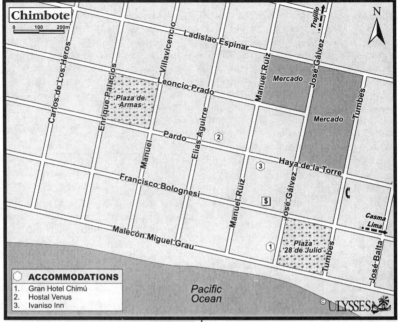

Chimbote

ACCOMMODATIONS
1. Gran Hotel Chimú
2. Hostal Venus
3. Ivaniso Inn

Pacific Ocean

Chimbote

In Peru, there are many places were everything seems just right in. Chimbote is definitely not one of them. Situated 400 kilometres north of Lima, at the mouth of Río Santa, Chimbote is the largest fishing port in the country and is known for its strong, foul fish odour. The town is of no interest to tourists except that this is where the road that travels through the spectacular Cañon del Pato (near Caraz, in the Callejón de Huaylas) ends.

Up until the middle of this century, Chimbote was just a little fishing village with a population of barely 4,000 residents, but in 1958 it became the first steel-making centre in the country. Today, this bustling port town numbers some 200,000 residents, but it has a reputation as a dangerous place to visit and many parts of the city are rife with noise and fetid odours. For quick stop-overs, however, there are a few quality hotels here, so staying here is not an altogether unpleasant experience. In 1991, a cholera epidemic broke out in Chimbote, sparked by a foreign ship anchored in the harbour, but this problem is now resolved.

Cañon del Pato ★★

Cañon del Pato means "canyon of the duck". Although there is no obvious explanation for the name, there is no question as to how the canyon was formed. It is the result of a combination of geological occurrences: the formation of the Andean cordillera, the erosion of the Río Santa valley between Cordillera Blanca and Cordillera Negra, and the runoff down the flanks of these two mountain chains caused by melting glaciers. The combination of these three factors acting over the course of a few million years created an impressive, one-kilometre-deep canyon in the

Río Santa valley. Part of the trip between Chimbote and Caraz features grandiose, simply awe-inspiring landscapes. The bus travels on the edge of precipices alongside steep rock walls, enters about 30 tunnels and crosses several waterways. Like the condor soaring to breathtaking heights, visitors are soon free of the memory of the putrid fumes and fetid, choking atmosphere of stagnant Chimbote. Unfortunately, this road is occasionally blocked, in which case travellers must find other ways to make the trip.

Callejón de Huaylas

Callejón means "corridor" in Spanish. The Callejón de Huaylas, a favourite destination of mountain climbers and hikers, lies between the Cordillera Blanca and the Cordillera Negra. Why are these mountain chains called Blanca and Negra? The answer is simply that the peaks of the Cordillera Blanca are usually capped with snow, while those of the Negra are only rarely so. In the Cordillera Blanca, the Peruvian glaciers have lost 25 to 50 percent of their mass since 1950, due to global warming.

The Callejón de Huaylas is surrounded by volcanoes. Some are still smoking and others are dormant, but sleep with one eye open awaiting the day when they will brutally and suddenly erupt.

The wind sighs through the mountains, like the soft melody of panflutes, and in the sheltered green valleys waterways gurgle and birds sing. Overhead, silence, storms, clouds, stars, the moon and the sun share the heavens. In this primordial landscape, mother nature is beautiful and cruel by turns. When her mood sours, she produces violent cataclysms that in a flash can destroy everything in their wake. These disasters remind humanity that the grandiose beauty of the countryside can suddenly release the destructive, unpredictable forces of nature, and so demands our greatest respect. May 31, 1970 is a date indelibly inscribed in the collective memory of Peruvians and proved to be just such an occasion. The earthquake lasted just over one minute but caused a monstrous landslide that took the lives of almost 20,000 people in barely 50 seconds. Approximately 60,000 people were killed in the Callejón region. Without a doubt, this was the most terrible natural disaster in the country's history.

Parque Nacional Huascarán ★★★

Declared a Biosphere Reserve by UNESCO, Parque Nacional Huascarán was created in 1975 to protect not only the fauna and flora of the region, but also the archeological sites found in it. Covering an area of 3,400 square kilometres, this park also encompasses the vast region of the Cordillera Blanca, including the tallest mountain in Peru, Huascarán.

Caraz

A small, quiet village situated about 70 kilometres north of Huaráz, Caraz enjoys a gentle, pleasant climate because of its moderate altitude of 2,270 metres. Caraz is one of the few villages that was spared by the terrible earthquake of 1970. People from all over the region liven up the village during the **Sunday market**.

Yungay

The little village of Yungay, 54 kilometres north of Huaráz and 12 kilometres south of Caraz, has been

THE DEPARTMENT OF ANCASH

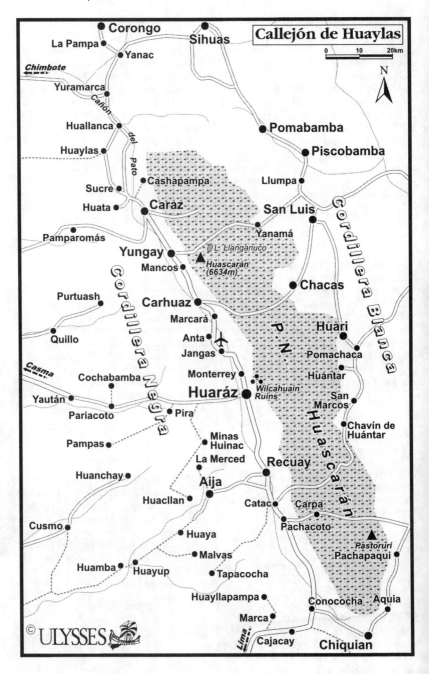

Callejón de Huaylas

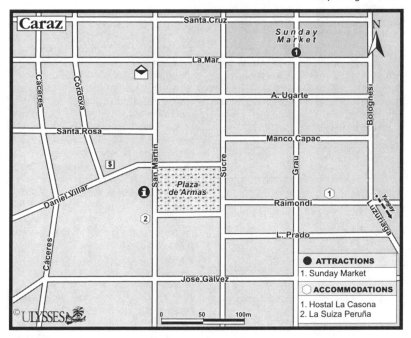

nature's victim several times. In 1872, an avalanche buried part of the village. In 1962, an earthquake devastated the region, but miraculously spared the village. However, this only foreshadowed a much graver misfortune that would hit place eight years later. Dates are remembered for different reasons – May 31, 1970, is permanently engraved in the memory of Peruvians, because it was on this day, at 3:30 on a bright spring afternoon that an earthquake measuring 7.7 on the Richter scale shook the Callejón de Huaylas, causing an enormous landslide that completely razed Yungay. In the horrifying panic that ensued, almost 20,000 men, women and children were buried alive under mud and rock. This terrible natural disaster is one of the saddest events Peruvian history. Some palm trees and a small monument commemorate the victims at what was once Yungay's Plaza de Armas. A half-swallowed bus can still be seen in the ground…

The town's cemetery is near the road that leads to the monument, on a hill topped by a giant statue of Jesus. Ironically, this is the high ground to which villagers fled to escape the slide.

Yungay once again courageously picked itself up from its ruins and rebuilt a few kilometres north of its original site. The new village is modern and not very attractive, but it is the beginning of a bumpy road that climbs 25 km up the mountain to Lagunas de Llanganuco.

Lagunas de Llanganuco ★★

The Lagunas de Llanganuco are two pretty lakes surrounded by superb mountains at an altitude of 3,850 metres. For a few *soles*, you can

THE DEPARTMENT OF ANCASH

rent a boat and sail along their green waters.

Llanganuco is also the departure point for one of the most popular hikes in the area, the one to Santa Cruz. The trek takes about five days and is ideal for beginners. It is recommended to contact an agency (see p 219).

Carhuaz

Not to be confused with Caraz, the quiet little village of Carhuaz is found some 30 kilometres north of Huaráz and is quite lively during the **Sunday market**.

Wilcahuain ★

The archaeological site of Wilcahuain is situated a little less than 10 kilometres north of Huaráz. It is a relic of Wari culture and is not very well maintained. The road to the site, however, features some pretty views.

Baños de Monterrey ★

For a rejuvenating afternoon, head to **Baños de Monterrey** *($1.50; every day 8am to 5pm)*, hot springs that are popular with tourists and Peruvians alike.

Huaráz ★

Searching for the colonial past in the dusty streets of old Huaráz is futile. Devastated by an avalanche of mud in 1945 and practically razed by the terrible earthquake of 1970 which claimed about 60,000 lives in the area, Huaráz was rebuilt and has become a busy, modern city of approximately 75,000 residents. Despite the vicissitudes of its recent past, the city enjoys a fabulous site on the banks of Río Santa, at an altitude of 3,060 metres, surrounded by some of the most majestic peaks in the Andean cordillera. Huaráz is considered Peru's "White Valley" because it serves as a base camp for Andean mountaineers who want to take on the challenges of the Cordillera Blanca. The best months to enjoy the pleasures of hiking and mountain climbing are from the end of May to the end of September. From November to March, rain showers are frequent and make trekking very unpleasant. The city especially comes to life during the **Thursday market**. Huaráz is also a good departure point for trips to the ruins of Chavín de Huantar.

Museo de Arqueológico de Ancash ★ *($2; every day 9am to 5pm)* exhibits ceramic objects from the Chavín, Wari, Chimú and Inca cultures. Some mummies that underwent cranial trepanation are also displayed. In the basement, there is a collection of photographs of Huaráz before it was devastated by the earthquake of 1970. Displayed outdoors behind the museum, monoliths produced by the Recuay are among the other curiosities housed at the museum.

Museo de Miniaturas del Perú ★ *($1; every day 9am to 5pm)* exhibits a model of the town of Yungay before it was buried by the landslide of 1970.

Travellers with a morning or an afternoon to spare can visit the **piscigranja** *($1; 9am to 5pm)*, ten minutes on foot from the downtown area. This trout hatchery is not at all spectacular, but it does supply the region's restaurants.

If you are looking for a view that fully captures the beauty of the Andes shouldn't miss the breathtaking panorama offered by the **Mirador de**

The stunning white facade of the Arequipa Cathedral occupies
the north side of Plaza de Armas. - *P. E.*

The Pisac ruins are believed to have been a fortress because of their strategic cliffside location and far-reaching view. - *P. E.*

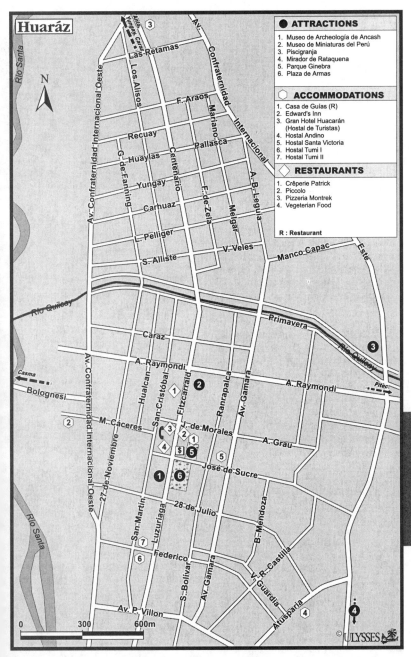

Huaráz

N

Rio Santa

ATTRACTIONS
1. Museo de Archeología de Ancash
2. Museo de Miniaturas del Perú
3. Piscigranja
4. Mirador de Rataquena
5. Parque Ginebra
6. Plaza de Armas

ACCOMMODATIONS
1. Casa de Guías (R)
2. Edward's Inn
3. Gran Hotel Huacarán
   (Hostal de Turistas)
4. Hostal Andino
5. Hostal Santa Victoria
6. Hostal Tumi I
7. Hostal Tumi II

RESTAURANTS
1. Crêperie Patrick
2. Piccolo
3. Pizzeria Montrek
4. Vegeterian Food

R : Restaurant

THE DEPARTMENT
OF ANCASH

0   300   600m

©ULYSSES

Rataquena ★★. The lookout is reached by a two-hour hike.

Chavín de Huantar

Although Chavín de Huantar is a simple little village lacking in tourist infrastructure, it has, however, given its name to the ruins of the Peru's earliest important civilization, the Chavín culture.

The Ruins of Chavín de Huantar ★★

In addition to hikers and trekkers, the area of the Callejón de Huaylas attracts archeology buffs who come to see the famous ruins of Chavín de Huantar. But what was the role of this city, of which only the ruins called Chavín remain? No one is able to answer this question, but it is certain that this city was as important a centre for Chavín culture as Rome was for the Romans, or even Cuzco for the Incas. Situated in the middle of nowhere 100 kilometres southeast of Huaráz, at an altitude of 3,190 metres between the Cordillera Blanca and the Cordillera Negra, these ruins once housed an important religious centre where priests, nobles and the civilization's elite officiated and dedicated themselves to propagating their belief in a strange haloed feline god. How pilgrims arrived at this spot without maps, roads or compasses remains a mystery.

These ruins were discovered in 1908 by Peruvian archeologist Julio C. Tello and are thought to have been built by the first large-scale civilization to develop in Peru. Since its discovery, the site has been the victim of several natural disasters, and consequentially most of the ruins are now buried about five metres underground. The last time Mother Nature struck down on this area was 1945, covering most of the site with a monstrous mudslide. As a result, only two hectares out of a total area of about 20 hectares are visible today.

The site is composed of a group of truncated pyramids between which were built narrow staircases, dark corridors, aqueducts that transported water and air ducts that whistled with the high-pitched notes of the wind. It is not difficult to imagine how the gloomy mysterious mazes, looked by torchlight. The site is now illuminated by an unreliable electrical system.

In total, 14 galleries wind through the site, only four of which are open to the public. The interior of the whole was probably inhabited by the leading social class or the priests who, it is thought, drugged themselves with San Pedro cactus to produce prophecies. The largest pyramid, named El Castillo by the Spanish, reaches a height of 10 metres and is supported by a square base of four 70-metre sides.

The main curiosity at Chavín de Huantar is inside the maze of subterranean galleries northwest of El Castillo. It is a monolith in the shape of a lance or knife, hence its name, *lanzón*. It is reached by descending the stone steps of a narrow staircase and then walking through a dark corridor at the end of which a flickering light unsteadily illuminates the strange, disturbing statue. According to some, it served as an altar on which animals or humans were sacrificed. As visitors approach the monolith, the features of a fantastic, supernatural being, half-man half-beast, sculpted into the stone of a 4.6-metre-tall granite slab, emerge: two bulging eyes, drooping ears, an owl's nose, a receding chin, a mouth full of razor-sharp fangs, a skull crowned by a tangle of interlaced snakes and felines. The obscure symbolism of these features and other unexplained designs can no doubt be traced back to human

Chavín Culture

Historians theorize that the Chavín culture arose toward 1000 BC, and was controlled by priests and elites who lived in the subterranean passageways of pyramids. These holy and noble men predicted the future by drugging themselves with a beverage made from San Pedro cactus, which caused strange hallucinations and perhaps even the civilization's decline – Chavín culture disappeared toward 200 BC, along with all of its secrets. Today, archeologists struggle to decipher mysterious symbols engraved on stone, but this is a very arduous task. If one day they do succeed in breaking the code, it will only be thanks to much patience and determination.

imagination itself, perhaps stimulated by the hallucinatory effects of excessive consumption of San Pedro cactus. In sum, it is a completely frightening idol that must have petrified people in the distant era of the Chavín. It is recommended to bring a small flashlight, since the electric lighting at the site sometimes fails.

Cabezas clavas, or "tenon heads", are also part of the mysterious world of Chavín culture. These are sculptures of human heads with sharpened fangs and bulging eyes that may have guarded the temple entrances. Only one of these is still attached to the wall of the main temple. The others have been torn from their mountings and buried by the natural catastrophes that have befallen the site, or were pillaged from inside the pyramids by *huaqueros*, or taken away to be displayed in Peruvian museums.

Two other monoliths, the **Raimondi stele** and the **Tello obelisk**, were discovered on the site. However, in order to protect them from the weather and vandalism, they were moved to the Museum of Anthropology and Archeology in Lima (see p 111).

The Tello Obelisk

The Tello obelisk was discovered on the Chavín site by none other than Julio Tello. A relic from a distant era, this large, prism-shaped block of stone displays a half-human half-animal figure with traits that bear a certain resemblance to those of a cayman, with feline teeth, a bird's tail and decorative motifs borrowed from the fauna and flora of the Amazon.

The Raimondi Stele

The Raimondi stele was found by accident in 1840 in the yard of a peasant who had himself discovered it some time earlier and had decided to use it as a table. It displays a mythical figure, a deified half-man half-feline, holding a kind of sceptre. This strange figure reappears in other cultures, including the Paracas, Pucará and Tiahuanaco, which were unquestionably later than and probably influenced by Chavín culture. These cultures succeeded each other through the centuries from 800 BC to AD 1000; the latter two were centred on the borders between present-day Peru and Bolivia.

THE DEPARTMENT
OF ANCASH

Puya Raimondi

One of the park's surprises is the Puya Raimondi, a giant plant that can grow to a height of 10 metres and live up to 100 years, but only blooms once. It is found at altitudes of about 4,500 metres, and it is unique to Peru and Bolivia. Puya Raimondi could easily be mistaken for a giant cactus, but it is actually a bromeliad. The best months to see this plant are May, October and November.

Puya Raimondi

Recuay

Set on the banks of the Río Santa, Recuay is a simple little village whose name designates an ancient culture of the region.

Pastoruri ★★

If you are not afraid of heights, visit the Pastoruri glacier. The bus that leaves from Huaráz drops passengers off at an altitude of almost 5,000 metres. From here, you must walk slowly – very slowly – the last 200 metres to the glacier, because the bus cannot be driven over the last stretch of the road. Alternatively, for a few *soles*, horses can be rented for this leg of the trip.

This is the only place in Peru where it is possible to ski, although it does not at all compare to North American or European ski resorts and there is no lift to the summit. For information, contact an agency or Casa de Guías (see p 218).

Chiquián

Chiquián, perched at an altitude of about 3,400 metres, is a little isolated

Cabeza clava

village with very little tourist infrastructure and serves as the departure point for hikers in the Huayhuash cordillera. For information contact an agency or La Casa de Guías (see p 218).

 ACCOMMODATIONS

During June, July and August, Huaráz hotels are often booked and the rates are higher. Conversely, during the rainy season, tou can bargain the prices down.

Barranca

Hostal Jefferson *($10; Jr. Lima 946)* rents relatively clean rooms and provides a rudimentary level of comfort.

Casma

Hostal Le Farol *($10; Tupac Amarú 450)* is an adequate place to spend the night in Casma.

Chimbote

Hostal Venus *($20; Haya de la Torre)* is suitable for travellers on tight budgets who want to make a quick stopover.

Ivaniso Inn *($60; pb, tv, hw, ℜ; Haya de la Torre 745)* offers modern, well-equipped rooms.

The old *hotel de turista*, **Gran Hotel Chimú** *($85; bkfst incl.; pb, hw, ℜ, tv; José Gálvez 109, ☎321-741)* is unquestionably the best hotel in town. The rooms are spacious and safe, and the restaurant has a good reputation.

Caraz

One block east of Plaza de Armas, **Hostal La Casona** *($10; corner of Raimondi and Jr. Grau)* is suitable for travellers with limited means.

La Suiza Peruña *($15; Jr. San Martín, between Jr. Grau and Jr. Bolognesi)*, on the southeast corner of Plaza de Armas, offers clean, comfortable rooms.

THE DEPARTMENT OF ANCASH

Monterrey

🦐 The Baños de Monterrey are owned by **Hotel Baños Termales Monterrey** *($50; pb, ℜ; Avenida Monterrey, ☎721-717)*. Located on top of the hill, next to the hot springs, this hotel is perfect for travellers who want to stay outside of Huaráz in an idyllic mountainside environment. Guests have free access to the springs.

El Patio *($50; pb, ℜ; Avenida Monterrey)* is in a colonial house just below the road to Baños de Monterrey. The clean, quiet rooms surround an interior courtyard.

Huaráz

Hostal Chong Roca *($10; Jr. de Morales 687)* is conveniently located and rents affordable rooms that offer a basic level of comfort. The staff is friendly.

La Casa de Guías *($7.50 per person, 10% discount for Hostelling International card holders; sb; Parque Ginebra 28-G, ☎721-811, ⌨722-306)* has a large dormitory with bunk beds. Simple, clean and cheap.

Edward's Inn *($12; Avenida Bolognesi 121, ☎/⌨722-692)* has been in operation for several years and seems to be hiker headquarters in the Callejón de Huaylas. The rooms are simple and safe. The owner is friendly and can help plan outings in the area. There is also laundry service.

Hostal Tumi I *($12; Jr. José de San Martín 1121, ☎721-784 or 721-913)* rents 18 austere rooms that will satisfy less-demanding travellers.

🦐 **Hostal Tumi II** *($25; pb, tv, hw, ℜ; Jr. José de San Martín 1085, ☎721-852 or 721-913)* is its neighbour's better half. It offers 80 clean, well-equipped, safe rooms on four floors.

Hostal Santa Victoria *($25; pb, ℜ; Avenida Gamarra 690, ☎722-422)* is located near Plaza de Armas and has clean, decent rooms, some of which have lovely views of the surrounding mountains.

Gran Hotel Huascarán *($45; pb, tv, ℜ; Avenida Centenario, ☎721-640, ⌨722-821)*, the local old *hotel de turista*, is the largest hotel in the city, but bigger is not necessarily better. The rooms are dated by about 20 years behind the times, although there is nothing to complain about in terms of the cleanliness of the place or the quality of the service. The restaurant (see p 231) has a good reputation, and the staff is friendly and helpful.

🦐 If you want to enjoy an atmosphere of intimacy, comfort, and good times during your visit to the Callejón de Huaylas, stay at the best hotel in the area: Swiss-run **Hostal Andino** *($60-$80; pb, hw, ctv, ℜ; Pedro Cochachin 357, Casilla 24, ☎721-662, ⌨722-830, andino@mail.cosapidata.com.pe)*, located just a five-minute's walk from downtown Huaráz. Some of the rooms have balconies where guests can lounge after a long day of hiking and enjoy a restful look at the splendid endless scenery. Some rooms also have fireplaces whose slow-burning logs heat the cool mountain nights. The entire place glistens with cleanliness. The hotel even has a computer that is hooked up to the Internet, guests can communicate with friends back home. The hotel also has its own tour agency, which organizes excursions of all kinds in the area. Dollars may be exchanged at the front desk, and chauffeured cars can be rented. Finally, the restaurant has a solid reputation and prides itself as the best in the city (see below). The staff are very obliging and speak French, English, German and, of course, Spanish.

 RESTAURANTS

Chimbote

If you like grill dishes, head to the little restaurant **La Fogata** *($; Villavicencio, between the Malecón and Bolognesi)*.

Chifa Canton *($; Bolognesi, at the corner of Villavicencio)* is a small, unpretentious Chinese restaurant.

The best restaurant in town is at **Gran Hotel Chimú** *($$-$$$; José Gálvez 109, ☎321-741)*. The prices are a bit steep, but the ingredients are fresh and lovingly prepared. Fish and seafood are of course the stars of the menu.

Huaráz

At the restaurant of **La Casa de Guías** *($; Parque Ginebra 28-G)*, tourists and hikers sit together at all hours of the day to dine on simple, nourishing fare.

For a fuss-free, healthy, affordable meal, opt for the restaurant simply called **Vegetarian Food** *($; upstair, just next to Telefónica del Perú)*. It serves a copious daily special at a reasonable price. The menu also lists a varied selection of dishes such as coffee brewed from roasted grains and vegetarian lasagna. The decor is unpretentious and the service is friendly.

Piccolo *($; Jr. Morales 632, at the corner of Avenida Luzuriaga, ☎726-360)* serves generous portions of pasta.

Pizzeria Montrek *($-$$; Luzuriaga 646)* offers a good selection of pizzas and pasta dishes, a simple, warm decor and friendly service.

Crêperie Patrick *($-$$; Luzuriaga 424, at the corner of Raimondi)* is named after its French owner. The establishment opens early in the morning to serve an affordable breakfast and stays open until late at night to serve rather fancy dishes such as duck à l'orange and fondue bourguignonne. It also has a good wine list.

The restaurant at **Gran Hotel Huascarán** *($$-$$$; Avenida Centenario, ☎721-640)* prepares tasty *pollo a la milanesa*, as well as other specialties from here and abroad. As a bonus, there is a pretty view of the mountains.

The most popular restaurant in the city is located under the same roof as the best hotel: **Hostal Andino** *($$-$$$; Pedro Cochachin 357, Casilla 24, ☎721-662)*. The kitchen cooks up all sorts of excellent things. The menu features, among other dishes, trout, steak, pasta, and, of course, cheese fondue. The ingredients are always fresh, prepared with care, attractively presented and served with a smile.

 ENTERTAINMENT

Tambo Taverna *(Jr. José de Lamar 776)* is popular with tourists and locals for drinks and dancing after a day of hiking.

Zona Blue Disco Pub Cafe *(Jr. Bolívar 653)* is one block from Plaza de Armas. In a true blue decor, visitors can enjoy varied music and happy hour, which is Friday nights between 8 and 10 o'clock.

The nightclub **El Sol** *(Avenida Luzuriaga, near Jr. Morales)* is mainly frequented by a young clientele that lets loose to the sounds of contemporary dance music.

TRUJILLO TO THE ECUADORIAN BORDER

he cultural richness of the North Coast should not be underestimated. Often bypassed by tourists visiting Peru, this region generally does not appear on mainstream itineraries. Hurried travellers usually visit the spectacular ruins at Machu Picchu, cross Lake Titicaca, fly over the mysterious Nazca Lines, climb the flanks of the Andes, or explore the luxurious Amazon rainforest. The flat desert surface of the coast north of Chimbote has only very sparse vegetation. Its lunar landscapes don't hold much allure. Yet here, on this ancient soil, stand fascinating sacred ruins of the little known Moche and Chimú cultures that are seldom seen by tourists.

In an era before the Incas, the great expansionist Andean people, conquered it, this coastal region was completely tamed by the brilliant Moche and Chimú cultures. Trujillo, the main city on the North Coast, proudly displays vestiges of its colonial past. It is the ideal point of departure for visiting the abandoned Chimú city of Chán-Chán, or the even older ruins of the Moche culture at Hauaca del Sol and Huaca de la Luna. Moreover, the North Coast has picturesque fishing villages hidden away along the coast. While waiting to sample the catch of the day, you can watch the skillful maneuvers of the pilots of the *caballitos de tortora* as they brave the Pacific waves.

The next important city to the north is Chiclayo, a mandatory stop if you wish to visit the site of Senor de Sipán, the most important archeological discovery in the Americas since Machu Picchu in 1911. The temperature rises progressively along the long stretches of deserted beach that lead north to Tumbes, the last large city before Ecuador.

FINDING YOUR WAY AROUND

Trujillo

By Plane

Aeroperú and Aerocontinente offer three flights daily to Trujillo from Lima starting at 5:30am. The cost is $55 one way for a trip that takes approximately an hour and a half. From Chiclayo, the price is $25 and the trip lasts 45 minutes. Two or three times a week there are flights to Trujillo departing from Iquitos. These flights take approximately two hours and cost about $55.

By Bus

The trip from Lima to Trujillo takes about nine hours. Departures are frequent and the fare is around $10.

Chiclayo to Trujillo is a three-hour bus ride that costs $4.

The trip from Cajamarca to Trujillo by bus takes approximately eight hours and costs about $7.

To get to Trujillo from Haráz by bus (via Chimbote) count on at least nine hours and a fare of about $9.

Huaca del Sol and Huaca de la Luna

It is strongly suggested to go though a local tourist agency (see p 238) to visit these ruins. There is no direct route to them using municipal transport.

Huaca Esmeralda

This other vestige of the past is situated in a rather run-down and crowded neighbourhood. It's best to go there in a group or with a tourist agency.

By Bus

Hop on the bus going to Huanchaco at the corner of Avenida Espana and Jr. Pizarro to the southeast of Plaza de Armas, and ask the driver to stop at the Mansiche church. The fare is only 35¢.

Chán-Chán

By Bus

It is dangerous to make this trip alone. Robberies have been reported in the last few years. As well as being safer, a trip to these ruins is also more interesting with a guide. Several agencies in Trujillo (see p 238) offer guided tours of Chán-Chán. If you insist on taking a chance, take the bus to Huanchaco from the corner of Avenida España and Jr. Pizarro, southeast of the Plaza de Armas. Ask to be dropped off 15 minutes later at the street leading to the site. From there it's a ten minute walk to the ruins. It's also possible to take this bus at Plaza de Toros, at the corner of Jr. Unión, but this part of the city is somewhat frenetic. The fare is the same; 40¢.

By Taxi

One way to save money is to share a taxi to the ruins. From Tujillo the fare is $4 to $5.

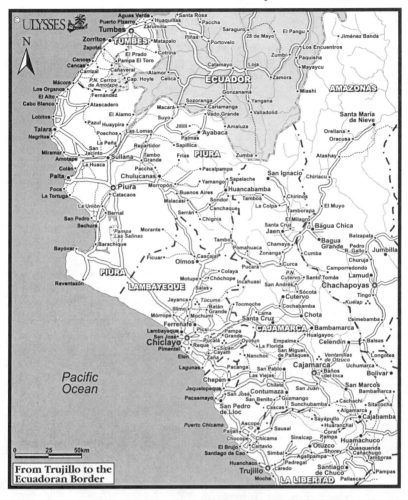

From Trujillo to the
Ecuadoran Border

Huanchaco

Take the Huanchaco bus on Avenida
España at the corner of Jr. Pizarro, on
the southeast corner of Plaza de Armas.
The trip takes about 20 min. for 40¢.

Huaca del Brujo and Huaca Prieta

It is best to go with an agency (see
p 238) to both sites.

Chiclayo

By Plane

Aeroperú and Aerocontinente offer
regular service to Chiclayo from Lima.
The trip takes 1.5 hrs. and costs about
$160, round trip. There is also air ser-
vice to Chiclayo from Tumbes for about
$20 one way.

By Bus

There is no central bus terminal for the many bus companies that go to Chiclayo. Each bus company has its own depot.

Many buses run from Lima to Chiclaya. The trip takes at least 12 hours for $10 to $12.

Sipán

It is best to go through a local tourist agency (see p 238) to visit this village, because bus service is irregular.

Lambayeque

By Bus

There are frequent departures for Lambayeque from the marketplace in Chiclayo. The trip takes less than 30 minutes and costs only 75¢.

Túcume

By Bus

There is bus service from Chiclayo to Lambayeque. The trip takes about 45 minutes and costs just under $1. The ruins of Túcume are one hour on foot, about one kilometre from the downtown area of the city.

Piura

By Plane

The flight from Lima takes approximately one hour and a half and costs about $90 one way.

By Bus

Piura is 15 hours from Lima by bus. The fare is about $15. Buses from Trujillo take seven hours and cost around $7.

Talara

By Bus

Talara is about three hours by bus from Tumbes at a cost of just under $4. Many of the buses going from Trujillo or Chiclayo to Tumbes stop in Talara.

Cabo Blanco

By Bus

Talara is the starting point for buses going to Cabo Blanco.

Tumbes

By Plane

There is only one flight per day from Lima. It takes about two hours and a half and costs around $70 one-way. The flight from Chiclayo takes an hour and costs about $30.

By Bus

Many buses go to Tumbes from Lima, Chiclayo, Trujillo and Puerto Pizarro. Lima is approximately 24 hours from Tumbes by bus, with a mandatory stop en route. It is obviously uncomfortable and exhausting, but it is much less expensive than the plane, between $17 and $25. Buses leave regularly from Chiclayo for Tumbes, a trip which takes nearly six hours and costs around $8.

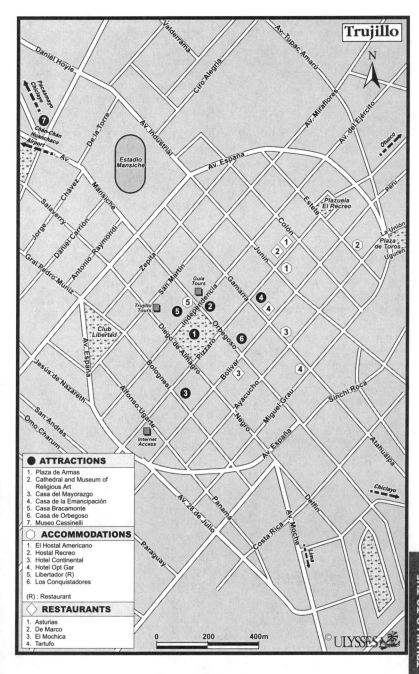

Trujillo

N

Estadio Mansiche

Plazuela El Recreo

Plaza de Toros

Guía Tours

Trujillo Tours

Club Libertad

Internet Access

● **ATTRACTIONS**

1. Plaza de Armas
2. Cathedral and Museum of Religious Art
3. Casa del Mayorazgo
4. Casa de la Emancipación
5. Casa Bracamonte
6. Casa de Orbegoso
7. Museo Cassinelli

◇ **ACCOMMODATIONS**

1. El Hostal Americano
2. Hostal Recreo
3. Hotel Continental
4. Hotel Opt Gar
5. Libertador (R)
6. Los Conquistadores

(R) : Restaurant

◇ **RESTAURANTS**

1. Asturias
2. De Marco
3. El Mochica
4. Tartufo

0   200   400m

©ULYSSES

Puerto Pizarro is less than 30 minutes away by bus at a cost of about $1.

Puerto Pizarro

By Bus

Buses shuttle from Tumbes to Puerto Pizarro for about 60¢.

PRACTICAL INFORMATION

Trujillo

Banking

The Banco de Credito is situated at 562 Gamarra Street. You can get cash advances on Visa credit cards here.

Interbanc is at the corner of Pizarro and Gamarra, on Pizarro. Cash advances on Visa are also available here.

Telecommunications

There is public phone service at 658 Bolívar at the corner of Bolívar and Gamarra.

Internet

Internet access is available on the corner of Pizarro, two streets southeast of the Plaza de Armas.

Tourist Agencies

Guía Tours *(519 Independecia, ☎245-170, ≈246-353)* is a well-established tourist agency offering standard tours of the city, the ruins at Chán-Chán, the Huacas de la Luna and del Sol, Huanchaco and the Huaca del

Brujo. Guía Tours also organizes excursions in the region of Chiclayo.

Trujillo Tours *(San Martin, at the corner of d'Almagro, ☎233-091, ≈257-518)* is another agency that organizes tours of the city and the nearby Moche and Chimú ruins.

Chiclayo

Banking

Banco de Credito is at 630 Balta Street. Cash advances on Visa credit cards are available here.

Tourist Agency

Indiana Tours *(556 Colón, ☎242-287, ≈240-833)* is a well-established agency offering excursions to the site of Señor de Sipán, the pyramids of Túcume, the Museo Brüning and to the area's picturesque villages. The staff is friendly and more than competent.

Piura

Telecommunications

There is a telephone on Loreto Street, on the corner of Lambayeque.

Tumbes

Banking

Interbanc is on the Plaza de Armas.

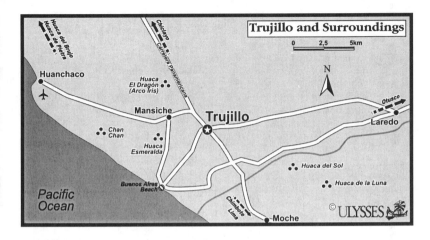

 EXPLORING

Trujillo

Trujillo, a vast oasis in the coastal desert, is the capital city of the department of La Libertad. With a population of 750,000, it is the largest coastal city except for Lima, and vies with Arequipa for the status of second-largest city in Peru. It is an appealing colonial city with the added attractions of nearby scenic beaches and ancient treasures that accumulated over its long secular history. You will appreciate both the charms of the city and the nearby ruins of the Moche and Chimú cultures. In Trujillo rain and fog are rare. It is almost always sunny.

Trujillo was founded in 1534 by Diego de Almagro. In the same year, Martin de Estete drew up plans for the city. However, it was Francisco Pizarro who, in the following year, officially gave it its status, naming it after his native city in Spain. In the next century, the Jesuits settled here with the mission of converting the native peoples living in the region.

Near the end of the seventeenth century, it was decided to encircle the city with ramparts to protect it from constant attacks by privateers and pirates who plundered the coast. It was here, that the first protests demanding independence were made, in 1820, and where Simón Bolívar took up residence to organize the revolution. At the beginning of the twentieth century, Raul Haya de la Torre, a native of the city, organized the APRA (Alianza para la Revolución Americana), a political party whose platform had major consequences for the entire region. This party opposed the interests of the land-owning hierarchy so effectively that the army confronted the militants in 1932. Nearly 4,000 residents were executed at the foot of the ramparts at the ruins of Chán-Chán.

This sad chapter in the history of Peru is now closed, but a feeling of patriotism still burns in the souls of the citizens of the department of La Libertad. Trujillo comes alive each January during the festival of the *marinera.*

Plaza de Armas

Plaza de Armas, in the centre of the city, is the largest urban plaza in Peru. It is centred around an elaborate and solemn monument built early this century to commemorate the heroes of independence and as a paean to liberty. Although the city developed rapidly, care was taken to preserve aspects of its glorious past. Trujillo's Plaza de Armas, like others in the country, is bordered by superb, pastel-coloured colonial mansions with majestic entrances and elegant windows protected by elaborately worked wrought-iron grills.

The **catedral** ★ has been reworked several times because of the earthquakes that have shaken the city. In spite of this, it has three naves and a lovely baroque façade. It contains a small **museo del arte religioso** hours vary).

Trujillo has several noteworthy colonial mansions. Among them are **Casa Urquiaga** ★ (446 Pizarro), **Casa de la Emancipación** ★ (610 Pizarro), **Casa Bracamonte** ★ (441 Independencia) and **Casa de Orbegoso** ★ (553 Orbeoso).

If you stay in Peru for a while, you will notice that each town or city seems to have its own distinct attraction. In Trujillo, it is the **Muséo Cassinelli** ★★ ($2.50; Mon to Fri 9:30am to 1pm and 4pm to 7pm, Sat and Sun 9:30am to 12pm; 601 Nicolás de Pierola), which is situated, oddly enough, in the basement of a service station. It displays many examples of precious pottery from the Nazca, Moche, Chimú, Chavín and other cultures.

Museo Arqueológico ★ ($1; every day, 9am to 4pm; at the corner of Ayacucho) has attractive ceramic items from the Moche, Chimú and Sicán coastal cultures.

Moche or Mochica Culture

Although Peru is inevitably associated with Inca civilisation, the development of this young republic has also been influenced by several older cultures and their respective history and traditions. Among these are the Moches, or Mochicas, as they are sometimes called.

Archaeologists prefer the term "Moche", which is the name of the valley where the ruins of this pre-Inca culture were discovered, but the name Mochica is commonly accepted.

This culture appeared around the first century AD, and dominated almost the entire north coast of Peru for 500 years before falling victim to the recurring weather phenomenon which exists even in our times: El Niño.

Following the example of the Nazcas in southern Peru, the Moche were able to cultivate the coastal desert by guiding the runoff waters from the western cordilleras into an irrigation system and by digging artesian wells.

Their ceramic art is the paragon of pre-Hispanic figurative art and constitutes a visual history of these fascinating pre-Inca people. Wonderfully illustrative of scenes from daily life, these sculptures have faces that vividly express emotions such as joy, jealousy, good spirits, or suffering. There are also representational figures of sea mammals that inhabit the coastal waters, as well as birds, and even of the *caballitos de tortora* that ride the waves of the Moche ceramics are also erotic in that they express very graphic sexual scenes between men and women and even between men and men. However,

The *marinera*

A fantastic sight, the *marinera* is a spellbinding dance which originated in Trujillo during the last century. Based on a blend of African, Spanish and Amerindian music, the *marinera* evokes contemporary Peru while calling to mind its mixed ancestry. In this dance of charm and seduction, the women court their partners to the rhythm of flamenco guitar and *cajón*, a wooden box used as a percussion instrument. Barefoot and wearing full, skirts trimmed with lace, the women swirl around the men who, bewitched, also spin and toss their hats or handkerchiefs into the air.

for reasons unknown, they do not depict sex between women. Sodomy was a common practice among the Moche. The penis is often depicted in exaggerated proportions on their pottery. To get a good look at these remarkably realistic works, visit the Larco de Pueblo Libre museum in Lima which has a collection of them.

In addition to ceramics, the Moche did admirable work with metal alloys, using gold, siver, copper and bronze. Among their practical inventions were the *caballitos de tortoras* which they used for fishing.

The Moche were not just peaceful artisans; they could also be cruel, violent and bloodthirsty. They sacrificed animals and humans to their idols. Among the torture imposed on the victims were dismemberment and castration.

The culture worshiped the cult of the god Ai-apaec, also named *El degollador*, the cut-throat, or *El decapitador*, the head-chopper. Part animal with a frightening expression, the god was depicted as holding a knife in the form of a crescent moon, or *tumi*, in the right hand, and grasping the hair of a freshly-severed head in the left.

Moche Ruins (see p 245)

Five kilometers southwest of Trujillo, on the left bank of the Río Moche, the **Temples of the Moon and the Sun** are striking examples of Mochica history and the splendor of a forgotten time. The two temples are pyramids of different sizes. Over the course of time, they have both suffered from the ravages of the Spanish conquest, the *huaqueros*, and the periodic downpours caused by the infamous ocean current, El Niño.

The **Huacas del Sol y de la Luna** *($1; every day from 9am to 4pm)* are shortened adobe pyramids with an access ramp. They are half a kilometer apart.

Huaca del Sol ★ ★

Huaca del Sol is a stepped adobe pyramid with polychromatic wall frescoes. Built on a rectangular base 228 metres long and 135 metres wide, it reaches a height of 48 meters. It is believed to be one of the Moches' most important sites for ritual ceremonies.

In the interior are superb red- and white-painted frescoes that illustrate *El decapitador* himself.

Takaynamo

Legend has it that the god of the Chimú, Takaynamo or Taykanamo, appeared on the horizon one day, heading a flotilla of balsa boats. He was accompanied by his whole family, numerous concubines and priests, and his entire army. This figure is often associated with Naymlap (see p 256), founder of the Sicán culture whose image decorates *tumis*. Takaynamo was the first ruler of the Chimú dynasty. He was followed in turn by his son, Guaquicraur, his grandson, Ñancenpinco, and seven kings whose names have been lost to history. The last sovereign, Michanzaman, was forced to abdicate to the Incas around 1470.

Huaca de la Luna

In front of Huaca del Sol are the remains of Huaca de la Luna. This adobe structure is as old as its neighbour and is 26 meters high and 80 meters in length. When the Spanish, opened up the bottom part of this pyramid in their never-ending search for hidden treasure and wealth, they discovered an object in the form of a half-moon with the figure of a woman inside it. Thus they named the place Hauca de la Luna.

Chimú Culture

The Chimú were the last people to be subjugated by the Incas. They appeared between AD 850 and 900, after the decline of the Moche civilization, and were influenced by Wari culture. Centred in Chán-Chán, they restored and improved upon the Moches' system of irrigation canals and artesian wells, and made the coastal desert bloom again.

In contrast to the Incas who venerated the sun, the Chimús worshiped the moon. This may be because these people, having chosen to live in an arid, desert-like area bordering the sea, noticed the important influence of the full moon which subjects the ocean to its gravitational pull each month. A bad omen for some fortunetellers, the muse

of poets, object of mystery for others, the Earth's satellite was, according to the beliefs of the Chimús, more important than its sun. In fact, during the period of the full moon, the surf is more powerful, the seas are rougher, and the creative force of the ocean is demonstrated by a healthy bounty of fish.

The Chimús were excellent sailors who navigated in balsa boats. They even went south to the Chincha Islands, near Ica, to harvest guano which they used as fertilizer. Some historians claim that the Chimú navigated as far as the Galápagos Islands, some 1,000 kilometers off the coast of what is now Ecuador.

Chimú ceramic art is monochromatic, mainly black. The culture's artisans were so good at working precious metals, that when the Incas defeated it, the smiths were deported to Cuzco to work for the Inca Empire.

Chimú Ruins

Chán-Chán ★★*($3; every day 9am to 4pm, the admission ticket is also valid for visits to Huaca del Dragón and Huaca Esmeralda)*, the adobe ruins of the capital of the Chimú nation are approximately five kilometres south of Trujillo. Its name is the result of a mispronunciation of the Chimú term, *Jian-Jian*, which means, "sun-sun". At its

Chán-Chán

peak, the capital governed a territory covering nearly 1,600 km north of Lima to the border of Ecuador. It was the empire's political and economic centre. The largest adobe city on the planet, it was probably also the biggest coastal city in pre-Columbian South America. Some historians credit it with a population of about 80,000, while others claim that it sheltered up to 250,000 people, some 50,000 more than Tenochtitlán in Mexico.

Located northwest of the valley of the Moche, the Chán-Chán ruins cover an area of 25 km², only of which a fifth is visible. The ruins themselves have a certain charm which contrasts with the harshness of its desert setting. However, the legacy of this period of unparalleled prosperity must have been much more spectacular at the height of this civilization. Today the site is eroded by desert wind and sand, and baked by merciless sun year-round.

Because its walls have no parapets, the city was probably not originally constructed as a military citadel, even though it served this purpose for several centuries. Slightly inward-sloping at the base, the massive walls are up to four metres wide and 12 m high.

The site is made up of 10 adjacent royal buildings *(ciudadelas)*, former residences of the Chimú line of kings. When each king died, his palace became his tomb. Buried with him were

his family, servants, and selected precious objects deemed necessary for his 'final voyage'. After the tomb was sealed, another palace was built for his son, the crown prince.

The different palaces, Tello, Velarde, Uhle and Tschudi, are named after archeologists who worked at the site.

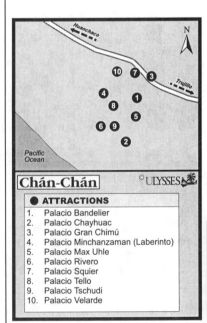

Chán-Chán

● ATTRACTIONS
1. Palacio Bandelier
2. Palacio Chayhuac
3. Palacio Gran Chimú
4. Palacio Minchanzaman (Laberinto)
5. Palacio Max Uhle
6. Palacio Rivero
7. Palacio Squier
8. Palacio Tello
9. Palacio Tschudi
10. Palacio Velarde

© ULYSSES

TRUJILLO TO THE ECUADORIAN BORDER

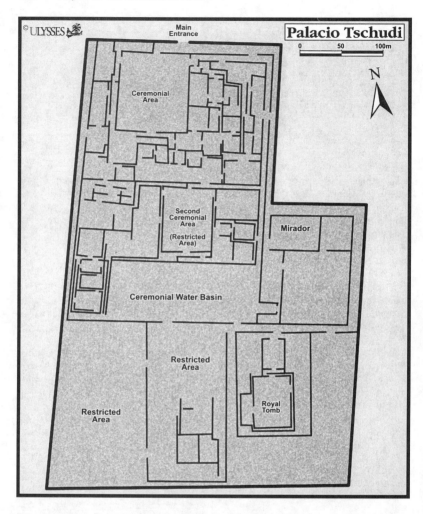

© ULYSSES

Main Entrance

Palacio Tschudi

0   50   100m

N

Ceremonial Area

Second Ceremonial Area

(Restricted Area)

Mirador

Ceremonial Water Basin

Restricted Area

Restricted Area

Royal Tomb

Tschudi

Tschudi, the only palace open to the public, is under constant renovation. It is entered by way of long adobe corridors that lead to an enormous ceremonial hall, that covers nearly 5,600 square metres. The walls are decorated with friezes of fish, mammals, strange animalistic figures and other mysterious divinities. The palace is divided into different sections which correspond to different social classes. Behind the palace, the enormous reservoir that the Chimú kept full of water is still visible. There is also a watchtower that looks out to sea.

Huaca del Dragón (Arco Iris) ★

The adobe ruins of Huaca del Dragón are five kilometres north of Trujillo. The

Huanchaco

walls of this ancient Chimú temple are decorated with handsome bas-relief frescoes depicting strange mythological creatures, including two-headed snakes. Unfortunately, the ruins have suffered damages from the torrential rains caused by El Niño.

Huaca Esmeralda

These adobe Chimú ruins were discovered in 1926 in what is now a rundown neighborhood in Trujillo. A few years later, and again in 1997, they suffered damage from the excessive rains caused by El Niño, but are being restored. Apart from the stylized images of supernatural creatures, there is not much of interest to tourists here.

Huanchaco ★

Ten kilometers to the west of Trujillo, Huanchaco is a small and extremely picturesque beach resort. Here, you can observe the resident fishermen straddling the waves of the Pacific in their

skiffs called *caballitos de tortora*. Every weekend the beaches are invaded by crowds of Peruvians in search of surf, sun and relaxation.

Caballitos de tortora are part of the ancient Moche heritage and have an odd resemblance to the small *tortora* boats used by Amerindians on Lake Titicaca. The skiffs at Huanchaco are constructed somewhat differently, since they have a flattened stern and raised prows. The paddler sits like a rider on horseback, hence the name *caballito.* The fishnet trails in the water behind the skiff.

Moche Ruins North of Trujillo

Nearly 40 kilometres north of Trujillo, the Pan American Highway enters the Chicama Valley and its handful of *haciendas* which are mainly involved in sugar-cane production. This seemingly ordinary valley conceals the ruins of the Moche culture, which are of great interest to archaeologists and travellers alike.

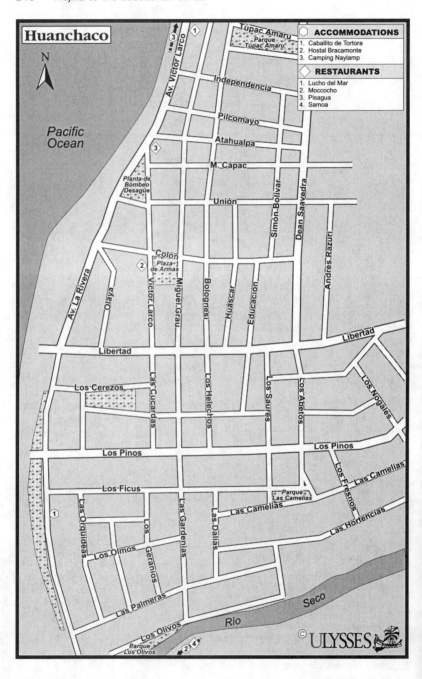

The first of these remains that will grab your attention is called **Huaca del Brujo** ★★, a recent discovery that lies slightly west of the Chicama valley on the coastal desert plateau near the ocean. When the age-old adobe walls of these Moche ruins were excavated from the desert sands, they revealed superbly painted, colorful designs. Among the subjects are captives taken during one of the Moches' conquests. Bound, castrated, submissive-looking men in chains... the images leave no doubt that the Moche could also be cruel, pitiless warriors. The site is very difficult to access because work on the dig is still underway. It is strongly recommended that you go there with a tourist agency (see p 238).

For over 5,000 years, **Huaca Prieta** has stood slightly over 12 metres high at the edge of the ocean, just next to the site of Huaca del Brujo. Apart from its view of the ocean, it doesn't really have much of interest.

Puerto Chicama ★

Twelve kilometers north of Huaca del Brujo lies the picturesque fishing village of Puerto Chicama. Although tourist services are rudimentary, the village attracts many surfers. Apparently, the breakers are the longest in the world.

Chiclayo ★

Called the *Capital de la amistad*, Chiclayo is a large modern city with a population of 300,000, located 640 kilometres north of Lima and 210 kilometres north of Trujillo. Its proximity to important archaeologic sites makes it a logical stop in the dry coastal desert. The most famous site in the area is the tomb of Señor de Sipán. Brought to light in 1987, this treasure

of a long-ago era is the most important archaeologic discovery since Machu Picchu in 1911. Further to the north, the ghostly adobe pyramids of Túcume can be visited.

Aside from the neoclassical cathedral designed by Gustave Eiffel, the city doesn't have anything exceptional. However, if you have a taste for the unusual, you will enjoy Chiclayo's *mercado modelo*. Though few articles of clothing and handicrafts on are on display, strolling peddlers will try to sell you just about anything. Tucked away in the market's maze, the **mercado do brujo** ★★ is most likely get your attention. This somewhat unusual part of the market displays a great variety of medicinal herbs, small pieces of animal parts, and unidentifiable foetuses preserved in formaldehyde. Many people come here hoping to find a cure for their illnesses.

Sipán ★★

Twenty-eight kilometres southeast of Chiclayo, in the middle of nowhere, lies Sipán, a desert village which became the focus of world attention in 1987 with the most important archeological find since Machu Picchu: a Moche mausoleum. Although the history of Moche culture is told through its magnificent ceramics and adobe ruins, this discovery gave archaeologists their first opportunity to study the tomb of a Moche ruler. Two years later, another intact tomb was excavated. These discoveries are considered very important by historians and archaeologists who can use the knowledge gained from them to reconstruct a much more detailed picture of the 1,200 years preceding the arrival of the Incas. Here is how it happened...

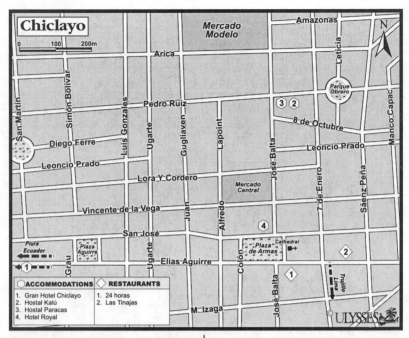

In early 1987, an abnormally large number of valuable archeological pieces were being circulated on the black market by an extremely active band of *huaqueros*. Once they became aware of this, archeologists were able to identify these precious objects and trace their point of origin close to Lambayeque, on the outskirts of Sipán. Lead by Peruvian archeologist Walter Alva, a research group quickly went to work attempting to unveil the secrets of the past. They first discovered a tomb which had unfortunately already been desecrated and pillaged by the *huaqueros.*

Nevertheless, the site was quickly barricaded and guards were posted to allow the archeologists to continue their work without disturbance. And then, Eureka! Another tomb was discovered intact, and thus the sepulchral slumber of the **Señor de Sipán** was interrupted.

Instead of being curled into a fetal position, the ruler lay on his back, in splendor, inside a large wooden coffin that was covered in bronze. His face was hidden by a finely-worked metal mask of gold-and-copper alloy. He wore a necklace made of silver and gold beads, the size and shape of peanuts. His upper body bore a gold chest-plate and other precious objects. At his feet lay three women with their feet cut off, a footless soldier, a priest, a boy of about ten and a dog. Archeologists believe that the bodies lying next to the Señor de Sipán had their feet amputated to prevent them from abandoning their leader.

Two years later, in 1989, a second tomb was discovered intact. Archeologists were excited to find the remains of another Moche monarch from an even earlier era than the Señor de Sipán.

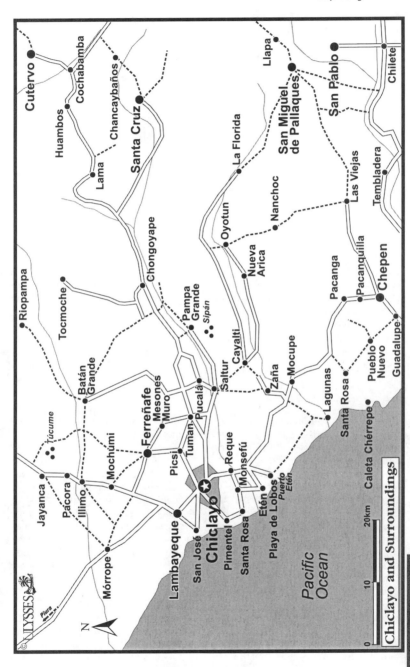

Chiclayo and Surroundings

Pacific Ocean

20km

TRUJILLO TO THE
ECUADORIAN BORDER

Sipán mask

More recently, a third untouched sepulcher was discovered; the dig is still in progress. Admission to the site costs about $1, and the hours are from 8am to 4pm. There is also a small *museo de sito* which displays some of the objects found here.

Pimentel ★

Pimentel is a little coastal fishing village, 14 kilometres west of Chiclayo, with a population of 20,000. The beach is bordered by an imposing jetty that extends out into the sea and was formerly used to unload goods going to Chiclayo by railway. The railroad has been out of service for a long time, but you can still stroll along the jetty and watch the perpetual rise and fall of the waves. Some of the *caballitos de tortora* are pulled up on the beach, while others are used for fishing a short distance offshore. At the foot of the jetty, modest stalls are set up to receive the catch of the day.

South of Pimentel, the road passes through the small village of Monsefú before arriving at Puerto Etén, another quaint fishing village. Puerto Etén is noted for an **antique locomotive** that has stood abandoned on its quay for decades.

Lambayeque

Ten kilometres north of Chiclayo, the quiet village of Lambayque has certainly seen better days, but it is worth mentioning because of Brüning's Museum.

Museo Arqueológico Brüning ★★★ *($2.50; every day 9am to 4pm)* owes its existence to Enrique Brüning, a German who came to Peru in 1884 to work in the sugar refineries. During the forty years he stayed in Peru, he developed an interest in Peruvian archeological artifacts and acquired a large number of precious works of art. Before returning to Germany, he sold his collection to the Peruvian government. Forty years later, in 1966, the museum named in his honour was finally opened in Lambayeque. The four-story museum is consecrated to the cultural richness of the coastal civilizations which flourished in the region well before the

Tumi

arrival of the Incas. The collection includes superb funeral masks, magnificent ceremonial vases, splendid erotic ceramics, finely-worked *tumis* and many other treasures of Moche, Chimú and lesser-known cultures. Also on display are a selection of items taken from the mausoleum of the Señor de Sipán. The rest of the mausoleum pieces can be seen in the Museo de la Nación in Lima (see p 114).

Lambayeque, or Sicán Culture

Not to be confused with the Señor de Sipán, the Señor de Sicán is tucked away near Tucumé. Sicán culture existed on the North Coast around the year 750. Archeologists believe that the Señor de Sicán might have been Takaynamo, the mysterious king of the Chimús. The Lambayeques constituted a very ancient regional cultural group that was probably enslaved by the Moches. The god, Naymlap, venerated by the ancient cultures of the region, is often confused with the Chimú divinity that belongs to a more recent era.

Túcume

To the north of Lambayque is Túcume, a little village known for its ghostly **pyramids ★**. With 26 pyramids spread out over 26 hectares, this fabulous legacy is one of the largest archeological complexes in the world. Unfortunately, it has deteriorated significantly because of the severe downpours caused by El Niño at the beginning of the century, in 1982-1983 and, again, in 1997. Norwegian Thor Heyerdahl is in charge of the excavations here. A small museum in Túcume displays a scale model of the site along with artifacts found in the area.

Zaña ★

Founded by the Spanish in 1563, the town of Zaña flourished rapidly, mainly because of the forced labor of the Amerindians who worked under inhumane conditions on the sugarcane plantations. When the natives were decimated by disease and overwork, the plantation owners simply replaced them with slaves from Africa. In con

trast to the misery of the slave workers, the residents of the town lived in splendor and spent their wealth so lavishly that, in the 17th century, Zaña rivalled the beauty and opulence of Trujillo. Naturally, this drew the attention of the pirates and privateers that plundered the coastal towns, and the city was eventually sacked by brigands. A natural disaster soon followed. On the night of March 15, 1720, there were such severe thunderstorms that the *río* overflowed and swept away roofs and walls of houses and even part of the church! Unable to rebuild after this catastrophe, the wealthy residents abandoned the city. Some people say the disasters that destroyed the city were a chastisement of the decadent lifestyle of the rich inhabitants. Today, the city is a "ghost town". The only residents are descendants of the slaves who were exploited by the Spanish. In spite of everything, Zaña has stood the test of time. Walls, arches and houses remain half-buried by the coastal desert sands that are swept against them by storms and hurricanes.

After Chiclayo, you can either continue through the desert to the border of Ecuador, or start the gradual climb of the Andes with a visit to the colonial city of Cajamarca (see p 259).

Piura

The first city built by the Spanish (1532), Piura is far up the north coast, about 1,050 kilometres from Lima. The city has been relocated several times because of Amerindian revolts and attacks by pirates who marauded along the coast. It was built at its present location in 1587. Piura is the native city of Miguel Grau who distinguished him-

self as a navigator in the War of the Pacific between Peru and Chile (see p 35).

Paita

In the colonial era, political differences often led to bloodshed, imprisonment or exile. A case in point is the fate of Manuela Saenz, known to her friends as Manuelita. She was the muse of Simón Bolívar during his years of glory. When he died, she refused his inheritance and came here to live out her life in exile.

Talara

This little fishing village was transformed by the discovery of "black gold". It is the largest producer of petroleum on the north coast. The population quickly grew to 50,000 and oil is produced at the rate of 60,000 barrels per day. It goes without saying that there isn't much here to attract tourists.

Cabo Blanco ★

Although few people have ever heard of the place, Cabo Blanco will forever be associated with the name of the famous author, Ernest Hemingway. It was here, at the local fishing club thirty kilometers north of Talara, that he wrote his great novel, *The Old Man and the Sea*. Hemingway truly enjoyed Cabo Blanco and its sports fishing. Apparently, he caught a 710 kilogram marlin here in 1953!

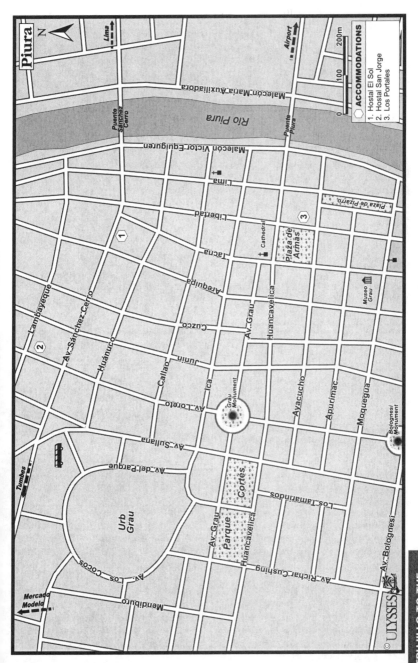

Piura

N

Lima

Río Piura

Malecón María Auxiliadora

Puente Sánchez Cerro

Puente Piura

Airport

Malecón Victor Equiguren

Lima

Libertad

Plaza de Pizarro

Tacna

Cathedral

③

Arequipa

Plaza de Armas

Cuzco

Huancavelica

Av. Grau

Museo Grau

Callao

Junín

Ica

Av. Loreto

Grau Monument

Av. Sánchez Cerro

Huánuco

Lambayeque

①

②

Ayacucho

Apurímac

Moquegua

Bolognesi Monument

Av. Sullana

Av. del Parque

Tumbes

Urb Grau

Cortés

Los Tamarindos

Av. Grau

Parque

Huancavelica

Av. Richar Cushing

Av. Los Cocos

Mendiburo

Mercado Modelo

Av. Bolognesi

© ULYSSES

ACCOMMODATIONS

1. Hostal El Sol
2. Hostal San Jorge
3. Los Portales

0 100 200m

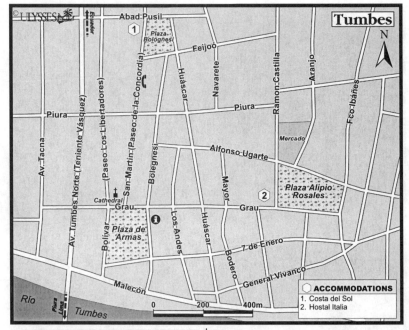

ACCOMMODATIONS
1. Costa del Sol
2. Hostal Italia

Tumbes

Tumbes is the point of entry into Ecuador and, like many border cities, it is a drug-trafficking centre. If you are stopping over here, you can visit the **Reserva Nacional Los Manglares**.

Puerto Pizarro

This sleepy fishing village some 10 kilometres northeast of Tumbes boasts a beautiful pristine beach, with neither hotels nor restaurants.

Crossing the Border

It is easy to cross the border into Ecuador. Upon arriving in the last Peruvian village, Aguas Verde, about three kilometres from the border, travellers must have their passports validated at the Peruvian immigration office *(open, in principle, from 9am to 12pm and from 2pm to 5pm)*. Next is the bus ride to the border. Then cross the bridge going into Huaquillas, where passports must be validated again.

ACCOMMODATIONS

Trujillo

Two blocks from the Plaza de Armas, **El Hostal Americano** *($10; sb; 792 Jr. Pizarro, ☎241-361)* will suit cash-strapped travellers looking for basic, inexpensive lodgings.

Also close to Plaza de Armas, **Hotel Internacional** *($10; sb; corner of Bolívar and Gamara, ☎245-392)* offers spartan rooms. Ideal for backpackers.

Slightly more expensive, **Hostal Recreo** *($25; pb, ℜ; 647 Estete, ☎246-991)* is a five-minute walk northeast of Plaza de Armas. The rooms here are not spectacular, but are clean and well-furnished. The staff is friendly.

Another mid-range hotel is the **Hotel Continental** *($25; pb, tv, hw, ℜ; 663 Gamarra, ☎241-607, ⊷249-881)*. This reputable, 15-year-old hotel offers clean, safe and simply furnished rooms. It is a five- minute walk from Plaza de Armas

Also well-known in Trujillo, **Hotel Opt Gar** *($40; pb, tv, hw, ℜ; 595 Jr. Grau, ☎242-192, ⊷235-551)* has been open for 24 years. It is a seven-story hotel with 66 clean, bright rooms.

Just two steps away from Plaza de Armas, **Los Conquistadores** *($70; bkfst incl., ctv, hw; 586 Diego de Almagro, ☎244-505, ⊷235-9172)* has been renovated in recent years and offers its clientele superior comfort that combines calm and security with charm. The rooms are clean and spacious and the staff is courteous and helpful.

Abobe

"Adobe" is the name given to a mixture of clay and straw that is formed into bricks and left to dry in the sun. The dry coastal climate has led each cultural group of desert dwellers to build their temples of adobe.

Treat yourself to a night at the best hotel in the city, the **Libertador** *($100; tv, hw, ≈, ℜ, ≈; 485 Jr. Independencia, ☎232-741, ⊷235-641, www.libertador.com)*. This flagship of a local hotel chain, in the heart of Trujillo on the Plaza de Armas, has everything you could want. The exterior of the hotel blends well with the colonial mansions which surround the plaza. It boasts superb openwork wooden balconies, wrought-iron grills on the windows and an imposing lobby entrance. Among the charms of this deluxe hotel are its lovely little swimming pool surrounded by plants and flowers, its intimate bar where you can sip a *pisco sour*, and its highly-acclaimed restaurant (see p 257). While the rooms are not spectacular, they are clean, well-furnished and air-conditioned. Try to get a room with a view of the Plaza de Armas. The staff is well-trained and very pleasant.

Huanchaco

The campground, **Naylamp** *($10; about ten minutes by foot northwest of Plaza de Armas)* will provide you with a spot to pitch your tent.

Hostal Sol y Mar *($15; 570 Los Ficus)* rents out cheap dingy rooms. It has a small swimming pool which is, unfortunately, surrounded by high concrete walls.

The rooms at **Hostal Bracamonte** *($25; pb, ℜ, ≈; 503 Jr. Los Olivos, ☎461-266, ⊷461-162)* are clean and safe, but their decor lacks charm. They either look out onto the swimming pool, or are nestled among flowers and greenery. Close to the airport and beach.

In the same price range, **Cacallito de Tortora** *($25; pb, ℜ; 219 Avenida La Rivera, ☎351-828)* is a hotel that has some of its rooms arranged around a small swimming pool behind a main building that faces the sea.

Naymlap

According to a legend similar to the one about the Lambayeques' god, Takaynamo, Naymlap, with his piercing almond eyes, came by sea with a flotilla of balsa boats, bringing his family, his wives, his army, and a sacred idol. After his death, he was reincarnated into a bird that flew off into eternity and is often depicted on *tumis*. His descendants governed the region without a hitch until, one day, the devil appeared as a beautiful woman and seduced the ruler into moving the sacred idol. This unleashed all the demons of hell, and a series of natural catastrophes followed: floods, droughts, and brutal climate changes afflicted the region and lead to its decline. Funny how these events resemble the more recent effects of El Niño.

Chiclayo

On the north side of Plaza de Armas, the aging **Hotel Royal** *($10, sb or $15, pb)* has certainly seen better days. The quality of the rooms is uneven. Some of the rooms are bright and charming with a view of the plaza, others are shabby and dark.

Not far from the Plaza de Armas, **Hostal Kuelap** *($15; pb, hw, ℜ, ctv; 1041 Juan Cuglievan, ☎273-331, ⇌228-431)* is a five story hotel with 30 modern, spacious and economically-priced rooms.

In the same vein, two neighbouring hotels close to the town market, **Hostal Kalú** *($15 to $20; pb, ℜ; Pedro Ruiz, between José Balta and 7 de Enero)* and **Hostal Paracas** *($15 to $20; pb, ℜ; Pedro Ruiz, between José Balta and 7 de Enero)*, offer essentially the same quality for the money.

Hotel Sipán *($60, bkfst incl. with ⊗, $70 bkfst incl. with ≡; pb, hw, ℜ, ≈; 150 Virgilio Dall'orso, ☎242-564 or 242-554, ⇌242-408, hsipan1@lullitec.com.pe)* is a three-story hotel with 50 very clean, safe and charming rooms. There is a lovely ter-race by the pool where you can relax after a swim.

El Gran Marques *($85-$130 bkfst incl.; pb, hw, ctv, ≈, ℜ; ☎249-582, ⇌249-161)* is four-story hotel a short distance from downtown. Its 50 rooms are bright, quiet and well-furnished. In addition to the pool on the ground floor, a second pool, a hairdressing salon, a sauna and a Turkish bath surround a spacious terrace on the roof. The establishment offers its guests a one-way taxi ride to the city centre from the hotel.

Undoubtedly, the best hotel in Chiclayo is the former *hotel de turista*, renamed **El Gran Hotel Chiclayo** *($80 - $135; pb, hw, ctv, ℜ, ≈; 115 Villareal, ☎234-911, ⇌223-961, www.business.com.pe/granhotel)*. Business travellers and vacationers alike will be pleased with the accommodations here. The rooms are spacious, bright, air-conditioned, ultra-clean, safe, and have mini-bars. The large pool and terrace are the ideal spot to relax and take a dip after a day of excursions.

Piura

Somewhat far from Plaza de Armas, **Hostal San Jorge** *($10-$15; sb; corner* *of Lambayeque and Loreto)* offers basic, inexpensive rooms.

A five-minute walk north of Plaza de Armas, **Hotel El Sol** *($25; pb, ℜ; corner of Sánchez Cerro and Tacna)* offers good value for the price

The prize for best hotel goes to a former *hotel de turista*, **Los Portales** *($85; pb, hw, ctv, ≈, ℜ)*. Situated on the Plaza de Armas, this establishment offers all the comfort expected of a superior hotel.

Cabo Blanco

The **village fishing club** *($40; pb, ℜ, ≈)* rents pleasant rooms that are usually occupied by avid fishermen.

Tumbes

Travellers on a tight budget can stay in the spartan rooms at **Hostal Italia** *($10; corner of Grau and Ramón Castilla)*.

Hostal Lourdes *($25; Bordero, between Alfonso Ugarte and Grau)* is conveniently located and has pleasant rooms.

Once again, the best place to stay in town is at a former *hotel de turista*. This time it's **La Costa del Sol** *($75; pb, tv, hw, ℜ; corner of San Martín and Abad Pusil)*.

 RESTAURANTS

Trujillo

For an inexpensive health-food restaurant, check out little **Naturaleza** *($; 455 Jr. Gamarra, ☎231-932)* and its friendly staff.

Tartufo *($; Plazuela Iquitos)* has a good selection of ice cream and sandwiches, and a pleasant little terrace with parasols.

The small charming cafe **Asturias** *($-$$; 739 Jr. Pizarro, ☎258-100)* serves simple, tasty meals in a dining room cooled by fans. The fruit juices are excellent.

Just next-door to Asturias, **De Marco** *($-$$; 725 Jr. Pizarro)* offers pasta dishes and pizza along with a few local specialties. They make a good *pisco sour*.

Close to the Plaza de Armas, **El Mochica** *($-$$: 462 Bolívar, ☎252-457)* has a large outdoor area and serves every sort of fish and seafood. The menu also includes chicken, beef and pork dishes. The *ceviche de mariscos* and the *chicharrón de mariscos* are outstanding. The service is unintrusive.

Seafood lovers, remember this name: **Restaurant Marisqeria** *($-$$; 337 Jr. Bolívar, ☎245-907)*. A short distance from Plaza de Armas, it is certainly worth taking the trouble go here for its many delicious fish and seafood dishes. Take a table near the window and feast your eyes upon the selection: *conchitas a la parmesana, tortilla de langostinos, escabeche de mero, filete de lenguado al ajo* or *arriz con mariscos*. What's more, it's one of the few places in town that offers *ceviche de camarones*.

Quiet atmosphere, efficient service and truly fresh ingredients make up the recipe for an outstanding culinary evening at the restaurant of the hotel **Libertador** *($$$; 485 Jr. Independencia, ☎232-741)*. Various local and exotic dishes are featured on the regular menu, to which the chef adds a fixed-

TRUJILLO TO THE ECUADORIAN BORDER

price menu with different regional specialties of the north coast each day.

Huanchaco

There is a series of popular restaurants along the beach. Although they don't offer much in the way of luxury, the menu is usually inexpensive and varies according to the catch of the day.

Close to the Hostal Bracamonte, **Samoa** *($; 517 Los Olivos)* recently opened in the wing of a house. This modest but very enjoyable restaurant serves a little of everything at very reasonable prices. The menu includes pasta dishes, hot dogs, hamburgers and, of course, *ceviches* and fish. There is a good selection of freshly-squeezed fruit juices, and the service comes with a smile.

If you like steamed fish, try **Moccocho** *($-$$; Plaza de Armas)*.

Pisagua *($-$$; 450 Avenida Larco)* is a small, unpretentious place that serves excellent *ceviches* and other ocean delicacies.

If the Pisagua is full, continue down Avenida Larco to **Lucho del Mar** *($-$$; Avenida Larco)*.

Chiclayo

With a name like **24 horas** *($; 884 Aguirre)* there's no doubt that this is *the* late night restaurant in Chiclayo. The food couldn't be simpler, cheaper or more filling. The decor is downright plain.

Las Tinajas *($-$$; 957 Elías Aguirre, ☎209-687)* is the name to remember for fresh fish and seafood dishes. The decor couldn't be simpler, but the food is excellent and the service is truly pleasant.

For more refined dining, try the large, bright dining room at the **Gran Hotel Chiclayo** *($-$$; 115 Villareal, ☎234-911)*. There is always a fixed-price menu that includes an appetizer, main dish, dessert and a beverage. The portions are large and the service is impeccable

 ENTERTAINMENT

Trujillo

On the edge of Plaza de Armas, **Las Tinajas** *(corner of Jr. Pizarro and Diego Almagro)* is the *rendez-vous* spot of travellers. A welcoming atmosphere, giant video screen, booming music and a wide variety of alcoholic drinks are in store.

Camana Pub *(791 San Martín)* is a good place to see the *marinera* danced. It also serves up *parilladas* and seafood.

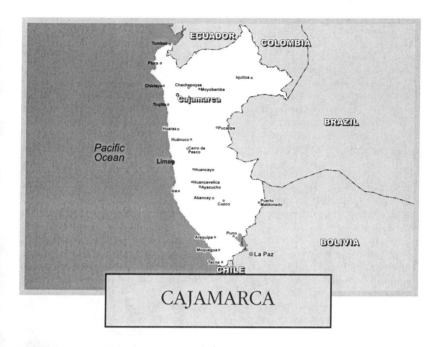

CAJAMARCA

I t was on November 16, 1532, a ghostly moonlit night, that Cajamarca, a city shrouded in legend, made its mark in history. The tragic fate of the Inca Empire was forever sealed here with the subjugation of its people. The city was the scene of the decisive war which would lead to the Incas' complete annihilation. Even though as much has been written about this clash of two worlds as blood has been spilled, a brief review of the events is in order.

The battle took place just after the Inca leader Huayna Cápac died of smallpox, which he probably caught from the Spanish conquerors. Cápac's death sparked a violent fratricidal war between Atahualpa, his illegitimate son and ruler of Quito, and Huáscar, his legitimate son of Inca blood, ruler of Cuzco. This war ended with Atahualpa and his men defeating Huáscar and his troops in Central Ecuador. Shortly after this glorious victory, Atahualpa settled in Cajamarca, where he rested in the thermal waters known today as the Baños del Inca. At the same time, Francisco Pizarro and his men had landed in Peru and were advancing towards Cajamarca to meet with Atahualpa.

Upon arriving in Cajamarca on Friday, November 15, 1532, Pizarro and his troops could not escape the bloody confrontation that was to ensue. At first, the city seemed to be deserted: there were only houses and tents as far as the eye could see. Pizarro asked his half-brother and an interpreter to request a meeting with the Inca. A meeting was set up and then cancelled, and finally postponed until the next day. Throughout the night, the Spanish became increasingly anxious. Pizarro emaciated and marked by the hardships of the past few months, and his face covered in sweat, convinced his men that they could bring about the fall of the Inca Empire through his tactics. Pizarro was undoubtedly influenced by the exploits of Cortez at Montezuma, Mexico, and probably thought that, since the sides were unequally matched, audacity could be just as effective as brute force, and that sometimes even the most audacious of plans work out. Pizarro's forces consisted of only about 180 men and a few horses, whereas Atahualpa led an army of approximately 25,000 men.

What caused the ensuing events? Apparently a priest, Luque, accompanied by an interpreter, appeared in front of Atahualpa unarmed to inform him about the existence of a heavenly power sent by God. While this was going on, Pizarro and his men were hiding and awaiting a signal. Priest Luque handed a bible to the Inca, who, of course, did not read or write. Puzzled, he looked at the bible, quickly flipped through it, and shook it close to his ear. Accounts of what followed have no doubt been distorted over time. It is said that Atahualpa either dropped the Bible or threw it to the ground. Regardless of what happened, it was enough to anger Priest Luque, who raised his voice, shook his fist and cried, "Let us avenge this insult hurled at Christ!" Upon hearing these words, the Spanish, knowing that they could not back down now, came out of hiding and slaughtered everyone in sight in a bloody killing frenzy. The Incas were unable to resist the Spanish conquerors' treacherous attack.

Under the pale sunlight, an unimaginably horrible and colossal battle began. The battlefield was filled with a confusing cacophony of bloodcurdling screams, harquebus shots, whinnying horses and clashing swords. And then, silence! Under a fine drizzle, corpses in bloody clothing and bodies stiffened by death lay scattered on the ground. Against all odds, a handful of Spaniards, greedy for gold and silver, came to defeat a people who had controlled practically all of South America.

The question remains: Why did the Incas fail to come to Atahualpa's rescue? Some say that the ruler was so powerful and respected that no one dared to make a move without his approval. Whatever the case, Atahualpa was taken prisoner, enabling the Spanish to keep his army at bay.

Surprisingly, Atahualpa was treated in an exemplary and respectful manner once he had succumbed to the Spaniards' underhanded tactics. He was allowed to keep his many concubines, his clothes and his apartments. The Inca leader quickly realized that it was gold which led the Spanish to venture to such a far-off land. He therefore made a deal with the Spanish: in exchange for his freedom, a room in his house would be filled with several tons of gold. This amount may have been exaggerated through oral tradition, but it is nevertheless indicative of the phenomenal amount of gold the Incas possessed. To the great pleasure and complete amazement of the *conquistadors*, the room slowly filled with this highly coveted precious metal. In the meantime, although Atahualpa was being secretly held in his apartments, he managed to pass messages to the outside. This is how he was able to give the order to execute Huáscar, who was being held prisoner by Atahualpa's troops, to prevent him from joining the Spanish.

Some time later, Pizarro heard a rumour that the Incas were secretly reorganizing and preparing for a counterattack to free Atahualpa. Furious, Pizarro went back on his word to free the Inca and instead set up a puppet court to judge him behind closed doors. The Inca leader stood trial for plotting against the Spanish, assassinating his brother

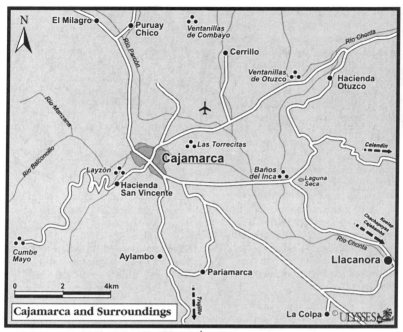

Cajamarca and Surroundings

and having had incestuous relationships with his sisters. He was sentenced without mercy: he was to be burnt at the stake. Atahualpa was very distressed about the cremation, since the fire would completely consume his body, and asked to convert to Catholicism. He was strangled instead. It was thus that Atahualpa, the last ruler of the Inca dynasty, died on August 29, 1533.

The news of Atahualpa's execution reached Europe, and many expressed their indignation at this despicable and heinous execution. However, the gold and riches from the Inca Empire soon poured into Spain and quickly put an end to the outcry over the ruler's death and this sad episode in the history of the Spanish conquest of South America.

Another version of the death of Atahualpa tells of one of the interpreters hired by the Spanish falling in love with one of the Inca's wives and devising a plot which, in the end, led to the Inca leader's death.

FINDING YOUR WAY AROUND

Cajamarca

By Plane

Aerocontinente and AeroCondor flights from Lima arrive in Cajamarca almost every day, but check with the airlines first, since schedules are subject to change. Flights from Lima take off early in the morning to avoid sudden changes in temperature or storms that may strike over La Sierra as much as possible. Flights are often late due to rain. The flight takes approximately 1.5 hours and costs about $80.

The airport is located 3 kilometres from downtown. It costs approximately $2.50 to get there by taxi, depending on your bargaining skills.

By Bus

Many buses go to Cajamarca from Lima, Chiclayo or Trujillo. Lima is 20 very long hours away from Cajamarca by bus. This trip is as uncomfortable and exhausting as you might expect, but at a fare of about $12, it is substantially cheaper than going by plane. Buses leave regularly from Trujillo to Cajamarca. The trip costs approximately $8 and takes 7 to 8 hours. Buses also ensure a daily link between Chiclayo and Cajamarca. This trip takes about 8 hours and costs $7 and $8.

Ventanillas de Otuzco and Cumbe Mayo

There is no regular bus service to these towns. Contact an agency for more information (see below).

El Baño del Inca

Buses go to El Baño del Inca regularly along Avenida Amazonas and stop at the corner of Jr. Dos de Mayo. Just hop on a bus with the sign *Baño del Inca* in its windshield. The trip takes approximately 15 minutes and costs under 50¢.

Chachapoyas and Kuelap

It is difficult to access this village and its ruins. Contact an agency for more information (see below).

PRACTICAL INFORMATION

Banking

The Banco de Credito is located on Jr. del Comercio at the corner of Apurímac. Visa advances are available.

The Banco Continental is located on 719 Jr. Tarapaca; the Interbanc is right beside it at no. 730.

Mail and Telecommunications

Telephone service is available in the Plaza de Armas.

Guided Tours

Cajamarca Tours *(323 Dos de Mayo, ☎922-813)* is an agency that belongs to the owners of the Hostal Cajamarca, and its offices are just adjacent. It offers typical excursions, including tours of the city, Las Veintanillas de Otzuco, Cumbe Mayo, El Baño del Inca and the Kuelap ruins. Cajamarca Tours runs the reservation office for AeroCondor Airlines.

EXPLORING

Cajamarca ★★

Located at an elevation of only 2,720 metres, Cajamarca, a quaint colonial city surrounded by mountains, is blessed with a pleasant climate. It is an ideal spot to get off the beaten track; because it is so deep in the northern Andes, it rarely sees hoards of tourists.

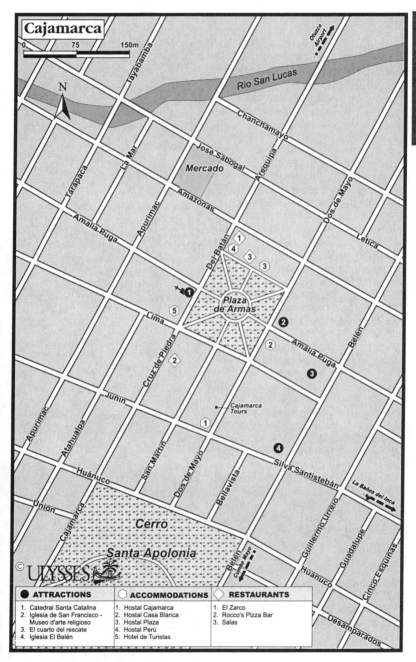

Cajamarca

0   75   150m

N

Río San Lucas

Onuzco Airport

Tayabamba

Chanchamayo

José Sabogal

Mercado

La Mar

Arequipa

Tarapaca

Apurimac

Amazonas

Dos de Mayo

Amalia Puga

Leticia

Del Batán

1
4
3
3

Plaza de Armas

Lima

5

1

2

2

Amalia Puga

Belén

Cruz de Piedra

2

3

Junín

Apurimac

Atahualpa

Cajamarca Tours

1

San Martín

Dos de Mayo

4

Silva Santistebán

La Baños del Inca

Huánuco

Bellavista

Unión

Cajamarca

Guillermo Urrelo

Guadalupe

Cinco Esquinas

Cerro

Santa Apolonia

Belén

Cumbe Mayo

Huánuco

© ULYSSES

Desamparados

● ATTRACTIONS	○ ACCOMMODATIONS	◇ RESTAURANTS
1. Catedral Santa Catalina	1. Hostal Cajamarca	1. El Zarco
2. Iglesia de San Francisco - Museo d'arte religioso	2. Hostal Casa Blanca	2. Rocco's Pizza Bar
3. El cuarto del rescate	3. Hostal Plaza	3. Salas
4. Iglesia El Belén	4. Hostal Perú	
	5. Hotel de Turistas	

Plaza de Armas

The ghost of the Inca leader Atahualpa still haunts the Plaza de Armas. In the centre of this square, the last member of the Inca dynasty was treacherously executed by the Spanish on August 29, 1533. Plaza de Armas is surrounded by several pretty colonial churches.

Construction of the **Catedral Santa Catalina** ★ began in the 15th century using Inca stone blocks, but was not completed until the late 20th century. This church is somewhat unusual, since it does not have a belfry. It is assumed that the nuns did not have enough money to build one.

Facing the Cathedral, **Iglesia San Francisco**, which dates back to the 17th century, is part of a convent that contains a small *museo del arte religioso (opening hours vary)*.

The only vestige of Inca architecture is *El cuarto del rescate* ★ *(722 Amalia Puga)*, the room where the Inca leader Atahualpa was held captive by the Spanish. This is not the room which was filled with gold and silver. While he was being held by the Spanish, Atahualpa offered to fill this room with gold and silver until it reached the red line on one of the walls. After reading and hearing so much about this famous room, it was somewhat disappointing. Three trapezium-shaped windows open outward and a door, also trapezium-shaped, lets you get a quick look at the inside, which is off limits.

Completed in the 18th century, the **Iglesia El Belén** ★★ has an incredible dome decorated with multicoloured sculptures. It has a small patio that adjoins the hospital.

The Outskirts of Cajamarca

Ventanillas de Otuzco ★

Located approximately 10 kilometres east of Cajamarca, Las Ventanillas de Otuzco is a regional pre-Columbian necropolis carved into the rocky cliffs.

El Baño del Inca ★

El Baño del Inca, a complex of water basins fed by various cold, warm and hot springs, is located 6 kilometres to the east of Cajamarca. According to legend, the place got its name after the Inca leader Atahualpa came here to recover from a war wound after defeating his half-brother, Huáscar, before being ambushed by Pizarro and his men.

Cumbe Mayo ★

At an altitude of 3,500 metres and 14 kilometres south-west of Cajamarca, Cumbe Mayo is a vast network of aqueducts carved out of rock, which once supplied the entire area with water.

Celendín

Celendín is a small, isolated village on the road to Chachapoyas, which has an average altitude of 2,620 metres. There is really nothing interesting in this town situated just over 100 kilometres east of Cajamarca, except that the festival of the Virgen del Carmen which takes place here every July 16.

Chachapoyas and Kuelap ★★

Off the tourist-beaten path, a poorly-kept road leads to Chachapoyas and the mysterious pre-Inca ruins of Kuelap. The Kuelap ruins were built on a hilltop in three levels. Some walls are nearly 20 metres high. The site is not looked after and is in dire need of restoration.

Moyobamba

Moyobamba, the capital of San Martín, is not a regular tourist destination. Perched at an altitude of just under 1,000 metres, Moyobamba is in an area that tourists are strongly advised **NOT** to visit because of terrorism. Moreover, drug-trafficking is an ever-present problem.

Tarapoto

A sleepy little town surrounded by lush vegetation, Tarapoto has a population of approximately 65,000 inhabitants and is located practically in the middle of the tropical rainforest, at an altitude of only 425 metres.

 ACCOMMODATIONS

Cajamarca

The **Hostal Plaza** *($10; sb; 669 Amalia Puga)* borders on La Plaza de Armas and provides spartan, economical lodging for travellers who are not too picky.

The **Hostal Peru** *($10; sb; 605 Amalia Puga)* is another inexpensive stop right next door to the Hostal Plaza. Very basic rooms, generally occupied by backpackers who don't mind roughing it.

The **Hostal Casa Blanca** *($25; pb, hw; 446 Jr. Dos de Mayo, ☎/≈922-141)* is a good bet if you are on an average

budget. It offers clean rooms and friendly service.

The old **Hotel de Turistas** *($30; pb, hw, ℛ; 773 Comercio, ☎922-470, ≈922-472)* also borders La Plaza de Armas and has approximately 50 clean, safe, but sparsely decorated rooms.

🛏 The best hotel in the city, **Hostal Cajamarca** *($45; pb, hw, ℛ; 311 Dos de Mayo, ☎921-432)* is only a short distance from La Plaza de Armas. A renovated period house, this hotel offers clean and quiet rooms that surround an attractive interior court.

🛏 The best hotel in the region, **La Laguna Seca** *($90-$115; pb, hw, ≈, ℛ; 1098 Avenida Manco Cápac, ☎823-149, ≈823-915)* is 6 kilometres from downtown Cajamarca, near El Baño del Inca. This former hacienda was converted into a luxury hotel with 41 rooms, which all have large baths that can be filled with thermal water. You can also rent horses or bicycles here. La Laguna Seca also has Turkish baths, a heated pool and thermal waters. There is a free airport shuttle service.

 RESTAURANTS

Cajamarca

There are not many quality restaurants in Cajamarca. Although the best restaurants are found in the best hotels, it is always possible to find a simple, filling meal without breaking the bank.

El Zarco *($; 170 Jr. del Batán)* does not look like much, but serves a variety of inexpensive, nutritious and tasty meals.

The restaurant of the **Hostal Cajamarca** *($-$$; 311 Dos de Mayo, ☎921-432)* is one of the best in the city, offering a wide variety of regional and international cuisine and friendly service in a relaxed ambiance.

Rocco's Pizza Bar *($-$$; 653 Jr. Cruz de Piedra)* is the place to wash down a pizza with a beer or a *pisco sour*.

The **Salas Restaurant** *($-$$; 637 Jr. Amalia Puga, ☎922-867)* faces Plaza de Armas and serves local cuisine in an informal setting.

For a bit of luxury, try the Peruvian and international specialities at the **La Laguna Seca Hotel** *($$-$$$; 1098 Avenida Manco Cápac, ☎823-149)*. Formal, classic setting, fresh food, friendly service and, as you might expect, rather high prices.

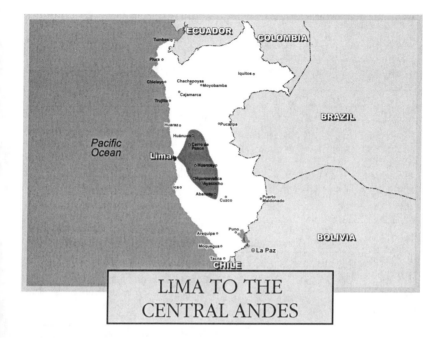

LIMA TO THE CENTRAL ANDES

O nce, a train left Lima regularly, threading its way gingerly along mountain rock faces, crossing fifty bridges over as many waterways, and passing through sixty tunnels to finally arrive some 300 kilometres further at Huancayo. Unfortunately, the train stopped making this run in 1991, and the most spectacular route from Lima to the central Andes is closed.

Only the truly reckless make this trip by car. The rest enjoy a passenger's view of the dramatic landscape from the bus, which provides efficient service in this region. Still, the central Andes are not much visited by travellers. The region is one of the poorest in the country and has few facilities for tourists. Since time immemorial, the main industry in the area has been mining. Early on, the Spanish forced indigenous people to work in the mines, reducing them to a state of slavery. In the middle of this century, foreign mining companies established themselves in cities like Cerro de Pasco and La Oroya. Then, in the early 1980s, the town of Ayacucho and the entire region were hit hard by the Shining Path guerilla war. Today, this bloody page of history seems to have turned, but infrastructure remains summary at best and the roads are still in poor condition, especially during the rainy season. Nonetheless, the villages are picturesque and the landscapes that unfurl before your eyes are simply sensational. The attentive traveller is sometimes treated to a glimpse of a little forlorn village clustered around the slender silhouette of its church, whose single bell summons the faithful.

FINDING YOUR WAY AROUND

La Oroya

By Bus

Buses from Lima travel about five hours to reach La Oroya. Budget about $5.

Buses leave Huancayo every day en route to La Oroya. Budget $2 for an hour-long trip.

Junín

By Bus

Buses leave La Oroya every day for Cerro de Pasco, via Junín. The fare is $1 for a trip of one-and-a-half hours.

Cerro de Pasco

By Bus

From La Oroya, buses reach Cerro de Pasco after a three-hour trip. It costs $2.

Huánuco and the Ruins of Kotosh

By Plane

There are irregular flights from Lima. The flight takes about one hour and costs approximately $60 one way.

By Bus

Many buses leave Lima regularly for Huánuco. The trip lasts about 10 hours and costs approximately $10.

From Huánuco, taxis may be hired for the trip to the ruins. Budget about $3, depending on your bargaining skills.

Tarma

By Bus

Tarma is about six hours by bus from Lima. The fare is about $5.

San Ramón - La Merced

By Bus

Buses leave Lima every day for La Merced by way of San Ramón. Count on spending $7 for a trip approximately nine hours long and get set for spectacular landscapes.

Jauja

By Bus

Many buses travel to Huancayo from Lima by way of Jauja. The trip takes about six hours for a fare of approximately $5.

Huancayo

By Bus

Buses make the trip from Lima to Huancayo in seven hours. Budget about $10. Spectacular landscapes.

Huancavelica

By Bus

Huancavelica is situated about 14 hours by bus from Lima. Departures

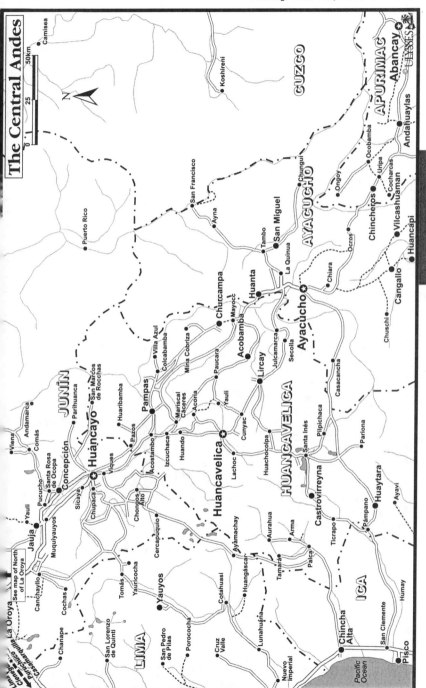

The Central Andes

0 25 50km

N

Camisea

Koshireni

CUZCO

APURIMAC

Abancay

© ULYSSES

Puerto Rico

San Francisco

Ayna

Ongoy

Ocobamba

Andahuaylas

Uripa

Cocharcas

Chinchejos

Vilcashuamán

Chungui

San Miguel

Tambo

La Quinua

Ocros

Chiara

Huancapi

Cangallo

AYACUCHO

Ayacucho

Chiara

Chuschi

LIMA TO THE
CENTRAL ANDES

Villa Azul

Churcampa

Huanta

Mayocc

Colcabamba

Mina Cobriza

Acobamba

Julcamarca

Secolla

Paucará

Lircay

JUNÍN

Parihuanca

San Marcos
de Rocchas

Huaribamba

Pampas

Pazos

Mariscal
Cáceres

Acoria

Yauli

Cunyac

Casacancha

HUANCAVELICA

Andamarca

Comas

Santa Rosa
de Ocopa

Concepción

HUANCAYO

Sicaya

Chupaca

Viques

Acostambo

Izcuchaca

Huando

Huancavelica

Lachoc

Huachocolpa

Santa Inés

Pilpichaca

Pariona

Huaytará

Ayaví

Viena

Andamarca

Pucucho

Muquiyauyos

Jauja

Yauli

Yauricocha

Tomás

Chupaca
Chongos
Alto

Cercapuquio

Ayamachay

Aurahua

Arma

Castrovirreyna

Ticrapo

Pampano

Chanape

Cochas

Canchayllo

San Lorenzo
de Quinti

Yauyos

Cotahuasi

Huangáscar

Tamará

Palca

HUANCAVELICA

See map of North
of La Oroya

La Oroya

LIMA

San Pedro
de Pilas

Porococha

Cruz
Valle

Lunahuaná

Nuevo
Imperial

Chincha
Alta

San Clemente

Humay

ICA

San Clemente

Pisco

Pacific
Ocean

are frequent and the fare is approximately nine $9.

By Train

Huancavelica is one of the few towns in the central Andes that can still be reached by train. The train leaves the station in Huancayo every day for Huancavelica. Although this line is not as spectacular as the defunct route between Huancayo and Lima, it is still very interesting. The train affords views of fabulous landscapes that will leave you simply awestruck.

Two trains shuttle between Huancayo and Huancavelica. The *autowagon* leaves Huancayo for Huancavelica at about 6am from Monday to Saturday and at about 2pm on Sunday. The trip lasts almost five hours and costs about $3. *El tren local* leaves Huancayo at about noon from Monday to Saturday. The trip is a bit longer and costs between $2 and $4, depending on the type of car chosen.

Ayacucho

By Plane

Most flights to Ayacucho leave Lima early in the morning to avoid the storms that can form in the mountains. The flight lasts about 45 minutes and costs approximately $50 one way. Delays are common.

By Bus

From Lima, the bus takes about 13 hours to reach Ayacucho. Budget about $12.

The Ruins of Wari - The Cave of Pikimachay

It is recommended to visit these two wonders with an agency.

Vilcashuamán

By Bus

Buses shuttle between Ayacucho and Vilcashuamán in about eight hours for approximately $6.

Andahuaylas

By Bus

From Ayacucho, buses reach Andahuaylas after 13 long hours for a $10 fare.

Abancay

By Bus

Abancay is about seven hours by bus from Cuzco. The fare is $8

 **PRACTICAL INFORMATION**

Huánuco

Tourist Information

There is a small tourist information office on Plaza de Armas.

Pachamanca

Pachamanca is a kind of underground barbecue. First, a hole is dug in the ground. A wood fire is lit in the bottom of the hole and covered with large stones. When the stones are very hot, a variety of meat is selected and cut (beef, chicken and pork), vegetables are added, and the whole is wrapped in leaves and placed in the hole, which is then refilled with earth. Diners wait patiently for the feast to be cooked to perfection.

Banking

Banco de Credito is located one block from Plaza de Armas on Dos de Mayo at the corner of Huánuco.

Telecommunications

The telephone is situated on 28 de Julio at the corner of Constitución.

Ayacucho

Banking

Banco de Credito is located on Plaza de Armas.

Mail and Telecommunications

The telephone and post offices are at the same address: Asamblea 293.

There is an Internet access provider on 28 de Julio, near the Iglesia de Santo Domingo.

Tour Agency

Wari Tours: Plaza de Armas, ☎913-315. This agency was established in Ayacucho several years ago and offers classic tours such as city tours, excursions to the ruins of Wari and Vilcashuamán, and to the cave of Pikimachay. Wari Tours organizes all sorts of excursions in the region.

 EXPLORING

Cieneguilla

Cieneguilla lies about 20 kilometres east of Lima on an Andean mountain road. Not much visited by tourists, this quiet little town is bustling on weekends, when *Limeños* flee the populous capital to relax outside the city and savour the local culinary specialty, *pachamanca*.

Cajamarquilla

The pre-Inca adobe ruins of Cajamarquilla are about eight kilometres east of Lima on the road to La Oroya. Like many other underappreciated Peruvian archeological sites, it is unfortunately very poorly maintained.

Puruchuco

Puruchuco has a site of pre-Inca adobe remains that date back to about the 3rd century AD. They were occupied much later by the Incas before the arrival of the Spanish. Toward the middle of the 20th century, the site was restored. It is presumed to have

LIMA TO THE
CENTRAL ANDES

been the home of a *curaca* (regional chief and functionary in service of the Inca Empire). A small museum on the premises houses some objects found at the site.

La Oroya

Perched at an altitude of more than 4,300 metres, the mining town of La Oroya is definitely not among the more attractive cities in the country. La Oroya subsists on the rich mineral deposits in the area, in particular those at the mines of Cerro de Pasco. Ore extracted from the deposits in this

region is processed in La Oroya before being transported to Lima by train.

La Oroya functions as a major transportation hub. This is where the road to Lima ends, and where roads heading in all directions through the central Andes – north, south and east – converge.

North of La Oroya

Junín

About 50 kilometres north of La Oroya, the little village of Junín, with its red-tile rooftops and the lake of the same

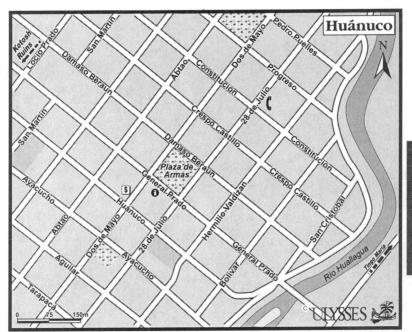

name, peeks out from the mountains at a height of some 4,100 metres. Although the town offers visitors few attractions, it has a place in Peruvian history. On August 5, 1824, Simón Bolívar and his valiant soldiers won a victory over Spanish troops at this very site.

Cerro de Pasco

The next town of significant size is situated even higher than Junín, and offers even fewer attractions. Perched at an altitude of 4,340 metres, Cerro de Pasco is a mining town that sprouted rapidly around 1940, when American companies established themselves in the region. This rapid development was interrupted in 1974, when the government decided to nationalize these enterprises. The minerals extracted here are still sent to La Oroya today to be refined before they are shipped to Lima.

Huánuco

After leaving Cerro de Pasco, the road runs up and down through the mountains, ending almost 100 kilometres further at Huánuco. Situated at the slightly lower altitude of 2,000 metres, alongside Río Huallaga, Huánuco is a quiet town that serves as the departure point for the ruins of Kotosh and Tingo María in the Selva.

The **ruins of Kotosh** stand barely five kilometres west of Huánuco. They are distinctive because of the presence of *el templo de las manos cruzadas* (temple of the crossed hands). The sculpture of the famous crossed hands can be seen at the Archeological Museum in Lima (see p 111). These ruins belonged to a civilization that preceded the Chavín era, but are unfortunately not very spectacular and poorly maintained. In 1960, Japanese archeologists began excavation of the site, but no one else has taken up the task for a very long time.

From Huánuco, the road continues its descent to Tingo María (see p 289) and the tropical forest.

Mini Feria

Toward the end of August, the square across from the church of Santa Ana is fenced in and a traditional Spanish *mini feria* is organized, during which brave (or foolhardy) participants try to outrun loose bulls. Here as elsewhere, the worst occasionally occurs and runners are stampeded or even gored to death.

East of La Oroya

Tarma

Compared to other central Andean towns, Tarma is quite populous. Its 100,000 residents live at an altitude slightly higher than 3,000 metres. Despite its significant population, it offers nothing particularly worth mentioning. At Easter, however, the city comes to life for *Semana Santa*.

San Ramón

The picturesque forsaken little village of San Ramón, about 80 kilometres east of Tarma, has a little over 5,000 residents and is rarely visited by tourists.

La Merced

Some 10 kilometres past San Ramón, the little village of La Merced stands on the horizon. Slightly more populous than San Ramón, it is not any more popular with visitors, who generally do not include this region on their itineraries.

South of La Oroya

Jauja

Jauja was the first capital of Peru. Perched at an altitude of 3,500 metres, about 40 kilometres from Huancayo, Jauja was designated the capital of the republic by Francisco Pizarro before he realized that, despite its fabulous mountain setting, the spot was difficult to defend against foreign attacks.

The Convent of Ocopa ★

The convent of Ocopa, erected in about 1725, is one of the oldest Franciscan missions in the country. Its library contains about 25,000 wonderful books, from here and abroad, which chronicle the history of the world through the centuries. Most of these books were individually bound by the missionaries, who battled wind and tides before settling here during the colonial era.

Huancayo

With about 100,000 residents, Huancayo, the capital of the department of Junín, is situated about 310 kilometres from Lima on the shores of Río Mantaro, at an altitude of 3,240 metres. The famous train that once linked the coast to the Sierra arrived here for the first time on August 24, 1908. It was also here that ex-president of the republic, Ramón Castilla, proclaimed the law abolishing slavery in 1854.

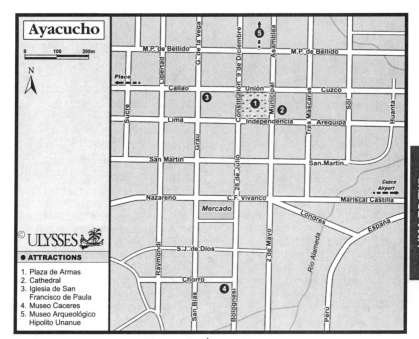

Ayacucho

0   100   200m

N

● **ATTRACTIONS**

1. Plaza de Armas
2. Cathedral
3. Iglesia de San Francisco de Paula
4. Museo Caceres
5. Museo Arqueológico Hipolito Unanue

©ULYSSES

The Sunday **market** enlivens the city and its surroundings. All sorts of crafts, articles of clothing that and other popular souvenir items can be found here.

Huancavelica

Situated in a rugged, isolated spot, the town of Huancavelica is not as famous as Potosí, even though its precious-metals were as important source of wealth for the Spanish as those of Potosí. Countless indigenous people died in the mines, whose sole purpose was to enrich the conquistadors and the royal coffers of Spain. Today, the town is in one of the poorest regions of the country, life expectancy is barely 50 years, and the infant mortality rate is among the highest in Peru.

Ayacucho ★

The history of Ayacucho dates back to 1536 and is linked directly to that of the capital of the Inca Empire. The preceding year, Cuzco had been subjected to repeated attacks by Manco and his troops who had laid it under siege. Simultaneously, Pizarro was quietly building Lima, the city of kings. As soon as he learned of the situation in Cuzco, however, he decided to protect his advantage by establishing a town between the two cities. Three years later, San Juan de la Frontera was born. In 1540, the town's name was changed to San Juan de la Victoria de Huamanga. Almost 300 years went by before Simón Bolívar renamed the town again, on February 15, 1825, calling it Ayacucho in honour of his victory in the battle of December 9, 1824.

Situated at an altitude of 2,740 metres, Ayacucho enjoys a pleasant climate,

Semana Santa

Millions of pilgrims from all over the country, and even from more far-off regions of the South American continent, to join together in celebration of the important annual religious holiday called *Semana Santa*. The week of festivities begins on Palm Sunday and includes a staging of the Passion of Christ, as well as nightly processions that light up the whole town. On the Saturday before Easter, a fair is held on the hill of Acuchimay, where people sing and dance all night as a prelude to the celebrations of Easter Sunday in the morning. The merrymaking includes corridas and horse races. It goes without saying that visitors who want to visit Ayacucho during this week must absolutely make hotel reservations well in advance.

with sunshine almost year-round, and a setting of pretty mountains. Unfortunately, the town is famous for being the birthplace of the Shining Path movement, which gained followers quickly and ultimately held the entire region under its thumb. This era is thankfully over, and travellers can now stroll around the town's streets, admiring its many reflections of the colonial era and its approximately 30 religious sanctuaries.

Ayacucho has about 30 churches that date from the colonial era. Most are closed or open only sporadically (there are simply not enough priests to lead all of these churches), and some are in a poor state of repair or undergoing restoration. However, all have a common denominator: despite their sober, faded façades, their interiors are richly decorated and ornamented with gold leaf.

It is unfortunately impossible to describe each of these temples, but visitors who take the time to see them are sure to make interesting discoveries.

Plaza de Armas is bordered by the cathedral, the university and the prefecture.

The **cathedral** *(on the west side of Plaza de Armas)* dates from the beginning of the 17th century and has three naves. Like the many other churches in town, its façade is modest, but its interior is lavishly decorated in the baroque style and covered in gold leaf.

The **church of San Francisco de Paula** *(Callao, corner of La Libertad)* has only one nave and stands solemnly one block northeast of Plaza de Armas. Its interior exhibits baroque characteristics and encloses one of the few wooden altars in the city that is not covered with gold leaf.

The **Museo Caceres** *($1; Mon to Sat 9am to noon and 2pm to 5pm)* is in an old house and displays furniture, paintings, and weapons from the colonial period.

The **Museo Arqueológico Hipolito Unanue** *($2; about 1 km north of Plaza de Armas)* contains a few ceramic pieces from Wari culture.

The Ruins of Wari or Huari

The Wari became exceptional masters of urban planning, despite being warlike. They were influenced by the Tiahuanaco and engaged in trade with the Nazca.

The **ruins of Huari** still stand, in the condition that might be expected, near Ayacucho. It is recommended that you visit the site with a specialized guide who can give you a deeper understanding of the significance of the ruins.

The Cave of Pikimachay

Situated about 24 kilometres from Ayacucho, this cave once enclosed the remains of a 20,000-year-old civilization. There is no longer anything to see inside its dark caverns, since all of the relics found here are now displayed in the country's many museums – mostly in Lima.

La Quinua

La Quinua is a quaint little village about 40 kilometres northeast of Ayacucho that comes to life during its Sunday market. A 44-metre **obelisk** stands near the village. Each metre represents one of the 44 years leading up to Peruvian independence. Ironically, the obelisk was built by a Spanish architect.

Huanta

Huanta is a small village located a few hours from Ayacucho that suffered greatly from Shining Path attacks when the revolutionary movement raged in the region. The town does not offer tourists anything spectacular and has very little infrastructure, but has a few simple hotels and restaurants.

Head to the little shop two steps from Plaza de Armas called **Licores de Frutas Nueva Esperanza** *(Jr. Razuhuillaca 220, ☎932-301, or from Lima ☎495-4556)* for a mixed drink. Try *leche de tuna*, which tastes a bit like the Irish drink called "Bailey's".

Vilcashuamán ★

Vilcashuamán is the name of the Inca ruins that stand about 100 kilometres from Ayacucho. These have lost much of their former charm and splendour from centuries of erosion, but will interest anyone who appreciates the old stone remains of vanished civilizations. You must get up very early in the morning to see the ruins and return to Ayacucho the same day.

Chincheros and Andahuaylas

These secluded, picturesque villages between Ayacucho and Abancay are rarely visited by tourists. During the rainy season, the roads are difficult to make out.

Abancay

Abancay is a remote Andean village in a narrow mountain pass that serves as a stopover for the bus from Ayacucho to Cuzco.

 ACCOMMODATIONS

Huancayo

Hostal Confort *($8; sb; Ancash 231)* is suitable for travellers with limited budgets.

There are two good hotels on Plaza Constitución: **Kiya Confort** *($25; pb, ℜ)* and **Presidente** *($25; pb, ℜ)*.

Ayacucho

The rooms at the little hotel **Central** *($8; sb; Jr. Arequipa)* are, as the name suggests, well situated in a central location and suitable for adventurers with tight budgets.

One block east of Plaza de Armas, the rooms at **Hostal la Colmena** *($8 sb, $10 pb; hw mornings only, ℜ; Jr. Cusco 140 ☎/≈812-146)* are set around a pretty interior courtyard. Some of them have small balconies.

One block further on the same street, **Gran Hotel Los Alamos** *($8 sb, $10 pb; hw mornings only, ℜ; Jr. Cusco 215, ☎/≈812-782)* offers basically the same rates as its neighbour.

A little under 10 minutes' walking distance from Plaza de Armas, **Hotel Valdelirios** *($20; tv, hw, pb, ℜ; Alameda Bolognesi 720, ☎913-908, ≈914-014)* occupies a charming colonial house. The rooms are clean, quiet, simple, and pleasant. Some are carpeted while others have hardwood floors.

Hostal San Francisco *($20 bkfst incl.; pb, hw, ℜ; Jr. Callao 290, ☎918-349, ≈914-501)* stands just a couple of steps from Plaza de Armas and offers about 40 simple, well-equipped, clean rooms with modern washrooms. Some rooms open onto small balconies.

Another establishment located near Plaza de Armas, **Hostal Santa Rosa** *($20; hw, pb, ℜ; Jr. Lima 166, ☎/≈812-083)* offers about twenty clean and decent rooms on two stories.

Without a shadow of a doubt, the best hotel in town is **Hotel Plaza** *($45-$55; tv, hw, pb, ℜ; Jr. 9 de Diciembre 102, ☎913-202, from Lima ☎421-470 or 423-091, ≈424-180)*. This old *hotel de turista* offers two types of lodging: the rooms in the centre of the main building are not overly exciting, but those overlooking Plaza de Armas have balconies and are spacious, bright, equipped with minibars, and much more comfortable

than the others. Of course, the better rooms cost a bit more. The staff is obliging, and the restaurant (see p 279) is the best in town. The establishment has its own bus and offers guests free customized shuttle service to and from the local airport.

Huanta

Hostal La Posada del Marques *($6 sb, $8 pb; Jr. Saenz Peña 160)* offers decent rooms in a colonial house.

 # RESTAURANTS

Huancayo

Good meals are offered at the restaurants of the hotels **Kiya Confort** *($-$$)* and **Presidente** *($-$$)*, which border Plaza Constitución.

Ayacucho

Just next to Fuente de Soda Max Max (see below), diagonally across from the Hotel Plaza, a little narrow alleyway leads to a large oven where fresh bread is sold at very economical prices *($; 28 de Julio 143)* from the early hours of the morning.

Fuente de Soda Max Max *($; 28 de Julio 139)* is a small restaurant that does not look like much, but serves all sorts of sandwiches and fresh orange juice at affordable prices, and is perfect for a quick, simple bite.

Polleria y Parrillada Niño *($; Jr. 9 de Diciembre 205)* is located across from the church of Santo Domingo and offers chicken or grilled meat dishes that may be savoured indoors or on the establishment's patio, which has a view of the mountains.

The **restaurant of the Hotel Plaza** *($-$$; Jr. 9 de Diciembre 102, ☎912-202)* offers a *menu del día* for about five dollars. Every Sunday, starting at 11am, a lavish buffet is served for the same price. The menu lists a variety of dishes.

Huanta

The restaurant **Central** *($; Avenida San Martín 116)* looks out onto Plaza de Armas. In a modern and bright setting it offers simple, affordable dishes.

The small, unpretentious restaurant **Samoa** *($; Jr. Oswaldo Regal 234, ☎832-151)*, located near the market, serves tasty steamed trout.

ENTERTAINMENT

Ayacucho

The "resto-pub-disco" **Peña Los Balcones** *(Jr. Asamblea 187)* has a tiny dance floor where local young people unwind to varied, upbeat music.

SHOPPING

For original carpets, visit **Las Voces del Tapiz** *(Plazuela de Santa Ana 82, ☎914-242)*, where Edwin Sulca Lagos creates unique works according to clients' wishes.

For Huamanga sculptures head to **Plazolete Santa Ana 12** *(☎814-278)*.

LIMA TO THE CENTRAL ANDES

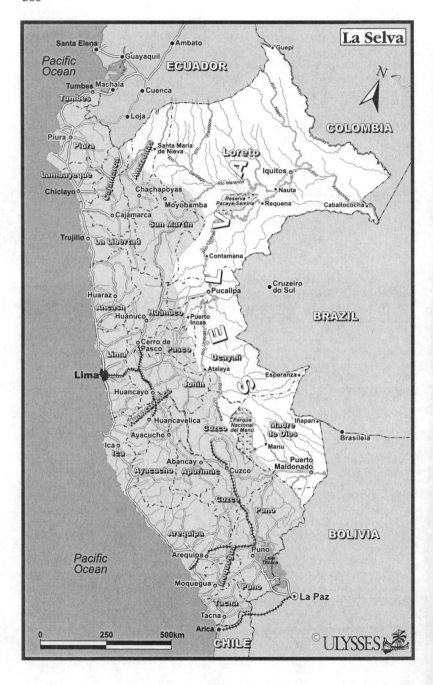

LA SELVA

The Selva, a formidable source of life and regenerator of water and energy, covers a little over 60% of Peru, but represents only a small portion of the enormous surface area of the planet occupied by tropical forests. Set along the equator between the tropics of Cancer and Capricorn, tropical rainforests constitute 14% of the Earth's surface, stretching over parts of South America, Central America, Africa, Asia, and the islands of the western Pacific.

At first glance, the rainforest seems nothing more than a huge labyrinth of flora, and all the trees look alike. But don't be fooled: from behind the dense forest foliage, innumerable eyes are watching, as many ears hear the slightest noise, and countless noses detect the presence of newcomers from miles away. A panoply of birds and animals are permanently camouflaged behind the ideal protection of this lush greenery. Large animals, like jaguars and

peccaries, are rarely spotted, since they flee at the least sense of danger. The conquistadors learned of these animals' timidity the hard way – those who survived the rigours of the forest almost died of starvation, and there are even stories that some were reduced to eating the leather of their belts stewed in herbs. Apart from the impressive variety of fauna that inhabits the Amazon, visitors are most likely to spot monkeys, birds and occasionally, snakes during a trek into the rainforest.

Despite their apparent similarity, a more careful look at the trees reveals that a great variety of species live symbiotically in this habitat.

If you look even closer, you will distinguish many colourful plants blooming in this favourable environment. The climate that characterizes the marvellous world of tropical forests permits an extraordinary array of plants to grow year-round.

Myth or Reality?

Toward the middle of 1997, some residents of the tiny village of Nuevo Tacna, in the Amazon forest, swore that they had seen a Dantesque reptile with the enormous dimensions of about 35 metres in length and 5 metres in width. This terrifying creature apparently shook the earth as it moved, ravaging everything in its path, before slinking into the muddy opaque rivers that course through the tropical forest... Believe it, or not!

Although the treetops receive intense sunshine, everything in the shade of the canopy subsists in half-light, so competition is intense. Some trees struggle for years before their neighbours topple over and they can finally flourish in the rays that trickle through the new opening.

Tropical rainforests are designated by various names, but whatever they are called, and wherever they are found, they are always places of mystery that evoke our fascination for the strange and unfamiliar. In Ecuador, the tropical forest is called the Oriente, while in Peru it is simply called the *Selva*, the Spanish word for "forest".

Europeans and Peruvians also call this region *infierno verde* ("green hell"), referring to the fates of adventurers of various eras who have disappeared without a trace in the forest's dense foliage and perpetually stifling heat.

Convinced that the forest concealed gold, cinnamon trees, and other priceless treasures, many explorers risked their lives to penetrate it. Few of them survived, and fewer emerged from the forest with their sanity intact.

In 1541, Francisco de Orellana led an armed expedition down the eastern Andes from Quito (Ecuador), cut his way through the forest by the blows of his sword, and reached Río Napo. He followed the course of this river to its confluence with the Amazon and then travelled the mighty Amazon to its mouth, thereby becoming, along with his troops, the first European to cross the entire South American continent from east to west by land and river.

When Orellana's expedition finally returned to Quito to tell of their formidable journey, the Spanish men convinced everyone that along the way they had engaged in furious combat with fierce warrior women. Of course, these claims were met with suspicion that soon devolved into ridicule. The next year, Orellana tried his luck again, but this time he disappeared into the green hell, never to return.

Nineteen years after Francisco de Orellana's Homeric journey, Viceroy Hurtado de Mendoza assigned Pedro de Ursúa to the head of another expedition whose mission was to pursue the eternal search for El Dorado. On September 27, 1560, Pedro de Ursúa and his men boarded a craft on Río Marañon and set out to find the source of their future wealth. Weeks passed, the expedition found nothing, and the soldiers became impatient. On the eve of the new year, 1561, a mutiny occurred. Led by Lope de Aguirre, the soldiers entered the room of Pedro de Ursúa and assassinated him. Fernando de Guzmán became the new captain, with Lope de Aguirre as his second-in-command. Aguirre nick-named the men *marañones* and refused to pledge allegiance to the king of Spain. He even wrote a letter to the king in which he addressed the

Fitzcarrald

The child of a Peruvian mother and a North American father, Isaias Fitzcarrald spent his youth in the department of Ancash before continuing his studies in Lima. He was accused of espionage during the Pacific War and had to flee into the Selva to escape his pursuers. Through hard work and perseverance, he profited from the latex boom and soon became a rich and influential business-man. He decided to pursue his insatiable quest for latex by travelling the waterways south of Iquitos and transporting his boat overland through the dense forest to another river. His courage was rewarded by the discovery of the isthmus that separates Río Ucayali from Río Madre de Dios. However, his exploration of the Amazon forest was short-lived – he drowned at the age of 36 during one of his expeditions. German director Werner Herzog made a film about this unique character, in the heart of the tropical forest under extremely difficult conditions, entitled *"Fitzcarraldo"*.

monarch in the familiar second person, a flagrantly disrespectful action. Added to this supreme insult, Aguirre specified to the king that he did not recognize the monarch's rights over the lands of the New World since he had not come himself to conquer them. Later, Aguirre assassinated his comrade, Fernando de Guzmán, and all those who engendered his mistrust. The survivors of the expedition finally reached the Atlantic Ocean and dropped anchor on the shores of Isla Margarita, in present-day Venezuela. At the end of this misadventure, the sword of Damocles fell in turn on Lope de Aguirre, who was murdered by his own men in a mutiny. *Aguirre, The Wrath of God*, a film by Werner Herzog, tells this fantastic tale and is available on videocassette.

After verifying Newton's hypothesis a few kilometres north of Quito, scientist Charles Marie de La Condamine decided to explore the mysterious world of the Amazon himself. In 1743, he travelled the length of Río Marañon and descended the Amazon to the Atlantic Ocean. During the expedition, Charles Marie de La Condamine described the river and its surroundings in minute detail. With this information, he was able to draw the first map that was relatively faithful to this vast, strange, unknown region, bequeathing to future cartographers a reliable basis for their work. As well, he collected objects for study, including poison arrows and many rare plant species such as quinine and a remarkably flexible, resinous plant called hevea that would revolutionize the nascent rubber industry.

The Formation of La Selva

Several million years ago, the Amazon region was covered by an inland sea that stretched from the Caribbean in the northeast to the Atlantic in the south, and in some places joined the Pacific in the west. The formation of the Andes, over 100 million years ago, isolated this sea from the Pacific, before gradually retreating to the east where it dried up. Meanwhile the forces of erosion acted on the Andes, covering the Amazon's peneplain with thick alluvial deposits. These deposits, regularly irrigated in the equatorial climate, permitted the emergence of exceptional wildlife. Much later, in the Quaternary, the glaciers that had amassed on the

Crossing the Colombian and Brazilian Borders

Although the idea of renting a boat in Iquitos to meander La Selva's muddy waters into Brazil or Colombia might seem romantic or exciting, travellers should never undertake this journey unaccompanied by a guide. Ignorance of local habits and customs, and of the forest's dense, complex network of rivers which lead to unknown destinations, can be dangerous in this exotic but inhospitable land. Two Japanese students who ignored this basic advice unfortunately learned its value at a high cost: they were assassinated by police officers guarding a border crossing in circumstances that are still unclear.

high Andean peaks melted due to an increase in average temperatures.

Countless waterways sprang to life, ran down the eastern flanks of the Andean cordillera toward the forest, merged and grew, ultimately combining to form Río Amazonas, the Amazon, which empties into the Atlantic Ocean at an immense delta.

These geological and climatic phenomena, in succession and in combination, created the environment in which the South American tropical forests as we know them today could flourish.

FINDING YOUR WAY AROUND

Despite the immense area it occupies, the Selva is difficult to reach. To visit the northern part, travellers usually head to the most populous city in the Peruvian Amazon, **Iquitos**. In the south, you must pass through **Cuzco** to reach **Puerto Maldonado**, which serves as a departure point for treks into the lush tropical forest.

There are daily flights from Lima and Miami to Iquitos, the northern departure point for Amazon excursions. Most travellers to the region buy all-inclusive packages ahead of time, but Iquitos and Cuzco are easy to reach on one's own and excursions into the forest may

be arranged from either of these cities. Prices vary according to the duration of the trip, the skill of the guides and the quality of the services. A three-day stay is the minimum time required for just a taste of the Amazon. The longer the trek, the further from civilization it takes you, and the better will be your chances of observing the rainforest and its wildlife inhabitants in their natural state.

Iquitos

By Plane

Airplanes and boats are the only two means of reaching Iquitos, and most travellers go by plane, unless they are already in La Selva. Aeroperú and Aerocontinente both offer regular one-and-a-half-hour flights from Lima to Iquitos. Budget $200 for round-trip airfare. There are also flights to Iquitos from the city of Pucallpa. Budget about $55 for a one-way ticket.

Airlines

Aeroperú: Prospero 248, ☎232-513

Aerocontinente: Prospero 331, ☎233-162

Save the Rainforest!

Although this message has often been repeated, it is never said enough. Tropical forests play a primary role in supplying the planet with sufficient oxygen and rain, and maintaining the ecological balance. They encompass innumerable plant species, some of which are used to cure human illnesses. Because of a lack of funding for research in this area, only a tiny percentage of these plants have been identified. It is very possible that the cures to many diseases could be found growing somewhere in the tropical forests. These resources are liable to disappear because of the ravages of deforestation and the oil industry. The tropical forests are in the process of being erased from the surface of the planet at an alarmingly rapid rate.

By Boat

Patient travellers can take a 15-hour-long boat ride from Pucallpa to Iquitos.

Tingo Maria

By Bus

There is a bus to Tingo María from Huánuco (see p 273); the trip takes four hours. Budget about $2 for a one-way fare.

Pucallpa

By Plane

Aeroperú and Aerocontinente fly to Pucallpa from Lima. The flight takes about one hour and costs approximately $75.

By Bus

The bus ride takes about 20 hours with an obligatory stop in Tingo María, and costs approximately $14. There are spectacular views. The town is difficult to reach in the rainy season.

Cuzco - Puerto Maldonado

By Plane

Travellers must fly to Cuzco before continuing on to Puerto Maldonado. Most flights to Cuzco from Lima, Arequipa and Juliaca leave early in the morning to avoid the abrupt changes in weather and the storms that can form over the Sierra in the afternoon. From Lima, the one-way fare is about $75 and the flight takes close to one hour. Aeroperú and Aerocontinente make this trip three times daily, starting at 5:30am. From Arequipa, the flight takes 25 minutes and costs about $35.

From Cuzco, Aeroperú offers daily flights of about 45 minutes to Puerto Maldonado for a fare of approximately $50.

Leticia (Colombia), Manaus - Tabatinga (Brazil)

Boats leave regularly from the dock in Iquitos for these towns, but before heading out on the *ríos* of the Amazon for Colombia or Brazil, inquire at the respective consulates as to which documents are required to cross their borders.

LA SELVA

PRACTICAL INFORMATION

What to Pack?

- Pants for the trip to the region
- Old pants for excursions. Jeans are not recommended because they are too tight and too heavy and dry very slowly; cotton pants are preferable.
- Underwear and socks for each day of the trip
- Cash in small denominations
- Binoculars
- Camera
- Fast film (at least 400 ASA)
- Sunglasses
- Insect repellent
- Raincoat
- Flashlight
- Sunscreen
- Long-sleeve shirt
- Biodegradable soap and shampoo
- Hat
- Compass
- Bathing suit

Iquitos

Banking

Banco de Credito is located on Plaza de Armas. This bank cashes traveller's cheques and offers Visa credit card cash advances.

Telecommunications

Jr. Arica, between Sargento Lores and Putamayo.

Mail

The post office is on Morona at the corner of Arica.

Tour Agencies

Paseos Amazonicos *(in Lima: Bajada Balta 131, Of. 4, Miraflores, ☎241-7576 or 241-7614, ⇌446-7996; in Iquitos: Pevas 246, ☎/⇌231-618)* is an agency that has its own small hotel, Ambassador (see p 293), and organizes short and longer excursions into the tropical forest, according to clients' wishes. The accredited guides are more than competent. Budget about $50 per person for one day and $100 per person per overnight stay.

Explorama *(Avenida La Marina 340, P.O. 446, ☎222-526, ⇌252-533)* has been in business for almost 40 years and owns three types of lodges and an environmental research laboratory. Budget about $180 per person per night and $725 per person for seven days.

Cumabeca Lodge & Expeditions *(Jr. Putamayo 263, Of. 1, ☎/⇌232-229)* offers affordable excursions into the Amazon. Budget about $40 per person per day or $75 per person per night.

Consulates

The **Brazilian consulate** is at Jr. Sgto. Lores 363. The **Colombian consulate** is at Jr. Putamayo 247.

Puerto Maldonado

Banking

Banco de Credito is on Plaza de Armas. This bank cashes traveller's cheques and offers Visa credit card cash advances.

Sloth

Telecommunications

The telephone office is on Puno, between Prada and Troncoso.

 EXPLORING

Northern La Selva

Iquitos ★★★

The town of Iquitos was founded in the middle of the 18th century by Jesuit missionaries, who were determined to convert the Yagua indigenous people. The town developed very slowly and had its glory day one hundred years later, when rubber was vulcanized in 1888. Together with the town of Manaus in Brazil, Iquitos prospered quickly thanks to latex extracted from the sap of the hevea, or rubber tree. Peru and Brazil held a monopoly over this lucrative industry for some time.

Many planters became rich during this era of wealth and prosperity, at the expense of the indigenous population.

In 1920, a brave, spirited Englishman succeeded in secretly importing hevea seeds to Great Britain. Shortly thereafter, these seeds were exported to Malaysia, where they soon acclimatized and formed many prosperous plantations that supplanted those of Peru and Brazil because of their greater accessibility (Malaysia is a peninsula, while the Amazon is almost impenetrable) and easier exploitation. Ultimately, South American rubber tree plantations were abandoned.

For a city that is only linked to the rest of the world by air and by river, Iquitos, the largest city in the Amazon basin, is surprisingly populous, bustling with some 355,000 souls and the many motorcycle taxis that travel its roads. It serves as a departure point for river trips into the fascinating tropical maze of the Amazon.

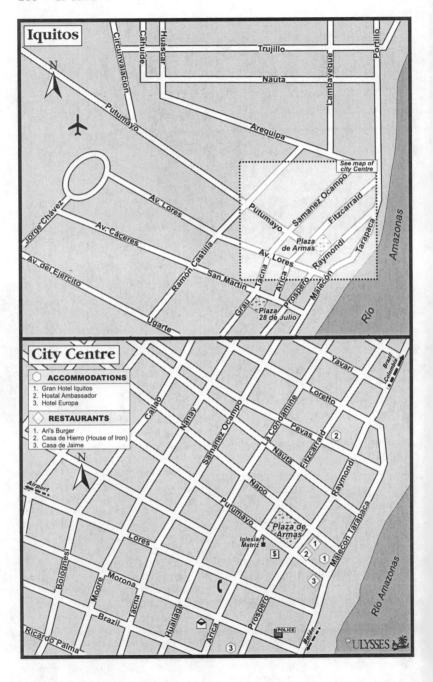

Beside Tikal in Guatemala, Machu Picchu is the only place in Latin America listed as a UNESCO Natural and Cultural World Heritage Site. - *P. E.*

The festival of the Virgen del Carmen takes place annually on July 16.
- *T. B.*

The **Iron House** ★ *(Plaza de Armas)* is a peculiar building constructed mainly of iron and other metal alloys, and is the product of the rather eccentric ambition of a rubber planter. Its history is more interesting than its architecture, however. When Iquitos was at the height of its development during the rubber boom, one of the new barons of the day, who had become rich by exploiting this then rare and precious resource, decided to import the separate pieces of a Paris house designed by Eiffel and reassemble them on the town's Plaza de Armas. The building now houses a small café.

A stroll along Malecón permits a view of a few buildings decorated with *azulejos* built during the flourishing years of the latex industry.

Belén is a floating shantytown made up of modest houses built on stilts to accommodate the seasonal rise of the river's water level.

La Laguna Quistococha and the Zoo

Laguna Quistococha is situated about 14 kilometres north of Iquitos. During the week, the area is calm and quiet, but on the weekend it is overrun by the many Peruvians who come here regularly to picnic on the shore and swim in the water. The zoo exhibits various animals that inhabit the tropical forest. Unfortunately, they are mostly kept in deplorable conditions. Buses leave regularly from Plaza 26 de Julio for the Laguna. Budget 50¢ for a 30-minute trip.

Tingo María

During the period when Peru was besieged by a wave of terrorism, it was not considered safe to visit Tingo María. Today, calm seems to have finally returned to the region, but the drug trade continues and does not appear to be abating. It is recommended to inquire with tourism organizations in Lima (see p 102) before travelling to the area. The town itself has few attractions and offers only minimal services. Curious travellers who come this far generally visit **Cueva de las Lechuzas**, a cave situated close to seven kilometres northwest of the town. The cave is inhabited by strange nocturnal birds of prey, which creates a rather dark and scary atmosphere that most people, except for speleology buffs who seek out this type of experience, find unpleasant.

Pucallpa

Pucallpa, a noisy, lively city, numbers almost 30,000 residents, but does not offer much in the way of tourist attractions despite being the capital of the province of Ucayali. It has only been linked with Lima by road since the beginning of the 20th century. Visitors who end up here can visit the tranquil **Laguna Yarinacocha**, where indigenous people sell crafts on the shore of the lagoon.

Southern La Selva

Puerto Maldonado

Deep in the humid tropical forest, Puerto Maldonado was founded June 12, 1902. It was subjected to floods whenever the river rose, until it was rebuilt on its present site in 1925. Puerto Maldonado experienced rapid growth during the rubber boom, but the local indigenous people organized an uprising after Fitzcarrald's death and the town was abandoned. Although it is accessible by plane, the town's infrastructure is summary at best. Neverthe-

LA SELVA

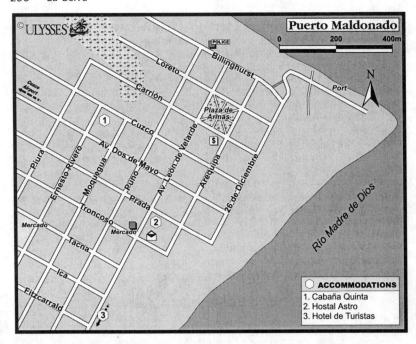

Puerto Maldonado

ACCOMMODATIONS
1. Cabaña Quinta
2. Hostal Astro
3. Hotel de Turistas

less, it is the departure point for excursions to Reserva Tambopata to the south and to Parque Nacional Manu to the west.

 PARKS

Parque Nacional Manu ★★★

Parque Nacional Manu stretches over the eastern flanks of the Andean cordillera and forms an almost untouched nature reserve of 18,800 square kilometres where animal and vegetable life abound. Over 1,000 species of bird have been sighted here, including the flamboyant *ara macao* and the cock-of-the-rock. As well, about 10 species of monkey, including the smallest primate on the planet, leap from branch to branch, and giant otters and black caymans frolic in the muddy water-

ways. There is also a diverse flora: more than 15,000 species of plant have been identified in the park.

Reserva Pacaya-Samiria ★★★

Washed by the waters of Río Pacaya and Río Samiria, the Reserva Pacaya-Samiria was established to protect the *païcha*, a giant catfish pushed to the brink of extinction by overfishing. This reserve stretches over 13,800 square kilometres and constitutes a veritable bosky bower in the middle of the lower tropical forest. Fascinating creatures inhabit the dense foliage of this leafy shelter of greenery, which is spongy and bushy at once, and through which a thousand and one waterways forge their way. Giant otters and river dolphins are just two of the animals visitors may observe here.

Jaguar

ACCOMMODATIONS

Hotels in the Amazon forest are not luxurious. Except for Iquitos, which has two or three places that meet the standards of an average modern hotel, lodgings consist of simple and sometimes meagre shelter.

Lodges

An original and popular way to visit La Selva is by staying in lodges.

Lodges are generally located on private property in the forest, on the shore of a river, and are made up of single- and double-occupancy cabins called *cabañas*. Like hotels, there are different categories of lodges, determined by the quality of services and amenities offered. Usually it is impossible to reach these lodges on your own, because the agencies that manage them from Lima, Iquitos and Cuzco rent out all available

rooms with their excursion packages. These packages include transportation from the airport to the hotel and full-board accommodation.

Before signing a contract for an excursion package, ask lots of questions, so you can avoid any unpleasant surprises.

- Does the guide speak English?
- Are meals (full board) included?
- What is the length of the stay?

Lodges near Iquitos

The agency **Paseos Amazonicos** *(in Lima: Bajada Balta 131, Of. 4, Miraflores, ☎241-7576 or 214-7614, ☞446-7996; in Iquitos: Pevas 246, ☎/☞231-618)* owns the two following lodges.

Sinchicuy Lodge is a little over an hour by boat from Iquitos. It consists of a main building that houses a bar and a dining room. A footbridge leads to the *cabañas*, which are equipped with comfortable beds and private bathrooms with cold-water showers. Many of La Selva's more tame animals, including some friendly monkeys, have free rein on the grounds. Meals are delicious, the welcome is inviting, and the service is impeccable.

The second lodge is much more rustic. It numbers about 10 *cabañas* with screen windows and thatch roofs set sleepily under the thick canopy of the trees. There is no electricity or hot water.

The agency **Explorama** *(Avenida La Marina 340, P.O. 446, ☎222-526, ⌐252-533)* manages the three following lodges as well as the ACEER complex.

Situated about 40 kilometres from Iquitos, the **Explorama Inn** is suited to travellers who want to get a taste of the tropical forest without feeling too disoriented. The cabins have screens and the food is good, but opportunities for wildlife viewing are rather limited compared to other places.

The **Explorama Lodge** opened about 40 years ago and was one of the first lodges built in the area. Located about 80 kilometres from Iquitos, it is slightly more rustic than the Explorama Inn.

On the banks of Río Napo, about 160 km from Iquitos, **Explornapo** is even cruder than the Explorama Lodge. It offers thatch-roofed *cabañas* summarily furnished with single beds covered by mosquito netting.

The **ACEER** Canopy Walkway offers a bird's eye view of the Amazon forest. ACEER (Amazon Center for Environmental Education and Research) is a non-profit organization whose goal is to protect the fascinating but fragile world of tropical forests. They have established an environmental studies laboratory near Explornapo. It is possible to stay at the research centre by making advance reservations. Several 500-metre-long suspension bridges have been built about 40 metres above the ground near the laboratory, and are ideal spots for taking in the sights and sounds of the birds that live in this environment.

Lodges near Puerto Maldonado

Cuzco Amazónico *(in Cuzco: Procuradores 48, ☎232-161)* is three quarters of an hour northeast of Puerto Maldonado by boat. It offers rustic accommodations and standard hikes in the Amazon.

Pantiacolla Tours *(in Cuzco: Plateros, pantiac@mail.com.cosapida.com.pe)* has garnered much praise from its guests. The lodgings are rustic, but the staff is quite expert and obliging, making the visit as pleasant as possible.

Manu Nature Tours *(in Cuzco: Avenida Pardo 1046, ☎252-721, ⌐234-793, postmaster@mnt.com.pe)* possesses the only lodge in Parque Nacional Manu. Its amenities let you visit the Amazon while maintaining a certain standard of comfort.

Situated about 60 kilometres, or three hours by boat, southeast of Puerto Maldonado, the **Explorer's Inn** *(in Cuzco: Peruvian Safaris, Plateros 365, ☎235-542)*, a lodge in the Reserva Tambopata-Candamo, offers *cabañas* that are best described as simple but comfortable.

Northern La Selva

Iquitos

Located a short distance from Parque 28 de Julio, **Hostal Lima** *($10; sb;*

Prospero 549) is another affordable option for travellers who are not too demanding.

Hostal Isabel *($10; sb; Brasil at the corner of the Malecón)* provides rooms that are simple and suitable for backpackers.

Also near Parque 28 de Julio, **Hostal Le Sitio** *($20; pb, ℜ; Ricardo Palma 541)* is one of the best values in the city. It has clean, safe, well-equipped rooms and a friendly staff.

Hotel Europa *($40; pb, ℜ; Brasil 222, ☎231-123)* is located three blocks from Plaza de Armas and offers simply decorated, sufficiently clean rooms.

Hostal Amazonas *($40; tv, ℜ, pb; Jr. Arica 108, ☎223-574, ⌐242-431)* borders Plaza de Armas and offers good value. The rooms are air-conditioned, clean and safe.

Hostal Ambassador *($40; pb, ℜ; Pevas 260, ☎233-110)* is owned by the proprietors of the Paseos Amazonicos agency (see p 286) and offers clean but unadorned rooms. Tourists who stay here are usually part of one of the agency's excursion groups. The agency owns its own bus and offers an airport pick-up service.

The view of the *río* from the spacious rooms of **Real Hotel Iquitos** *($45; pb, ℜ; Malecón Tarapacá, ☎231-011, from Lima: ☎241-2202, ⌐241-8149)* is their main advantage. However, they are in serious need of a fresh coat of paint and new furniture.

El Dorado *($50; pb, ctv, ≈, ℜ; Jr. Napo 362, ☎237-326 or 231-742, ⌐232-203)* is among the better hotels in the city. The swimming pool is a plus any time of day. Although the rooms are a bit sterile, they are spacious, modern and safe.

Located one block from the Real Hotel Iquitos, **Hotel Victoria Regia** *($50; pb, tv, ℜ; Palma 352 at the corner of Prospero)* rents clean, modern, but unoriginal rooms set around a swimming pool.

Five blocks from Plaza de Armas, **Hotel Río Grande** *($60; ctv, pb, ℜ; Jr. Prospero 644, ☎231-694, ⌐224-312)* is another of Iquitos' better hotels and offers clean, air-conditioned rooms.

Tingo María

La Cabaña *($8; sb; Raimondi 342)* is suitable for backpackers who are not too particular. The simple rooms are relatively clean.

The best hotel in the area is located outside the town: **Turistas** *($25; pb, ℜ, ≈; on the road to Huánuco)*.

Pucallpa

If you are down to your last pennies, you might wan to stay in the modest, austere rooms of **Hostal Mori** *($8; sb; Jr. Independencia 114)*.

Hostal Mercedes *($20; pb, ℜ; Raymondi 610)* offers simple, comfortable rooms at reasonable rates.

Sol del Oriente *($60; pb, ℜ; Avenida San Martín 552, ☎575-154)* is the best hotel in town. Its rooms are clean, modern, and safe, and the pool is refreshing.

LA SELVA

Southern La Selva

Puerto Maldonado

Hostal Astro *($10; sb; Velarde 617)* is a low-budget shelter for travellers who are short on cash.

La Cabaña Quinta *($20; pb, ℜ; Cuzco 535)* is one of the best deals in town. The rooms are simple but clean, and the staff is friendly.

Hotel de Turistas *($30; pb, ℜ; near Río Tambopata, ☎571-029)* rents out the best rooms in town: they are clean, come with air conditioners and have a view of the *río*.

 RESTAURANTS

Dining in the Amazon does not involve drinking from fancy wine glasses or savouring the delights of Peruvian cuisine. Restaurants offer affordable daily menus or simple, filling individual items.

Northern La Selva

Iquitos

The interior of the Iron House (see p 289) has been transformed into a small, unpretentious **café** *($; Plaza de Armas)* that serves simple, economical dishes.

You can have nutritious Chinese food at **Wai Ming** *($; Plaza 28 de Julio)* in an unpretentious decor.

Adventurers can be found at all hours of the day lounging under the breeze created by ceiling fans at **Ari's Burger** *($-$$; Plaza de Armas)*. The breakfasts are inexpensive, and although the spot is known for its variety of hamburgers, the menu also includes chicken, fish and meat dishes.

For a quick, no-fuss bite, head to **La Casa de Jaime** *($-$$; Malecón)*. The menu includes fish, chicken and pasta.

Pucallpa

The small restaurant **Don José** *($; Jr. Ucayali)* is across from Hostal Mercedes and offers simple, affordable dishes.

Southern La Selva

Puerto Maldonado

Most restaurants in town seem to serve the same thing: simple dishes that vary from day to day. Places to try are **Kalifa** *($; Piura)* and **Le Hornito** *($; Plaza de Armas)*.

GLOSSARY

GREETINGS

Goodbye	*adiós, hasta luego*
Good afternoon and good evening	*buenas tardes*
Hi (casual)	*hola*
Good morning	*buenos días*
Good night	*buenas noches*
Thank-you	*gracias*
Please	*por favor*
You are welcome	*de nada*
Excuse me	*perdone/a*
My name is...	*mi nombre es...*
What is your name?	*¿cómo se llama usted?*
yes	*no*
no	*sí*
Do you speak English?	*¿habla usted inglés?*
Slower, please	*más despacio, por favor*
I am sorry, I don't speak Spanish	*Lo siento, no hablo español*
How are you?	*¿qué tal?*
I am fine	*estoy bien*
I am American (male/female)	*Soy estadounidense*
I am Australian	*Soy autraliano/a*
I am Belgian	*Soy belga*
I am British (male/female)	*Soy británico/a*
I am Canadian	*Soy canadiense*
I am German (male/female)	*Soy alemán/a*
I am Italian (male/female)	*Soy italiano/a*
I am Swiss	*Soy suizo*
I am a tourist	*Soy turista*
single (m/f)	*soltero/a*
divorced (m/f)	*divorciado/a*
married (m/f)	*casado/a*
friend (m/f)	*amigo/a*
child (m/f)	*niño/a*
husband, wife	*esposo/a*
mother	*madre*
father	*padre*
brother, sister	*hermano/a*
widower widow	*viudo/a*
I am hungry	*tengo hambre*
I am ill	*estoy enfermo/a*
I am thirsty	*tengo sed*

DIRECTIONS

beside	*al lado de*
to the right	*a la derecha*
to the left	*a la izquierda*
here	*aquí*
there	*allí*
into, inside	*dentro*
outside	*fuera*
behind	*detrás*
in front of	*delante*
between	*entre*
far from	*lejos de*
Where is ... ?	*¿dónde está ... ?*
To get to ...?	*¿para ir a...?*
near	*cerca de*
straight ahead	*todo recto*

MONEY

money	*dinero / plata*
credit card	*tarjeta de crédito*
exchange	*cambio*
traveller's cheque	*cheque de viaje*
I don't have any money	*no tengo dinero*
The bill, please	*la cuenta, por favor*
receipt	*recibo*

SHOPPING

store	*tienda*
market	*mercado*
open	*abierto/a*
closed	*cerrado/a*
How much is this?	*¿cuánto es?*
to buy	*comprar*
to sell	*vender*
the customer	*el / la cliente*
salesman	*vendedor*
saleswoman	*vendedora*
I need...	*necesito...*
I would like...	*yo quisiera...*

batteries	*pilas*
blouse	*blusa*
cameras	*cámaras*
cosmetics and perfumes	*cosméticos y perfumes*
cotton	*algodón*
dress jacket	*saco*
eyeglasses	*lentes, gafas*
fabric	*tela*
film	*película*
gifts	*regalos*
gold	*oro*

handbag	*bolsa*
hat	*sombrero*
jewellery	*joyería*
leather	*cuero, piel*
local crafts	*artesanía*
magazines	*revistas*
newpapers	*periódicos*
pants	*pantalones*
records, cassettes	*discos, casetas*
sandals	*sandalias*
shirt	*camisa*
shoes	*zapatos*
silver	*plata*
skirt	*falda*
sun screen products	*productos solares*
T-shirt	*camiseta*
watch	*reloj*
wool	*lana*

MISCELLANEOUS

a little	*poco*
a lot	*mucho*
good (m/f)	*bueno/a*
bad (m/f)	*malo/a*
beautiful (m/f)	*hermoso/a*
pretty (m/f)	*bonito/a*
ugly	*feo*
big	*grande*
tall (m/f)	*alto/a*
small (m/f)	*pequeño/a*
short (length) (m/f)	*corto/a*
short (person) (m/f)	*bajo/a*
cold (m/f)	*frío/a*
hot	*caliente*
dark (m/f)	*oscuro/a*
light (colour)	*claro*
do not touch	*no tocar*
expensive (m/f)	*caro/a*
cheap (m/f)	*barato/a*
fat (m/f)	*gordo/a*
slim, skinny (m/f)	*delgado/a*
heavy (m/f)	*pesado/a*
light (weight) (m/f)	*ligero/a*
less	*menos*
more	*más*
narrow (m/f)	*estrecho/a*
wide (m/f)	*ancho/a*
new (m/f)	*nuevo/a*
old (m/f)	*viejo/a*
nothing	*nada*
something (m/f)	*algo/a*

quickly	*rápidamente*
slowly (m/f)	*despacio/a*
What is this?	*¿qué es esto?*
when?	*¿cuando?*
where?	*¿dónde?*

TIME

in the afternoon, early evening	*por la tarde*
at night	*por la noche*
in the daytime	*por el día*
in the morning	*por la mañana*
minute	*minuto*
month	*mes*
ever	*jamás*
never	*nunca*
now	*ahora*
today	*hoy*
yesterday	*ayer*
tomorrow	*mañana*
What time is it?	*¿qué hora es?*
hour	*hora*
week	*semana*
year	*año*

Sunday	*domingo*
Monday	*lunes*
Tuesday	*martes*
Wednesday	*miércoles*
Thursday	*jueves*
Friday	*viernes*
Saturday	*sábado*
January	*enero*
February	*febrero*
March	*marzo*
April	*abril*
May	*mayo*
June	*junio*
July	*julio*
August	*agosto*
September	*septiembre*
October	*octubre*
November	*noviembre*
December	*diciembre*

WEATHER

It is cold	*hace frío*
It is warm	*hace calor*
It is very hot	hace mucho calor
sun	*sol*
It is sunny	hace sol
It is cloudy	*está nublado*

rain	*lluvia*
It is raining	*está lloviendo*
wind	*viento*
It is windy	*hay viento*
snow	*nieve*
damp	*húmedo*
dry	*seco*
storm	*tormenta*
hurricane	*huracán*

COMMUNICATION

air mail	*correos aéreo*
collect call	*llamada por cobrar*
dial the number	*marcar el número*
area code, country code	*código*
envelope	*sobre*
long distance	*larga distancia*
post office	*correo*
rate	*tarifa*
stamps	*estampillas*
telegram	*telegrama*
telephone book	*un guia telefónica*
wait for the tone	*esperar la señal*

ACTIVITIES

beach	*playa*
museum or gallery	*museo*
scuba diving	*buceo*
to swim	*bañarse*
to walk around	*pasear*
hiking	*caminata*
trail	*pista, sendero*
cycling	*ciclismo*
fishing	*pesca*

TRANSPORTATION

arrival	*llegada*
departure	*salida*
on time	*a tiempo*
cancelled (m/f)	*anulado/a*
one way ticket	*ida*
return	*regreso*
round trip	*ida y vuelta*
schedule	*horario*
baggage	*equipajes*
north	*norte*
south	*sur*
east	*este*
west	*oeste*
avenue	*avenida*
street	*calle*

highway	*carretera*
expressway	*autopista*
airplane	*avión*
airport	*aeropuerto*
bicycle	*bicicleta*
boat	*barco*
bus	*bus*
bus stop	*parada*
bus terminal	*terminal*
train	*tren*
train crossing	*crucero ferrocarril*
station	*estación*
neighbourhood	*barrio*
collective taxi	*colectivo*
corner	*esquina*
express	*rápido*
safe	*seguro/a*
be careful	*cuidado*
car	*coche, carro*
To rent a car	*alquilar un auto*
gas	*gasolina*
gas station	*gasolinera*
no parking	*no estacionar*
no passing	*no adelantar*
parking	*parqueo*
pedestrian	*peaton*
road closed, no through traffic	*no hay paso*
slow down	*reduzca velocidad*
speed limit	*velocidad permitida*
stop	*alto*
stop! (an order)	*pare*
traffic light	*semáforo*

ACCOMMODATION

cabin, bungalow	*cabaña*
accommodation	*alojamiento*
double, for two people	*doble*
single, for one person	*sencillo*
high season	*temporada alta*
low season	*temporada baja*
bed	*cama*
floor (first, second...)	*piso*
main floor	*planta baja*
manager	*gerente, jefe*
double bed	*cama matrimonial*
cot	*camita*
bathroom	*baños*
with private bathroom	*con baño privado*
hot water	*agua caliente*
breakfast	*desayuno*
elevator	*ascensor*

air conditioning	*aire acondicionado*		
fan	*ventilador, abanico*		
pool	*piscina, alberca*		
room	*habitación*		

NUMBERS

1	*uno*	30	*treinta*
2	*dos*	31	*treinta y uno*
3	*tres*	32	*treinta y dos*
4	*cuatro*	40	*cuarenta*
5	*cinco*	50	*cincuenta*
6	*seis*	60	*sesenta*
7	*siete*	70	*setenta*
8	*ocho*	80	*ochenta*
9	*nueve*	90	*noventa*
10	*diez*	100	*cien*
11	*once*	101	*ciento uno*
12	*doce*	102	*ciento dos*
13	*trece*	200	*doscientos*
14	*catorce*	300	*trescientos*
15	*quince*	400	*quatrocientoa*
16	*dieciséis*	500	*quinientos*
17	*diecisiete*	600	*seiscientos*
18	*dieciocho*	700	*sietecientos*
19	*diecinueve*	800	*ochocientos*
20	*veinte*	900	*novecientos*
21	*veintiuno*	1,000	*mil*
22	*veintidós*	1,100	*mil cien*
23	*veintitrés*	1,200	*mil doscientos*
24	*veinticuatro*	2000	*dos mil*
25	*veinticinco*	3000	*tres mil*
26	*veintiséis*	10,000	*diez mil*
27	*veintisiete*	100,000	*cien mil*
28	*veintiocho*	1,000,000	*un millón*
29	*veintinueve*		

INDEX

OTHER ULYSSES GUIDES

Acapulco (Mexico)
Ulysses Due South guide offers a fresh look at Acapulco, the most famous Mexican resort: Acapulco Bay, its beaches, restaurants and captivating nightlife are all in there, but so are the neighbouring mountains, as well as an enlightened look at the people and history of this spot.
Marc Rigole, Claude-Victor Langlois   150 pages, 5 maps
$14.95 CAN $9.95 US   £6.99
2-89464-062-5

The Islands Of The Bahamas
Vacationers will find extensive coverage of the big favourites of New Providence (Nassau) and Grand Bahama (Freeport) with their spectacular beaches, glittering casinos and great scuba diving, but they will also find the most extensive coverage of the Out Islands. Here island-hoppers enjoy world-class fishing, scuba diving and boating, friendly people and pristine deserted beaches.
Jennifer McMorran   288 pages, 25 maps
8 pages of colour photos
$24.95 CAN $17.95 US   £12.99
2-89464-123-0

Belize
This tiny Central American country encompasses part of the ancient Ruta Maya and is rimmed by spectacular coral reefs. Its archaeological and natural treasures make it an explorer's paradise. Practical and cultural information will help you make the most of your vacation.
Carlos Soldevila   208 pages, 10 maps
$12.95 US
2-89464-179-6

Cancún & Cozumel (Mexico)
The entirely man-made resort of Cancún on the Yucatán Peninsula attracts visitors from the world-over. They come to enjoy a unique travelling experience with fabulous archaeological sites, the last remnants of the Mayan civilization, and the island of Cozumel, a scuba-diver's paradise, both close by.
Caroline Vien, Alain Théroux   200 pages, 20 maps
$17.95 CAN $12.95 US   £8.99
2-89464-040-4

Cartagena, 2nd edition
Here is the new edition on this colonial jewel. Declared a World Heritage Site by UNESCO, Cartagena boasts historic charm, cultural riches, luxurious hotels, beautiful beaches and the possibility of exciting excursions, all the ingredients for an extraordinary vacation.
Marc Rigole   128 pages, 10 maps
$12.95 CAN $9.95 US   £6.50
2-89464-018-8

Costa Rica
This fresh look at Costa Rica provides travellers with the most extensive choice of practical addresses, no matter what their budget while also placing special emphasis on eco-tourism, independent travel and the culture, history and natural wonders of this Central American gem.
Francis Giguère, Yves Séguin   368 pages, 35 maps
8 pages of colour photos
$27.95 CAN $19.95 US   £13.99
2-89464-144-3

Cuba, 2nd edition
Already a second edition for this unique guide to Cuba. The island's spirit is revealed, from colonial Havana, to the world-heritage site of Trinidad and to Santiago with it Afro-Cuban culture. The guide also covers the famous beaches and provides travellers with countless shortcuts and tips for independent travel in Cuba.
Carlos Soldevila   336 pages, 40 maps
8 pages of colour photos
$24.95 CAN $17.95 US   £12.99
2-89464-143-5

Dominican Republic
The most complete reference to this Caribbean hot spot: excursions, historical information, cultura details, addresses of restaurants, shops and hotels, road maps and city plans.
Pascale Couture, Benoit Prieur
250 pages, 20 maps
8 pages of colour photos
$24.95 CAN $17.95 US   £12.99
2-89464-064-1

Ecuador and the Galápagos Islands
All the major sites of this South American country are explored including extensive coverage of the capital city, Quito, but also the extraordinary Galapagos Islands. Hundreds of addresses for all budgets as well as countless useful hints for discovering this fascinating and ancient land of the Incas.
Alain Legault 300 pages, 25 maps
8 pages of colour photos
$24.95 CAN $17.95 US   £12.99
2-89464-059-5

El Salvador
This guide provides everything the traveller needs to discover this fascinating Central American country explanation of cultural and political contexts, advice on how to travel in the area, descriptions of the various attractions, detailed lists of accommodation, restaurants, entertainment.
Eric Hamovitch   152 pages, 7 maps
$22.95 CAN $14.95 US   £11.50
2-921444-89-5

Guadeloupe, 3rd edition
This is the only guide to provide such extensive cultural and practical coverage of this destination. Th charm of this dramatically beautiful Caribbean island is revealed along winding picturesque roads throug typical villages and towns. Magnificent colour plates help to identify Guadeloupe's birds and plants.
Pascale Couture   208 pages, 15 maps
8 pages of colour photos
$24.95 CAN $17.95 US   £12.99
2-89464-135-4

Guatemala
Historic peace talks have once again allowed tourism to develop in Guatemala, providing a spectacu glimpse at a country whose native traditions are so strong and omnipresent.
Carlos Soldevila, Denis Faubert   336 pages, 30 maps
$24.95 CAN $17.95 US   £12.99
2-89464-175-3

Honduras, 2nd edition
The prospects for tourism in Honduras are among the brightest – promising travellers a first-ra vacation, whether they are in search of spectacular deserted beaches, fascinating archaeological sit or supreme diving locations. This guide offers numerous suggestions for outdoor adventure plus practi tips and information on everything from A to Z.
Eric Hamovitch   224 pages, 20 maps
$24.95 CAN $17.95 US   £12.99
2-89464-132-X

Martinique, 3rd edition
A perfect marriage of cultural and practical information provides the best coverage of Martinique. Numerous tours lead across the island of flowers, from Fort-de-France to Saint-Pierre, with stops in Grande Anse and Montagne Pelée. Everything you need to know about hiking and water sports. Magnificent colour plates help to identify birds and plants.
Claude Morneau   256 pages, 18 maps
8 pages of colour photos
$24.95 CAN $17.95 US   £12.99
2-89464-136-2

Nicaragua
Once a headline-maker the world over, Nicaragua is more often featured in the "Travel" section these days. Besides the capital city of Managua and the popular resort of Montelimar, this guide traverses the whole country, discovering the touching cities of León and Granada, among other places, along the way.
Carol Wood   224 pages, 15 maps
$24.95 CAN $16.95 US   £11.50
2-89464-034-X

Panamá, 2nd edition
Famous for its impressive canal, Panamá offers magnificent beaches on two different oceans, nestled in a diverse ethnic and cultural environment. This guide will help the traveller discover an infinite variety of landscapes, with unequalled flora and fauna.
Marc Rigole, Claude-Victor Langlois   208 pages, 16 maps
3 pages of colour photos
$24.95 CAN $16.95 US   £11.50
2-89464-005-6

Peru
Ulysses reveals the stunning scenery of this varied land: the Inca Trail and the ancient Inca city of Macchu Pichu, the depths of the Amazon rainforest, the high reaches of the Cordillera Blanca, modern and bustling Lima and beautiful Arequipa. An insightful portrait and a thorough how-to section round out the guide.
Alain Legault   352 pages, 60 maps
8 pages of colour photos
$17.95 US
2-89464-122-2

Puerto Vallarta (Mexico)
What began as a tiny fishing village nestled between sea and mountains has blossomed into one of the Mexican Riviera's most splendid resorts. This guide reveals the splendour of Puerto Vallarta, from its luxuriant flora to its quaint tile-roofed houses and countless excellent restaurants.
Richard Bizier, Roch Nadeau   160 pages, 5 maps
$14.95 CAN $9.95 US   £6.50
2-89464-039-0

Saint Martin - Saint Barts, 2nd edition
Jewels of the French and Dutch Caribbean, Saint Martin and Saint Barts offer a kaleidoscope of attractions – beautiful beaches, charming villages, first-class tourist facilities – and they have been combined for this guide. Whether it's international Saint Martin or tiny Saint Barts, or both, this handy pocket guide has all the great restaurants, luxurious hotels, outdoor activities, plus a glossary, maps and a historical overview.
Pascale Couture   192 pages, 10 maps
$16.95 CAN $12.95 US   £8.99
2-89464-071-4

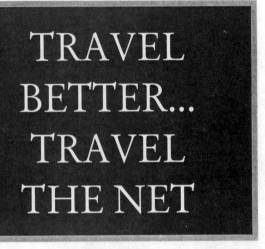

ORDER FORM

☐ Affordable B&Bs in Québec $12.95 CAN $9.95 US	☐ Louisiana . . . . $29.95 CAN $21.95 US
☐ Atlantic Canada . . . . $24.95 CAN $17.95 US	☐ Martinique . . . . $24.95 CAN $17.95 US
☐ Beaches of Maine . . . . . . $12.95 CAN $9.95 US	☐ Montréal . . . . $19.95 CAN $14.95 US
☐ Bahamas . . . . $24.95 CAN $17.95 US	☐ New Orleans . . . . $17.95 CAN $12.95 US
☐ Belize . . . . $16.95 CAN $12.95 US	☐ New York City . . . . $19.95 CAN $14.95 US
☐ Calgary . . . . $17.95 CAN $12.95 US	☐ Nicaragua . . . . $24.95 CAN $16.95 US
☐ Canada . . . . $29.95 CAN $21.95 US	☐ Ontario . . . . $24.95 CAN $14.95US
☐ Chicago . . . . $19.95 CAN $14.95 US	☐ Ottawa . . . . $17.95 CAN $12.95 US
☐ Chile . . . . $27.95 CAN $17.95 US	☐ Panamá . . . . $24.95 CAN $16.95 US
☐ Costa Rica . . . . $27.95 CAN $19.95 US	☐ Peru . . . . $27.95 CAN $19.95 US
☐ Cuba . . . . $24.95 CAN $17.95 US	☐ Portugal . . . . $24.95 CAN $16.95 US
☐ Dominican Republic . . . . . $24.95 CAN $17.95 US	☐ Provence - Côte d'Azur . . $29.95 CAN $21.95US
☐ Ecuador Galapagos Islands $24.95 CAN $17.95 US	☐ Québec . . . . $29.95 CAN $21.95 US
☐ El Salvador . . . . $22.95 CAN $14.95 US	☐ Québec and Ontario with Via . . . . $9.95 CAN $7.95 US
☐ Guadeloupe . . . . $24.95 CAN $17.95 US	☐ Toronto . . . . $18.95 CAN $13.95 US
☐ Guatemala . . . . $24.95 CAN $17.95 US	☐ Vancouver . . . . $17.95 CAN $12.95 US
☐ Honduras . . . . $24.95 CAN $17.95 US	☐ Washington D.C. . . . . . . $18.95 CAN $13.95 US
☐ Jamaica . . . . $24.95 CAN $17.95 US	☐ Western Canada . . . . $29.95 CAN $21.95 US
☐ Lisbon . . . . $18.95 CAN $13.95 US	

☐ Acapulco . . . . $14.95 CAN $9.95 US	☐ Cancun Cozumel . . . . . . $17.95 CAN $12.95 US
☐ Belize . . . . $16.95 CAN $12.95 US	☐ Puerto Vallarta . . . . $14.95 CAN $9.95 US
☐ Cartagena (Colombia) . . . $12.95 CAN $9.95 US	☐ St. Martin and St. Barts . . $16.95 CAN $12.95 US

ULYSSES TRAVEL JOURNAL

☐ Ulysses Travel Journal . . . . $9.95 CAN
(Blue, Red, Green, Yellow, Sextant) $7.95 US

ULYSSES GREEN ESCAPES

☐ Cycling in France . . . . . . $22.95 CAN   ☐ Hiking in Québec . . . . . . $19.95 CAN
                        $16.95 US $13.95 US
☐ Hiking in the
   Northeastern U.S. . . . . . . $19.95 CAN
                        $13.95 US

TITLE	QUANTITY	PRICE	TOTAL

Name _____	Subtotal
Address _____	
_____	Canadian postage & handling* 4,00 $
_____	
Payment : ☐ Cash ☐ Visa ☐ MasterCard	Subtotal
Card number _____	GST in Canada 7%
Signature _____	
	TOTAL

ULYSSES TRAVEL PUBLICATIONS
4176 St-Denis,
Montréal, Québec, H2W 2M5
(514) 843-9447 fax (514) 843-9448
www.ulysses.ca
*$15 for overseas orders

U.S. ORDERS: **GLOBE PEQUOT PRESS**
P.O. Box 833, 6 Business Park Road,
Old Saybrook, CT 06475-0833
1-800-243-0495 fax 1-800-820-2329
www.globe-pequot.com